Labour in History and Society

This series explores various forms of labour relations across the world, and over a broad temporal period from antiquity to the present. The editors invite contributions from researchers in a range of disciplines, including history, sociology, economics, anthropology and philosophy, and encourage an interdisciplinary approach which will make use of historical and social science methodologies. Covering different types of labour relations, from commodified labour for the market, to tributary labour for the polity and reciprocal labour for the household, the series aims to examine dominant classes such as masters, rulers and capitalists in order to unveil the dialectical relationship not only between employers and employees, but also between elites and the 'subaltern'. Providing insights from multiple disciplines, the series will examine aspects of race, gender and caste, as well as trade unionism, unpaid labour and precarious work. It will present a range of perspectives: both global and local; regional and national; micro and macro, and will include case studies and contributions from across the globe.

Mario Grassi

The Silk Industry in Early Modern Piedmont

The Fabric of Innovation

palgrave
macmillan

Mario Grassi
Dipartimento di Scienze Storiche Geografiche
e dell'Antichità DiSSGeA
University of Padua
Padua, Italy

ISSN 2731-9474 ISSN 2731-9482 (electronic)
Labour in History and Society
ISBN 978-3-032-15352-4 ISBN 978-3-032-15353-1 (eBook)
https://doi.org/10.1007/978-3-032-15353-1

This Palgrave Macmillan imprint is published by the registered company Springer Nature Switzerland AG.
The registered company address is: Gewerbestrasse 11, 6330 Cham, Switzerland

Preliminary note on original documents translation:
Except where otherwise noted, all translations are the author's own.

Source of Funding

Funded by the European Union. Views and opinions expressed are however those of the author(s) only and do not necessarily reflect those of the European Union or the Research Executive Agency. Neither the European Union nor the granting authority can be held responsible for them. Project: 101108617—SILKRAA—HORIZON-MSCA-2022-PF-01.

Acknowledgments

It has now been ten years since I first set foot in an archive, searching for names, facts, and traces of the silk industry in Piedmont. Today, at last, the fruit of that long journey comes to life.

Over the past decade, I have accumulated countless debts of gratitude toward people on both sides of the Atlantic. Beyond a collective heartfelt thanks to colleagues, friends, and family, I am especially grateful to Luciano Allegra, who first introduced me to the world of archives. I am equally grateful to Paola Bertucci, Andrea Caracausi, Manuela Martini, and Luca Molà, who accompanied my journey with patience and care, offering guidance and encouragement throughout the years. I am also deeply grateful to Maurice Aymard, Cinzia Lorandini, Giorgio Riello, Leonard Rosenband, Raffaella Sarti, Ilja Van Damme, and Stefania Montemezzo for their careful reading and invaluable feedback. At different times and in different places, they helped guide my research with remarkable insight. I also wish to express my sincere gratitude to the anonymous reviewers, whose thoughtful comments greatly helped to improve this work.

To Sally Massmann—and to our *Wahlverwandtschaften*—goes my deepest thanks for her tireless attention to the proofreading of this volume. Furthermore, I remain especially indebted to my dear friend Mario Sanseverino, who has read every word I have written over the years.

A warm acknowledgment also goes to the staff of the Archivio di Stato di Torino and the Archivio Storico della Città di Torino, as well as to Olga Cardellino, who kindly granted me access to the documents preserved in the parish archive of the Santissima Annunziata.

To conclude, this research, its development, and the writing of this book would not have been possible without the resources and the generous hospitality of the Scuola Superiore di Studi Storici of the University of the Republic of San Marino, the Macmillan Center at Yale University, the Laboratoire de recherche historique Rhône-Alpes at Université Lumière Lyon 2, the Universities of Padua and Turin, and—last but certainly not least—the support of the European Union through a Marie Skłodowska-Curie Postdoctoral Fellowship. As for the quality of the research, I leave that judgment to the readers. I take full responsibility for it.

This book is dedicated to the cherished memory of Franco Monetti, a familiar figure in the archives, who—though we barely crossed paths—taught me resilience when I most needed it.

Competing Interests The author has no competing interests to declare that are relevant to the content of this manuscript.

Contents

About the Author

Mario Grassi is a Marie Skłodowska-Curie Post-doc Fellow, pursuing a project entitled "The Silk Route Across the Alps. Craftsmen Migrations, Commercial Exchanges & Social Relations Between France & Italy in the Early Modern Period" (SILKRAA) at the University of Padua, in collaboration with Yale University, the University Lumière Lyon2, and the Como Silk Museum. During his PhD at the Scuola Superiore di Studi Storici of the University of the Republic of San Marino, he presented an in-depth prosopography of the society employed in the production of silk artifacts in Piedmont during the eighteenth century, a research that was awarded the Walter Maturi prize 2021 by the Deputazione Subalpina di Storia Patria. His current research, in addition to the socio-economic history of the silk industry, covers the history of migration, gender and violence, food and material culture.

Abbreviations

Archive Abbreviations

APSA	Archivio Parrocchiale della Santissima Annunziata
ASCT	Archivio Storico della Città di Torino
AST, C	Archivio di Stato di Torino, Corte
AST, SR	Archivio di Stato di Torino, Sezioni Riunite
Art.	Articolo (section)
b.	Busta (folder)
c.	Carta (folio)
Cat.	Categoria (category)
Coll.	Collezione (collection)
fasc.	Fascicolo (file)
m.	Mazzo (bundle)
NSI	Non soggetto a Insinuazione—Not subject to registration in the Insinuazione office
n.d.	Not dated
v.	Volume

Weights[1]

1 rubbo	25 libbre
1 libbra	12 once
1 oncia	8 ottavi

[1] A *rubbo* corresponded to 9.222 kilograms; a *libbra* to 0.369 kilograms; and an *oncia* to 30.74 grams.

Coinage

1 doppia piemontese	2 scudi piemontesi
1 scudo piemontese	6 lire piemontesi
1 lira piemontese	20 soldi
1 soldo	12 danari

List of Figure

List of Pictures

List of Maps

List of Tables

CHAPTER 1

The Ecosystem of Innovation: An Introduction

1 The Glass Beads Paradox

> From time immemorial Montreuil-sur-Mer's specialized industry had been the imitation of English jet jewellery and of the black glass jewellery of Germany. This industry had always languished because of the high price of the raw materials, which affected the worker's pay. When Fantine returned to Montreuil-sur-Mer an amazing transformation had taken place in this production of 'black ware'. Towards the end of 1815 a man, a stranger, had come and set up business in the town, and had the idea of substituting shellac for resin in the manufacturing process and, for bracelets in particular, using metal clasp links that were simply pinched together instead of soldered. This very small change had been a revolution. (Hugo 2016, 147)[1]

[1] "De temps immémorial, Montreuil-sur-mer avait pour industrie spéciale l'imitation des jais anglais et des verroteries noires d'Allemagne. Cette industrie avait toujours végété, à cause de la cherté des matières premières qui réagissait sur la main-d'œuvre. Au moment où Fantine revint à Montreuil-sur-mer, une transformation inouïe s'était opérée dans cette production des 'articles noirs'. Vers la fin de 1815, un homme, un inconnu, était venu s'établir dans la ville et avait eu l'idée de substituer, dans cette fabrication, la gomme laque à la résine et, pour les bracelets en particulier, les coulants en tôle simplement rapprochée aux coulants en tôle soudée. Ce tout petit changement avait été une révolution" (Hugo 1862, 36–37).

M. Grassi, *The Silk Industry in Early Modern Piedmont*, Labour in History and Society,
https://doi.org/10.1007/978-3-032-15353-1_1

The narrative of Montreuil-sur-Mer in *Les Misérables* by Victor Hugo offers a striking example of how technological innovation is both essential and yet insufficient to transform a community's destiny. A seemingly minor detail—the replacement of resin with shellac and the simplification of the technique for making glass beads for costume jewelry—becomes the engine of a productive shift that Hugo describes as a true *revolution*. This is a word that, in post-revolutionary France, is anything but incidental. The most significant transformation, however, happens on a social level: "Before Père Madeleine's arrival,[2] the whole place was languishing. Now everything there was sustained by the wholesomeness of the working life. A strong circulation is entirely beneficial and reaches everywhere. Unemployment and poverty were unknown. There was no pocket so obscure that it had not a little money in it, no home so poor that it had not a little gladness in it" (Hugo 2016, 148–149).[3] But innovation alone cannot guarantee lasting change. Without a social structure capable of harnessing its potential and institutions that can turn economic progress into a collective endeavor, change risks remaining superficial or quickly fading away. The case of Montreuil-sur-Mer thus becomes emblematic: while technology can set transformation in motion, it is ultimately the community—with its social, economic, and cultural dynamics—that determines whether it will last. Indeed, with the departure of Père Madeleine, the town's fragile equilibrium crumbles, and its prosperity swiftly declines.

Hugo's account is, undoubtedly, a work of fiction. Yet the insight with which he intertwines Valjean's story with the manufacturing of beads in Montreuil-sur-Mer offers a significant perspective for reflecting on the relationship between technological and social history. Innovation, while both a driver and a consequence of deep social, cultural, political, and economic shifts—and even when recognized on an international scale—is not, by itself, enough to guarantee lasting economic development. Hugo's fictional narrative provides a privileged starting point for exploring this

[2] Père Madeleine is the alias of the protagonist of *Les Misérables*, Jean Valjean, who becomes a respected mayor and factory owner in *Les Misérables*.

[3] "Avant l'arrivée du Père Madeleine, tout languissait dans le pays; maintenant tout y vivait de la vie saine du travail. Une forte circulation échauffait tout et pénétrait partout. Le chômage et la misère étaient inconnus. Il n'y avait pas de poche si obscure où il n'y eût un peu d'argent, pas de logis si pauvre où il n'y eût un peu de joie" (Hugo 1862, 40–41).

dynamic through a historical lens, focusing on a real case of innovation and transformation: the history of the silk industry in early modern Piedmont.

2 A Success Story? The Silk Industry in Piedmont

This study focuses on the history of the silk industry in the early modern era. It is the story of a transformation that profoundly shaped the global textile industry, rooted in a centuries-old tradition. The story of an industry geographically concentrated in a relatively small area, yet one that, during the early modern period, set the international standard for the quality of silk thread. The story of technological integration into a local production system, where social, political, cultural, and material forces converged to favor its acceptance. The story of a sector that, through the essential role of the artisan, aimed at both national economic development and international success, leveraging the superior quality of its signature product, known as *organzino alla piemontese* - a silk thread superior to any produced in Europe or much of the world at the time. The story of a local brand that found recognition too late, in a world that was rapidly changing. The story of a society that placed its hopes in this industry, only to have its dreams shattered.

Like Père Madeleine's glass beads, Piedmontese silk embodies the paradox of excellence that is not enough to secure lasting prosperity. No matter how refined or *révolutionnaires* technical and product innovations may be, they must address the deep-rooted issues in the society in which they emerge, the global political and economic networks they inevitably become part of, and the broader transformations—institutional, cultural, and political—that coexist with technological changes and shape their trajectory. In Piedmont's case, organzine became the symbol of an economy built on quality, yet one that could not withstand local tensions and global shifts. In this case, technological innovation was not a turning point in itself but rather "merely a keystone," to use De Grazia's words: change occurs when cumulative processes unfold, driven by the convergence of creative ideas and actions across different fields, generating new combinations of knowledge with tangible—material, institutional, psychological—effects (De Grazia 2013, 9).

From this perspective, the case of Piedmont is more than just a fragment of economic history; it becomes a prism through which to explore the intricate interplay of technology, society, and culture. This volume does not follow the grand narrative of industrial progress, nor does it rely on sweeping economic theories or demographic models to interpret the forces shaping industrial development. Instead, it adopts a micro-analytical approach, enabling the examination of the case study from multiple perspectives: from within and without, from above and below, from up close and at a distance. By analyzing Piedmont's silk industry through this lens, it is possible to transcend the conventional view of economic development as a linear sequence of achievements and failures. Instead, it is seen as a dynamic web of local and global forces, aspirations and challenges, technical excellence and structural vulnerabilities.

This volume invites reflection on the meaning of progress and the fragile balance between innovation and social context. The history of Piedmontese silk—marked by both extraordinary flourishing and ultimate decline—demonstrates that the value of a technology or the fame of a product cannot be considered in isolation from the human, political, and economic environment in which it emerges. The success of an innovation depends not only on its technical merit but on a broader vision—one that integrates the local with the global, the technological with the human, and the immediate with the future-oriented. In the intricate history of Piedmontese silk, it is clear how quality and innovation, powerful as they may be, remain inseparably woven into the fabric of social and cultural transformation.

After all, only by turning over a finely woven fabric can the structure of its weave truly be seen—the small knots, the irregular threads, and, to the trained eye, the very labor of the hand that crafted it.

3 Dealing with the Concept of Innovation

About ten years ago, Gabriele Balbi and Cecilia Winterhalter (2013) published a book titled *Antiche novità. Una guida transdisciplinare per interpretare il vecchio e il nuovo* (Ancient Novelties: A Transdisciplinary Guide to Interpreting the Old and the New). The book aimed to address crucial issues in social research such as the relationship between old and new, tradition and innovation, continuity and change. While most of the case studies focus on contemporary sociological topics, they never lose sight of the book's central objective: proposing research approaches that help understand change by softening the rigid dichotomy between old and new. As De Grazia (2013) stated in the introduction, the humanities must examine the interplay between old and new to deepen our understanding of human action, the motives, and the forces that drive society in one direction or another—or resist change altogether. This idea recalls Gramsci's concept of *interregnum*, in which "the old is dying, and the new cannot be born." In moments like these, an atmosphere of uncertainty and conflict emerges, where the forces of the past and future collide and merge, creating a liminal state—a fertile ground for innovation but also for the resurgence of resistance and nostalgia (Gramsci 1975; Hoare and Nowell-Smith 1971, 276). Fundamentally, the old and the new coexist and constantly influence each other in every sphere, forcing societies—often inclined to see the old as the past and the new as the future—to confront the long-standing tension between tradition and innovation. As Hobsbawm and Ranger (1983) argued in their seminal work *The Invention of Tradition*, tradition is not necessarily tied to the past but rather to the cultural and symbolic framework of the society in which it emerges. Sometimes, tradition facilitates innovation by drawing parallels with the familiar; at other times, it fuels resistance by framing change as something foreign to the traditional, thereby fostering opposition to the new. At the heart of these dynamics lies the delicate boundary between continuity and change—a boundary that, when examined closely, seems more linguistic than empirically verifiable. Change can only be fully understood when viewed as a cumulative process of ideas and creative actions that generate innovative solutions by reconfiguring existing knowledge. This is the essence of innovation: it is never entirely "new" when one considers the extent to which it builds on the "old." It is neither pure transformation nor mere continuity. In this book, technological innovation is only a fragment of a much broader picture. It is a dynamic force deeply rooted in the past, introduced into a specific geopolitical and historical context through the interplay of evolving social, economic, and political factors. Once introduced, innovation triggers qualitative transformations in products, reshaping socio-economic structures and redefining local production and commerce. However, the forces driving change do not simply fade once an innovation is adopted. Instead, they continue to evolve, making it necessary to reassess innovation through institutional frameworks that define its features, limitations, and potential.

Innovation has been a recurring theme in economic history since the early modern period, as demonstrated, for example, by the widespread influence of the *Encyclopédie* in the eighteenth century (Brewer 2011). This topic has fascinated generations of historians (Bloch 1935; Cipolla 1965, 1974; Kuhn 1962; Braudel 1979) and continues to engage scholars today (Mokyr 1990, 2002, 2012, 2016; Davids and De Munck 2014; Godin 2015; Hahn 2020; Bertucci 2021, 2023; Smith 2022). Much of historiography has linked technological advancements to economic success and industrial progress, often placing machines at the center of the narrative (White 1962; Walton 2020)—at times with hopeful enthusiasm, at others with barely concealed apprehension (Mumford 1934). Yet in recent years, narratives surrounding the "Industrial Revolution" have been increasingly questioned—gradually but steadily. The role of machinery is being reexamined and recontextualized as new research challenges established assumptions, seeking to problematize innovation without falling into the trap of an uncritical, dehumanizing technological determinism (Mokyr 1990, 2002; Smith and Marx 1994; Acemoglu and Johnson 2023).

A key perspective for understanding the scope of these dynamics is offered by Kaiserfeld in *Beyond Innovation* (2015), where he places the social dimension at the center of the discussion on the introduction and management of innovation. By focusing on the role of institutions, he presents a critical view of progress through an interdisciplinary approach, demonstrating that technological innovation is deeply embedded in social structures. Kaiserfeld's methodological proposal, while widely recognized in science and technology studies, has remained relatively underexplored in other research domains. Nevertheless, it holds a significant place in the long-standing debate on the role of institutions in technological innovation, particularly in relation to the complex issue of economic development. Social sciences have frequently highlighted the ambiguous and context-dependent role of institutions in economic development. Over the past three decades, this topic has been the focus of extensive research. On the one hand, scholars have demonstrated that institutions play a crucial role in economic development; on the other, they have raised fundamental questions about which forms of governance best foster economic expansion and how institutions emerge and evolve (Kanani and Larizza,

2021). Over time, research has emphasized institutions as central drivers of economic development (Hall and Jones 1999; Acemoglu et al. 2001; Acemoglu and Johnson 2005; Acemoglu and Robinson 2010; Baland et al. 2020), highlighting two key issues: firstly, the strong dependence of economic performance on institutional policy decisions (North 1989, 1990; Sabel and Zeitlin 1997); and secondly, the hypothesis that institutional quality is a determining factor in either economic stagnation or growth (Kapur and Webb 2000; Chang 2011; Baland et al. 2020).

When these themes are examined in the context of the early modern world, the prevailing forms of government—such as lordships or monarchies—might suggest a direct link between the economic success or failure of state policies and the ruler's authority. Instead, in this context, an equally crucial role is played by the mechanisms of governmental oversight and the political influence of mercantile elites, who either support or are supported by centralized power (North and Thomas 1973; Acemoglu et al. 2005; Torvik 2020; Rössner 2016, 2020). Traders, with their extensive domestic and international networks, played a decisive role in shaping economic policies and, consequently, in determining the success of local products in global markets (Caracausi and Jeggle 2014). Technical and institutional innovations are closely tied to the characteristics of new products, playing a decisive role in the emergence and expansion of what is commonly referred to as the "consumer society." Since at least the late twentieth century, this subject has been at the forefront of numerous studies often shaped by a Western-centric perspective and driven by an implicit search for origins (Baudrillard 1970; Braudel 1979; Trentmann 2016). This focus has diverted attention from the cultural and social dynamics that fundamentally reshaped lifestyles, habits, and tastes throughout history, while simultaneously fueling debates over whether the consumer society originated in early modern Great Britain (McKendrick et al. 1982; Goldthwaite 1987; Clunas 1991; Jardine 2006). More recently, innovative methodological approaches have emerged (De Vries 2008), stimulating intense debate on the subject. What can be stated with reasonable certainty, however, is that a strong link exists between the development of consumer society and the demand for specific material qualities in products traded on international markets. This dynamic reinforced the connection between locality and product in a world where quality—particularly in the textile sector—was ideally guaranteed by the reputation of local manufacturing traditions (Massa 1970; Molà 1994, 2000; Battistini 2003; Poni 2009).

The study of product quality is intrinsically linked to the history of labor and the institutional organizations that regulated it. The qualitative attributes that made certain products particularly desirable were, in fact, guaranteed through the organization of labor, supported by the guild systems that operated across a large part of early modern Europe (De Munck 2011). As institutions characterized by distinctive dynamics—such as long apprenticeship periods, high registration fees, and rigorous master exams—guilds played a pivotal role in both artisan training and production oversight, mediating between governing authorities and the workforce. Within the artisanal workshop, these mechanisms reinforced the connection between the value of labor and the value of the product (Lis and Soly 2012; Belfanti 2018; Maitte 2009, 2016, 2021), ensuring that wages were closely tied to the socially defined status of the individual (Trivellato 1999; Caracausi 2011; Grassi 2026). Amidst debates that have portrayed guilds either as obstacles to economic development (Ogilvie 2004, 2008, 2011, 2014, 2019) or as key players in fostering growth (Epstein 1998, 2008; Epstein and Prak 2008; Prak and Wallis 2020), a particularly compelling perspective has emerged from recent Castilian and Catalan historiography (Franch Benavent 2014; Franch Benavent et al. 2016; Solà Parera 2019; Nieto Sánchez 2021; Hidalgo Fernández and Nieto Sánchez 2024). Building on studies related to the "return of the guilds" (Lucassen et al. 2008), this historiography has emphasized the importance of studying the behaviors and motivations of the guilds in relation to the socio-economic contexts in which they emerge, operate, and disappear, expanding the types of sources used and suggesting the avoidance of generalizations (Sonenscher 1989; Ago 1998, 2000; Trivellato 2000; Nieto Sánchez and Zofío Llorente 2015; Ferrer-Alòs 2022). This research has, in fact, proposed studying the history of labor as a response to economic history, often dominated by numbers and formulas, shifting toward a history that takes into account practices and their interactions. Within this framework, gender dynamics play a crucial role in shaping the processes of innovation, revealing how technological change is deeply embedded in social and cultural structures (Blake and Hanson 2005; Alsos et al. 2013). The division of labor, the transmission of expertise, and the recognition of skill were all influenced by gendered hierarchies that determined access to training, remuneration, and professional visibility (Sarti et al. 2018; Zucca Micheletto 2022). Women, though frequently undervalued or rendered invisible by institutional and social structures, nonetheless contributed significantly to the development and diffusion of technical knowledge

(Groppi 1996; Humphries and Sarasúa 2012; Bellavitis 2021). Their participation was essential to maintaining quality standards and ensuring the continuity of production. The goal, therefore, is to offer a reconstruction of economic and social dynamics, free from the stereotypical lens that has often portrayed them in a simplistic light. As Musso (2023) has recently argued, following the insights of Dal Pane (1968), labor history is not only all-encompassing—the history of labor conceived as the history of humankind (Lucassen 2021)—but it must also account for the motivations driving individual choices. It is in this space, in fact, that personal and professional lives intertwine.

In this sense, the history of Piedmontese silk serves as a lens through which to reconsider long-term economic and social transformations. It encourages a shift beyond deterministic narratives of technological progress, embracing instead a more nuanced and complex perspective—one that recognizes the multiple forces shaping the adoption and success of innovation.

4 The Piedmontese Silk Industry: An Innovation Ecosystem Between Micro and Macro

Based on these premises, the study explores how innovation can be effectively analyzed from a historical perspective. Among the various possible approaches, the concept of the "innovation ecosystem" has been chosen—a term introduced into the scientific landscape by Moore (1993) and Adner (2006) to describe how businesses interact in a competitive environment characterized by rapid and transformative technological changes. Since its introduction, the concept has gained both widespread recognition and criticism (Oh et al. 2016; Ritala and Almpanopoulou 2017; Baiyere 2018; De Vasconcelos Gomes et al. 2018). However, while initially developed within business studies, subsequent interpretations suggest that it holds valuable insights for other fields as well. In particular, Granstrand and Holgersson (2020) have recently defined an innovation ecosystem as "the evolving set of actors, activities, and artifacts, and the institutions and relations, including complementary and substitute relations, that are important for the innovative performance of an actor or a population of actors" (Granstrand and Holgersson 2020, 3). Their definition significantly broadens the potential applications of this concept: through this interpretative lens, the case of the Piedmontese silk industry is analyzed as an innovation ecosystem—an intricate network of technological, social, cultural, and economic interactions. These elements, deeply rooted in tradition, have coexisted and influenced each other, enabling the local silk industry to establish a lasting reputation and a durable legacy—despite its inherent economic fragility. Applying this framework rests on three key principles: an innovation ecosystem consists of various actors, connections, and resources, all essential for transforming an idea into meaningful large-scale impact. The effectiveness of each component within the innovation ecosystem is shaped by its interaction with other elements in the system, and a change in one part of the innovation ecosystem sparks a series of reactions across the whole system.

Yet, applying this definition raises a significant issue, particularly when considering the context of the ancien régime: how do the dynamics of the innovation ecosystem interact with the geographical and political space in which innovation takes place? Moreover, how does the innovation ecosystem engage with the broader global dynamics in which it is inevitably embedded? In other words, what role does space play within an innovation ecosystem?

A useful framework for addressing these questions can be found in the historiographical methodology of micro-spatial history, recently introduced by De Vito and Gerritsen (2018). Drawing on the microhistorical tradition developed by nineteenth- and twentieth-century scholars, this approach reconsiders the spatial dimension of historical processes and fosters a dialogue between the micro and macro scales (Galtung 1990; Revel 2006; De Vito 2019; Trivellato 2023). However, while this study builds on De Vito and Gerritsen's reflections on the spatial configuration of historical processes—particularly the role of space in shaping actors, artifacts, institutions, and relationships—its methodological foundations lie in the Italian tradition of social microhistory (Ginzburg 1976, 1994, 2019; Grendi 1977, 1993; Ginzburg and Poni 1979; Levi 1985; Revel 2006; Lanaro 2011). This approach privileges the reconstruction of social relations, and individual trajectories as a means of interpreting broader structures of power, economy, and culture. The biographical–prosopographical perspective and the spatial sensitivity inspired by De Vito and Gerritsen are therefore considered complementary dimensions of analysis in this study, illuminating how local practices and institutional frameworks are shaped by their material and geographical settings. Within this integrated framework, the Piedmontese silk industry is examined as a dynamic social organism—an innovation ecosystem in which people, places, and institutions interact to generate and sustain change, moving beyond linear narratives of progress and decline, revealing the dense web of relationships and spatial interconnections that shaped Piedmont's silk economy over time.

5 The Fabric of Innovation: Contents

The volume consists of nine chapters, each exploring the relationship between innovation and social transformation.

Chapter 2 examines the link between tradition and innovation in the manufacturing production of the ancien régime, presenting the case study of the Piedmontese silk industry as the latest branch of a long-standing global tradition. To underpin this perspective, the chapter traces the introduction of silk to Europe and Italy, providing the necessary context to understand the rapid rise of Piedmont's silk industry, despite its late start compared to the well-established Italian textile centers of the late Middle Ages. While Italy's prominence in the silk trade declined in the seventeenth century, Piedmont took a different path, specializing in the production of silk yarns. These yarns were highly sought after by competing industries at least until the mid-nineteenth century.

Chapters 3 and 4 introduce two key perspectives—technological and institutional—both of which contributed to the initial success of the Piedmontese silk industry. These chapters demonstrate that importing technologies and developing innovative techniques alone are not sufficient to reach a leading economic position. A strategic plan must consider human capital, whose worldview was shaped in a historical period before the introduction of innovation. Through a detailed analysis of the phases of diffusion and development of new techniques and technologies related to the innovative production of high-quality silk goods, examined in a comparative perspective with other Italian and international contexts, these chapters explore the interplay between technological and institutional innovation. Technical progress, in fact, requires a legislative framework to shore up its implementation, function, and long-term sustainability. In this context, the mercantilist policies introduced in France by Colbert—and their adaptation in Piedmont under Minister Truchi di Levaldigi in the late seventeenth century—illustrate the positive role of collaboration between state institutions and the merchant class in driving industrial innovation and securing a leading economic position on the international market. By addressing the complex political role of merchants, the chapters also show how they were both agents of change and custodians of monopolistic practices. While they sought profits in international markets and aimed to influence state policies, merchants also had to navigate tensions with artisans and their role in trade. The attempt to subjugate artisans' labor clashed with the phenomenon of the founding (or, in some cases, re-founding) of guilds, institutions that allowed distinct phases of technological advancement to coexist.

Through a prosopographical analysis of the merchant and artisan classes, the fifth, sixth, and seventh chapters explore the strategies, roles, impact, reactions, and concrete participation of individuals in innovation within commerce and production. Chapter 5 looks at the role of traders. By reaping the benefits of the thriving silk industry, these traders managed to reshape their social, political, and economic roles, gradually expanding their market influence by financing manufacturing enterprises. This process fostered the emergence of the industrial capitalist entrepreneur. The collaboration between entrepreneurs and the government led to two significant developments: the establishment of royal manufactories and the possibilities for exploiting the labor of individuals housed in charitable institutions, involving both adults and children. Turning to the world of craftsmen, Chap. 6 reaches the peak of its bottom-up approach through a microhistorical reconstruction of artisan life. The intertwined life stories of Pierre Millori, his son Pietro, and his daughter-in-law Anna Maria Pajsio shed light on the interaction between innovation and labor in the silk sector. They highlight the fundamental role played by factors such as artisan mobility, professional training, and gender in shaping the introduction and management of innovation in the Piedmontese silk industry. Lastly, the subject of Chap. 7 is the city of Turin, the capital of the Savoyard state and the nerve center of production and trade. This chapter brings to life the streets, squares, and alleyways, revealing the close links between product innovation and urban transformation. It highlights how social variables have often been viewed through lenses clouded by stereotypes, while archival evidence reveals a far more complex and diverse story than traditional narratives suggest.

The last section looks at the bigger picture and places the case study within an international context. Chapters 8 and 9 examine the success of the Piedmontese silk industry within the broader global history of textiles and its outcomes in the modern era—marking the decline of Piedmont's silk ambitions. This "decline" should not be understood as an isolated or exceptional collapse. Rather, it reflected a broader realignment of the Italian silk economy at the turn of the nineteenth century—similar contractions and reconfigurations were observable in other major centers such as Milan, Venice, and Bologna, as the entire peninsula adjusted to new market structures and industrial logics. Specifically, the study examines how the emergence of the Lyonnais fashion system and the rise of cotton production reshaped the market, relegating Piedmontese silk production to the role of a semi-finished goods supplier for the international market. Amid desperate attempts to recover and to address the serious consequences of the late eighteenth-century crisis, Chap. 8 highlights how the economic policies and technological innovations failed to keep pace with changing times. Finally, Chap. 9 delves into the complex relationship between the silk industry and the social, political, and cultural transformations that unfolded before, during, and after the French Revolution—a period that had unique consequences for Piedmont. Global political upheavals left little room for Piedmontese silk production. Only with Napoleon's annexation of Piedmont into the French Empire did the region's silk industry, albeit under difficult conditions, regain access to Lyon—turning Piedmont into a productive colony. However, the world after Napoleon's fall was changed fundamentally, even as Piedmont was abruptly returned to the ancien régime. In analyzing the socio-economic dynamics that unfolded during this turbulent period, this conclusion highlights how the interaction between technological innovation, social organization, and state policy shaped both the strengths and limitations of Piedmont's manufacturing model.

From a broader perspective, this collapse can also be interpreted as the structural crisis of a state-managed form of commercial capitalism. As Banaji (2019) suggests, such systems were inherently unstable: their concentration of mercantile capital under state control generated short-term growth but undermined long-term accumulation. In Piedmont, this imbalance between public authority and private enterprise reached a breaking point, revealing the limits of a hybrid model that had once sustained the region's economic prominence. In this sense, Piedmont's silk experience adds a vital piece to the socio-economic dynamics that characterized early nineteenth-century Italy, when long-standing textile systems were redefined by global trade, new technologies, and the restructuring of regional economies.

To conclude, the Epilogue returns to the "Glass Beads Paradox" first outlined in the opening chapter, weaving together the threads of the volume's central argument, and reflecting on how the reconstruction of Piedmont's silk industry illuminates the enduring tension between innovation, adaptation, and decline in the making of modern industrial societies.

Bibliography

Acemoglu, Daron, and Simon Johnson. 2005. Unbundling institutions. *Journal of Political Economy* 113 (5): 949–995.

Acemoglu, Daron, and Simon Johnson. 2023. *Power and progress. Our 1000-year struggle over technology & prosperity*. London: Hodder and Stoughton.

Acemoglu, Daron, and James A. Robinson. 2010. The role of institution in growth and development. *Review of Economics and Institutions* 1 (2): 1–33.

Acemoglu, Daron, Simon Johnson, and James A. Robinson. 2001. The colonial origins of comparative development: An empirical investigation. *American Economic Review* 91 (5): 1369–1401.

Acemoglu, Daron, Simon Johnson, and James A. Robinson. 2005. The rise of Europe: Atlantic trade, institutional change, and economic growth. *American Economic Review* 95 (3): 546–679.

Adner, Ron. 2006. Match your innovation strategy to your innovation ecosystem. *Harvard Business Review* 84 (4): 98–107.

Ago, Renata. 1998. *Economia barocca: mercato e istituzioni nella Roma del Seicento*. Rome: Donzelli.

Ago, Renata. 2000. Le fonti notarile del XVII secolo: alcune istruzioni per l'uso. *Mélanges de l'École française de Rome. Italie et Méditerranée* 112 (1): 31–44.

Alsos, Gry A., Elisabet Ljunggren, and Ulla Hytti. 2013. Gender and innovation: State of the art and a research agenda. *International Journal of Gender and Entrepreneurship* 5 (3): 236–256.

Baiyere, Abayomi. 2018. Fostering innovation ecosystems - note on the 2017 ISPIM innovation forum. *Technovation* 69:1.

Baland, Jean-Marie, François Bourguignon, Jean-Philippe Platteau, and Thierry Verdier. 2020. Economic development and institutions. An introduction. In *The handbook of economic development and institutions*, ed. Jean-Marie Baland, François Bourguignon, Jean-Philippe Platteau, and Thierry Verdier, 1–20. Princeton: Princeton University Press.

Balbi, Gabriele, and Cecilia Winterhalter, eds. 2013. *Antiche Novità. Una guida transdisciplinare per interpretare il vecchio e il nuovo*. Naples: Orthotes.

Battistini, Francesco. 2003. *L'industria della seta in Italia nell'età moderna*. Bologna: Il Mulino.

Baudrillard, Jean. 1970. *La société de consommation: ses mythes, ses structures*. Paris: Gallimard.

Belfanti, Carlo Marco. 2018. Branding before the brand: Marks, imitations and counterfeits in pre-modern Europe. *Business History* 60 (8): 1127–1146.

Bellavitis, Anna. 2021. Arricchire I questionari: la storia del lavoro di Angela Groppi. *Genesis* 20:13–25.
Bertucci, Paola. 2021. Spinners' hands, imperial minds: Migrant labour, embodied expertise, and the failed transfer of silk technology across the Atlantic. *Technology and Culture* 62 (4): 1003–1031.
Bertucci, Paola. 2023. *In the land of marvels. Science, fabricated realities and industrial espionage in the age of the grand tour.* Baltimore: John Hopkins University Press.
Blake, Megan K., and Susan Hanson. 2005. Rethinking innovation: Context and gender. *Environment and Planning A* 37 (4): 681–701.
Bloch, Marc. 1935. Avènement et conquêtes du moulin à eau. *Annales d'histoire Économique et Sociale* 7:538–563.
Braudel, Fernand. 1979. *Civilisation matérielle, économie et capitalisme.* Paris: Colin.
Brewer, Daniel. 2011. The Encyclopédie: Innovation and legacy. In *New essays on Diderot*, ed. James Fowler, 47–58. Cambridge: Cambridge University Press.
Caracausi, Andrea. 2011. The just wage in early modern Italy: A reflection on Zacchia's "De Salario seu Operariorum Mercede". *International Review of Social History* 56 (S19): 107–124.
Caracausi, Andrea, and Christof Jeggle, eds. 2014. *Commercial networks and European cities, 1400–1800.* London: Routledge.
Chang, Haj. 2011. Institutions and economic development: Theory, policy and history. *Journal of Institutional Economics* 7 (4): 473–498.
Cipolla, Carlo M. 1965. *Guns, sails, and empires: Technological innovation and the early phases of European expansion, 1400–1700.* New York: Minerva.
Cipolla, Carlo M. 1974. *Storia economica Europa preindustriale.* Bologna: Il Mulino.
Clunas, Craig. 1991. *Superfluous things. Material culture and social status in early modern China.* Cambridge: Polity Press.
Dal Pane, Luigi. 1968. *La storia come storia del lavoro: discorsi di concezione e di metodo.* Bologna: Patron.
Davids, Karel, and Bert De Munck, eds. 2014. *Innovation and creativity in late medieval and early modern European cities.* London: Routledge.
De Grazia, Victoria. 2013. Prefazione. Il vecchio e il nuovo, crisi e interregni. In *Antiche Novità. Una guida transdisciplinare per interpretare il vecchio e il nuovo*, ed. Gabriele Balbi and Cecilia Winterhalter, 5–10. Naples: Orthotes.
De Munck, Bert. 2011. Guilds, product quality and intrinsic value. Towards a history of conventions in historical social research. *Historical Social Research* 36 (4): 103–124.
De Vasconcelos Gomes, Leonardo A., Ana Lucia Figueiredo Facin, Mario Sergio Salerno, and Rodrigo Kazuo Ikenami. 2018. Unpacking the innovation ecosys-

tem construct: Evolution, gaps and trends. *Technological Forecasting and Social Change* 136:30–48.
De Vito, Christian G. 2019. History without scale: The micro-spatial perspective. *Past & Present* 242 (2): 348–372.
De Vito, Christian G., and Anne Gerritsen, eds. 2018. *Micro-spatial histories of global labour*. London: Palgrave Macmillan.
De Vries, Jan. 2008. *The industrious revolution. Consumer behavior and the household economy, 1650 to the present*. Cambridge: Cambridge University Press.
Epstein, Stephan R. 1998. Craft guilds, apprenticeship, and technological change in preindustrial Europe. *The Journal of Economic History* 58 (3): 684–713.
Epstein, Stephan R. 2008. Craft guilds in the pre-modern economy: A discussion. *Economic History Review* 6181:155–174.
Epstein, Stephan R., and Maarten Prak, eds. 2008. *Guilds, innovation and the European economy, 1400–1800*. Cambridge: Cambridge University Press.
Ferrer-Alòs, Llorenç. 2022. El gremio cuando interesa. Producción y comercialización de pañuelos de seda en Manresa (Cataluña) en el siglo XVIII. *Studia Historica: Historia Moderna* 44 (1): 409–444.
Franch Benavent, Ricardo. 2014. Los maestros del colegio del arte mayor de la seda de Valencia en una fase de crecimiento manufacturero (1686–1755). *Hispania* 74 (1): 41–68.
Franch Benavent, Ricardo, Daniel Muñoz Navarro, and Luis Rosado Calatayud. 2016. La reproducción de los maestros y las transformaciones de las condiciones sociales de los miembros del Colegio del Arte Mayor de la Seda de Valencia en el siglo XVIII. *Revista de Historia Industrial* 25 (65): 15–50.
Galtung, Johan. 1990. Macro-history as metaphor for biography: An essay on macro and micro history. *Biography* 13 (4): 283–299.
Ginzburg, Carlo. 1976. *Il formaggio e i vermi*. Turin: Einaudi.
Ginzburg, Carlo. 1994. Microstoria: due o tre cose che so di lei. *Quaderni Storici* 86 (2): 511–539.
Ginzburg, Carlo. 2019. Ricordando Carlo Poni. Una rilettura de "Il nome e il come". *Quaderni Storici* 161 (2): 552–556.
Ginzburg, Carlo, and Carlo Poni. 1979. Il nome e il come. Scambio ineguale e mercato storiografico. *Quaderni Storici* 40 (1): 181–190.
Godin, Benoît. 2015. *Innovation contested. The idea of innovation over the centuries*. London: Routledge.
Goldthwaite, Richard A. 1987. The empire of things. Consumer demand in renaissance Italy. In *Patronage, art and society in renaissance Italy*, ed. Francis W. Kent and Patricia Simons, 153–175. Oxford: Oxford University Press.
Gramsci, Antonio. 1975. *Quaderni del Carcere*. Edited by Valentino Gerratana. Turin: Einaudi.
Granstrand, Ove, and Marcus Holgersson. 2020. Innovation ecosystems: A conceptual review and a new definition. *Technovation* 90–91 (102098): 1–12.

Grassi, Mario. 2026. The Main purpose. Bargaining, wages and gender in the 18th century Piedmontese silk manufacture. In *A historical casebook of wage formation: Wage determination and wage bargains of the pre industrial world*, ed. Giulio Ongaro, Judy Z. Stephenson, and Luca Mocarelli. Cham: Palgrave Macmillan.

Grendi, Edoardo. 1977. Micro-analisi e storia sociale. *Quaderni Storici* 35 (2): 506–520.

Grendi, Edoardo. 1993. *Il cervo e la repubblica. Il modello ligure di antico regime.* Turin: Einaudi.

Groppi, Angela, ed. 1996. *Il lavoro delle donne.* Rome-Bari: Laterza.

Hahn, Barbara. 2020. *Technology in the industrial revolution.* Cambridge: Cambridge University Press.

Hall, Robert E., and Charles I. Jones. 1999. Why do some countries produce so much more output per worker than others? *Quarterly Journal of Economics* 114 (1): 83–116.

Hidalgo Fernández, Francisco, and José Antolín Nieto Sánchez, eds. 2024. *Artesanos. Una historia social en España (siglos XVI-XIX).* Ciudad Real: Ediciones de la Universidad de Castilla-La Mancha.

Hoare, Quintin, and Geoffrey Nowell-Smith. 1971. *Selections from the prison notebooks of Antonio Gramsci.* London: Lawrence & Wishart.

Hobsbawm, Eric, and Terence Ranger. 1983. *The invention of tradition.* Cambridge: Cambridge University Press.

Hugo, Victor. 1862. *Les Misérables.* Vol. 2.2. Paris: Pagnerre.

Hugo, Victor. 2016. *Les Misérables.* Translated by C. Donougher. London: Penguin.

Humphries, Jane, and Carmen Sarasúa. 2012. Off the record: Reconstructing women's labor force participation in the European past. *Feminist Economics* 18:39–67.

Jardine, Lisa. 2006. *Affari di genio. Una storia del Rinascimento europeo.* Rome: Carocci.

Kaiserfeld, Thomas. 2015. *Beyond innovation: Technology, institution and change as categories for social analysis.* Cham: Palgrave Macmillan.

Kanani, Alma, and Marco Larizza. 2021. Institutions matter for growth and prosperity today more than ever. *World Bank Blogs.* https://blogs.worldbank.org/governance/institutions-matter-growth-and-prosperity-today-more-ever. Accessed 20 August 2024

Kapur, Devesh, and Richard Webb. 2000. Governance-related conditionalities of the IFIs. *G-24 discussion paper series* 6.

Kuhn, Thomas S. 1962. *The structure of scientific revolutions.* Chicago: University of Chicago Press.

Lanaro, Paola, ed. 2011. *Microstoria. A venticinque anni da L'eredità immateriale.* Milan: FrancoAngeli.

Levi, Giovanni. 1985. *L'eredità immateriale. Carriera di un esorcista nel Piemonte del Seicento*. Turin: Einaudi.
Lis, Catharina, and Hugo Soly. 2012. *Worthy efforts: Attitudes to work and workers in pre-industrial Europe*. Leiden-Boston: Brill.
Lucassen, Jan. 2021. *The story of work: A new history of humankind*. New Haven: Yale University Press.
Lucassen, Jan, Tine De Moor, and Jan Luiten Van Zanden. 2008. The return of the guilds: Towards a global history of the guilds in pre-industrial times. *International Review of Social History* 53 (16): 1–14.
Maitte, Corine. 2009. *Les chemins de verre. Les migrations des verriers d'Altare et de Venise (XVIe-XIXe siècles)*. Rennes: Presses Universitaires de Rennes.
Maitte, Corine. 2016. Le travail invisible dans les familles artisanales (XVIIe-XVIIIe siècle). *Mélanges de l'École française de Rome - Italie et Méditerranée modernes et contemporaines* 128:1.
Maitte, Corine. 2021. Rémunérer et compter le travail sur les chantiers Médicis (fin xvie siècle-début xviie siècle). *Histoire & Mesure* 36 (1): 3–36.
Massa, Paola. 1970. *L'arte genovese della seta nella normativa del XV e del XVI secolo*. Genoa: Atti della Società Ligure di Storia Patria.
Mckendrick, Neil, John Brewer, and John H. Plumb. 1982. *The birth of a consumer society. The commercialization of eighteenth-century England*. Bloomington: Indiana University Press.
Mokyr, Joel. 1990. *The lever of riches: Technological creativity and economic Progress*. Oxford: Oxford University Press.
Mokyr, Joel. 2002. *The gifts of Athena: Historical origins of the knowledge economy*. Princeton: Princeton University Press.
Mokyr, Joel. 2012. *The enlightened economy. An economic history of Britain 1700–1850*. New Haven: Yale University Press.
Mokyr, Joel. 2016. *A culture of growth: The origins of the modern economy*. Princeton: Princeton University Press.
Molà, Luca. 1994. *La comunità dei lucchesi a Venezia: immigrazione e industria della seta nel tardo Medioevo*. Venice: Istituto Veneto di Scienze, Lettere ed Arti.
Molà, Luca. 2000. *The silk industry of renaissance Venice*. Baltimore and London: Johns Hopkins University Press.
Moore, James F. 1993. Predators and prey: A new ecology of competition. *Harvard Business Review* 71 (3): 75–86.
Mumford, Lewis. 1934. *Technics & civilization*. New York: Harcourt, Brace and Co.
Musso, Stefano. 2023. Il senso di fare storia del lavoro oggi in Italia. *Passato e Presente* 119:5–14.
Nieto Sánchez, José Antolín. 2021. A propósito del monopolio gremial: Toledo, 1700–1837. *Investigaciones de Historia Económica/Economic History Research* 18 (1): 12–25.

Nieto Sánchez, José Antolín, and Juan Carlos Zofío Llorente. 2015. Los gremios de Madrid durante la Edad Moderna: una revisión. *Áreas* 34:47–61.
North, Douglass C. 1989. Institutions and economic growth: An historical introduction. *World Development* 17 (9): 1319–1332.
North, Douglass C. 1990. *Institutions, institutional change and economic performance*. Cambridge: Cambridge University Press.
North, Douglass C., and Robert P. Thomas. 1973. *The rise of the western world: A new economic history*. Cambridge: Cambridge University Press.
Ogilvie, Sheilagh. 2004. Guilds, efficiency, and social capital. Evidence from German protoindustry. *Economic History Review* 57 (2): 286–333.
Ogilvie, Sheilagh. 2008. Rehabilitating the guilds. A reply. *Economic History Review* 61 (1): 175–182.
Ogilvie, Sheilagh. 2011. *Institutions and European trade: Merchant guilds, 1000–1800*. Cambridge: Cambridge University Press.
Ogilvie, Sheilagh. 2014. The economics of guilds. *Journal of Economics Perspectives* 28 (4): 169–192.
Ogilvie, Sheilagh. 2019. *The European guilds: An economic analysis*. Princeton: Princeton University Press.
Oh, Deog-Seong, Fred Phillips, Sehee Park, and Eunghyun Lee. 2016. Innovation ecosystems: A critical examination. *Technovation* 54:1–6.
Poni, Carlo. 2009. *La seta in Italia, una grande industria prima della rivoluzione industriale*. Bologna: Il Mulino.
Prak, Maarten, and Patrick Wallis, eds. 2020. *Apprenticeship in early modern Europe*. Cambridge: Cambridge University Press.
Revel, Jacques. 2006. *Giochi di scala: la microstoria alla prova dell'esperienza*. Rome: Viella.
Ritala, Paavo, and Argyro Almpanopoulou. 2017. In defense of 'eco' in innovation ecosystem. *Technovation* 60–61:39–42.
Rössner, Philipp R., ed. 2016. *Economic growth and the origins of modern political economy. Economic reasons of state 1500–2000*. London: Routledge.
Rössner, Philipp R. 2020. *Freedom and capitalism in early modern Europe. Mercantilism and the making of the modern economic mind*. Cham: Palgrave Macmillan.
Sabel, Charles, and Jonathan Zeitlin, eds. 1997. *World of possibilities. Flexibility and mass production in Western industrialization*. Cambridge: Cambridge University Press.
Sarti, Raffaella, Anna Bellavitis, and Manuela Martini, eds. 2018. *What is work? Gender at the crossroads of home, family, and business from the early modern era to the present*. Oxford: Berghahn.
Smith, Pamela H. 2022. *From lived experience to the written word: Reconstructing practical knowledge in the early modern world*. Chicago: University of Chicago Press.

Smith, Merritt R., and Leo Marx, eds. 1994. *Does technology drive history? The dilemma of technological determinism*. Boston: MIT Press.

Solà Parera, Àngels, ed. 2019. *Artesanos, gremios y género en el sur de Europa (siglos XVI–XIX)*. Vilassar de Dalt: Icària.

Sonenscher, Michael. 1989. *Work and wages: Natural law, politics and the eighteenth-century French trades*. Cambridge: Cambridge University Press.

Torvik, Ragnar. 2020. Formal institutions and development in low-income countries: Positive and normative theory. In *The handbook of economic development and institutions*, ed. Jean-Marie Baland, François Bourguignon, Jean-Philippe Platteau, and Thierry Verdier, 103–136. Princeton: Princeton University Press.

Trentmann, Frank. 2016. *Empire of things. How we became a world of consumers, from the fifteenth century to the twenty-first*. London: Allen Lane.

Trivellato, Francesca. 1999. Salaires et justice dans les corporations vénitiennes au XVIIe siècle: le cas des manufactures de verre. *Annales* 54 (1): 245–273.

Trivellato, Francesca. 2000. *Fondamenta dei vetrai. Lavoro, tecnologia e mercato a Venezia tra Sei e Settecento*. Rome: Donzelli.

Trivellato, Francesca. 2023. *Microstoria e storia globale*. Rome: Officina Libraria.

Walton, Steven A. 2020. *Fifty years of medieval technology and social change*. London: Routledge.

White, Lynn, Jr. 1962. *Medieval technology and social change*. Oxford: Oxford University Press.

Zucca Micheletto, Beatrice. 2022. A difficult matching. In *Female artisans, technical knowledge and inventions in early modern Savoy-Piedmont. The republic of skill*, ed. David Garrioch, 223–245. Boston: Brill.

CHAPTER 2

The Italian Silk Road and Piedmontese Backwardness

1 Introduction

During the early modern period, the silk industry emerged as one of the most lucrative economic sectors. Its significant profitability fueled intense competition, not only among silk-producing nations but also among individual merchants eager to expand their market reach. In this competitive environment, treatises and pamphlets on the latest technological innovations in silk production were common, often authored by entrepreneurs and intellectuals (Stockland 2017). Among these writings, those of Antonio Zanon—a native of Friuli deeply connected to the silk trade through his family's business—stand out for their wide dissemination and editorial success (Griselini 1770; Luzzatto 1927; Molesti 1974; Cargnelutti 2009). A forward-thinking and enlightened entrepreneur, Zanon devoted his later years to intellectual pursuits, with a particular focus on advancing agriculture and industry. Between 1763 and 1767, he published 115 dissertations in epistolary form, compiled into 7 volumes under the title *Dell'Agricoltura, dell'arti, e del commercio in quanto unite contribuiscono alla felicità degli Stati* (On Agriculture, Arts, and Commerce, and How Their Union Contributes to the

M. Grassi, *The Silk Industry in Early Modern Piedmont*, Labour in History and Society,
https://doi.org/10.1007/978-3-032-15353-1_2

Happiness of States). The first volume is dedicated entirely to general trade and commerce, while the second focuses on the preeminent commercial sector of the era: silk. In the first eight letters, Zanon gathers accounts and testimonies that trace the historiographical tradition of silk's remarkable success. The ninth letter then shifts to describe what was considered at the time the pinnacle of silk production: the Piedmontese industry.

> Among all the peoples of Italy, the Piedmontese were the last to cultivate silk, despite their land and climate being perfectly suited for such production. (…) Yet their rulers deserve full recognition for having, in an astonishingly short time, elevated it to remarkable heights while also teaching us the true method of silk production.[1] (Zanon 1763, 144)

This statement highlights the dual nature of Piedmont's relationship with the silk industry and its broader impact on the sector's advancement. Zanon, on the one hand, highlights the region's initial delay compared to Italy's well-established silk production. On the other, he acknowledges Piedmont's crucial contribution to perfecting the most advanced manufacturing techniques. In his treatise, supporting the revival of Friuli's silk industry, he presents the Piedmontese model as the culmination of a long historical process, emphasizing that such achievements were made possible by centuries of accumulated expertise and global refinement of production practices. Indeed, the history of silk production is marked by rapid socio-economic transformations, rooted in a long-standing tradition of manufacturing and trade. Beyond its enduring economic significance, silk has, since its introduction to Europe, been deeply connected to the exchange of knowledge, technologies, and people, reflecting the dynamism of the ancien régime economy. Through the development of production chains and the expansion of trade networks aimed at international markets, numerous European cities secured prominent positions in the global economy as early as the medieval period.

[1] "Fra tutti gli altri popoli d'Italia gli ultimi a coltivare la seta furono i piemontesi, quantunque la terra, ed il clima (…) sieno attissimi, a tale prodotto. Ma que' sovrani hanno la gloria intera d'averlo in breve corso d'anni ridotto ad una incredibile moltiplicazione; e nello stesso tempo insegnato a noi il vero modo di lavorare la seta" (Zanon 1763, 144).

Recent studies on innovation, across diverse research fields, have highlighted the dynamics and tensions between tradition and novelty, continuity and change, and the interplay of the old with the new (Hall and Rosenberg 2010; Balbi and Winterhalter 2013; Forti et al. 2020; Hernes and Feuls 2023). These studies reveal that these elements do not operate in rigid opposition but instead adapt, overlap, and intertwine, giving rise to entirely new outcomes. Applying this perspective to the history of the Piedmontese silk industry underscores how its development emerged from the convergence of traditional knowledge (whether technical, cultural, economic, etc.) accumulated over time and a series of both major and minor innovations that progressively transformed the sector. Understanding the role of tradition in fostering innovation begins with contextualizing the "before"—that is, identifying the enduring features transmitted across generations within the industry. This chapter aims to trace the initial steps of the process that enabled Piedmont to develop what Zanon famously described as "the true method" for working with silk.

To achieve this, the chapter first outlines the key aspects of the centuries-old history of silk production in Europe and Italy, paying particular attention to Piedmont's slow emergence of silk manufactories. It then examines the contributions of the Italian silk tradition that inspired the House of Savoy to take the first step toward the development of this new sector. Framing the new through the lens of the old challenges the notion of a sharp divide between "before" and "after" driven by innovation. Instead, it highlights a continuity that weaves together tradition and novelty, avoiding idealized portrayals of progress or reductive interpretations of resistance, and offering a more balanced understanding of the transformative processes at work.

2 From *Serindia* to the Mediterranean

The introduction of silk to Europe is shrouded in legend. Archaeologists, historians, philologists, and linguists have dated and mapped evidence of silk artifacts in the ancient world, showing that the exchange of goods between Europe and Asia—including silk fabrics—was already underway well before the Christian era (Thorley 1971; Michelazzi 2018). However, the narrative changes when the introduction of silk production into

Europe is analyzed. By the early centuries CE, some centers in Eastern Europe under Byzantine rule had established small-scale private production of silk textiles and fabric dyeing. Yet, the raw material still arrived from East Asia via Persian intermediaries. Frequent conflicts between the Romans and Persians disrupted this supply chain, often leading to shortages of raw silk (Lopez 1945; Oikonomidès 1986; Muthesius 1997; Daryaee 2003; Beckwith 2009).

The most renowned account of how silkworms were introduced to Europe via Byzantium comes from Procopius of Caesarea.[2] According to the author, around the 550s CE, Nestorian monks brought the first silk moth eggs to Emperor Justinian (482–565). This story, later repeated by numerous chroniclers (Bussagli 1992),[3] regardless of its legendary elements, reflects a key historical development: the establishment of silkworm cultivation in Byzantine territories and the emperor's efforts to achieve self-sufficiency in silk production. While most of the silk thread processed in Byzantine workshops continued to be imported from the Middle East, the industry grew stronger. The Byzantines began cultivating mulberry trees and expanding silkworm farming in Greece and southern Italy, aiming to develop manufacturing hubs, particularly in the Peloponnese (Lopez 1945; Laiou 2002; Jacoby 2004; Galliker 2014; Manolova 2020). The subsequent Islamic expansion disrupted the established order, challenging Byzantium's maritime trade supremacy and transforming the Mediterranean in the seventh and eighth centuries into a stage for battles and conquests (Heers 2005; Wickham 2023). Such disruptions were compounded by conflicts between populations that, following the fall of the Western Roman Empire, had taken control of the mainland. Starting with the conquest of North Africa in the seventh century, Arab populations introduced sericulture and silk weaving to Egypt, Tunisia, and Morocco (Spring and Hudson 2002)—techniques that later spread to Al-Andalus in the following centuries (Martín i Ros 1999; Gayo García and Arteaga 2005; Partearroyo Lacaba 2005, 2007; Feliciano 2014; Jacoby 2017; Lopez-Marigorta 2023). Moreover, in this context, Jewish enclaves also played a key role in the dissemination of silk production techniques. These communities were well established in major manufacturing cities in Byzantine Greece and southern Italy (Cassuto 1912; Ferorelli 1915; Munkácsi 1939; Summo 1939; Colafemmina 2000). While evidence is

[2] Procopius of Caesarea, *The Wars of Justinian*, IV.17.1–7.

[3] For example, Theophylactus Simocatta, *Historiae*, VII.9.

limited, some isolated sources highlight the importance of the *Radhanites*, ninth-century Jewish traders, who facilitated commerce between India, China, Byzantium, and the court of Charlemagne, engaging in extensive trade networks (Jacobs 1919; Foltz 1998; McCormick 2002; Toch 2013).

The development of sericulture in the Italian peninsula, rooted in Byzantine traditions, shaped by Jewish migratory and commercial networks, and influenced by Arab conquests in southern Italy, appears to converge around a pivotal historical moment: the *Regnum Siciliae* under Ruggiero II of Hauteville (1095–1154) (Simonsohn 1997; Giardina 2017). The Normans settled in a region where the Byzantines had cultivated sericulture for centuries, and by conquering southern Italy, they brought an end to the period of Saracen incursions, integrating a rich and diverse socio-economic fabric in which silk was highly valued (Simonsohn 1997). After conquering Corfu, Corinth, and Thebes, Ruggiero II captured a large number of Jewish silk workers and brought them to Palermo. According to the chronicle of Nicetas Choniates, the Theban and Corinthian workforce was so essential to the *Rex Siciliae* that, during peace negotiations with Byzantine Emperor Manuel I Komnenos (1118–1180) after the Byzantine reconquest of Corfu, Ruggiero II made sure that the textile workers would not be released.[4]

The turbulent geopolitical landscape likely prompted some weavers, along with their families, to migrate up the peninsula, seeking refuge in other Italian cities, with Lucca standing out (Battistini 1993, 2003; Mainoni 2000; Del Punta and Rosati 2017; Casarino 2018). The significance of the Tuscan city in Italy's silk industry is undeniable. By the mid-twelfth century, the trade in Lucca's silk fabrics was flourishing (Battistini 1998; Mainoni 2000) likely due to its strategic location on the Via Francigena, the principal communication route between Italy and France (Perotti 1998; Rivolin 2002). During the thirteenth century, Lucchese merchants participated in fairs in Champagne, Montpellier, England, Sicily, and Genoa, among other locations (Molà 1994). The success of Lucca and its silk industry is also linked to the growing commercial dominance of the so-called maritime republics (Jacoby 2000; Mainoni 2000; Orlando 2021). Between the twelfth and thirteenth centuries, the ships of Amalfitans, Genoese, Venetians, and Pisans came to dominate key European merchant ports, securing control over the Mediterranean (Orlando 2021). Throughout the thirteenth century, Lucca relied on

[4] Niketas Choniates, *Chronikè Dièġèsis*, III 13.10.

Genoa and Pisa for both the supply and distribution of raw materials, with silk arriving from southern Italy, Sicily, and the Eastern Mediterranean (Cordero di San Quintino 1840; Ferretto 1900; Boldorini 1962; Massa 1970; Battistini 1998; Mainoni 2000). In contrast, Venice played a more limited role in the development of Lucca's manufacture during that period, focusing primarily on the silk trade with Byzantium and the Arab territories (Dini 1993). In addition to its primacy in Italian and European silk weaving, by the thirteenth century, Lucca had begun to lead the way in silkworm breeding and thread processing techniques, ahead of other Italian regions (Dini 1993). This was likely the result of continuous exchanges between Lucca and southern Italy, the Caspian region, Syria, Persia, Turkestan, and, to a lesser extent, Spain (Molà 1994; Battistini 1998). Beyond Lucca, few Italian centers in the thirteenth century could boast silk production that extended beyond their city walls. Only the silk produced in Lucca, Venice, Genoa, and Bologna could meet foreign demand, despite the existence of smaller workshops, such as those in Milan, which primarily served local needs. However, while Genoa and Venice focused on trade and limited luxury production, and Bologna on more common goods, Lucca stood out for its ability to diversify its production (Molà 2000). By the early fourteenth century, the Lucchese silk industry, which had experienced a significant boost with the introduction of the innovative circular silk spinning mill, witnessed the unintended spread of know-how as skilled laborers migrated to other Italian centers following the conquest of Lucca by the mercenary Uguccione della Faggiola in 1314 (Bini 1853–1854; Livi 1881; Green 1986; Molà 1994).

This shift allowed other medieval cities where silk manufacturing had already developed to gradually expand their market share, gain greater renown, and establish themselves as prominent centers of Renaissance production. Francesco Balducci Pegolotti, a Florentine merchant active in several European cities during the 1300s, notes that the Venetian silk trade reached unprecedented levels in the fourteenth century, following the migration of Lucchese silk workers. Notably, Venice had already established a guild of silk weavers by the 1260s, and by the 1340s, Venetian silk was being regularly traded in major cities such as Florence, Nîmes, Montpellier, Paris, London, the cities of Flanders, and even Lucca. Meanwhile, as Balducci Pegolotti stated in his *Pratica della mercatura* (The Practice of Commerce) in the fourteenth century, Bologna, following the Lucchese exodus, managed to increase both the quantity and quality of its silk production (Evans 1936; Dini 1993; Molà 1994, 2000;

Jacoby 2000). In the same period that Venetian and Bolognese silk manufacturing flourished, Genoa experienced a transformation in its production, fully taking shape only in the fifteenth century, when the statutes of the Genoese Silk Guild were formalized in 1432. During this time, a shift in Genoese merchants' commercial practices, supported by favorable tax policies for domestic silk production and the prohibition of silk imports from regions outside the Republic's domain—with some exceptions (Gioffrè 1967; Comba 1992)—encouraged the uninterrupted and consistent growth of the industry. A similar development occurred in Florence's silk industry. Upon their arrival, the Lucchese exiles were integrated into the multifaceted *Por Santa Maria* guild, steadily gaining importance and autonomy. For nearly a century, the *Por Santa Maria* guild concentrated primarily on commercial activities. It was only in the early fifteenth century, following a significant reform of its statutes, that the guild shifted its focus toward production. In a short period, the Florentine silk industry achieved remarkable levels of quality, and by the end of the fifteenth century, the city's luxurious silks and gold-threaded fabrics were being traded not only across Italy but also in markets as far afield as Catalonia, Spain, Turkey, Barbary, Geneva, Avignon, London, Antwerp, Lyon, and Montpellier (Dei 1985; Franceschi 2000).

By the mid-fifteenth century, the Duchy of Milan had also entered the market of silk production, a sector it had previously found difficult to access (Grillo 1994). In 1442, Filippo Maria Visconti (1392–1447) accepted an offer from Pietro di Bartolo, a Florentine silk weaver, to establish a silk factory in the city. Visconti, who had previously attempted but failed to control the port of Genoa, arousing the ire of both Venetians and Florentines, seized the opportunity to distance Milan from rival cities, introducing "the complete craft and mastery of silk production"[5] into the city. This marked the beginning of a production sector that would soon become self-sustaining, including the establishment of animal-powered spinning mills and, in a single unsuccessful case, a hydraulic spinning facility during the early years of the Sforza reign (Zanoboni 2001). In particular, the development of sericulture in Milan is credited to Ludovico il Moro (1452–1508), Duke of Milan during the final decades of the fifteenth century—where his moniker, "Il Moro," is believed to have originated from the word for mulberry tree in the local dialect, highlighting his

[5] "Universum laborerium totamque artem sirici" (Verga 1916, IX).

connection to silkworm farming (Verga 1917; Comba 1992; Mainoni 1994).

By the end of the fifteenth century, the silk industry in Italy had become firmly entrenched in the four cities that, according to Braudel (1949), remained the center of wealth and trade throughout the Mediterranean in the following century: Venice, Genoa, Milan, and Florence (Dini 1993).

Despite the commercial dominance of the four major silk-producing cities, the most significant technological innovation in the industry until the seventeenth century came from Bologna. Up to that point, Bologna had been involved in the production and export of high-quality silk fabrics, although these were of somewhat lower quality compared to those produced in competing cities (Molà 2000). The introduction of the hydraulic silk spinning mill, originally developed in Lucca (Crippa 1990; Molà 1994), enabled Bolognese manufacturers to process significantly larger quantities of material, in a more uniform manner, requiring less labor and time, thereby substantially improving the quality of Italian silk yarn. The secret of the *alla bolognese* silk spinning mill was closely guarded within the city's walls for several centuries. It only spread beyond Bologna at the end of the fifteenth century, gradually diffusing into neighboring states and lordships during the sixteenth century (Molà 2000; Righi 2016; Comino and Gasparetto 2020). At the same time, sericulture in the Vicenza and Verona areas had also reached a remarkable level, providing raw materials for the Venetian silk industry and producing semi-finished goods that were exported across the Alps (Demo 2000, 2001, 2003; Molà 2000; Caracausi 2004; Vianello 2004).

From the sixteenth century onward, the spread of silk manufacturing accelerated, with numerous cities across Italy becoming major centers for silk production. It was during this historical moment that cities such as Ferrara, Modena, Siena, Perugia, Naples, Catanzaro, and Messina became key players in the Italian silk trade. This expansion shifted the fragile balance that had allowed the traditional silk capitals to dominate both domestic and international silk trade. As a result, medieval cities with long-established silk traditions began to undergo rapid transformations—seeking greater autonomy in raw material production and aiming to acquire advanced technologies for producing high-quality silk fabrics (Molà 2000).

3 An Early Modern World Draped in Italian Silk

During the Renaissance and early modern periods, Italian silk was unmatched throughout Europe. However, this does not mean that other parts of Europe did not begin to establish their own silk production centers. For example, in several cities of the Muslim Iberian Peninsula, known as Al-Andalus, a flourishing silk industry had been established as early as the eighth and ninth centuries. Malaga, Seville, Cordoba, Jaen, Murcia, and notably Valencia were among the cities producing large quantities of silk fabrics, which were then sold by Muslim merchants across northern Africa and Eastern Europe (Franch Benavent and Navarro Espinach 2017; Owen Crocker et al. 2022). This flourishing industry began to decline with the *Reconquista*, only to revive later due to the "mercantile colonization" by Italian traders (commonly referred to as Genoese merchants) and the export of silk manufactures to the New World across the Atlantic (Massa 1970; Constable 1990, 2004; Subrahmanyam 1996; Navarro Espinach 1999; Molà 2000). Valencia became a particularly important center for silk production where, by the end of the fifteenth century, around 200 handlooms operating in the "Genoese" style were in use. Prosopographical studies have shown that roughly a thousand silk weavers were working in the city (May 1957; Lamb 2005; Navarro Espinach 2016, 2017; Iradiel Murugarren et al. 2016). Over the centuries, the silk guild evolved from the modest *Gremi de Velluters* (founded in 1479) into the prestigious *Colegio del Arte Mayor de la Seda* (1686), a transformation that underscores not just survival but the flourishing and growing power of the silk industry. By the eighteenth century, Valencia had indisputably become the leading silk production center on the Iberian Peninsula (Navarro Espinach 1996, 2022; Franch Benavent and Muñoz Navarro 2024; González Fons 2024).

Similarly, in medieval France, the development of silk manufacturing began, probably on a domestic scale, primarily for urban consumption, especially for haberdashery (Farmer 2017). A key turning point came with the intersection of small-scale local manufacturing and the major fairs that, from the twelfth century, attracted merchants and commodities from across Christian Europe. The Champagne fairs, characterized by significant attendance, meticulous organization, and exemption from customs duties, offered an excellent opportunity for merchants from all over to make lucrative transactions (Bautier 1992, 1993; Taitz 1994; Molà 2000; Farmer 2017). The success of these fairs paved the way for the emergence of new trading events, gradually replacing those held in the Duchy of Champagne. Among these, the Lyon fair soon established itself as a central marketplace for Italian silks in France (Brésard 1914; Gascon 1956; Dini 1993; Greville Pounds 1994). It was not until the fifteenth century, with the arrival of Florentine, Venetian, and Lombard spinners, dyers, and weavers in Provence and Languedoc, that the foundations of the silk industry began to take shape in France, with Lyon emerging as the hub for Tuscan merchants and bankers (Gascon 1956; Poni 1999). Initially, local production only met domestic demand and was not yet renowned for its quality. However, within a few years, silk-related trades began to flourish in Orange, Carpentras, Nîmes, Marseille, Tours, and Lyon, reaching as far as Flanders—particularly to Bruges, already famous throughout Europe for its fine textiles (Galoppini 2009). Within a few decades, the industry expanded from Bruges to Antwerp, Utrecht, and Amsterdam (Barbour 1950; Molà 2000; Pietsch and Jolly 2012).

The ambition to establish silk weaving industries in France, capable of participating in the global commercial network, can be traced back to King Louis XI (1423–1483). In 1466, with the privileges granted to the "new manufacture of velvets and silk fabrics,"[6] the monarch sought to protect and promote Lyon's silk industry, though this plan encountered significant obstacles (Rondot 1894). It was, in fact, the objections of Lyon's own merchants—who met the costs of transporting goods between Lyon and Tours, the royal court's location until the sixteenth century—that led the king to relocate the industry to Tours in 1470 (Collas 2015). Meanwhile, in Lyon, efforts shifted to consolidating the city's role as a commercial hub by prohibiting French merchants from attending competing fairs in Geneva and blocking foreign traders from passing through France upon their return from these events. Despite these measures, Italians continued to establish new banking offices in Lyon, which, thanks to its strategic position for trade between northern and southern Europe, would eventually become a key center for commerce (Canestrini 1857; Molà 2000; Drouault 2007; Collas 2015). The relocation of the French silk industry to Tours coincided with a significant migration of artisans, mostly Italians, who settled along the Loire River (Levasseur 1916). However, the measures of *le Roi Prudent* proved short-lived, as the Italian Wars, triggered by Charles VIII's (1470–1498) invasion of Italy in the 1490s, soon overshadowed earlier initiatives.

[6] "Nouvelle magniffacture de vellours et draps de soye" (Rondot 1894, 36).

The first true flourishing of the French silk industry did not occur until the rise of the Valois-Angoulême dynasty and more specifically under King Francis I (1494–1547), a prominent figure of the French Renaissance. In the 1530s, at the king's request, numerous Italian artisans, including Bartolomeo Naris and Étienne Turquet, likely of Piedmontese origin, arrived in Lyon (Ozanam 1836; De Valous 1868; Boucher 1994).[7] To "support and promote the emerging silk production of Lyon"[8] (Ozanam 1836, 8–9), Francis I imposed heavy taxes on Italian and Spanish fabrics in 1536, granting Lyon a monopoly on the import and trade of silk. This was part of a broader fiscal plan, which culminated in a ban on the import of foreign silk fabrics into France, with the sole exceptions being Venetian, Florentine, and Lucchese silks. Over time, the influence of Italian artisans who had contributed to establishing the silk industry in France gradually waned (Gascon 1971; Ciriacono 2018). Within a few decades, the industry saw a growing dominance of French capital and labor, especially from Avignon and Tours. The growing association between silk and France was further underscored by the founding of silk spinning mills in Vienne, designed to supply the raw materials for the burgeoning industry (Chicco 1995). Yet, the outbreak of the French Wars of Religion under the later Valois rulers again hindered the progress of the French silk industry, which would only see a revival after the accession of Henry IV of Bourbon (1553–1610). Under his reign, numerous requests for patents, monopolies, and subsidies were granted, allowing the French silk industry—particularly in Lyon—to recover, stabilize, and thrive. This laid the groundwork for the fiscal modernization introduced by Jean Baptiste Colbert (1619–1683) in the latter half of the seventeenth century (Ciriacono 2018). In a relatively short period, Lyon transformed from a major market for silks produced by Italian artisans to the leading producer of fabrics made by French hands. However, it is important to note that the limited quality and quantity of silk filaments produced in France did not meet the needs of weavers or the demands of merchants. Despite efforts

[7]The French translation of the Italian names Bartolomeo Narice and Stefano Turchetti. While Naris was probably of Ligurian or Piedmontese origin, Turquet's Piedmontese origins are rather certain: according to Ozanam (1836), Turchetti/Turquet was originally from Cherasco, whereas De Valous (1868) states that he was born in Chieri.

[8]"Pour favoriser et encourager les fabriques naissantes de Lyon." *Edict du Roy de France François sur les draps d'or, d'argent & de Soye, & pareillement sur toutes especes de crepes, passemens, rubans, ceintures, franges, pannes, tissures, & autres ouvrages de fil d'or, d'argent ou de Soye,* Valence-sur-Rhône, Charles Barbier Imprimeur & libraire, 1687, p. 3–24.

to develop sericulture, reeling, and spinning within France, most of Lyon's textiles were still produced using Italian silk. In fact, the Italian peninsula underwent a significant industrial transformation between the sixteenth and seventeenth centuries, with a focus on the expansion of sericulture and twisting, alongside the gradual decline of weaving (Rosso 1992; Poni 1999).

In the context of the economic expansion associated with the silk industry, England was among the latecomers. With its tumultuous medieval history and an adverse climate for the development of sericulture,[9] England had failed to develop a domestic silk industry and become dependent on foreign silk fabrics. Yet, this did not prevent the English nobility from consuming large quantities of silk (Muthesius and King 2004; Monnas 2018), and the booming trade in this sector had caught the interest of the Crown. Despite this, attempts to establish silk factories under the York and Tudor monarchs had proven unsuccessful. In the early modern period, the English silk weaving industry benefited from the growing anti-Protestant policies of France after the battle of Lepanto (1571) and the St. Bartholomew's Day Massacre (1572), which prompted many Protestant artisans to leave French territories and settle across the Channel, in Queen Elizabeth I's realm (Warner 1921; Jack 1977). Nevertheless, despite the growth of silk weaving workshops and the trade in silk fabrics in London, Canterbury, and Norwich, it was not until the revocation of the Edict of Nantes in 1685 that a true turning point was reached. This coincided with the migration of French Huguenots and the foundation of a major weaving center in Spitalfields (Guitteau 1942; Clay 1984; Rothstein 1987, 1993; Scouloudi 1987; Luu 1997, 2005, 2008; Luu and Goose 2003; Levy Peck 2005; Hilaire-Pérez and Verna 2006; Joblin 2024), significantly boosting English silk production and setting the stage for the industrial ventures of the Lombe brothers. Amidst legend and documented history, the Lombe brothers succeeded in uncovering the technological secrets of Europe's leading silk industry of the eighteenth century, which had flourished in the Piedmontese territories of the Kingdom of Sardinia.

[9] The only reference to mulberry sericulture practices in Great Britain dates back to the reign of James I Stuart (1603–1625), but it remains an isolated case (Levy Peck, 2005).

4 From Lagging Behind to Leading the Way: Silk in Piedmont

Medieval Piedmont was not immune to the allure of silk and its production processes. As early as 1299, the ledger of the Countess of Savoy[10] recorded the purchase of *vermes facientes sericum* (literally "worms making silk").[11] Yet, this entry should likely be seen as a trivial interest of the countess (Cibrario 1854), as there is no documentary evidence to suggest the introduction of sericulture to Piedmont before the fifteenth century. However, research has shown that a substantial group of merchants from Asti had been involved in the trade of silks and other goods since the thirteenth century (Vernazza 1883; Comba 1988). Nevertheless, in the fourteenth century, it was wool and cotton that enjoyed particular fame in Piedmont, with the establishment of fabric manufacturing in Chieri. This small town, located just outside Turin and along the road to Asti, developed a thriving production of cotton fabrics, as well as blended cotton-wool and cotton-linen textiles during the Renaissance. This was an ambitious venture, given its dependence on imported raw materials, yet it allowed the rise of a skilled class of weavers, specializing in

[10] Many scholars identify Sibylle de Baugé (1255–1294), the first wife of Amedeo V (1253–1323), Count of Savoy, as the person in question. However, Luigi Cibrario argues—despite inconsistencies in his account throughout the book—that the expense was actually incurred by Marie de Brabant (?–1338), the count's second wife. Sibylle, in fact, is believed to have died in 1294 (Cibrario 1854, 1855).

[11] "Account of Nicolaus de Fago, clerk, concerning the expenses of the household of the lady countess, recorded by his own hand from Sunday, on the feast of the Apostles Peter and Paul, in the year of Our Lord 1299. In that same week, 20 *danari* were paid to a messenger sent to *Gebenna* to procure silkworms" (Computus Nicolai de Fago clerici de expensis hospicii dominae comitissae facta per manum suam a die dominica per festum apostolorum Petri et Pauli anno Domini MCC nonagesimo nono. In ipsa septimana soluti fuerunt vigenti danarios uni misso Gebennas quaestitum vermes facientes sericum). The record is cited by numerous scholars. In particular, De Bossi claims to have personally examined the document, stating: "I think that the art of raising silkworms was practiced in your region (Switzerland) before it was in Piedmont. My opinion on this matter is based on the fact that in the year 1299, Sibylle de Baugé, wife of Amedeo V, sent a messenger to Geneva to procure silkworm eggs, as evidenced by the expense account of her household steward or *maître d'hôtel*, the original of which is still preserved in the archives of the city of Turin. This document on the origins of silk in Piedmont is the oldest I have been able to discover, and as it may be of interest to the history of your homeland, I am sending it to you." Nevertheless, the same author also reports the existence of a controversy regarding the word *Gebenna*, which remains uncertain between Geneva, Genoa, and Cévennes (De Bossi 1843, 461–463).

medium-quality fabrics with broad market appeal, even reaching foreign markets, particularly in Lyon and Geneva. This was made possible through the mediation of Asti's merchants and their Piedmontese colleagues, who had increasingly turned to the textile trade (Giordano 1895; Patrone Nada 1966; Allegra 1987; Comba 1988).

Despite the absence of conclusive evidence of silk manufacturing in fourteenth-century Piedmont, it is likely that some form of silk spinning was already practiced around Racconigi. The involvement of the Peirolero family—natives of Racconigi—among the *seatearii* who helped establish Genoa's Silk Guild in 1432 suggests that silk manufacturing was already present in the region. According to the guild's statutes, the Peirolero brothers, *Jacobus et fratres*, were credited with introducing the craft to Genoa. Later records document several Racconigi artisans who were active in Genoa, holding significant positions within the city's guild (Di Tucci 1948; Massa 1970; Comba 1988, 1992). The presence of *mercatores* (merchants) and *operatores* (workers) from Racconigi in Genoa suggests that silk production and trade may have already been established in Piedmont, within the orbit of the Genoese market, as early as the fourteenth century—despite the first solid evidence of a silk manufactory in Racconigi dating only to 1463 (Comba 1992). By the fifteenth century, Racconigi had become part of a wider network of Italian silk-producing cities, and in the centuries that followed, it would emerge as Piedmont's leading silk production center (Destefanis 1942; Chierici and Palmucci Quaglino 1993; Chierici 2004, 2007). In Turin, the first attempts to establish silk manufactories occurred in the 1440s. Milan played a pivotal role in this development: in 1447, the city's authorities permitted the establishment of a silk workshop within the city walls, run by Andrea de Bigniaco, a Milanese *dorerius* (gold thread maker). As part of the agreement, his wife was tasked with teaching the city's women how to spin and weave silk. A similar initiative occurred in 1453, when a company consisting of the Milanese Antonio Panigarola, Martino Grassi, and the Racconigi native Leone de Alba selected Turin as the location for their venture "for establishing, maintaining, and practicing the art of silk fabric production."[12] These three noblemen took responsibility for providing machinery and ensuring that all interested citizens—regardless of gender—could learn

[12] "Pro faciendo, fundendo et manutenendo (...) artem pannorum siricorum seu sete" (Comba 1992).

the art of weaving and spinning. Their efforts infused new energy into Turin's stagnant silk market (Comba 1988, 1992).

A turning point in the field occurred, however, only in the sixteenth century, when silk-related crafts and trade began to be boosted by the establishment of profitable sericulture in the region. The introduction of mulberry cultivation in Piedmont is often attributed to the foresight of Bernardino I of Savoy-Racconigi (?–1526). As reported in a document attributed to Niccolò Balbo, "at that time, the lord of Racconigi, ancestor of the modern lords, encountered mulberry cultivations in Vicenza - a city under Venetian control - while traveling in Venice. Inspired by this, he brought skilled workers to plant them in Piedmont, just as had been done there"[13] (Destefanis 1942, 35). This emerging agricultural activity soon had to face the devastation brought by the invasion of French and Spanish mercenary armies during their campaigns in Italy. After claiming the Duchy of Milan based on a distant, hereditary right, Francis I was defeated by Charles V of Habsburg (1500–1558) in the 1519 contest for the imperial throne. In the following decades, northern Italy, under French dominion and encircled by the vast Habsburg Empire, became the backdrop for constant military movements. The death of Francesco II Sforza (1495–1535) reignited French ambitions, leading to an invasion of the Duchy of Savoy and the occupation of Turin. It was only with the Peace of Cateau-Cambrésis in 1559 that hostilities between the French Crown and the Empire over Italian territories were brought to an end, allowing the House of Savoy to regain its Piedmontese lands and establish its capital in Turin in 1563.

Amidst the ongoing conflicts, the development of a thriving agricultural and manufacturing industry seems unlikely. A decisive push toward economic transformation in Piedmont seems to have come from Emanuele Filiberto I (1528–1580), known as the Iron Head Duke (*Testa 'd fer*), who promoted policies to foster sericulture and establish silk manufacturing facilities in Piedmont, including those for spinning and weaving silk (Duboin 1849, 496—April 30, 1567; Arese 1922). Although the actual impact of these policies is still debated (Merlin 1988), the sixteenth century clearly marked the beginning of a new economic era for the region.

[13] "Al tempo il signor di Raconisio, padre delli moderni signori, andando in Vinetia, gli occorse di veder in Vicenza, città suddita ai Veneziani, tal redditi di moroni; ne tolse esempio et conducette (in Piedmont) persone pratiche a piantarne come fu fatto" (Destefanis 1942, 35).

Despite the critical assessment of the Venetian ambassador Giovan Francesco Morosini, who dismissed the developing Piedmontese silk industry as a subordinate branch of the Genoese and Milanese manufactories (Firpo 1983), the century witnessed the granting of monopolies and subsidies for all sectors of the silk industry: from mulberry cultivation and silkworm farming to the installation of looms and the processing of silk byproducts (Arese 1922; Rosso 1992).

Following the death of Emanuele Filiberto I, his son, Carlo Emanuele I (1562–1630), inherited and advanced his father's vision for the development of the silk industry. This vision was also embraced and expanded by Emanuele Filiberto's daughter-in-law, Caterina Michela of Habsburg (1567–1597), daughter of Philip II of Spain, a fact reflected in the final verses of the poem *La Sereide*, composed by Alessandro Tesauro in 1585 to commemorate their wedding (Masoero et al. 1999; Raviola and Varallo 2013).

E dal cielo a tal grazia altra s'aggiunge,	And from the sky, another grace is bestowed upon us,
Che d'armi micidiali il lampo abbaglia	As the radiant gleam of lethal weaponry dazzles
Col lume suo quest'alma Caterina,	This soul, Caterina,
Ch'a noi pace conferma, e pace apporta	Who affirms peace for us and carries peace
(…)	(…)
Giungi dunque a tant'opre, a tanti studj,	Embark now on so many endeavors, in various studies,
Che 'l maturo tuo senno inventa e impone	Where your mature wisdom conceives and imposes
A pro de' servi tuoi, quest'altro ancora:	Yet another enterprise for the benefit of your subjects:
Segua adjutrice mano al buon consiglio;	Let the guiding hand be assisted by good counsel;
Onde il dominio tuo, come d'ogn'altra	Thus may your rule, like any other thing
Cosa che dia natura, e l'arte adorni,	Imbued with nature and adorned by art,
De' serici lavor porti anco il vanto	Also boast the pride of silken works

Book II, vv. 1757–1763

The work, dedicated to Caterina Michela and inspired by Emanuele Filiberto's achievements in sericulture, combines epic and bucolic poetry. In free hendecasyllabic verses, it recalls the origin of the silkworm, wishing success to the Spanish Infanta in advancing the silk industry in her new homeland.

Tesauro's vision swiftly materialized. The tentative and unsteady steps that had characterized the sixteenth-century Piedmontese silk industry began to solidify and gain confidence in the final decades of the century. In 1592, it was Caterina Michela herself who issued the first rudimentary regulations for the reeling process (Duboin 1850, 138—June 5, 1592), aiming to ensure the quality of raw silk (Rosso 1992). While limited to the separation of slightly joined cocoons (*doppioni gentili*), fully joined cocoons (*doppioni grossi*), and intact cocoons (*galette vere*), the Duchess of

Savoy laid the foundation stone for a transformation that, within a century, would elevate Piedmontese silk to worldwide renown, establishing "the cornerstone around which the Piedmontese regulations for the silk industry would grow" (Arese 1922, 7; Rosso 1992, 44).

5 Conclusions

This marks the beginning of our story, where the Piedmontese journey converges with the ancient tradition of silk production, with Piedmont swiftly emerging as the foremost innovator in the global silk industry in a little over a century. New technologies, techniques, and organizational structures—social, commercial, and professional—were the very features that had defined the medieval and Renaissance successes of many silk-producing cities, and they enabled Piedmont to attain the pinnacle of European silk production during the ancien régime. Piedmont offered the international market the finest silk thread: the *organzino alla piemontese*. However, this was not a spontaneous blossoming from an unknown seed but rather a graft. The "true method" of producing silk threads, as Zanon argued, was revealed to the world by the Piedmontese, representing the culmination of centuries of knowledge transfer and technological development. It is no coincidence that the Friulian intellectual, in his treatise, linked the impetus provided by the House of Savoy to that begun a century earlier by the Persian Shah Abbas the Great (Zanon 1763, 150; Steinmann 1987; Matthee 1999; Quinn 2015).

In this ever-turning cycle, materiality and knowledge are as crucial as the social, political, and economic factors that drive innovation. The quality of silk achieved in Piedmont during the early modern period forever reshaped the global production of this precious fiber. Yet, it was the product of centuries of global textile innovation. It is within this continuity that the Piedmontese experience should be understood—a synthesis that, through innovation, reshapes the past in service of what is yet to come.

Bibliography

Allegra, Luciano. 1987. *La città verticale. Usurai, mercanti e tessitori nella Chieri del Cinquecento.* Milan: FrancoAngeli.

Arese, Giovanni. 1922. *L'industria serica piemontese dal secolo XVII alla metà del XIX.* Turin: Bona.

Balbi, Gabriele, and Cecilia Winterhalter, eds. 2013. *Antiche Novità. Una guida transdisciplinare per interpretare il vecchio e il nuovo*. Naples: Orthotes.

Barbour, Violet. 1950. *Capitalism in Amsterdam in the seventeenth century*. Baltimore: Johns Hopkins University Press.

Battistini, Francesco. 1993. La gelsibachicoltura e la trattura della seta in Toscana (secc. XIII-XVIII). In *La seta in Europa secc XIII-XX*, ed. Simonetta Cavaciocchi, 293–299. Florence: Le Monnier.

Battistini, Francesco. 1998. *Gelsi, bozzoli, caldaie. L'industria della seta in Toscana tra città, borghi e campagne (secc. XVI-XVIII)*. Florence: Olschki.

Battistini, Francesco. 2003. *L'industria della seta in Italia nell'età moderna*. Bologna: Il Mulino.

Bautier, Robert-Henri. 1992. *Commerce méditerranéen et banquiers italiens au Moyen Âge*. Hampshire: Brookfield.

Bautier, Robert-Henri. 1993. Provins et les foires de Champagne. In *De l'histoire de la Brie à l'histoire des réformes: mélanges offerts au chanoine Michel Veissière*, ed. Michèle Bardon, 153–174. Paris: Fédération des Sociétés Historiques et Archéologiques de Paris et d'Ile-de-France.

Beckwith, Christopher I. 2009. *Empires of the silk road: A history of Central Eurasia from the Bronze Age to the present*. Princeton: Princeton University Press.

Bini, Telesforo. 1853–1854. *I lucchesi a Venezia. Alcuni studi sopra i secoli XIII e XIV*. Lucca: Felice Bertini.

Boldorini, Alberto M. 1962. Santa Croce di Sarzano e i mercanti lucchesi a Genova (secc. XIII-XIV). *Atti della Società Ligure di Storia Patria* 76:77–90.

Boucher, Jacqueline. 1994. *Présence italienne à Lyon à la Renaissance: du milieu du XVe à la fin du XVIe siècle*. Lyon: Éditions LUGD.

Braudel, Fernand. 1949. *La Méditerranée et le monde méditerranéen à l'époque de Philippe II*. Paris: Colin.

Brésard, Marc. 1914. *Les foires de Lyon aux XVe et XVIe siècles*. Lyon: Académie des Sciences, Belles-Lettres et Arts de Lyon.

Bussagli, Mario. 1992. *Indica et serindica. Scritti di storia dell'arte dell'India e dell'Asia centrale*. Rome: Bardi.

Canestrini, Giuseppe. 1857. L'arte della seta portata in Francia dagli italiani. A proposito del libro: I lucchesi a Venezia di Telesforo Bini. *Archivio Storico Italiano* 6 (2): 3–24.

Caracausi, Andrea. 2004. *Nastri, nastrini, cordelle. L'industria serica nel padovano secc. XVI-XIX*. Padua: Cleup.

Cargnelutti, Liliana. 2009. Zanon Antonio, economista e imprenditore. In *Nuovo Liruti. Dizionario biografico dei friulani, II, L'età veneta*, ed. Cesare Scalon, Claudio Griggio, and Ugo Rozzo, 2625–2634. Udine: Forum.

Casarino, Giacomo. 2018. Lucchesi e manifattura serica a Genova tra XIV e XVI secolo. In *Genova, solo mercanti? Artigiani, corporazioni e manifattura tra Quattro e Cinquecento*, ed. Giacomo Casarino, 103–149. Florence: Aracne.

Cassuto, Umberto. 1912. Un ignoto capitolo di storia ebraica. In *Judaica: Festschrift zu Hermann Cohens siebzigstem Geburtstage*, 389–404. Verlag von Bruno Cassirer.

Chicco, Giuseppe. 1995. *La seta in Piemonte 1650–1800. Un sistema industriale d'ancien régime*. Milan: FrancoAngeli.

Chierici, Patrizia. 2004. Racconigi: una città industriale d'antico regime tra fonti scritte e iconografiche. *Il tesoro delle città. Strenna dell'Associazione Storia della Città* 2:127–133.

Chierici, Patrizia, ed. 2007. *Un filo di seta, le fabbriche magnifiche in provincia di Cuneo*. Caraglio: Edizioni Nerosubianco.

Chierici, Patrizia, and Laura Palmucci Quaglino, eds. 1993. *Le Fabbriche Magnifiche. La seta in provincia di Cuneo tra Seicento e Ottocento*. Cuneo: L'arciere.

Cibrario, Luigi. 1854. *Origini e progresso delle instituzioni della Monarchia di Savoia. Parte I: Storia*. Torino: Stamperia Reale.

Cibrario, Luigi. 1855. *Origini e progresso delle instituzioni della Monarchia di Savoia. Parte II: Specchio Cronologico*. Torino: Stamperia Reale.

Ciriacono, Salvatore. 2018. *Luxury production, technological transfer and international competition in early modern Europe*. Leipzig: Leipziger Universitätsverlag.

Clay, Christopher G. A. 1984. *Economic expansion and social change: England, 1500–1700*. Cambridge: Cambridge University Press.

Colafemmina, Cesare. 2000. Hebrew inscriptions of the early medieval period in southern Italy. In *The Jews of Italy. Memory and identity*, ed. Bernard D. Cooperman and Barbara Garvin, 65–81. Bethesda: University Press of Maryland.

Collas, Rolande. 2015. *L'avancée dans les métiers de la soie; L'exemple de Tours: XVIe-XVIIe siècles*. Hallennes-lez-Haubourdin: The Book Edition.

Comba, Rinaldo. 1988. *Contadini signori e mercanti nel Piemonte medievale*. Rome-Bari: Laterza.

Comba, Rinaldo. 1992. Dal velluto all'organzino: produzioni seriche nel Piemonte rinascimentale. In *Torino sul filo della seta*, ed. Giuseppe Bracco, 11–38. Turin: Archivio Storico della Città di Torino.

Comino, Stefano, and Alessandro Gasparetto. 2020. Silk mills in the early modern Italy. *Advances in Historical Studies* 9:284–294.

Constable, Olivia Remie. 1990. Genoa and Spain in the twelfth and thirteenth centuries: Notarial evidence for a shift in patterns of trade. *The Journal of European Economic History* 19:635–656.

Constable, Olivia Remie. 2004. *Housing the stranger in the Mediterranean world: Lodging, trade, and travel in late antiquity and the Middle Ages*. Cambridge: Cambridge University Press.

Cordero di San Quintino, Giulio. 1840. Cenni intorno al commercio dei Lucchesi coi Genovesi nel XII e XIII secolo. In *Atti della Reale Accademia Lucchese di Scienze, Lettere e Arti*. Lucca: Bertini.
Crippa, Flavio. 1990. Il torcitoio circolare da seta: evoluzione, macchine superstiti, restauri. *Quaderni Storici* 73:169–212.
Daryaee, Touraj. 2003. The Persian Gulf trade in late antiquity. *Journal of World History* 14 (1): 1–16.
De Bossi, Benigno. 1843. Vers à soie. In *Bulletin de la Classe d'agriculture de la Société des Arts de Genève*, 458–465. Genève: Imprimerie de P.A. Bonnant.
De Valous, Vital. 1868. *Étienne Turquet et les origines de la fabrique lyonnaise. Recherches et documents sur l'Institution de la Manufacture des étoffes de soie 1466–1536*. Lyon: Augustine Brun.
Dei, Benedetto. 1985. *La cronica dall'anno 1400 all'anno 1500*. Edited by Roberto Barducci. Florence: Francesco Papafava Editore.
Del Punta, Ignazio, and Maria Ludovica Rosati. 2017. *Lucca, una città di seta: produzione, commercio e diffusione dei tessuti lucchesi nel tardo Medioevo*. Lucca: Fazzi.
Demo, Edoardo. 2000. La produzione serica a Verona e Vicenza tra quattro e cinquecento. In *La seta in Italia dal Medioevo al Seicento. Dal baco al drappo*, ed. Luca Molà, Reinhold C. Mueller, and Claudio Zanier, 305–323. Venice: Marsilio.
Demo, Edoardo. 2001. Mercati e manifatture nel Veneto tardo medievale. *Reti medievali* 2:1–10.
Demo, Edoardo. 2003. Sete e mercanti vicentini alle fiere di Lione nel XVI secolo. In *La pratica dello scambio. Sistemi di fiere, mercanti e città in Europa (1400–1700)*, ed. Paola Lanaro, 177–200. Venice: Marsilio.
Destefanis, Gina. 1942. Notizie sull'arte della seta e sulla "Università dei Filatoieri" in Racconigi nei secoli XVI, XVII e XVIII. *Bollettino della Società per gli studi storici, archeologici ed artistici della provincia di Cuneo* 21:53–75.
Di Tucci, Raffaele. 1948. Lineamenti storici dell'industria serica genovese (statuti inediti del 1432). *Atti della Società Ligure di Storia Patria* 71:19–77.
Dini, Bruno. 1993. L'industria serica in Italia. Secc. XIII-XV. In *La seta in Europa secc XIII-XX*, ed. Simonetta Cavaciocchi, 91–123. Florence: Le Monnier.
Drouault, Célia. 2007. Le travail de la soie, une voie pour l'exercice de la liberté individuelle des femmes à Tours au XVIIIe siècle. *Annales de Bretagne et des Pays de l'ouest* 144:159–168.
Duboin, Felice Amato. 1849. *Raccolta per ordine di materie delle leggi cioè editti, patenti, manifesti, ecc. emanate negli stati di terraferma sino all'8 dicembre 1798 dai sovrani della real casa di Savoja, t. 16, v. 18*. Turin: Arnaldi.
Duboin, Felice Amato. 1850. *Raccolta per ordine di materie delle leggi cioè editti, patenti, manifesti, ecc. emanate negli stati di terraferma sino all'8 dicembre 1798 dai sovrani della real casa di Savoja, t. 17, v. 19*. Turin: Baricco ed Arnaldi.

Evans, Allan, ed. 1936. *Balducci Pegolotti Francesco, La pratica della mercatura*. Cambridge: The Medieval Academy of America.

Farmer, Sharon. 2017. *The silk industries of medieval Paris. Artisanal migration, technological innovation, and gendered experience*. Philadelphia: University of Pennsylvania Press.

Feliciano, María J. 2014. Medieval textiles in Iberia: Studies for a new approach. In *Envisioning Islamic art and architecture. Essays in honor of Renata Holod*, ed. David J. Roxburgh, 46–65. Leiden-Boston: Brill.

Ferorelli, Nicola. 1915. *Gli Ebrei nell' Italia meridionale dall'Età Romana al Secolo XVIII*. Turin: Il Vessillo Israelitico.

Ferretto, Arturo. 1900. I genovesi in Oriente nel carteggio di Innocenzo IV. *Giornale storico e letterario della Liguria* 1:353–368.

Firpo, Luigi, ed. 1983. *Relazioni di ambasciatori veneti al senato. Tratte delle migliori edizioni disponibili e ordinate cronologicamente*. Vol. 11. Turin: Bottega d'Erasmo.

Foltz, Richard. 1998. Judaism and the silk route. *The History Teacher* 32:9–16.

Forti, Enrico, Maurizio Sobrero, and Andrea Vezzulli. 2020. Continuity, change, and new product performance: The role of stream concentration. *Journal of Product Innovation Management* 37 (3): 228–248.

Franceschi, Franco. 2000. I forestieri e l'industria della seta fiorentina fra medioevo e rinascimento. In *La seta in Italia dal Medioevo al Seicento. Dal baco al drappo*, ed. Luca Molà, Reinhold C. Mueller, and Claudio Zanier, 401–416. Venice: Marsilio.

Franch Benavent, Ricardo, and Daniel Muñoz Navarro. 2024. La organización del trabajo artesanal en la Valencia del siglo XVIII: La función de los gremios en una ciudad industrial. In *Artesanos: Una historia social en España (siglos XVI-XIX)*, ed. Francisco Hidalgo Fernández and José Antolín Nieto Sánchez, 91–129. Ciudad Real: Ediciones de la Universidad de Castilla-La Mancha.

Franch Benavent, Ricardo, and Germán Navarro Espinach, eds. 2017. *Las rutas de la seda en la historia de España y Portugal*. Valencia: Universitat de València.

Galliker, Julia L. 2014. Middle *Byzantine silk in context: Integrating the textual and material evidence*. PhD thesis: University of Birmingham.

Galoppini, Laura. 2009. *Mercanti toscani e Bruges nel tardo Medioevo*. Pisa: Pisa University Press.

Gascon, Richard. 1956. Nationalisme économique et géographie des foires. *Cahiers d'Histoire* 3:253–287.

Gascon, Richard. 1971. *Grand Commerce et vie urbaine au XVIe siècle, Lyon et ses marchands*. Paris: Mouton.

Gayo García, María Dolores, and Ángela Arteaga. 2005. Análisis de colorantes de un grupo de tejidos hispanomusulmanes. *Bienes culturales: revista del Instituto del Patrimonio Histórico Español* 5:123–146.

Giardina, Andrea. 2017. *Storia mondiale dell'Italia*. Rome-Bari: Laterza.

Gioffrè, Domenico, ed. 1967. *Liber institutionum cabellarum veterum communis Ianue*. Acta Italica 12.
Giordano, Luigi. 1895. *L'università dell'arte del fustagno di Chieri*. Turin: Tipografia San Giuseppe degli Artigianelli.
González Fons, Paula. 2024. Tejiendo el saber: Los aprendices del gremio de velluters de Valencia, 1570-1682. In *Artesanos: Una historia social en España (siglos XVI-XIX)*, ed. Francisco Hidalgo Fernández and José Antolín Nieto Sánchez, 159–181. Ciudad Real: Ediciones de la Universidad de Castilla-La Mancha.
Green, Louis. 1986. *Castruccio Castracani: A study on the origins and characters of a fourteenth-century Italian despotism*. Oxford: Clarendon Press.
Greville Pounds, Norman J. 1994. *An economic history of medieval Europe*. London: Routledge.
Grillo, Paolo. 1994. Le origini della manifattura serica in Milano (1400-1450). *Studi storici: rivista trimestrale dell'Istituto Gramsci* 35:897–916.
Griselini, Francesco. 1770. Elogio della Società d'Agricoltura pratica di Udine, Al Signor Antonio Zanon. In *Antonio Zanon. Dell'Utilità morale, economica e politica delle Accademie di Agricoltura, Arti e commercio*. Udine: Gallici.
Guitteau, Joanne P. 1942. Influence of the Huguenot refugees on English manufactures. *The Social Studies* 33 (6): 264–267.
Hall, Bronwyn, and Nathan Rosenberg. 2010. *Handbook of the economics of innovation*. Amsterdam: North-Holland.
Heers, Jacques. 2005. *Chute et mort de Constantinople (1204–1453)*. Paris: Perrin.
Hernes, Tor, and Miriam Feuls, eds. 2023. *A research agenda for organisational continuity and change*. Cheltenham: Elgar.
Hilaire-Pérez, Liliane, and Catherine Verna. 2006. Dissemination of technical knowledge in the Middle Ages and the early modern era: New approaches and methodological issues. *Technology and Culture* 47 (3): 536–565.
Iradiel Murugarren, Francisco Paulino, Germán Navarro Espinach, David Luis Igual, and Concepción Villanueva Morte, eds. 2016. *Identidades urbanas Corona de Aragón - Italia: redes económicas, estructuras institucionales, funciones políticas (siglos XIV-XV)*. Zaragoza: Prensas de la Universidad de Zaragoza.
Jack, Sybil M. 1977. *Trade and industry in Tudor and Stuart England*. London: Allen & Unwin.
Jacobs, Joseph. 1919. *Jewish contributions to civilization: An estimate*. Philadelphia: Jewish Publication Society of America.
Jacoby, David. 2000. Dalla materia prima ai drappi tra Bisanzio, il Levante e Venezia: la prima fase dell'industria serica veneziana. In *La seta in Italia dal Medioevo al Seicento Dal baco al drappo*, ed. Luca Molà, Reinhold C. Mueller, and Claudio Zanier, 265–294. Venice: Marsilio.

Jacoby, David. 2004. The silk trade of late Byzantine Constantinople. In *550th anniversary of the Istanbul University*, ed. Sümer Atasoy, 129–144. Istanbul: Istanbul University Press.

Jacoby, David. 2017. The production and diffusion of Andalusi silk and silk textiles, mid-eighth to mid-thirteenth century. In *The chasuble of Thomas Becket. A biography*, ed. Shalem Avinoam, 142–151. Munich: Hirmer.

Joblin, Alain. 2024. Trois refuges huguenots aux XVIe et XVIIe siècles: Calaisis, Hollande, Angleterre. *Revue du Nord* 449 (2): 23–42.

Laiou, Angeliki E., ed. 2002. *The economic history of Byzantium from the seventh through the fifteenth century*. Washington: Dumbarton Oaks.

Lamb, Venice. 2005. *Looms past and present around the Mediterranean and elsewhere*. Hertingfordbury: Roxford Books.

Levasseur, Émile. 1916. *Ordonnances des Rois de France: règne de François I*. Paris: Imprimerie Nationale.

Levy Peck, Linda. 2005. *Consuming splendor: Society and culture in seventeenth-century England*. Cambridge: Cambridge University Press.

Livi, Giovanni. 1881. I mercanti di seta lucchesi in Bologna nei secoli XIII e XIV. *Archivio Storico Italiano* 7 (4): 29–55.

Lopez, Robert Santino. 1945. Silk industry in the Byzantine Empire. *Speculum* 20 (1): 1–42.

Lopez-Marigorta, Eneko. 2023. How al-Andalus wrapped itself in a silk cocoon: The ṭirāz between Umayyad economic policy and Mediterranean trade. *Mediterranean Historical Review* 38 (1): 1–23.

Luu, Lien B. 1997. French-speaking refugees and the foundation of the London silk industry in the 16th century. *The Huguenot Society Journal* 26 (5): 564–576.

Luu, Lien B. 2005. *Immigrants and the industries of London*. Farnham: Ashgate.

Luu, Lien B. 2008. Immigrants and the diffusion of skills in early modern London: The case of silk weaving. *Documents pour l'histoire des techniques* 15 (1): 32–42.

Luu, Lien B., and Nigel Goose, eds. 2003. *Immigrants in Tudor and Stuart England*. Sussex: Liverpool University Press.

Luzzatto, Fabio. 1927. *Antonio Zanon e la legislazione agraria della Repubblica veneta*. Udine: Doretti.

Mainoni, Patrizia. 1994. La seta a Milano nel XV secolo: aspetti economici e istituzionali. *Studi storici: rivista trimestrale dell'Istituto Gramsci* 35:871–896.

Mainoni, Patrizia. 2000. La seta in Italia fra XII e XIII secolo. Migrazioni artigiane e tipologie seriche. In *La seta in Italia dal Medioevo al Seicento. Dal baco al drappo*, ed. Luca Molà, Reinhold C. Mueller, and Claudio Zanier, 376–390. Venice: Marsilio.

Manolova, Violeta. 2020. Development of sericulture in byzantine cities 11th-13th century. *Études Balkaniques* 56 (2): 209–226.

Martín i Ros, Rosa María. 1999. Los tejidos en Europa. De Carlomagno al año 1000. In *Cataluña en la época carolingia: arte y cultura antes del románico (siglos IX y X)*, ed. Jordi Camps Sòria, Eduard Carbonell Esteller, and Montserrat Pagès Paretas, 265–269. Barcelona: Generalitat de Catalunya.

Masoero, Mariarosa, Sergio Mamino, and Claudio Rosso, eds. 1999. *Politica e cultura nell'età di Carlo Emanuele I. Torino, Parigi, Madrid*. Florence: Olschki.

Massa, Paola. 1970. *L'arte genovese della seta nella normativa del XV e del XVI secolo*. Genoa: Atti della Società Ligure di Storia Patria.

Matthee, Rudolph P. 1999. *The politics of trade in Safavid Iran. Silk for silver, 1600–1730*. Cambridge: Cambridge University Press.

May, Florence Lewis. 1957. *Silk textiles of Spain: Eighth to fifteenth century*. New York: Hispanic Society of America.

McCormick, Michael. 2002. *Origins of the European economy: Communications and commerce AD 300–900*. Cambridge: Cambridge University Press.

Merlin, Pierpaolo. 1988. Gli Stati, la giustizia e la politica nel ducato sabaudo della prima metà del Cinquecento. *Studi Storici* 29 (2): 503–525.

Michelazzi, Emilia. 2018. *Roma e il misterioso popolo della seta*. Bologna: Pàtron.

Molà, Luca. 1994. *La comunità dei lucchesi a Venezia: immigrazione e industria della seta nel tardo Medioevo*. Venice: Istituto veneto di scienze, lettere ed arti.

Molà, Luca. 2000. *The silk industry of renaissance Venice*. Baltimore: Johns Hopkins University Press.

Molesti, Romano. 1974. *Il pensiero economico di Antonio Zanon*. Milan: Giuffrè.

Monnas, Lisa. 2018. A study in contrasts: Silk consumption in Italy and England during the fifteenth and sixteenth centuries. In *Threads of global desire: Silk in the pre-modern world*, ed. Dagmar Schäfer, Giorgio Riello, and Luca Molà, 149–186. Woodbridge: Boydell.

Munkácsi, Ernst. 1939. *Der Jude von Neapel. Die historischen und kunstgeschichtlichen Denkmäler des süditalienischen Judentums*. Zürich: Die Liga.

Muthesius, Anna. 1997. *Byzantine silk weaving AD 400 to AD 1200*. Vienna: Fassbaender.

Muthesius, Anna, and Stacie M. King. 2004. *Collected textile studies: Donald King*. New York: Pindar Press.

Navarro Espinach, Germán. 1996. *El col.legi de l'àrt major de la seda de València*. Valencia: Consell Valenciá de cultura.

Navarro Espinach, Germán. 1999. *Los orígenes de la sedería valenciana (siglos XV-XVI)*. Valencia: Ayuntamiento de Valencia.

Navarro Espinach, Germán. 2016. Italianos, franceses y alemanes en la Zaragoza de los Reyes Católicos (1479-1516). In *Identidades urbanas, Corona de Aragón - Italia: redes económicas, estructuras institucionales, funciones políticas (siglos XIV-XV)*, ed. Paulino Iradiel, Germán Navarro Espinach, David Igual Luis, and Concepción Villanueva Morte, 245–262. Zaragoza: Prensas de la Universidad de Zaragoza.

Navarro Espinach, Germán. 2017. Valencia en las rutas de la seda del mediterráneo occidental (siglos XIII-XV). In *Las rutas de la seda en la historia de España y Portugal*, ed. Ricardo Franch Benavent and Germán Navarro Espinach, 99–128. Valencia: Universitat de València.

Navarro Espinach, Germán. 2022. Textiles in the crown of Aragon: Production, commerce, consumption. In *Textiles of medieval Iberia. Cloth and clothing in a multi-cultural context*, ed. Gale R. Owen, María Barrigón Crocker, Nahum Ben-Yehuda, and Joana Sequeira, 93–122. Woodbridge: The Boydell Press.

Oikonomidès, Nicolas. 1986. Silk trade and production in Byzantium from the sixth to the ninth century: The seals of Kommerkiarioi. *Dumbarton Oaks Papers* 40:33–53.

Orlando, Ermanno. 2021. *Le Repubbliche Marinare*. Bologna: Il Mulino.

Owen Crocker, Gale R., María Barrigón, Nahum Ben-Yehuda, and Joana Sequeira, eds. 2022. *Textiles of medieval Iberia. Cloth and clothing in a multi-cultural context*. Woodbridge: The Boydell Press.

Ozanam, Jean-Antoine-François. 1836. *Origine de la soie et des étoffes fabriquées avec cette matière*. Lyon: Léon Boitel.

Partearroyo Lacaba, Cristina. 2005. Los tejidos del periodo almohade. In *Los almohades: problemas y perspectivas*, ed. Patrice Cressier, Luis Molina, and María Isabel Fierro Bello, 305–352. Madrid: Consejo Superior de Investigaciones Científicas.

Partearroyo Lacaba, Cristina. 2007. Tejidos andalusíes. *Artigrama: Revista del Departamento de Historia del Arte de la Universidad de Zaragoza* 22:371–420.

Patrone Nada, Anna Maria. 1966. L'arte del Fustagno in Chieri. In *Statuti dell'arte del Fustagno in Chieri*, ed. Vittorio Balbiano di Aramengo, 157–187. Turin: Deputazione subalpina di Storia Patria.

Perotti, Antonella. 1998. *La via Francigena in Canavese. Pellegrini, monaci e mercanti sulle strade del Medioevo*. Santhià: GS Editrice.

Pietsch, Johannes, and Anna Jolly, eds. 2012. *Netherlandish fashion in the seventeenth century*. Riggisberg: Abegg-Stiftung.

Poni, Carlo. 1999. The circular silk mill: A factory before the industrial revolution in early modern Europe. *History of Technology* 21:65–85.

Quinn, Sholen A. 2015. *Shah Abbas: The King who refashioned Iran*. London: Oneworld.

Raviola, Blythe Alice, and Franca Varallo, eds. 2013. *L'infanta. Caterina d'Austria, duchessa di Savoia (1567–1597)*. Rome: Carocci.

Righi, Laura. 2016. Produzione di seta e trasferimenti tecnologici tra legislazione e frodi: il caso di Bologna dal XIV al XVI secolo. *Archivio Storico Italiano* 174 (4): 639–668.

Rivolin, Joseph-Gabriel. 2002. Il Gran San Bernardo e la via Francigena: pellegrini e mercanti in Valle d'Aosta nel Medioevo. In *Carte di viaggi e viaggi di carta. L'Africa, Gerusalemme e l'Aldilà*, ed. Giusi Baldissone and Marco Piccat, 121–125. Novara: Interlinea.

Rondot, Natalie. 1894. *L'Industrie de la Soie en France*. Lyon: Imprimerie Mougin-Rusand.
Rosso, Claudio. 1992. Dal gelso all'organzino: nascita e sviluppo di un'industria trainante. In *Torino sul filo della seta*, ed. Giuseppe Bracco, 39–66. Turin: Archivio Storico della Città di Torino.
Rothstein, Natalie. 1987. Huguenots in the English silk industry in the eighteenth century. In *Huguenots in Britain and France*, ed. Irene Scouloudi, 125–140. London: Palgrave Macmillan.
Rothstein, Natalie. 1993. The successful and the unsuccessful Huguenot, another look at the London silk industry in the 18th and early 19th centuries. *The Huguenot Society Journal* 25 (5): 439–450.
Scouloudi, Irene, ed. 1987. *Huguenots in Britain and France*. London: Palgrave Macmillan.
Simonsohn, Shlomo. 1997. *The Jews in Sicily (383–1300)*. Leiden-Boston-Cologne: Brill.
Spring, Chris, and Julie Hudson. 2002. *Silk in Africa*. Washington: University of Washington Press.
Steinmann, Linda K. 1987. Shah'Abbas and the Royal Silk Trade 1599–1629. *Bulletin of the British Society for Middle Eastern Studies* 14 (1): 68–74.
Stockland, Étienne. 2017. Patriotic natural history and sericulture in the French Enlightenment (1730–1780). *Archives of Natural History* 44 (1): 1–18.
Subrahmanyam, Sanjay, ed. 1996. *Merchant networks in the early modern world, 1450–1800*. London: Routledge.
Summo, Giuseppina. 1939. *Gli Ebrei in Puglia dall'XI al XVI secolo*. Bari: Cressati.
Taitz, Emily. 1994. *The Jews of medieval France: The Community of Champagne*. Westport, CT: Greenwood Press.
Tesauro, Alessandro. 1585. *La Sereide*. Turin: Herede Bevilacqua.
Thorley, John. 1971. The silk trade between China and the Roman Empire at its height, circa A.D. 90–130. *Greece & Rome* 18:71–80.
Toch, Michael. 2013. *The economic history of European Jews*. Leiden-Boston: Brill.
Verga, Ettore. 1916. Origini dell'organizzazione dell'Arte della Seta in Milano—Secolo XV. Comune di Milano. *Annuario storico-statistico per il 1915* 32 (2): IX–XXV.
Verga, Ettore. 1917. *Il Comune di Milano e l'arte della seta dal secolo decimoquinto al decimottavo*. Milan: Stucchi Ceretti.
Vernazza, Giuseppe. 1883. Della seta negli Stati del Re, al Conte di Lemie, Giuseppe Ignazio Ghiliossi senatore, giudice nel Consolato, procuratore nel Real Consiglio del Commercio. *Giornale linguistico di archeologia, storia e letteratura* 34:I–XII.
Vianello, Francesco M. 2004. *Seta Fine e Panni Grossi: Manifatture e Commerci nel Vicentino, 1570–1700*. Milan: FrancoAngeli.

Warner, Frank. 1921. *The silk industry of the United Kingdom. Its origin and development.* London: Dalcassian Publishing Company.
Wickham, Chris. 2023. *The donkey and the boat: Reinterpreting the Mediterranean economy, 950–1180.* Oxford: Oxford University Press.
Zanoboni, Maria Paola. 2001. "Noctis tempore rapuit et exportavit rotam". Disavventure dell'unico mulino da seta ad energia idraulica di Milano. *Storia Economica* 6 (1): 149–183.
Zanon, Antonio. 1763. *Dell'Agricoltura, dell'Arti e del Commercio in quanto unite contribuiscono alla felicità degli Stati. Lettere di Antonio Zanon, t. 2.* Venice: Fenzo.

CHAPTER 3

The Piedmontese Avant-Garde: Innovations in Techniques and Technologies

1 Introduction

The study of the dynamics of technology and technique dissemination among countries has long been at the center of historiographical interest (Mokyr 1990; Belfanti 2006; Epstein 2013; Prak and Van Zanden 2013; Brioist and Hilaire-Pérez 2016; Zucca Micheletto 2017; Garrioch 2022), although opinions on this subject have occasionally diverged (Bertucci 2021). However, one thing seems certain: within the limits of their power, ancien régime governments sought every possible opportunity to adopt innovations in production—while having to deal with the socio-economic realities of their time. For instance, deeply rooted in tradition, manual craftspeople frequently (and sometimes successfully) resisted the introduction of new machinery, fearing job losses. Yet machinery traveled, along with the knowledge necessary to build, operate, and repair it. This transfer could take various forms, in which the roles of the key actors—governments, experts, artisans, and even the objects themselves—could shift dramatically (Eiras Roel and Rey Castelao 1994).

One strategy, for example, was to take advantage of the arrival of migrants who were forced to flee their regions in a quest to survive. These people—such as the Sicilian Jews in the ninth and tenth centuries, the Lucchese in the fourteenth century, and the Huguenots in the sixteenth century—came from areas where specific technologies were used to produce goods renowned for their quality. Despite the xenophobic tensions

M. Grassi, *The Silk Industry in Early Modern Piedmont*, Labour in History and Society,
https://doi.org/10.1007/978-3-032-15353-1_3

these migrants often faced in new environments, city governments frequently chose to welcome them in order to capitalize on the innovations they could introduce. Sometimes, they designated urban quarters to accommodate these newcomers, therefore fostering the city's economic growth, as was the case in Venice, Antwerp, and London, for instance (Magdelaine 1994; Molà 1994; Simonsohn 1997; Harris 1998; Hilaire-Pérez and Verna 2006; Carnino et al. 2016). That said, these attraction policies often entailed an element of luck, as the success of these types of initiatives depended on several key factors. For example, these necessitated a crisis in the home country that prompted migration in the first place and for the migrants to have valuable expertise recognized by the governments of the cities receiving them. Lastly, but crucially, foreign governments needed to be willing to acknowledge the potential of welcoming migrants as a way of fostering their own economic development (Poussou 1994).

The second case involves governments seeking to acquire skills and technologies through the often illicit and unscrupulous appropriation of knowledge. To achieve this aim, they might either attempt to obtain a "descriptive object," detailed enough to allow reconstruction of machinery and repetition of movements or look for artisans capable of replicating, through their expertise and skill, the intricate features of machines and the gestures required to bring them to life and exploit their full potential (Epstein 2013). For example, in archives and libraries, it is not uncommon to find manuals, treatises, and *Teatri di Machine* (Theaters of machines)—sometimes depicting actual machines (Hilaire-Pérez and Dolza 2002; Dolza and Marchis 2007; Bertucci 2023). These books were intended, supposedly, to preserve and disseminate knowledge about artisanal production. Nevertheless, many of these were aimed at a noble and wealthy audience; they were often luxuriously produced, in large formats, with elaborate illustrations, and minimal text. The idea that these volumes could enable their owners to successfully replicate the machines they described seems almost fanciful (Dolza and Vérin 2004; Dolza and Marchis 2007). By contrast, other technical manuals—such as recipe books and sewing guides—were far more successful in making knowledge accessible through the printed page (Jütte 2015; Plebani 2016; Fraser 2020; Uchacz 2020; Garrioch 2022; Smith 2022). Another category of descriptive objects, almost entirely composed of written text, comprised legal texts and statutes. Collections of local regulations were often transmitted across borders, potentially inspiring competing industries. For instance, French legal texts were well known in Piedmont and vice versa, as were the legal codes of Venice, Amsterdam, London, and Madrid—thanks to the presence of ambassadors and travelers (Poni 1981; Biagioli 2006a, b; Rial Costas 2017; Dauchy 2018; Pihlajamäki et al. 2018). Finally, evidence points to the circulation of prototypes, machine parts, and scale models, disseminated through complex networks that remain largely unknown (Chicco 1995; Popplow 2002; Epstein 2013; Brioist and Hilaire-Pérez 2016). Yet, the success of dissemination via descriptive objects appears fraught with challenges, and many questions remain unanswered: how could these objects be obtained? Once in the hands of local mechanics, could they truly reproduce the machines described? How would they know which materials were appropriate or the correct dimensions? These questions remain the subject of ongoing debate (Long 2003; Epstein 2013; Smith 2022). By contrast, when governments sought to attract foreign artisans known for their expertise, this proved to be a far more reliable means of acquiring a machine or technique. This strategy was actually considered by many European governments, despite the existence of laws that categorically prohibited the migration of skilled labor, under penalty of fines, corporal punishment, or even death. Ironically, these were usually the same states that sought to acquire the latest innovations in production by encouraging such migration (Davids and De Munck 2014). These practices resemble what has traditionally been referred to as "industrial espionage," whereby governments funded the travel of artisans, artists, and intellectuals (both religious and secular) to study the processes of foreign industries and bring their secrets back home (Harris 1998; Bertucci 2013).

Finally, a third option involved the decision of people with the expertise to leave their homeland. Fully aware of the potential for social and economic recognition through their expertise—at times newly invented, at others established in the country they came from but unknown elsewhere—artisans would take the daring move of crossing political borders. They would seek privileges granted by kings, lords, and governments, often risking diplomatic tensions and sometimes their very lives (Biagioli 2006a, b).

This schematic overview is neither exhaustive nor strictly applicable to the long history of know-how dissemination (Dolza 2007; Schulz 2007). However, identifying these patterns reveals that the history of the spread of techniques and technologies is, in essence, a history of movement. Sometimes it was slow and took centuries, at others it was rapid and immediate—where the person with the specific knowledge and expertise remains at the heart of the process.

Examining the numerous social, economic, and political factors involved in this dissemination allows for a reinterpretation of events and documents related to the development of the silk industry in Piedmont. There is a need for a critical approach that reflects the human element in the transmission, evolution, and spread of techniques and technologies. As Bertucci (2021) has recently demonstrated, artisans' full mastery of particular know-how and the fact that they actually relocate somewhere else are not, per se, sufficient to transplant a new technique successfully in a different backdrop. By reconstructing the phases of the dissemination of the *alla piemontese* reeling method in Georgia—through the remarkable story of Gioanna Camosso, and on the basis of the reports sent by the governor of the American colony to the trustees, the historian challenges earlier theories on the transfer of techniques (Harris 1998; Jeremy 1998; Ash 2010). Bertucci demonstrates that dissemination fundamentally relies on the individual possessing the know-how, shaped by a specific context, embedded in a particular institutional framework, and influenced by distinct socio-economic dynamics. At the heart of her analysis is the lived experience of the workforce, making "embodied expertise" the result of a "gradually acquired practical intelligence, perfected through lifelong interaction with the (…) machine, and constructed by (…) regulations issued by the state" (Bertucci 2021, 1006).

Building on these premises, this chapter does not reproduce the workshop sequence of the production process (Fig. 3.1) but instead follows the logic of innovation, adopting an analytical order that reconstructs the causal links between technological change and shifts in productive organization. The following sections explore how silk production techniques and technologies were introduced and evolved within the Savoyard domains, enabling the local manufacturing industry to secure a prominent position in the international market during the seventeenth and eighteenth centuries. Innovation is examined through a detailed reconstruction of the introduction and implementation of new technical and technological advances, which became the cornerstone of the Piedmontese silk industry's success, establishing it as a global leader in silk production—while also acknowledging the vital role of the people behind these developments.

Phase	Process	Brief description
1	Mulberry cultivation	Planting mulberry trees to feed silkworms.
2	Silkworm breeding	Raising silkworms from eggs to the cocoon stage.
3	Cocoon harvesting and sorting	Collecting, drying, and grading cocoons by quality and size.
4	Reeling	Unwinding silk filaments from cocoons to obtain raw silk threads.
5	Winding	Transferring silk from skeins onto bobbins to prepare for twisting.
6	Z-Twisting	Applying the first twist to strengthen the combined filaments.
7	Doubling	Combining two or more silk filaments to form a stronger and more uniform thread.
8	S-Twisting	Giving the second, tighter twist to produce durable organzine yarn for weaving.
9	Conditioning and measuring	Checking weight, humidity, and quality of the silk thread.
10	Dyeing	Coloring the silk threads.
11	Warping	Arranging and aligning threads on the loom to form the warp.
12	Loom preparation	Threading each warp yarn through the heddles and reed to prepare the loom.
13	Weaving	Interlacing warp and weft threads to create fabrics.
14	Inspection	Final quality check.
15	Trade	sale/export of the finished silk fabric.

Fig. 3.1 Synthetic reconstruction of the workshop phases of silk fabric production and quality control (*Source*: author's elaboration based on Battistini, Francesco. 2003. *L'industria della seta in Italia nell'età moderna*. Bologna: Il Mulino)

2 Beautiful, or Rather, Marvelous Machines: The Hydraulic Spinning Mill and the Stocking Frame

An anonymous travel diary, dating back to the late seventeenth century and belonging to an English merchant in Italy, surfaced from the depths of the Bodleian Library in Oxford approximately 50 years ago.[1] The unknown traveler meticulously recorded the stages of his journey, which began in Genoa in 1677 and concluded in Florence the following year, where he visited all the major silk manufacturing centers of northern Italy along the way. With a discerning expert eye, the traveler identified

[1] Oxford Bodleian Library, *Mss. Rawlinsoniani*, D. 1510.

variations in silk-spinning machinery across different cities, classifying them into two fundamental categories: the *Genoese/Milanese-style* mills and those *exactly alla bolognese*. This classification depended on the presence or absence of key technological features such as a hydraulic wheel, a mechanical winding machine (*incannatoio*), and spools (*rocchetti* and *rocchelle*) instead of reels for the initial winding process (Guenzi and Poni 1987). In certain local manufactories, such as in Genoa, the absence of advanced "exactly *alla bolognese*" technology had caused significant industrial delays in the production of high-quality silk thread. Yet upon reaching Turin, the traveler observed a remarkable diversity of machinery, noting the coexistence of both "*Genoese/Milanese*" and "exactly *alla bolognese*" mills. Through his journey, the author vividly portrays a dynamic landscape of technological innovation, offering a more nuanced perspective on the spread of the hydraulic silk spinning mill—one of early modern European governments' most sought-after machines. In Piedmont, this technology would achieve such renown that it earned a distinguished entry in Diderot and D'Alembert's *Encyclopédie* (Diderot and D'Alembert 1765, 268–306).

For centuries, it is highly likely that skeins of raw silk were transferred directly to the loom, making reeling the only process preceding silk weaving, which resulted in mediocre outcomes (Crippa 2000). The growing demand for light, finely woven, and dyed fabrics required additional processing of the yarn to achieve a more uniform, resilient, and finely spun product with a rounded shape—qualities that improved its resistance to dyeing and weaving (Crippa 2000). Unlike other fibers such as hemp, flax, wool, or cotton, which could be spun using spindle and distaff, silk required a more labor-intensive manual spinning process. A solution to these production challenges came from the East between the twelfth and thirteenth centuries, with the introduction of the "simple spinning wheel" to Europe.[2] This tool allowed silk to be wound onto spools while imparting a twist more efficiently. However, the twist remained uneven due to the independent movement of the spindle and the thread (Crippa 2000). While production improved, it was still unable to keep pace with the growing demand for silk yarns. This prompted inventors and experts to develop a machine capable of multiplying the actions of the "simple spinning

[2] A possible depiction of the "simple spinning wheel" was identified by Flavio Crippa in the stained glass windows of Chartres Cathedral (Crippa 1990a, 174).

wheel." This was a circular silk spinning mill, the forerunner of the hydraulic silk spinning mill later perfected in Bologna—and its renowned Piedmontese counterpart (Crippa 1990a; Molà 2000; Righi 2016; Comino and Gasparetto 2020).

With the advent of this new technology, it proved impossible to transfer raw silk skeins directly from the reel to the spinning mill. Instead, the skeins had to be wound onto spools because the irregularity of manually wound threads would have forced workers to frequently stop the spinning mill due to the fragility and inconsistency of the silk filaments. The solution came with the invention of the mechanical winding machine (Picture 3.1), which, utilizing the motion of a wheel, enabled a more uniform transfer of raw silk from skein to spool. In the mechanical winding machine, the raw silk skeins were fixed onto lightweight, movable frames known in

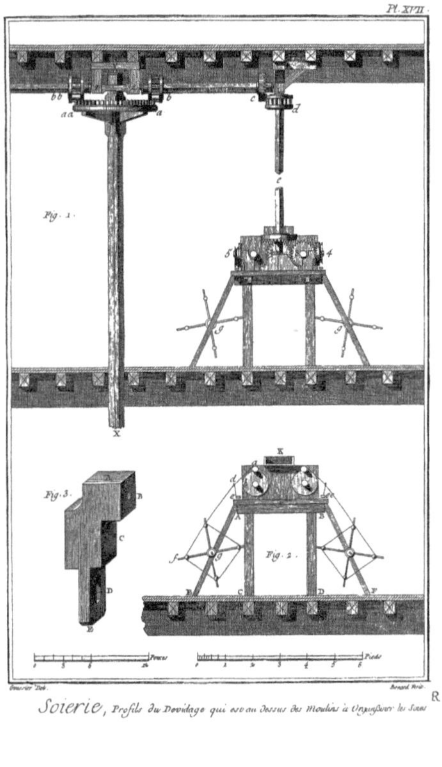

Picture 3.1 Profile of the winding machine over a hydraulic spinning mill. (*Source*: Diderot and D'Alembert 1772, *Planche XVII*. Bibliothèque nationale de France. Gallica. https://gallica.bnf.fr/ark:/12148/bpt6k3252515)

Piedmont as *tavelle* or *aspini* (Picture 3.2) (Poni 1976).[3] Once placed in the mechanical winding machine, the silk thread, guided by a spiral-ended metal rod (the *barbino*), was wound uniformly onto a spool designed to fit the spindles of the spinning mill, called *rocchetto*. Not only did the mechanical winding machine allow for a more even winding process, reducing the risk of breakage, but it also enabled the simultaneous production of multiple spools, drastically increasing efficiency. Because it was often possible to operate both the spinning mill and the winding machine via the motion of a central shaft, the winding machinery was frequently installed in spaces

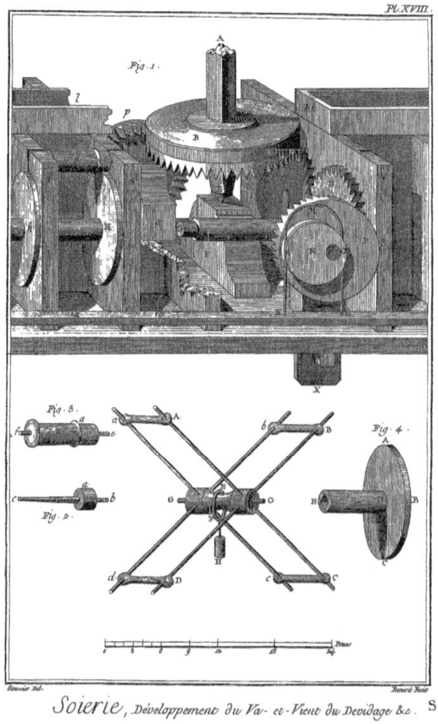

Picture 3.2 Detailed view of the mechanism of the winding machine (top). A *tavella* (bottom). (*Source*: Diderot and D'Alembert 1772, *Planche XVIII*. Bibliothèque nationale de France. Gallica. https://gallica.bnf.fr/ark:/12148/bpt6k3252515)

[3] In Piedmont, no documents have been found so far to support Carlo Poni's claim that "in Turin, the tavelle are also called *guindoli*" (Poni 1976, 25).

above the spinning mill—such as small rooms or attics (Picture 3.3) (Crippa 2000).[4]

Once the silk was wound onto spools, it could move on to the spinning mill. Hydraulic spinning mills (*filatoio*) were composed of two distinct elements called *piante*: one designed for the initial throwing of the thread (*pianta da filato*) and the other for twisting the thrown silk (*pianta da torto*). Initially, the silk spools were fixed onto the spindles attached to the outer frame of the *pianta da filato*. Through circular motion, the thread underwent torsion (defined as a Z-twist or right-hand twist) and was collected onto specific supports known as *rocchelle*, large spools that replaced

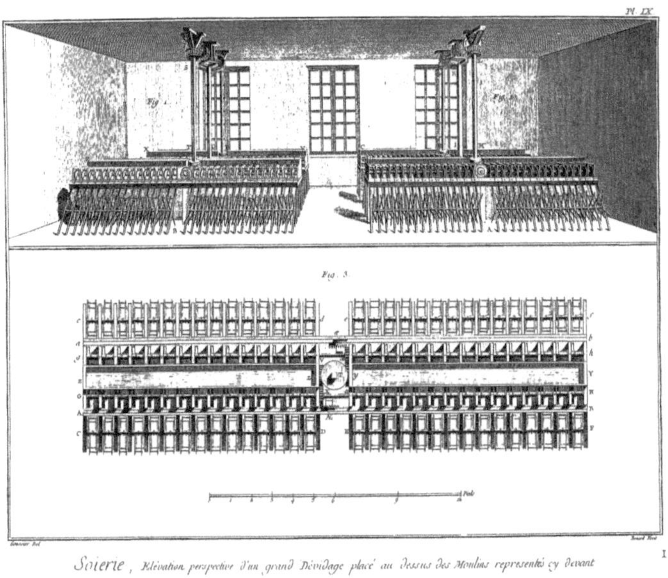

Picture 3.3 Plan and perspective view of a winding machine positioned over a hydraulic spinning mill. (*Source*: Diderot and D'Alembert 1772, *Planche IX*. Bibliothèque nationale de France. Gallica. https://gallica.bnf.fr/ark:/12148/bpt6k3252515)

[4] In the late sixteenth century, in Bologna, not only the spinning mill but also the winding machine began to be powered by hydraulic energy. This was achieved through a system of gears that connected the shafts of both the spinning mill and the winding machine to a water-driven wheel, replacing the previous manual winding process. As a result, work at the winding machine was reduced to retying broken threads and replacing *tavelle* and *rocchetti*, a task often assigned to apprentices (Poni 2009).

reels for collecting the thread.[5] Once this process was completed, the *rocchelle* were removed from the machinery to proceed to the next stages of processing. Some of the yarns produced during the throwing stage were sold, but a second process was necessary to transform them into organzine yarn. The thread collected on the *rocchelle*, although more solid, could still not withstand the motion of the *pianta da torto*, which would reverse the prior twist while applying a new one. Thus, the yarn needed to undergo a second winding process, known as doubling (*binatura*)—made with a specific machinery, the doubling machine (*macchina binatrice*), which resembled a winding machine. The process involved combining two twisted threads from two *rocchelle* onto a new spool (Poni 1976; Crippa 1990a).[6] Once wound together, the yarn was ready for transfer to the *pianta da torto*, where the re-twisting process (defined as S-twist or left-hand twist) took place. The threads on the spools inserted into the machinery were reeled off the spools by the mill's rotation, simultaneously undergoing torsion and being collected onto reels (Crippa 1990a, b; Cordero et al. 2008; Poni 2009; Marchis 2016, 2018). At this point, the organzine was ready to move, as skeins, to subsequent stages of processing like dyeing and weaving (Picture 3.4).

Working around the *pianta da filato* and *pianta da torto* was both complex and hazardous. Besides assembling and disassembling components, workers had to re-knot broken threads during the throwing and twisting process. To perform this task, the spinning mill had to be stopped, which could not be done abruptly due to what is known as the "flywheel effect." Components such as reels and spools also often fell down, which at best resulted in damage to the components themselves and, at worst, caused physical injuries to workers. Fires were another frequent risk, often sparked by oil-based lighting. Once set alight, these fires were difficult to extinguish because of the wooden structure and design of the spinning mill, which caused flames to spread easily and rapidly (in other words, a chimney effect) (Poni 1976; Crippa 1990a).

The Savoy government's ambition to reform silk production by focusing on high-quality organzine spun using the hydraulic spinning mill dates

[5] "*Rocchelle* are a type of spool, but somewhat larger and placed horizontally. On the *rocchelle*, the silk from the spools is unwound in the spinning mill" (Carena 1854, 428). AST, C, *Materie economiche*, Cat. IV, m. 23 di II addizione, fasc. "Descrizione del machinismo ed ordegni de' filatoj di seta" (n.d., but 1724).

[6] Among Leonardo da Vinci's papers, there are also designs for doubling machines (Crippa 1990a, 187).

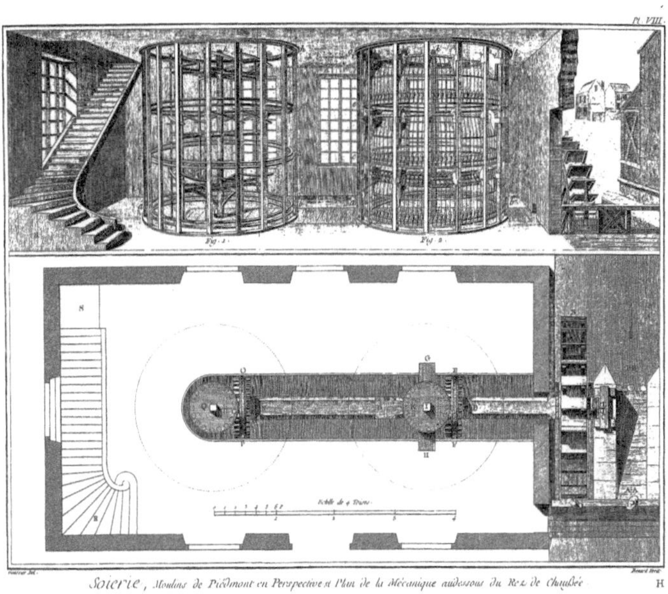

Picture 3.4 Plan and perspective view of the Piedmontese hydraulic spinning mills: on the left, the *pianta da filato*; on the right, the *pianta da torto*. (*Source*: Diderot and D'Alembert 1772, *Planche VIII*. Bibliothèque nationale de France. Gallica. https://gallica.bnf.fr/ark:/12148/bpt6k3252515)

back to the 1660s. This initiative was championed by two key figures: Giuliano Pilla degli Alberti, a merchant from Piacenza, and Gio Francesco Galleani. Piacenza, strategically located along the Po River and a significant commercial hub, had experienced a boom in mulberry cultivation and silkworm farming under Duke Ranuccio II Farnese (1630–1694). By the 1660s, the city still lacked hydraulic spinning mills (Artocchini 1972; Poni 2009).[7] So, it is likely that the Piedmontese government's interactions with Piacenza were aimed at establishing connections to attract skilled Bolognese spinners to work in Piedmont. Letters sent to Turin, detailing careful inquiries, highlight early contacts with Giuliano Pilla

[7] This argument appears to be supported by an account found in the travel diary preserved at the Bodleian Library of Oxford (Guenzi and Poni 1987). This merchant stated in 1678: "In Piacenza they have ye tavelle and ye spinning bobbins wanting only the water to make them exactly alla Bolognese." Oxford Bodleian Library, *Mss. Rawlinsoniani,* D. 1510.

degli Alberti, a local merchant with notable ties in both the mercantile community and among craftsmen skilled in building advanced machinery. The cautious nature of these discussions is reflected in the correspondence regarding the construction of a hydraulic spinning mill in Piedmont in late 1662, indicative of the significant political risks involved. Despite these efforts, progress was slow, and communication ceased unexpectedly the following year, with only a brief update stating that installation was about to begin (Chicco 1995).

Meanwhile, during this same period, the hydraulic spinning mill technology for twisting silk threads did find its way to Piedmont, thanks to Gio Francesco Galleani (Rosso 1992). While Galleani's origins remain unclear, sources consistently describe him as a "traitor" to the citizens of Bologna.[8] It is uncertain whether he was born in Bologna and brought the secrets of the hydraulic spinning mill to Turin or was a Piedmontese native who worked in Bolognese hydraulic spinning mills before returning to his homeland with the necessary skilled knowledge. However, one thing is certain: in 1663, he wrote to Turin expressing his desire to introduce the production of "true Bolognese-style organzine" using water. In October 1663, Galleani petitioned the municipal authorities for a property in *borgo Dora*.[9] Galleani, in fact, was not the sole driving force behind the enterprise: while the factory was constructed on land owned by the City of Turin, the financial support came from some of the city's most prominent bankers (Rosso 1992).[10] By 1665, the hydraulic spinning mill in *borgo*

[8] Even in the last decades of the eighteenth century, the Piedmontese silk spinner Francesco Bal, whose memoirs were discovered by Maria Carla Lamberti, wrote during his time in Bologna: "I spent two days exploring the city; the soldier, as best he could, accompanied me and acted as my guide. (…) In the square, there is an ancient bell tower." He said to me, "Pay close attention and try to read that large white plaque if you can." I replied, "You would need a telescope." "I will explain it to you: our Piedmont owes its silk mills to the man depicted up there. He was a Bolognese inventor who, unappreciated in his homeland, moved to Turin. The government rewarded him, while Bologna hanged him in effigy. Piedmont has grown rich thanks to this industry, and the Bolognese laugh about it" (Lamberti 1994, 155–156).

[9] ASCT, *Ordinati (1661–1663)*, v. 194, c. 209r, October 13, 1663.

[10] The newly ennobled Count Bartolomeo Canera and Baron Carlo Bianco, along with their business partners Girolamo Quaglia and Pietro Francesco Tonso—who would later become the first representatives of the Consulate of Commerce—were the main financiers of the enterprise, with Galleani serving as little more than a figurehead. While the venture initially depended on the financial backing of these four bankers, who provided an annual lease of "one hundred gold *doppie*," Gio Francesco's public role and the success of his spinning mill must have quickly generated substantial returns. This prosperity eventually allowed his

Dora was probably operational. This venture was very successful and lucrative, and within a little over a decade, two additional Galleani hydraulic spinning mills were established in Piedmont. This expansion solidified the family's status as the owners of the largest number of spinning mills in the Duchy of Savoy.[11]

The exceptional quality achieved by Piedmontese silk production not only spurred on the development of technologies tied directly to its manufacturing but also paved the way for the introduction of other innovative machinery. These advancements enabled merchants and artisans to gain entry to new and unexpected markets, such as the production and trade of silk stockings crafted using new, ad hoc machinery: the stocking frames.

The origins of hand-knitting remain shrouded in mystery, though it likely emerged from the need for fabrics with greater elasticity than those produced by early rudimentary looms (Norbury 1963; Belfanti 2005; Caracausi 2008). Throughout the Renaissance and early modern period, stockings and socks were crafted by hand using knitting needles—a labor-intensive process. The quality of the finished product depended heavily on the skill of the artisan and the type of thread used, resulting in items that varied in sophistication, elasticity, and elegance (Belfanti 2005). The invention of the knitting frame revolutionized this craft in the late sixteenth century. While historical records are limited, the credit for this innovation is widely attributed to William Lee, a clergyman from Nottinghamshire. In 1589, Lee constructed a machine capable of producing knitted stockings. However, according to tradition, his creation failed to gain favor with Queen Elizabeth I, who twice refused to grant him a patent. Frustrated by the lack of support in England, Lee relocated to France, bringing his workers and machines with him. There, he found favor with King Henry IV, who, unlike the English queen, granted him the patent. Settling in Rouen, Lee established a workshop with royal patronage. Unfortunately, his fortunes changed after Henry IV's

son, Gio Girolamo, to take over the business after his father's death, having in the meantime freed himself from the burden of the tenants. AST, SR, *Insinuazione Torino*, 1670, v. 7, c. 533.

[11] In 1670, the Galleani's silk mill of Venaria Reale (TO) was built, followed in 1676 by the still-existing "Red Silk Mill" (Filatoio Rosso) in Caraglio (CN). By 1708, the Galleani counts, sons of Giovanni Francesco, were recorded as the owners of a total of 14 silk spinning mill machines, all water-powered: by the early eighteenth century, the *borgo Dora* facility already had five machines, the one in Venaria had another five, and the Caraglio mill four (Chicco 2002).

assassination, as the privileges he had enjoyed were revoked. William Lee died a few years later in France. It was Lee's brother, James, who returned to England and succeeded in establishing several stocking frame workshops in and around London. In doing so, James brought a resolution—albeit a tumultuous and at times legendary one—to the story of the first frame-stocking maker (*calzettaio*) (Pasold 1975; Lewis 1986). Even so, it seems that France's first workshop for silk stockings made on frames did not open until 1666. Located at the Château de Madrid in the Bois de Boulogne, this enterprise was founded under the direction of Colbert, the influential minister of Louis XIV (1638–1715) (Duchesne and De Grandsaigne 1912).

The development of the silk stocking industry in Piedmont was significantly influenced by John Hanford's trip, undertaken in the 1660s with the aim of introducing the English stocking frame to Italian authorities (Lowry 2003). Hanford arrived in Milan in 1663, but after facing significant resistance from both the government and local guilds (Cooke and Tavman-Yilmaz 1999), he redirected his efforts to Turin, hoping for more favorable opportunities under the Savoyard court (Belfanti 1996; Cooke and Tavman-Yilmaz 1999). Duke Carlo Emanuele II of Savoy (1634–1675) welcomed Hanford's proposal, granting him a fifteen-year monopoly, the right to establish workshops throughout the kingdom, and tax exemptions for himself, his family, and ten families of skilled silk stocking makers. The first stocking frame was introduced in the Savoyard capital in 1666 (Belfanti 2005). However, it was not until a few years later, likely after Hanford's patent expiring, that the combination of skilled French labor migrating to Piedmont and the already high quality of Piedmontese silk that led to Turin-made stockings gaining a significant share of foreign markets.[12] Piedmont thus began to compete alongside Venice and Genoa in the ready-to-wear stocking market (Belfanti 1996, 2005), manufacturing standardized goods that were sold with simple labels such as "men's," "women's," or "children's," bypassing the traditional commission system.[13]

While many details about the exact design of the stocking frame remain unknown, research has provided enough information to offer a plausible reconstruction of how it operated (Griselini 1768, 102–175). The frame,

[12] AST, C, *Materie Economiche*, Cat. IV, m. 1 d'addizione, fasc. 3, 1724 and 1725.
[13] AST, C, *Materie Economiche*, Cat. IV, m. 7, fasc. 47, 1730.

compact and vaguely resembling a school desk, could produce stockings of various sizes and qualities through a system of needles moved by pedals and weights (Picture 3.5). After adjusting the number of needles, the artisans had to skillfully synchronize their movements to achieve the correct fabric consistency, using beat-up strokes like those required on a weaving loom. It is also known that the machine produced flat stockings (not cylindrical ones) and that the needles had hooks at their tips and were arranged in rows on both sides of the frame. The first row of stitches had to be manually created and attached individually to each needle (along the stem, not at the hook), while the thread was fixed to the hooks on the opposite side of the frame. A system of weights kept the thread tensioned evenly, ensuring consistent depth of stitches. Once set up, a bar was used to press the fabric, allowing the already-formed stitches to catch onto the needles

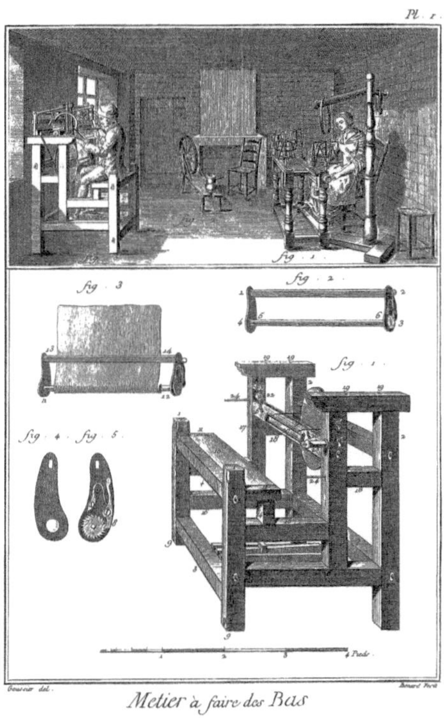

Picture 3.5 Silk stocking maker's workshop (top) and silk stocking frame (bottom). (*Source*: Diderot and D'Alembert 1763, *Planche I*. Bibliothèque nationale de France. Gallica. https://gallica.bnf.fr/ark:/12148/bpt6k321265x)

beneath (Picture 3.6). Beyond its complex operation, there is no doubt that this was a state-of-the-art, costly machine, difficult to construct and challenging to operate. In addition to considerable physical strength, it required a high degree of coordination between the movements of the hands, feet, knees, and even the artisan's forehead (Cruxent Pruna 1960).

The invention of a specialized frame also brought about the profession of the silk stocking maker. Silk stockings produced on the frame could be made much more quickly than by hand, allowing skilled workers to produce a pair of stockings in just over a day. By contrast, a hand-knitter, even the fastest, would need at least a month to make the same quantity, with less uniformity and precision (Griselini 1768).

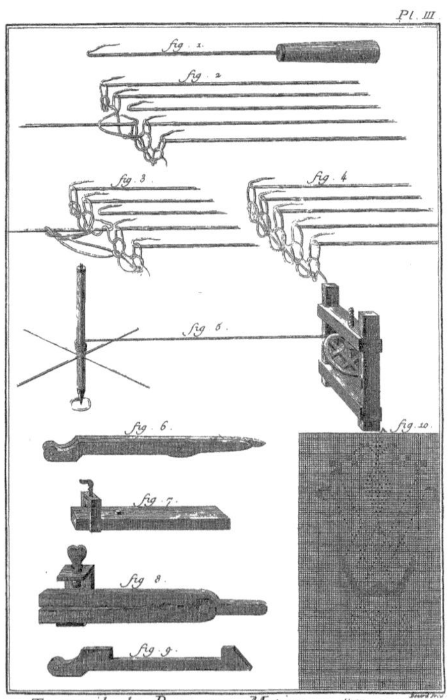

Picture 3.6 Needle mechanism of the stocking frame. (*Source*: Diderot and D'Alembert 1763, *Planche III*. Bibliothèque nationale de France. Gallica. https://gallica.bnf.fr/ark:/12148/bpt6k321265x)

3 The Role of Technology in the Development of New Techniques: The Piedmontese Silk Reeling Method

Gio Francesco Galleani's expertise in silk production was widely acknowledged during the reign of Carlo Emanuele II. In 1667, he was appointed "chief inspector of the factory and operations for raw and thrown silks"—a role established by the duke to standardize the production of raw silk in order to promote its transformation into organzine within the state.[14] Thus, Galleani was entrusted with the task of traveling through towns and villages across Piedmont to promote an innovative reeling method capable of producing raw silk so robust that it allowed the water-powered machinery to operate continuously. This minimized the need to stop and re-tie broken threads and became known as the *alla piemontese* reeling method.

Reeling, in its most basic form, involved placing silkworm cocoons in a basin of hot water over a stove to separate the filaments and extract a usable thread for weaving. The heat from the water caused the protein structure of the filament to break down, allowing the thread to untangle, thus enabling it to be collected into a skein. However, reeling methods varied widely across time and regions. For instance, there were notable differences between the reeling techniques used in northern and southern Italy during the Renaissance and the early modern period—even if the scarcity of sources makes it difficult to trace the history of the dissemination of the machinery used in this process (Zanier 1994).

Calabria and Sicily were among the first places in Italy to see the development of sericulture, and they likely inherited techniques from the Arab-Byzantine tradition for transforming the cocoon into raw thread—as evidenced by the trade of raw silk with the North African coasts since the Middle Ages (Molinari 1994). Yet, the development of reeling techniques in Europe remains unclear. It is possible that the Byzantines brought small "Chinese-style" reeling machines to southern Italy as part of the broader introduction of sericulture (Battistini 2003), therefore making the subsequent technological developments a Calabrian-Sicilian innovation (Malanima 2009). If this is the case, how can the use of similar machinery

[14] AST, SR, *Camerale Piemonte*, art. 539 Consegne bigatti e semenze d'essi, fasc. 5, June 16, 1667.

in Bursa during the early modern period be explained (Zanier 2000; Montemayor 1996)? For now, these remain unresolved questions (Kuhn 1988; Zanier 1994; Ma 2005).

Based on current knowledge, one of the key differences between reeling methods in the South and North of Italy during the early modern period was the machinery employed. In the North, even before the development of the Piedmontese reeling method, a small basin placed over a stove was used to extract the thread, which was then collected on a small reel. By contrast, in the South, at least from the fourteenth century, a larger machine was used—called *grande mangano* due to its large reel (about two meters in diameter). Even in the eighteenth century, the silk guild regulations in Palermo stipulated that the reel "should not be less than nine *palmi* in length, nor more than ten *palmi*"[15] (Laudani 1989, 121).

The stark contrast between the two types of machinery led to the development of distinct, machine-dependent labor dynamics that not only influenced the organization of labor but also had a profound impact on the production system overall. Operating the *grande mangano* required at least four workers: the *maestro trattore* (master silk reeler), the *voltatore* (master turner), one *discepolo* (an apprentice who was preferably male), and at least one woman. The women involved in the reeling process, known as *cacciasete*, were responsible for untangling the thread in the basin, while the male workers operated the large reel to collect the thread (Molinari 1994). Additionally, due to the scale of the machinery and the fiscal interests tied to production, in southern Italy, the reeling process often took place in public spaces designated for this purpose (Aymard 1965; Chorley 1965; Capalbo 1988; Laudani 1989, 1993, 1996; Ciccolella 2003; Ragosta 2009; Morreale 2021). In contrast, in the North, the reeling machine was primarily encountered in rural dwellings, where usually two or three women, generally referred to as *filatrici*, operated it (Chicco 1992).

With the installation of the first hydraulic silk spinning mills in Piedmont, it soon became apparent that the quality of the raw silk produced by using the traditional reeling method was not good enough to be processed by the innovative machinery. For the hydraulic spinning machines to operate smoothly without frequent interruptions caused by broken or uneven threads, the raw silk skeins needed both to be highly

[15] "Considering that a Sicilian palmo is equivalent to 0.258 meters, the *grande mangano* must have measured approximately two and a half meters" (Laudani 1989, 121).

durable and to maintain their fineness and uniformity. As Poni (1981) put it, the thread needed to be "thin and round." Achieving this quality required direct intervention during the reeling phase. This led to the development of an innovative method for extracting the thread from the cocoons and creating the raw silk skein, which became known as the reeling method *alla piemontese.* The transition from the traditional northern Italian reeling method to the "Piedmontese" one is well documented in the *Registro di visita e delli atti per il regolamento della fabrica delle sette* (Register of Inspections and Proceedings for the Regulation of the Silk Manufacture).[16] One of the most interesting documents on the spread of silk reeling techniques in Piedmont, the volume contains a transcription of the control phases and conversations between Galleani, artisans, and local community representatives between June 16 and June 30, 1667. As the document reveals, in that year the new *alla piemontese* reeling method was still far from widespread. After all, the ducal decree mandating the shift from the old to the new reeling method had only been issued in May, amid the installation of the silk reeling mills (*filande*) (Picture 3.7). This short timeframe made it impossible to modernize all the facilities, prompting the duke to refrain from imposing fines and penalties for that year (Chicco 1995).

So, how did the new reeling method work? The most comprehensive answer comes from the law enacted shortly after the installation of the first hydraulic spinning mill in *borgo Dora*, titled *Lettere Patenti di S.A. (…) pel perfezionamento della filatura della seta* (Letters Patent of His Highness (…) for the improvement of silk spinning), which aimed at perfecting the silk spinning process (Duboin 1848, 138—May 14, 1667). Since the state-of-the-art machinery required high-quality raw material to benefit the country's economic growth, the law demonstrates how the launch of new technology can lead to the development of innovative techniques. From May 14, 1667, the "Piedmontese method" became the only reeling method allowed in the Savoy territories, otherwise people risked heavy fines. The law was a true reform, regulating every phase of the reeling process and clearly separating the traditional methods from the production of raw silk intended for higher-level processing (Chicco 1995). The text clearly reveals the rapid changes taking place. It records that by 1667, the innovative reeling method had already been developed, and a specific apparatus had been created to ensure the final product was of unparalleled

[16] AST, SR, *Camerale Piemonte*, art. 539 Consegne bigatti e semenze d'essi, fasc. 5, June 16, 1667.

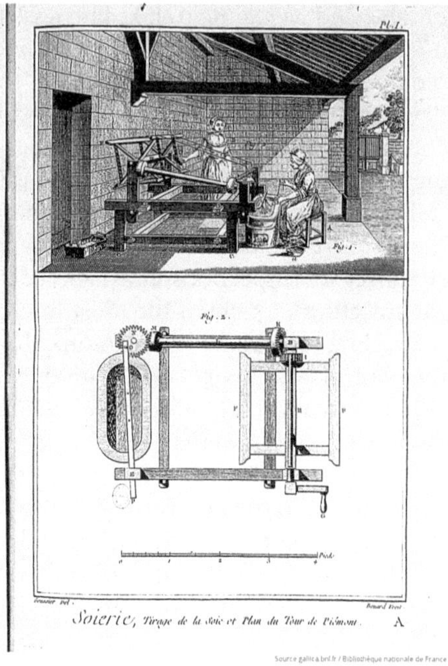

Picture 3.7 *Alla piemontese* silk reeling in a silk reeling mill (top) and perspective of an *alla piemontese* silk reeling machine (bottom). (*Source*: Diderot and D'Alembert 1772, *Planche I*. Bibliothèque nationale de France. Gallica. https://gallica.bnf.fr/ark:/12148/bpt6k3252515)

quality: the *bacinella alla piemontese* ("Piedmontese" basin) (Picture 3.7 and Picture 3.8). The 1667 decree mandated that all the silk reeling mills install only *alla piemontese* machinery, characterized by an oval, thin basin, one-quarter of a yard deep, surrounded by a wooden cover, and equipped with devices with wheels and a shelf to protect the raw silk from the smoke rising from the stove beneath the basin. The Letters Patent, publicly read aloud to ensure their content was understood by all, established the general rules for reeling and spinning and imposed a fine of 50 *lire* for violating any of the directives. For the first time, after an emphasis on the importance of notifying the authorities about the names of the workers responsible for reeling and sorting the cocoons, a guide for female reelers (*filatrici*) was also introduced. This guide stipulated that no more than 40 cocoons should be placed in the basin at a time, with a maximum of 10 or 12 threads per filament joined. The water was to be changed at least three times a day, and the strands drawn from the cocoons had to be twisted at

Picture 3.8 Plan of an *alla piemontese* silk reeling machine and utensils. (*Source*: Diderot and D'Alembert 1772, *Planche II*. Bibliothèque nationale de France. Gallica. https://gallica.bnf.fr/ark:/12148/bpt6k3252515)

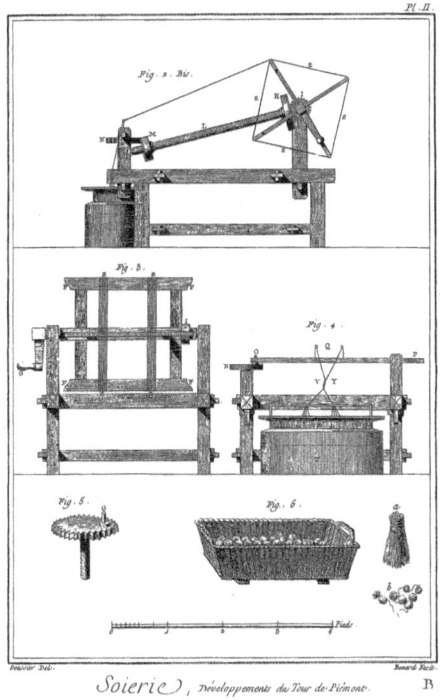

least eight times before being collected on the reel, ensuring they were well-twisted, dry, and tough. A skilled reeler was also necessary to turn the spindle and collect the raw silk. The law concluded by stressing fair remuneration for the workers in the silk reeling mills: under the new regulations, their pay would no longer be based on the quantity of silk processed but on a daily rate and a fair price. This approach was taken to encourage them to exercise all necessary care—an important incentive to prevent the sloppiness that could result from piece-rate compensation.

The *alla piemontese* reeling method thus transformed the industry at multiple levels, influencing not only the machinery but the whole production system. It established a control structure that encouraged workers to enhance the quality of the raw silk, maximizing the benefits of the hydraulic mill innovation.

4 The Quality Challenge, or How to Maintain Prestige

> Turin enjoys the highest reputation and price (for its silk); indeed, one could argue that its exceptional organzines cannot be compared to any others, as they lack a fixed price. Producers value them at their discretion, and they are of such refinement, perfect consistency, and exquisite craftsmanship that, for certain manufacturers, they are purchased at any cost.[17] (Zanon 1763, 239–240)

This mid-eighteenth century quotation comes from Antonio Zanon, who (not without a hint of envy) remarked that achieving the quality of the *alla piemontese* organzines was "more something to be wished for than realistically hoped for"[18] (239–240). Zanon's observation underscores the exceptional quality of Piedmontese silk and its ability to command a premium price—a price he deemed justified. Nevertheless, the hydraulic spinning mills and the *alla piemontese* reeling method alone were insufficient to secure the international acclaim that Piedmontese silk enjoyed in the early modern era. Significant obstacles still impeded its path to success and included ensuring a steady supply of intact cocoons, maintaining consistent quality, and building buyers' trust. These challenges were overcome through innovative techniques and tools, which propelled Piedmontese silk to unprecedented levels of excellence.

The problem of supplying intact cocoons to the silk reeling mills was solved through the introduction of cocoon drying methods. While both sericulture and silk reeling were primarily rural activities, the widespread availability of mulberry trees and families' ability to raise silkworms far exceeded the number of silk reeling mills available for the initial raw silk processing. Many farming families, in fact, did not engage in reeling themselves but instead sold the cocoons they harvested. Yet, to ensure that the cocoons could be processed intact, they had to be transformed into raw silk within 10–15 days after their formation. Otherwise, the silkworm's metamorphosis into a butterfly and its emergence from the cocoon would

[17] "Torino gode bene il primo grado di riputazione e di prezzo; anzi, può dirsi, che i suoi orsoj sopraffini non sono da mettersi in comparazione di tutti gli altri in grado veruno, perché non hanno veramente determinato prezzo. I fabbricatori di questi li valutano a loro arbitrio, e sono di finezza tale, di così perfetta eguaglianza, e sì squisitamente lavorati che, per certe manifatture, ad ogni prezzo vengono comperati" (Zanon 1763, 239–240).

[18] "Ma ella è cosa piuttosto da desiderarsi, che da potersi sperare" (Zanon 1763, 240).

literally break the silk threads, resulting in a low-quality product and compromising the whole supply chain. As the market for organzines expanded and quality controls increased, countermeasures became necessary. Cocoon drying could be achieved through three methods. The first technique, safer and more common, involved boiling water in a bain-marie process. Using a cauldron, the cocoons were steamed and then left to dry on wooden boards after the silkworm had died. This method appears to have been developed only in the eighteenth century, as no earlier treatises mention it. From the early seventeenth century, however, sun-drying and oven-drying methods were documented. Sun-drying, a less reliable method, involved exposing the cocoons to the sun for several hours, during which they had to be rotated (Corcucci 1581; Caracausi 2004; Crippa 2000). Finally, the last option was oven drying. A risky technique, yet one that preserved quality while ensuring the death of the larvae. That said, oven drying was recommended exclusively for Piedmontese workers, who were considered the most skilled. But for others, it was discouraged due to the serious risk of ruining entire batches of cocoons, given the difficulty in controlling both the oven's temperature and drying time.[19] Despite the risks, its speed and reliability spawned the development of specialized ovens. In the late 1760s, Constans de Castellet, a French expert, invented an oven capable of maintaining a consistent temperature, earning him a medal and the title of *Ispettore Generale delle Filature e Filatoi negli Stati del Re di Sardegna* (Inspector of Piedmontese Silk Manufactories from the King of Sardinia) (De Castellet 1766; Crippa 1993).

Once the integrity of the cocoons was ensured and the reeling process completed, the next challenge was quality control of the raw silk. The raw silk skeins reaching the market were classified according to their quality, which was assessed through visual and tactile inspection. The ability to recognize quality was made possible, thanks to the accumulated inspector's experience. Furthermore, buyers knew that the threads in the skeins could not be perfectly homogeneous—within certain limits. If the discrepancies exceeded these limits, the buyer could resort to legal action through the commercial judicial system (Tolaini 2023). In Piedmont, the growing

[19] By the late seventeenth century, the Piedmontese had already gained recognition for their superiority in silkworm cocoon drying. Chapter five of the *Lettere Patenti* of May 14, 1667, states: "To store the cocoons for two or three months without deterioration, skilled men will be appointed to treat them in the oven, although many in the region are already experienced in this practice" (Duboin 1848, 138—May 14, 1667).

reputation of local silk quality led to more thorough inspections of the yarn, honing the techniques of conditioning—namely, the systematic evaluation of skeins ready for sale. Conditioning, which simply means "drying," involved aging the skeins for 24/48 hours in heated environments to allow for weighing or to highlight any defects caused by additives used in production (such as oil, egg whites, sand, etc.). Once inspected, if the skeins proved faulty, appropriate action was taken. Otherwise, they would be placed in controlled environments to regain the proper level of humidity before being returned to their owner. While there are no direct testimonies to confirm this theory, it is likely that conditioning was already practiced in other parts of Italy, given the high value placed on silk and the risk of purchasing counterfeit yarns. Moreover, with the advent of the first hydraulic spinning machines and the growing need for homogeneous and durable threads, the use of conditioning must have increased accordingly. In Piedmont, this technique had been in practice since at least the late 1600s,[20] but a significant advance came in the 1720s with the opening of a "public space suitably arranged under the custody of a responsible person appointed by the Consulate, who, after weighing the silk in the presence of the parties and recording the details, would expose it to conditioning according to the instructions provided by the Consulate" (Duboin 1848, 166—April 8, 1724). This marked the creation of the first public conditioning institution in Europe—an institution that, several decades later, would find fertile ground in Lyon (Tolaini 2023). However, public conditioning was met with resistance from merchants, who frequently criticized the inadequacy of the public facilities and the incompetence of those supervising the process (Chicco 1995). In other words, a more objective system for conditioning was needed, and the solution came from Isaac François Matthey, an inventor of probable Genevan origins. Throughout his life, he had been involved in various sectors of industry, from lime production to saltworks—and silk as well—and earned the title of *Regio Macchinista* (Royal Machinist) in Piedmont (Bertucci 2007, 2023). It was Abbé Nollet who, through his account of a trip to Italy funded by the French *Bureau of Commerce*, reported Matthey's invention

[20] Taking into account an edict issued by the Consulate of Commerce in 1684, which granted the spinner the right to let the silk season in a suitable place if it was not properly dried, and likewise allowed the merchant, upon receiving it, to do the same for a period of 24 hours in dry weather and 48 hours in humid conditions (Duboin 1848, 148—October 15, 1684).

of two scientific instruments. These devices were designed to address the issues raised by merchants and ensure that the flourishing Piedmontese silk industry could maintain its reputation by guaranteeing the sale of high-quality yarn. Matthey invented a hygrometer to measure the silk-skein humidity after conditioning and what would later be known as a *provino*, an instrument to determine the yarn's quality grade (Bertucci 2007, 2023). As a matter of fact, while conditioning could determine weight, it could not assess the actual quality of the skein. It was also not uncommon for organzines sold as superfine to include lower-quality threads (Tolaini 2023). Matthey's invention consisted of a small spool, driven by a crank, that wound a standard length of yarn (400 *aune*)[21] and allowed measurement of its weight in grades. When expressed in *denari*, this value indicated the quality of the silk sample. This method greatly simplified the silk weighing process, cutting both time and costs, introducing a scientific measurement through mechanical technology, and allowing buyers to assess the quality of the silk before purchasing (Tolaini 2023). Although the sample machine was initially available only to a few merchants, within a few decades it became widely used, reaching Lyon, Paris, and the silk cities of Provence (Poni 1997).

Thus, behind the name *organzino alla piemontese* lay a production world founded on unparalleled quality assurance, supported by practical elements and scientific research. In conjunction with commercial interests, these factors ensured the presence of the finest, most durable silk on the international market, ready for the subsequent stages of production.

5 Conclusions

The developments in techniques and technologies in Savoyard Piedmont set in motion a series of advancements that would establish a production paradigm for the modern age on an international scale. "Now, only the machine of Piedmont performs this marvel,"[22] declared the anonymous writer of the entry on silk in the *Encyclopédie*, praising the quality of the silk products achieved by Piedmontese industry in the 1770s. Yet machines

[21] "Aona. Auna. is a unit of length, equivalent to two braccia in the braccio a panno fiorentino system and approximately two rasi in the Piedmontese system. It is used in France and other regions, measuring 3 feet and 8 points in length" (Sant'Albino 1859, 121).

[22] "Or la machine de Piémont seule opere cette merveille" (Diderot and D'Alembert 1765, 273).

are only part of the equation, because without the living artisan, the blueprint remains a mere drawing, the law's text remains an insightful ideal, and the model is merely a mute sculpture. While some people, such as Galleani, Hanford, or Matthey, have become famous names in history, the examples of dissemination presented here are not individual inventions. Rather, they represent techniques and technologies embedded within a context of "modification by many hands," in which changes in market demands, imitation, and adaptation play a key role (Garrioch 2022, 1–2). It should be pointed out that these "many hands" belonged to artisans with embodied expertise—arguably the most reliable method of transferring techniques and machines in the modern era.

Mind, eye, and hand—observation, practice, contact with materials, machinery, and those who know how to operate, maintain, and optimize it—are all essential elements in this context, directly influencing the spread of innovations. As the cases presented demonstrate, for innovations to succeed, they must first be accepted at social and institutional levels. Secondly, they should not be seen as finite achievements by the societies that adopt them; on the contrary, they must be viewed as works in progress, subject to improvement. These are not paradigms, but experiments—regardless of the ultimate success they might achieve. Possessing a machine capable of producing a highly sought-after product, along with the presence of those who can build it to perfection and operators who know how to use it optimally, is not enough. The launch of new machinery also requires the development of new techniques, which can radically reshape prior traditions and practices. The decision taken in this volume to begin with machines and subsequently address techniques reflects how, historically, technological innovation prompted the redefinition of traditional working methods. Furthermore, as the case of the stocking frame demonstrates, the process of redefining technique can, in turn, facilitate the introduction of further machinery that, by benefiting from results achieved for different purposes—such as improvements in the quality of organzine—can be used to its full potential, thereby making the state's trade more competitive in other markets.

The hoped-for (though not guaranteed) outcome is the success of the product—and the *organzino alla piemontese* is a perfect example of a successful product. It quickly became indispensable for luxury manufactories across much of Europe. However, maintaining that reputation is no easy task, particularly in a world such as that of the ancien régime, where states were adept at devising intricate plans for appropriate technologies. To address this challenge, scientific inventions emerged, capable of measuring the quality—and (by extension) the true value—of the product. In this context, science underpins craftsmanship, providing data that confirms the reliability of the "made in"—traditionally regarded as a trustworthy indicator of a specific level of quality (Belfanti 2019).

Bibliography

Artocchini, Carmen. 1972. *Appunti per una storia dell'industria tessile piacentina.* Piacenza: Tipografia Fogliani.

Ash, Eric. 2010. Introduction: Expertise and the early modern state. *Osiris* 25 (1): 1–24.

Aymard, Maurice. 1965. Commerce et production de la soie sicilienne aux XVIe-XVIIe siècles. *Mélanges de l'école française de Rome* 77 (2): 609–640.

Battistini, Francesco. 2003. *L'industria della seta in Italia nell'età moderna.* Bologna: Il Mulino.

Belfanti, Carlo Marco. 1996. Fashion and innovation: The origins of the Italian hosiery industry in the sixteenth and seventeenth centuries. *Textile History* 27 (2): 132–147.

Belfanti, Carlo Marco. 2005. *Calze e maglie. Moda e innovazione nell'industria italiana della maglieria dal Rinascimento a oggi.* Mantua: Tre Lune.

Belfanti, Carlo Marco. 2006. Between mercantilism and market. Privileges for invention in early modern Europe. *Journal of Institutional Economics* 2:1–20.

Belfanti, Carlo Marco. 2019. *Storia culturale del made in Italy.* Bologna: Il Mulino.

Bertucci, Paola. 2007. *Viaggio nel paese delle meraviglie. Scienza e curiosità nell'Italia del Settecento.* Turin: Boringhieri.

Bertucci, Paola. 2013. Enlightened secrets. Silk, intelligent travel, and industrial espionage in eighteenth-century France. *Technology and Culture* 54 (4): 820–852.

Bertucci, Paola. 2021. Spinners' hands, imperial minds: Migrant labour, embodied expertise, and the failed transfer of silk technology across the Atlantic. *Technology and Culture* 62 (4): 1003–1031.

Bertucci, Paola. 2023. *In the land of marvels. Science, fabricated realities and industrial espionage in the age of the grand tour.* Baltimore: Johns Hopkins University Press.

Biagioli, Mario. 2006a. From print to patents: Living on instruments in early modern Europe. *History of Science* 44 (2): 139–186.

Biagioli, Mario. 2006b. Patent republic: Representing inventions, constructing rights and authors. *Social Research: An International Quarterly* 73 (4): 1129–1172.

Brioist, Pascal, and Liliane Hilaire-Pérez. 2016. L'Europe des techniques. In *Histoire des techniques. Mondes, sociétés, cultures (XVIe-XVIIIe siècle)*, ed. Guillaume Carnino, Liliane Hilaire-Pérez, and Aleksandra Kobiljski, 101–141. Paris: Presses Universitaires de France.

Capalbo, Cinzia. 1988. Mercato esterno e tradizione di mestiere. La produzione della seta a Cosenza tra Sette e Ottocento. *Meridiana* 3:73–96.

Caracausi, Andrea. 2004. Nastri, nastrini, cordelle. L'industria serica nel padovano secc. XVI-XIX. Padua: Cleup.

Caracausi, Andrea. 2008. *Dentro la bottega. Culture del lavoro in una città d'età moderna*. Venice: Marsilio.

Carena, Giacinto. 1854. *Prontuario di vocaboli attinenti a parecchie arti, ad alcuni mestieri, a cose domestiche, e altre di uso comune per saggio di un vocabolario metodico della lingua italiana*. Naples: Del Fibreno.

Carnino, Guillaume, Liliane Hilaire-Pérez, and Aleksandra Kobiljski, eds. 2016. *Mondes, sociétés, cultures (XVIe-XVIIIe siècle)*. Paris: Presses Universitaires de France.

Chicco, Giuseppe. 1992. L'innovazione tecnologica nella lavorazione della seta in Piemonte a metà Seicento. *Studi Storici* 33:195–215.

Chicco, Giuseppe. 1995. *La seta in Piemonte 1650–1800. Un sistema industriale d'ancien régime*. Milan: FrancoAngeli.

Chicco, Giuseppe. 2002. Città e campagna: una partita aperta. In *Storia di Torino IV*, ed. Giuseppe Ricuperati, 273–290. Turin: Einaudi.

Chorley, Patrick. 1965. *Oil, silk and enlightenment: Economic problems in XVIIIth century Naples*. Naples: Istituto Italiano per gli Studi Storici.

Ciccolella, Daniela. 2003. *La seta nel Regno di Napoli nel XVIII secolo*. Naples: Edizioni Scientifiche Italiane.

Comino, Stefano, and Alessandro Gasparetto. 2020. Silk mills in the early modern Italy. *Advances in Historical Studies* 9:284–294.

Cooke, William D., and Mine Biret Tavman-Yilmaz. 1999. Hand knitting, frame knitting and rotary frame knitting in the 17th, 18th and 19th centuries. A question of identification. *Textile History* 30 (2): 199–206.

Corcucci, Giovanni. 1581. *Il vermicello della seta*. Rimini: Simbeni.

Cordero, Mario, Lucia Dessi, and Vittorio Marchis, eds. 2008. *Storie di fili di seta, ovvero non tutti i bruchi diventano farfalle*. Milan: Silvana.

Crippa, Flavio. 1990a. Il torcitoio circolare da seta: evoluzione, macchine superstiti, restauri. *Quaderni Storici* 73 (1): 169–212.

Crippa, Flavio. 1990b. Lo "stuarsidor" torcitoio circolare da seta. *Il coltello di Delfo* IV:41–45.

Crippa, Flavio. 1993. Stufatura ed essiccazione. La conservazione del bozzolo per la trattura. In *Le fabbriche magnifiche. La seta in provincia di Cuneo tra Seicento e Ottocento*, ed. Patrizia Chierici and Laura Palmucci Quaglino, 87–92. Cuneo: L'arciere.

Crippa, Flavio. 2000. Dal baco al filo. In *La seta in Italia dal Medioevo al Seicento. Dal baco al drappo*, ed. Luca Molà, Reinhold C. Mueller, and Claudio Zanier, 3–33. Venice: Marsilio.

Cruxent Pruna, Jaime. 1960. La invasión francesa y la introducción del telar de tejidos de punto en España. *Revista Técnica de la Industria de Géneros de Punto* V (4): 5.

Dauchy, Serge. 2018. French law and its expansion in the early modern period. In *The Oxford handbook of European legal history*, ed. Heikki Pihlajamäki, Marcus Dubber, and Mark Godfrey, 760–781. Oxford: Oxford University Press.

Davids, Karel, and Bert De Munck, eds. 2014. *Innovation and creativity in late medieval and early modern European cities*. London: Routledge.

De Castellet, Jean-Baptiste Constans. 1766. *L'arte di moltiplicare la seta, o sia trattato sopra gelsi, l'educazione de' bachi, e la filatura delle sete*. Milan: Agnelli.

Diderot, Denis, and Jean Le Rond D'Alembert. 1763. Encyclopédie, ou dictionnaire raisonné des sciences, des arts et des métiers. In *Recueil de Planches, sur les Sciences, les Arts Libéraux et les Arts Méchaniques, avec leur explication*, vol. 2. Paris: Briasson, David, Le Breton and Durand.

Diderot, Denis, and Jean Le Rond D'Alembert. 1765. *Encyclopédie, ou dictionnaire raisonné des sciences, des arts et des métiers*, v. 15. Neuchâtel: Samuel Faulche & Co.

Diderot, Denis, and Jean Le Rond D'Alembert. 1772. Encyclopédie, ou dictionnaire raisonné des sciences, des arts et des métiers. In *Recueil de Planches, sur les Sciences, les Arts Libéaux et les Arts Méchaniques, avec leur explication*, vol. 11. Paris: Briasson.

Dolza, Luisa. 2007. Utilitas et delectatio: libri di tecniche e teatri di macchine. In *Il Rinascimento italiano e l'Europa. Produzione e tecniche*, ed. Philippe Braunstein and Luca Molà, 115–144. Costabissara: Colla.

Dolza, Luisa, and Vittorio Marchis. 2007. Choses rares & exquises. Dalle arti all'industria: Il Crystal Palace e il suo background. In *Arti Tecnologia Progetto. Le esposizioni d'industria in Italia prima dell'Unità*, ed. Giorgio Bigatti and Sergio Onger, 9–44. Milan: FrancoAngeli.

Dolza, Luisa, and Hélène Vérin. 2004. Illustrating mechanics: The enigma of theater of machines during the Renaissance. *Revue D'histoire Moderne et Contemporaine* 51 (2): 7–37.

Duboin, Felice Amato. 1848. *Raccolta per ordine di materie delle leggi cioè editti, patenti, manifesti, ecc. emanate negli stati di terraferma sino all'8 dicembre 1798 dai sovrani della real casa di Savoja, t. 15, v. 17.* Turin: Baricco ed Arnaldi.

Duchesne, Henri-Gaston, and Henry De Grandsaigne. 1912. *Histoire du Bois de Boulogne. Le Château de Madrid d'apres documents inédits des Archives Nationales, des Archives de la Seine et des Mémoires manuscrits ou imprimés.* Paris: Daragon.

Eiras Roel, Antonio, and Ofelia Rey Castelao. 1994. *Les migrations internes et à moyenne distance en Europe, 1500–1900.* Santiago de Compostela: Xunta de Galicia, Consellería de Educación e Ordenación Universitaria.

Epstein, Stephan R. 2013. Transferring technical knowledge and innovating in Europe, c. 1200-c. 1800. In *Technology, skills and the pre-modern economy in the east and the west*, ed. Maarten Prak and Jan Luiten Van Zanden, 25–67. Leiden-Boston: Brill.

Fraser, Elisabeth A. 2020. The mobility of people and things in the early modern Mediterranean. In *The art of travel.* London: Routledge.

Garrioch, David, ed. 2022. *The republic of skill. Artisan mobility, innovation, and the circulation of knowledge in premodern Europe.* Leiden-Boston: Brill.

Griselini, Francesco. 1768. *Dizionario delle arti e de'mestieri.* Venice: Fenzo.

Guenzi, Alberto, and Carlo Poni. 1987. Sinergia di due innovazioni. Chiaviche e mulini da seta a Bologna. *Quaderni Storici* 64:111–128.

Harris, John R. 1998. *Industrial espionage and technology transfer: Britain and France in the eighteenth century.* Aldershot: Ashgate.

Hilaire-Pérez, Liliane, and Luisa Dolza. 2002. Inventions and privileges in the eighteenth century: Norms and practices. A comparison between France and Piedmont. *History of Technology* 24:21–44.

Hilaire-Pérez, Liliane, and Catherine Verna. 2006. Dissemination of technical knowledge in the Middle Ages and the early modern era: New approaches and methodological issues. *Technology and Culture* 47 (3): 536–565.

Jeremy, David J. 1998. *Artisans, entrepreneurs and machines: Essays on the early Anglo-American textile industries, 1770s–1840s.* Aldershot: Ashgate.

Jütte, Daniel. 2015. *The age of secrecy: Jews, Christians, and the economy of secrets, 1400–1800.* New Haven: Yale University Press.

Kuhn, Dieter. 1988. Textile technology: Spinning and reeling. In *Science and civilisation in China*, ed. Joseph Needham, 247–436. Cambridge: Cambridge University Press.

Lamberti, Maria Carla. 1994. *Vita di Francesco Bal scritta da lui medesimo.* Milan: FrancoAngeli.

Laudani, Simona. 1989. "Li posti delli mangani", Note sulla seta siciliana tra Sette e Ottocento. *Meridiana* 6:109–144.

Laudani, Simona. 1993. Tra mutamenti e continuità: i Consolati della seta ed il sistema manifatturiero in Sicilia (XVIII-XIX secolo). In *La seta in Europa secc XIII-XX*, ed. Simonetta Cavaciocchi, 407–416. Florence: Le Monnier.

Laudani, Simona. 1996. *La Sicilia della seta: economia, società e politica.* Catanzaro: Meridiana Libri.

Lewis, Peta. 1986. William Lee's stocking frame: Technical evolution and economic viability 1589–1750. *Textile History* 17 (2): 129–147.

Long, Pamela O. 2003. *Openness, secrecy, authorship: Technical arts and the culture of knowledge from antiquity to the renaissance.* Baltimore: The Johns Hopkins University Press.

Lowry, Priscilla. 2003. *The secrets of silk: From textiles to fashion.* Austin: St John's Press.
Ma, Debin, ed. 2005. *Textiles in the Pacific, 1500–1900. The Pacific world: Lands, peoples and history of the Pacific, 1500–1900.* Burlington: Ashgate.
Magdelaine, Michelle. 1994. La diaspora des protestants français à la fin du XVIIe siècle. In *Les migrations internes et à moyenne distance en Europe, 1500–1900*, ed. Antonio Eiras Roel and Ofelia Rey Castelao, 553–560. Santiago de Compostela: Xunta de Galicia, Consellería de Educación e Ordenación Universitaria.
Malanima, Paolo. 2009. Crescita e ineguaglianza nell'Europa preindustriale. *Rivista di Storia Economica* 2:189–212.
Marchis, Vittorio. 2016. *Storia delle macchine. Tre Millenni di cultura tecnologica.* Rome-Bari: Laterza.
Marchis, Vittorio. 2018. Lo spionaggio tecnologico nell'Italia del Seicento e del Settecento. *GNOSIS* 2:169–179.
Mokyr, Joel. 1990. *The lever of riches: Technological creativity and economic progress.* Oxford: Oxford University Press.
Molà, Luca. 1994. *La comunità dei lucchesi a Venezia: immigrazione e industria della seta nel tardo Medioevo.* Venice: Istituto veneto di scienze, lettere ed arti.
Molà, Luca. 2000. *The silk industry of Renaissance Venice.* Baltimore: Johns Hopkins University Press.
Molinari, Alessandra. 1994. La produzione e il commercio in Sicilia tra il X ed il XIII secolo: il contributo delle fonti archeologiche. *Archeologia Medievale* 21:99–119.
Montemayor, Julian. 1996. La seda en Toledo en la Época Moderna. In *España y Portugal en las rutas de la seda. Diez siglos de producción y comercio entre Oriente y Occidente*, ed. Celia Fernández Corral, 120–132. Barcelona: Universitat Autònoma de Barcelona, Servei de Publicacions.
Morreale, Antonino. 2021. *Manifatture di seta a Palermo. Baroni e mercanti, filatori e tessitori, mastre e lavoranti (1550–1650).* Palermo: Torri del Vento.
Norbury, James. 1963. Nota sulla lavorazione a maglia e sui tessuti di maglia. In *Storia della tecnologia III*, ed. Charles Singer, Alfred R. Hall, Eric J. Holmyard, and Trevor I. Williams, 187–192. Turin: Boringhieri.
Pasold, Eric W. 1975. In search of William Lee. *Textile History* 6:7–17.
Pihlajamäki, Heikki, Albrecht Cordes, Serge Dauchy, and Dave Deruysscher. 2018. *Understanding the sources of early modern and modern commercial law: Courts, statutes, contracts and legal scholarship.* Leiden: Brill.
Plebani, Tiziana. 2016. Dal lavoro alla disciplina. Precettistica e libri di ricami. In Conduct literature for and about women in Italy. *Prescribing and describing life*, ed. Helena Sanson and Francesco Lucioli, 303–323. Paris: Garnier.
Poni, Carlo. 1976. All'origine del sistema di fabbrica: tecnologia e organizzazione produttiva dei mulini da seta nell'Italia settentrionale (sec. XVII-XVIII). *Rivista Storica Italiana* 88:444–497.

Poni, Carlo. 1981. Misura contro misura: come il filo di seta divenne sottile e rotondo. *Quaderni Storici* 16 (3): 385–423.

Poni, Carlo. 1997. Standard, fiducia e conversazione civile: misurare lo spessore e la qualità del filo di seta. *Quaderni Storici* 3:717–734.

Poni, Carlo. 2009. *La seta in Italia, una grande industria prima della rivoluzione industriale.* Bologna: Il Mulino.

Popplow, Marcus. 2002. Models of machines: A 'missing link' between early modern engineering and mechanics? Max-Planck Institut für Wissenschaftsgeschichte Preprints 22.

Poussou, Jean Pierre. 1994. Les migrations internes et à moyenne distance en France à l'époque moderne et au XIXe siècle. In *Les migrations internes et à moyenne distance en Europe, 1500–1900*, ed. Antonio Eiras Roel and Ofelia Rey Castelao, 205–224. Santiago de Compostela: Xunta de Galicia, Consellería de Educación e Ordenación Universitaria.

Prak, Maarten, and Jan Luiten Van Zanden, eds. 2013. *Technology, skills and the pre-modern economy in the east and the west.* Leiden: Brill.

Ragosta, Rosalba. 2009. *Napoli, città della seta. Produzione e mercato in età moderna.* Rome: Donzelli.

Rial Costas, Benito. 2017. Marketing a new legal code in fifteenth-century Castile: A case study of the interactions between crown, law and printing. In *Books in motion in early modern Europe. Beyond production, circulation, and consumption*, ed. Daniel Bellingradt, Paul Nelles, and Jeroen Salman, 87–109. Cham: Palgrave Macmillan.

Righi, Laura. 2016. Produzione di seta e trasferimenti tecnologici tra legislazione e frodi: il caso di Bologna dal XIV al XVI secolo. *Archivio Storico Italiano* 174 (4): 639–668.

Rosso, Claudio. 1992. Dal gelso all'organzino: nascita e sviluppo di un'industria trainante. In *Torino sul filo della seta*, ed. Giuseppe Bracco, 39–66. Turin: Archivio Storico della Città di Torino.

Sant'Albino, Vittorio. 1859. *Gran dizionario piemontese-italiano.* Turin: L'Unione tipografico-editrice.

Schulz, Knut. 2007. La migrazione di tecnici, artigiani e artisti. In *Il Rinascimento italiano e l'Europa. Produzione e tecniche*, ed. Philippe Braunstein and Luca Molà, 89–114. Costabissara: Colla.

Simonsohn, Shlomo. 1997. *The Jews in Sicily (383–1300).* Leiden: Brill.

Smith, Pamela H. 2022. *From lived experience to the written word: Reconstructing practical knowledge in the early modern world.* Chicago: University of Chicago Press.

Tolaini, Roberto. 2023. Qualità e differenziazione: per una fenomenologia delle misure della seta (XVII-XIX secoli). *RiSES - Ricerche di Storia Economica e Sociale* 9 (1-2): 123–153.

Uchacz, Tianna Helena. 2020. Reconstructing early modern artisanal epistemologies and an "undisciplined" mode of inquiry. *Isis* 111 (3): 606–613.

Zanier, Claudio. 1994. *Where the roads met. East and west in the silk production processes (17th to 19th century)*. Kyoto: Istituto Italiano di Cultura, Scuola di Studi sull'Asia Orientale.

Zanier, Claudio. 2000. Un protettore scomodo. San Giobbe e la seta. In *La seta in Italia dal Medioevo al Seicento. Dal baco al drappo*, ed. Luca Molà, Reinhold C. Mueller, and Claudio Zanier, 153–210. Venice: Marsilio.

Zanon, Antonio. 1763. Dell'Agricoltura, dell'Arti e del Commercio in quanto unite contribuiscono alla felicità degli Stati. In *Lettere di Antonio Zanon*. Venice: Fenzo.

Zucca Micheletto, Beatrice. 2017. Privilegi economici, corporazioni e rapporti di potere negli stati sabaudi (1680-1799): una ricerca in corso. *RiSES - Ricerche di Storia Economica e Sociale* 3 (1–2): 139–161.

CHAPTER 4

Beyond Technology. Law, Institutions, and the Challenge of Innovation

1 Introduction

On January 21, 1742, after a more than 70-year hiatus, a Venetian ambassador was solemnly received at the court of Turin. The long-standing dispute over the title of "King of Cyprus," which had embroiled the House of Savoy and the Most Serene Republic of Venice in a centuries-long, bloodless conflict, was resolved, thanks to the Venetian ambassadorship of Marco Foscarini in Rome between 1737 and 1740 and papal mediation. The shutters of Palazzo Biandrate Aldobrandino di San Giorgio, the historic residence of Venetian ambassadors in Turin, were reopened. It was there that Foscarini composed what is still remembered as a masterpiece of Venetian diplomatic tradition: the *Relazione di Savoja* (Account of Savoy) dedicated to King Carlo Emanuele III of Savoy (1701–1773) and presented to the Venetian Senate on March 1, 1743 (Valsecchi 1959; Venturi 1969, 1970; Firpo 1983). While adhering to the structure and addressing the traditional themes of seventeenth-century ambassadorial reports, Foscarini chose to devote an entire section to praising the economic policies of Vittorio Amedeo II (1666–1732), the ruler who, citing the ambassador, had successfully "set his sights on commerce" (Firpo 1983, 1017). Foscarini acknowledged that the brevity of his stay in Turin had not allowed him to form a complete picture of Savoyard economic strategy. He also admitted that a diplomatic report was an unconventional medium for a detailed analysis of the dynamics that had enabled Piedmont to

M. Grassi, *The Silk Industry in Early Modern Piedmont*, Labour in History and Society,
https://doi.org/10.1007/978-3-032-15353-1_4

double its revenues during Vittorio Amedeo II's reign. Nevertheless, he was eager to offer the Venetian Senate what he considered a succinct formula for this success. He informed them about Vittorio Amedeo II's creation of a new institutional body, the Consulate of Commerce; the promulgation of "excellent edicts" to improve silk production and quality and, last but not least, a keen awareness of the needs of his subjects (Firpo 1983, 1024).

Integrating innovation into a long-standing tradition, along with the success in importing and adapting techniques and technologies, was vital for Piedmont to achieve a high level of quality in the silk industry. These were vital but insufficient prerequisites. In fact, the Savoyard government sought, sometimes successfully and sometimes unsuccessfully, to create and maintain a sufficiently flexible economic policy, capable of adapting to the rapid changes in an increasingly open world, such as that of the eighteenth century, by establishing new institutions and engaging in legislative activity. Building on Hupfel's methodological approach (2019) in his study of the French and English governments' economic policies in the silk industry, this analysis will explore, from a top-down perspective, the processes that led to the creation of a legislative and institutional framework that enabled Piedmontese silk to gain international recognition. These processes were deeply embedded in the broader social, political, and economic dynamics that shaped Europe between the sixteenth and eighteenth centuries, positioning Piedmont's history as a key factor in understanding the shifting relations among European states during this period of radical change.

A good example of this is the Piedmontese version of the "mercantilist partnership" (Rosenberg and Birdzell 1986, 113–144; De Goey and Veluwenkamp 2002) between the merchant class and the government, inspired by the actions of the French minister Colbert and promoted in Piedmont by the minister Truchi di Levaldigi. Rather than a harmonious alliance, recent scholarship interprets such arrangements as a form of state-mediated capitalist accumulation, in which the state both enabled and constrained private enterprise, channelling commercial capital into production while subordinating private interests to public control—a dynamic particularly evident in the silk industry, where governments and entrepreneurs jointly shaped economic activity under constant negotiation and persistent asymmetries (Banaji 2019; Franceschi 2020). Seen in this light, the Savoyard experience exemplified a hybrid configuration, where collaboration and conflict coexisted within a framework of state regulation.

This symbiotic yet structurally asymmetric relationship was legitimized by the establishment, at the end of the seventeenth century, of the *Consolato di Commercio* (Consulate of Commerce)—a new legal entity that fortified the strong link between market and political power and operated as a key instrument of state-managed commercial capitalism (Symcox 1983; Cerutti 1992, 2003). This institution was closely linked to the government's increasing focus on issues related to the silk industry, a valuable resource constantly at risk of causing problems from both intrinsic and external factors affecting Piedmontese society. Indeed, the government's legislative activity evolved at kaleidoscopic speed between the late seventeenth and early eighteenth centuries.

During these same years—and notably later than in most other European regions—the guild system began to take shape in Piedmont. Its emergence was closely linked to the merchants' growing ambition to expand their influence in international commerce and to consolidate their social and political standing within the Savoyard state. As these ambitions increasingly intersected with ducal authority, the formation of guilds took place within a framework of top-down regulation, where economic organization and state oversight evolved in close interaction. This dynamic makes the Piedmontese case a revealing example of how professional specialization and political centralization interacted in the early modern economy. In Piedmont, corporate institutions were created to integrate production and trade within an administrative framework already shaped by fiscal and legislative control, revealing the mechanisms through which the state sought to channel private initiative through legally defined bodies, using guilds as instruments of supervision as much as of representation. Seen in this light, the Piedmontese experience acquires broader significance within the European debate on the role of guilds in economic development—a question that has long divided historians (Sacco 1930; Guenzi et al. 1999; Massa and Moioli 2004; Prak and Van Zanden 2013; Bellavitis 2018; Ogilvie 2019). Far from following a uniform model, guilds displayed highly diverse institutional and socio-economic functions across regions and periods, making any general judgment on their long-term economic impact inherently problematic (Hafter 2007; De Munck 2022).

Finally, the focus will shift to the Savoy government's legislative activity regarding the silk industry, driven by the intense economic dispute with England. After appropriating the technology of the hydraulic silk mill, England sought to establish itself on the international stage by exploiting raw Piedmontese silk. This conflict prompted the creation of the *Nuovo regolamento del setificio*, published on April 8, 1724. The mechanisms set in motion during this period ultimately culminated in this manifesto, which became the global paradigm for high-quality silk production in the years that followed.

This chapter will examine the process of creating and reforming institutional bodies related to silk production, a process that had significant economic and political implications (Prato 1908; Quazza 1957; Sabel and Zeitlin 1997). The purpose of the new laws governing the production and sale of silk, the new institutions managing the industry, the new regulations, and the fines related to labor organization and techniques was to develop the industry. But they also play an active role in defining the social roles of the classes involved in the production and commercialization of silk products. These measures contributed to shaping the fundamental aspects of the representation of a centralized state focused on the figure of the monarch. Piedmontese silk thus became the flagship industry of the House of Savoy, turning the sector into one worthy of investing in bureaucratic, economic, and social terms. Silk was a source of profit that demanded continuous attention—a precious gem, which for over a century would remain the exclusive domain of the Savoyard court.

2 The Foundations of a Mercantilist Partnership: The *Consolato di Commercio*

In their *How the West Grew Rich*, the famous and, to some extent, controversial work (Engerman 1994), Rosenberg and Birdzell (1986) emphasized the importance of institutions as catalysts of economic transformation, focusing on the spaces for initiative and negotiation that merchants gradually conquered during the transition from feudalism to capitalism. Their argument resonated with a broader current of thought—most notably advanced by Douglass North and Robert Thomas (1973)—that placed institutional incentives and property-rights arrangements at the core of long-term economic growth. North's later works (1989, 1990, 2000) refined this approach by linking institutional change to processes of learning and adaptation, while Acemoglu and Robinson (2012) further developed the discussion through their distinction between "inclusive" and "extractive" institutions, proposing a framework that links economic performance to the distribution of political power. Inclusive institutions foster participation and innovation by granting access to resources and opportunities to a broad segment of society, whereas extractive institutions concentrate authority and wealth in the hands of a few, often ensuring short-term control at the expense of long-term growth. Applying such models to early modern economies therefore requires careful contextualization, acknowledging both their explanatory power and their limitations. Although the institutions of the early modern period cannot be directly equated with those described by North or Acemoglu, they reveal similar underlying logics of incentive, regulation, and participation. From this perspective, early commercial tribunals offer a useful lens through which to examine how economic and political actors negotiated authority within evolving state structures. In Piedmont, the *Consolato di Commercio* (Consulate of Commerce) embodied this dynamic, functioning simultaneously as an instrument of incentive, regulation, and participation in the governance of commerce. This conceptual background does not imply a linear progression from institutional design to economic success but rather highlights the tensions inherent in any attempt to coordinate private initiative and public control.

Building on this theoretical framework, the evolution of commercial courts offers a concrete illustration of these dynamics. Their origins can be traced back to ancient times: across the world, from East Asia to the Mediterranean, institutional bodies emerged to regulate, protect, and adjudicate the production and exchange of goods—ranging from leather to grain, from bronze to wool (Mitchell 1904; Ago 1998; Mazzarella 2020). The first records of financial control in the territories of the Duchy of Savoy date back to the *Statuta Sabaudiae*, promulgated in 1430 by the first Duke of Savoy, Amedeo VIII (1383–1451) (Sacco 1930). The text reveals some leitmotifs that will be repeated, mutatis mutandis, until the end of the ancien régime—such as the need for control over merchants and artisans' activities, and attention to issues like remuneration and working hours. In the fifteenth century, the Savoyard court was based in Chambéry, where the duke had established a specialized council for commercial and maritime affairs, delegating the oversight of trade and navigation cases in the port of Nice (Duboin 1848, 102–106—July 28, 1448; December 9, 1528; July 22, 1531; August 2, 1531). Despite these early developments, the creation of a significant administrative structure in the Piedmont region would not occur until the French occupation of the city (1536–1559), with the establishment of the *Parlamento* (Parliament) and the *Camera dei Conti* (Chamber of Accounts) in 1539 (Merlin 1998).

With the Peace of Cateau-Cambrésis (1559), Duke Emanuele Filiberto I reconquered Piedmont—taking control of territories devastated by war, where much of the artisan population had fled and the economy was collapsing (Duboin 1848, 11—April 20, 1561). Realizing the strategic importance of the city of Turin, the main crossroads between French and Italian territories, the duke decided to move the capital of his domains from Savoy to Piedmont (Merlin 1992, 1995, 1998). He supported the project with plans for the economic recovery of the region through incentives and tax exemptions for foreign workers who would settle in Piedmont (Duboin 1848, 11—April 20, 1561).

The relocation of the capital and the court prompted substantial commercial interests (Raviola 2015). The duke immediately realized that the administrative legacy inherited from the French period needed to be embraced and new legislation under his authority passed to reflect the emerging socio-economic structure of the city's merchant class (Merlin 1998). One year after the Savoy family's triumphant entry into Turin in 1563, a special judge for commercial disputes, called *Conservatore de' mercanti*, was established—though unfortunately no records of this role remain (Duboin 1848, 43). The initiative to develop the economy in the duchy's Piedmontese territories was ambitious. Its foundations, in addition to their formal outlines in the *Prammatica* of 1565 (Borelli 1681, 685–691—April 1, 1565; Muzzarelli 2020), became more robust with the creation of a board of experts in arts and manufactures, designated by the duke (Duboin 1848, 1—January 20, 1566). This played a crucial role in consolidating Savoy power in the city and provided fresh impetus to the reform process (Merlin 1998; Quazza 1957). In the early decades of the seventeenth century, under the reign of Carlo Emanuele I, further measures were introduced, including registering all artisans according to their trade and electing a council. Composed of artisans themselves, the council was responsible for enforcing production rules (based on common sense and the experience of the most skilled), and had the authority to fine and punish violators. The ducal order acquired a significance that far exceeded that of previous regulations, establishing a rudimentary framework for what would later evolve into the guilds of Turin (Cerutti 1992). Nevertheless, in the years that followed, control over the crafts remained unclear.[1] For much of the century, it was the Chamber of Accounts, serv-

[1] With few exceptions. The *Magistrato sopra le arti* (Magistrate overseeing the arts) of the Albergo di Virtù is considered by Duboin to be an internal figure within the Council of the

ing as the main financial institution of the Savoy state, that handled the issuance of laws to regulate the emerging silk industry (Merlin 2021). However, there was still no institutional body dedicated to the control, oversight, and economic development of industries and manufactures.

By the 1650s, a new wind was blowing from the Kingdom of France, marking the end of the period of Mazzarino's term as Prime Minister and the introduction into state financial administration of his ambitious successor, Jean Baptiste Colbert. Having risen to the position of Prime Minister in 1661, Colbert succeeded, following in the footsteps of his predecessors, in involving the government in every aspect of managing the French domestic economy. He shook up the institutional structure of production, thus offering one of the greatest examples of mercantilist policy under the ancien régime (Cole 1931; Boissonade 1932; Mira 1964; Minard 1997, 1998, 2000, 2008; Dessert 2019). Perhaps due to geographical proximity, commercial interests, or the success of Colbert's economic policies, mercantilist ideals also began to flourish in Piedmont only a few years later. It was in this context that the person who would later be referred to as the "Savoyard Colbert" emerged: Giovanni Battista Truchi di Levaldigi (Cibrario 1830, 67–68; Firpo 1983, 938). Despite some research casting doubt on the actual contribution of Truchi's actions in the state and the possibility of directly comparing French and Piedmontese mercantilism in this period (Prato 1920; Stumpo 1979), the strong desire for economic recovery in the duchy—particularly through the silk industry—is apparent. Truchi represented a local financial class that, by asserting its presence in state institutions, became a full participant in the driving force aimed at strengthening Piedmont's economy (Prato 1920; Stumpo 1979; Rosso 1992, 2018). During these years, merchants, financiers, and bankers converged on Turin from all the major Piedmontese centers, collecting taxes, providing credit, and handling money transactions with the leading European markets (Stumpo 1979). Furthermore, in 1663, traders succeeded in founding a religious congregation, the *Pia Congregazione dei banchieri, negozianti e mercanti* (Pious Congregation of Bankers, Shopkeepers and Merchants), which, within a few years, began to make demands for greater economic and political power (Cerutti 1992; VV 1986).

eponymous Charitable Institution (1848, 70—September 13, 1587). This role likely held a certain degree of state recognition in commercial matters (Duboin 1848, 123—June 16, 1619).

From this perspective, the establishment of the commercial tribunal known as the Consulate of Commerce, one of the key bodies responsible for overseeing production and trade in Piedmont, is a pivotal innovation. It was founded during the regency of Madama Reale Giovanna Battista di Savoia-Nemours (1644–1724), who assumed power after her husband's death and served as regent for the future duke (Cerutti 1992, 2003; Arnaldi di Balme and Ruffino 2019; Guardamagna 2021). The institution, characterized by summary procedures, responded to the growing demands of the merchants' congregation, which saw an increasing number of members each year. Among her first actions, the regent authorized the creation of the Consulate in 1676 (Abrate 1960; Stumpo 1979; Cerutti 1992). The connection between the new institution and the silk industry is evident from the analysis of the Consulate's composition at the time of its founding. The Consulate included the two bankers who financed the establishment of the Galleani spinning mill in *borgo Dora* in the 1660s, as well as merchants of textiles and dyeing materials (Duboin 1848, 82—November 25, 1676). Thus, in this first period, the Consulate was, per se, a guild-like institution, primarily focused on resolving issues arising among members of the textile trade (Cerutti 2003). With the support of the new institution, the Regent promulgated a new decree on June 20, 1677, regarding the regulations for various trades, especially silk production and dyeing (Duboin 1848, 29—June 20, 1677). The text established the assignment of workers, the procedure for joining the emerging guild entourage, and imposed practical rules on the conduct of professions, but only those relevant to the Consulate's members (Duboin 1848, 82—November 25, 1676; Stumpo 1979).

Nevertheless, the history of this institution was marked by difficulties. Its creation, in fact, undermined the control over production and sales held by the Municipality and the Chamber of Accounts. As a result, it eroded the power of their members—who missed no opportunity to express their discontent. Despite representing a key moment in economic development, the new institution remained inconsistent throughout the regency of Maria Giovanna Battista, hindered by persistent complaints and resistance (Cerutti 1992; Naldi et al. 2011; Devoti 2021). The issue resurfaced in 1687, after the disputed dismissal of the regent and ascent of Vittorio Amedeo II to the throne (Navire 2008). It is true that the young duke inherited a more stable and prosperous economic and administrative state of affairs than the one left by Carlo Emanuele II. Yet the Piedmontese silk industry remained subject to favoritism, privileges, and the self-interest of craftsmen and merchants. Clear and decisive action was needed to end this disarray and ensure that the growing success of European trade would not be hindered by fraud or other abuses. At the same time, tensions between the Municipality and the Consulate had grown, forcing the duke to act (Cerutti 1992). Consequently, he brought the Consulate of Commerce's tribunal under the control of the Senate, limiting the mercantile class to a consultative role while, in practice, removing authority from the Municipality. It was only with the *Regie Costituzioni* (Royal Constitutions) of 1723 that control of the Consulate was restored to the merchants through a reform that reinstated its summary judicial system, also known as the *mercantile* system (Cerutti 2003). The pace of change was persistent. By 1733, just a decade later, the merchants themselves had stepped down from leadership of the Consulate. The state officials' persistent opposition throughout the 1720s had greatly limited their influence, while the chance to join the city's aristocracy through the Consulate had become increasingly out of reach due to new membership criteria set by a rising administrative elite (Monestarolo 2006). Only bankers, whose role had become largely symbolic, stayed in the tribunal, though their involvement was limited to a purely consultative role (Cerutti 1992).

The foundation of the Consulate, a new arm of ducal power, was a decisive response from absolute authority to the challenges of the mid-seventeenth century. Under Minister Truchi and the regency of Maria Giovanna Battista, the foundations of a mercantilist partnership were established in Piedmont, which would come to define the reign of Vittorio Amedeo II. During this period, the emerging group of traders gained increasing importance in the kingdom's economic development. However, establishing an innovative institution does not necessarily ensure its effective performance, as the case of the Consulate of Commerce demonstrates. It faced the internal tensions of a society fiercely fighting to retain its fragile power embodied by its own social class, turning the new mercantile tribunal into a potential tool for both social mobility and market control. While the involvement of merchants in the Consulate facilitated the adoption of innovations aimed at advancing the silk sector, it also had significant consequences for Piedmontese society—particularly for the artisan class.

3 The Pendulum of Power: Merchants, Guilds, and Journeymen

Following the establishment of the Consulate of Commerce, another phenomenon of growing importance took shape: the rise of craft guilds.[2] As Cerutti (1992) pointed out, guilds flourished in Piedmont only between the seventeenth and eighteenth centuries, amid the ongoing struggle between Turin's municipal power and ducal authority. Since the Consulate of Commerce functioned both as a tribunal for commercial disputes and as an administrative arm of royal authority responsible for approving commercial privileges and manufacturing regulations, it is clear that Savoyard guilds evolved within a framework of strict state supervision. As elsewhere in the Italian peninsula, these corporations were known during the early modern period as *Università*[3]—collective bodies formally recognized by the sovereign power, endowed with legal personality and governed by their own internal regulations. The royal sanction of their statutes was the legal condition of their existence, defining the limits of corporate autonomy to internal matters such as apprenticeship, workshop discipline, and the distribution of labor (Sewell 1980). In this system, corporate authority was strictly subordinated to the prerogatives of the sovereign administration. Guilds possessed no political autonomy and operated under the close supervision of the Consulate of Commerce, which acted as both regulator and arbiter of their activities. Any collective initiative—be it the revision of statutes, petitions for privileges, or the settlement of internal disputes—had to pass through the Consulate and receive royal approval. This arrangement marked a decisive departure from the late-medieval "jurisdictional state" model typical of Italian city-states: in Piedmont, guilds no longer functioned as autonomous civic bodies but as instruments of royal economic governance, integrated into the increasingly centralized machinery of Savoyard administration (Mozzarelli 1988; Borelli 1999; Caligaris 1999; Lanaro 1999; Massa and Moioli 2004).

Among the various sectors endowed with a formal guild organization, the silk industry best exemplified how the Savoyard model of corporative regulation combined state intervention with professional representation.

[2] Unlike other Italian regions, where powerful guilds had flourished since the Middle Ages, Piedmont developed only a handful of geographically concentrated guilds, each overseeing limited aspects of production (Allegra 1987; Cerutti 1992).

[3] In early modern Italy, the term università, derived from the Latin universitas, denoted a legally recognized collective body or corporation (Quaglioni 1998).

Within this sector, however, the distribution of corporate structures was far from uniform. Only a few occupations were granted formal guild statutes: reelers never formed a guild of their own, while silk spinners—though nominally affiliated with the guilds of Turin and Racconigi—and silk dyers were organized into craft bodies only in formal terms. In practice, however, these groups appear to have operated mainly under the regulations imposed by the central government, most notably through the Manifesto of April 8, 1724, which established uniform rules for the entire silk industry.[4] By contrast, the guilds representing the upper tiers of production and trade—such as the *Università dei mastri mercanti tessitori in oro, argento e seta* (Guild of Master Merchant Weavers in Gold, Silver, and Silk), the *Università dei mercanti in seta* (Guild of Silk Merchants), and the *Università dei mastri calzettai* in seta (Guild of Master Silk Stocking Makers)—were more clearly defined and institutionally stable.

What was the reason for this difference? The most evident explanation lies in the central role of weaving and trading activities within the city. The number of spinners working with hand-operated spinning mills gradually declined following the establishment of the hydraulic spinning mills in *borgo Dora*, and dyers were forced to move their activities outside the city walls as early as the seventeenth century. On the contrary, merchants, silk weavers, and sock makers had—and continued to have throughout the eighteenth century—numerous active workshops in the city. For instance, in 1679, there were over 200 master silk weavers in Turin[5]—making the guild one of the largest in the city.[6] Furthermore, two other factors seem to have helped encourage the demand for official statutes for these guilds. Firstly, master craftsmen underwent a process of proletarianization and lost commercial power, and secondly, official legislation lacked specific regulations regarding production activities, work organization, and product sales. In structural terms, a broad, sectoral—or "umbrella"—form of guild organization was initially adopted in Piedmont, which sought to unite production and commerce within the same institutional framework (Epstein 1998; Pfister 2008). The *Università dei mastri mercanti tessitori in oro, argento e seta* (Guild of Master Merchant Weavers in Gold, Silver, and Silk), founded in 1687 as the first silk-related guild following the foundation of the Consulate of Commerce, exemplified this model by

[4] AST, C, *Materie economiche*, Cat. III, m. 1 da ordinare, fasc. 14, April 4, 1791.

[5] APSA, *Università dei mastri vellutai*, v. 4, 1677–1795.

[6] AST, SR, *Consolato di Commercio*, Congreghe, m. 32b, 1687–1700.

integrating the interests of both artisans and merchants. This configuration corresponds to some extent to what Borelli (1999) identifies as the "sectoral guild" typical of late medieval Italian textile cities, in which related crafts were grouped under a single institutional body. During the first half of the eighteenth century, however, this model evolved into a more differentiated system of phase-specific guilds. This transformation—from a comprehensive to a function-based structure—reflected, to some extent, broader developments observable in other Italian textile centers, where the expansion of urban markets and the consolidation of state administration favored increasingly specialized and hierarchically defined forms of corporate representation.

The ambiguous position of the weavers, acting both as producers and as traders, is evident from the very name of the *Università* itself—and it was precisely this ambiguity that led merchants to seek emancipation from the world of production (Ago 1998). Yet the disputes within the Consulate of Commerce and the complex dynamics created by the War of the Spanish Succession delayed any concrete action. The silk merchants' first request to establish an independent guild, separate from that of the craftsmen, was submitted to the Consulate only in June 1714. This solicitation was made amidst the complex economic and political landscape of the time. When the changes brought about by the Treaty of Utrecht allowed the Savoyard domains to rise from a duchy to a kingdom, the political structure and borders of the Savoyard state were suddenly altered. Territories previously under Milanese control were incorporated, while the fortunes of Piedmontese silk abroad were on the rise. The new borders had prompted Emperor Charles VI of Habsburg (1685–1740), in Milan, to prohibit the import of foreign-made silk fabrics to promote domestic production and prevent the altered borders from significantly affecting state trade. The matter was taken very seriously in nearby Turin, where merchants, experts, and guild representatives were consulted to assess the potential damage from this decision and what steps, if any, should be taken. Although the damage was considered minimal, the issue highlighted the importance of silk fabric trading for the newly established kingdom and, even more, the need for an independent body to oversee it.

Furthermore, in the same year, some Piedmontese merchants requested a privilege from the government to introduce the production of *lustrato*,[7]

[7] A shiny silk fabric, where the glossy surface is achieved by applying heat, pressure, a chemical treatment, or by using polishing substances (Burnham 1980, 65).

a particular type of fabric, with state support. In June 1714, the merchants of Turin offered to do their best to promote this new type of production, using the chance to distance themselves from the producers.[8] According to the merchants, the lack of appropriate legislation for those wishing to enter the profession had allowed many artisans, employed in other sectors, to also take up weaving. The upshot was the production of poor-quality fabrics and harm to the reputation of the state's industries. The draft statutes for the creation of a guild exclusively for silk merchants focused on traditional issues, such as apprenticeship regulations, registration requirements, and the management of shops by widows in the event of a merchant's death. Nevertheless, a significant difference from traditional proposals for guild statutes emerged: the ninth and tenth articles were wholly dedicated to regulating the relationship between merchants and master weavers. Through the statute, the merchants outlined the challenges their businesses faced due to weavers who, in times of difficulty, would sell or pawn the silk supplied to them. Interestingly, with the statute's approval, if weavers wanted to sell fabrics made from silk they had purchased, they would be required to join the proposed *Università dei mercanti in seta* (University of Silk Merchants). Otherwise, they would have to rely on the merchants' commissions. This petition did not result in the establishment of the Silk Merchants' Guild, as shown by the submission of similar requests in 1720 and 1738 (Duboin 1848, 312–313). However, this merely reinforced a process already underway: by the early eighteenth century, most weaving was already being done on commission from merchants, effectively making master weavers dependent on them.

In the following years, both merchants and some weavers continued to produce and sell silk fabrics until the publication of a new royal decree on July 23, 1730. Paragraph 17 of the new law was a significant change compared to the past, limiting the maximum number of looms each artisan could manage simultaneously to four (Duboin 1848, 50—July 23, 1730).[9]

This change was based on previous complaints made by some master weavers to the king, advocating for the restriction of looms per master—a similar law had been in place in Lyon since 1703 (Garden 1970). The goal, as stated by the weavers, was to "eliminate the numerous and

[8] AST, C, *Materie economiche*, Cat. IV, m. 7, June 4, 1714.

[9] Similar restrictions on the number of looms were also introduced in Lyon (Garden 1970) and other Italian centers, aiming to balance production and preserve fabric quality (Massa 1992; Della Valentina 1999).

harmful abuses introduced (into the craft) (…) and promote the fair distribution of the common good."[10] This request did have consequences. The masters in leadership positions within the guild council at the time opposed it, presumably driven by their own interests—as argued by the requesting masters (Cerutti 1992; Della Valentina 1999). When this new regulation was implemented, all weavers were forced to seek commissions exclusively from merchants because they were no longer able to meet their direct customers' fabric production requirements by themselves. For the many masters already working for merchants, the workload would inevitably be distributed more equitably. On the other hand, for the few masters still trading, it meant losing control over the market.

The implementation of this law, however, also hindered the merchants. Realizing their substantial inability to meet the growing demand within the confines of these restrictions, they were forced to turn to the king for further concessions and privileges. The merchants sought to bypass the four-loom rule. Their goal was to allow the most skilled masters to weave their silk, thus introducing the finest fabrics produced in the city into the market, fulfilling numerous orders, maintaining the reputation of the Turin manufactures, and ensuring future sales. In the disputes between merchants and weavers, trust proved to be crucial in the merchants' arguments (Holmström 2002), contrasting with the obvious need for all artisans to support themselves through their craft. Alongside the loss of the freedom to operate more than four looms and to produce and sell independently, the master craftsmen were categorized by the merchants into two groups: the capable and loyal ones, and the inexperienced and undisciplined ones. The former lacked enough looms to handle the high volume of orders, while the latter received less and less work from the merchants. The concentration of orders in the hands of the merchants, the dependent position of the weavers, and the resulting economic consequences forced artisans to face an increasing scarcity of resources. In order to support themselves and their families, many silk weavers made the decision to leave the kingdom in search of opportunities in other states. Sometimes they had to abandon their families back home, leaving them dependent on charitable organizations for assistance.[11]

In this regard, the 1733 reform of the Consulate of Commerce played a crucial role. This measure definitively excluded the merchant class from

[10] AST, C, *Materie economiche*, Cat. IV, m. 7, fasc. 49, December 11, 1730.

[11] AST, C, *Materie economiche*, Cat. IV, m. 8, fasc. 3, 1738–1739.

the ranks of the Consulate, effectively reducing the political influence of merchants and traders, and relegating them to the economic sphere. The new Consulate, made up of judicial members, opted for a distinct approach, favoring the institutional separation of the two guilds once and for all. A year later, and not without prolonged disputes between representatives of the respective parties, the statutes of the University of Silk Merchants were published in August 1738,[12] and the renovated statutes of the University of Master Weavers of Gold, Silver, and Silk were republished in June 1739 (Picture 4.1). Both of these events were accompanied by the edict imposing limits on the number of looms (Duboin 1848, 312–324—August 28–29, 1738; June 10–18, 1739). The Savoyard case thus evolved from a broad, comprehensive guild—typical of medieval and early modern Italian textiles—to phase-based corporations, each representing a specific function within the silk industry.

It would also appear possible to identify similar dynamics by reading the documents related to the production of silk stockings on the loom. In the 1720s, both Piedmontese silk merchants and silk stocking makers sold large quantities of silk stockings produced on looms to France, Switzerland, Milan, Genoa, the major centers of Rome and Naples, and the ports of Nice, Savona, and Finale Ligure, through which the Piedmontese products likely reached the coasts of Spain and Portugal.[13] Thus, silk stocking makers were also hybrid figures involved in both production and sales. The lack of legislation regulating the organization of labor and the presence of merchants engaged in selling stockings likely favored the merchants' attempt to create dependence between the two professional categories. As was the case with fabrics, merchants sought to dominate the activity of producers in the case of stockings as well. Following the radical redefinition of the merchants' political role in 1733, concerned about being excluded from the commercial world and relegated only to the productive phase, silk stocking makers found a solution by founding a guild. This organization was aimed at preserving their dual role as artisans and merchants and protecting themselves from the monopolistic goals of the merchants. On these premises, the statute allowing the foundation of the *Università dei mastri calzettai in seta* (University of Master Silk Stocking Makers) was accepted on March 17, 1734.

[12] AST, C, *Materie economiche*, Cat. IV, m. 8, fasc. 2, 1738.
[13] AST, C, *Materie economiche*, Cat. IV, m. 6 d'addizione.

Picture 4.1 Coat of arms of the *Università dei mastri tessitori in oro, argento e seta* of Turin. Anonymous copper engraving (*Source*: AST, SR, *Consolato di Commercio*, m. 67, Patente di Gio Antonio Simonetti, October 10, 1791. Courtesy of the State Archives of Turin)

However, the act of foundation brought a new, significant issue to light: the inadequacy of the new legislation regarding hiring journeymen. The rising labor costs (Caligaris 2001) and the fact that the statute favored the inheritance of the profession must have seemed like an insurmountable barrier for journeymen who had entered the profession as newcomers. In an effort to cut production costs, the masters preferred to hire apprentices rather than already trained journeymen who, over time, could have become competitors. These factors led to the creation of a large group of journeymen for life, trapped in their jobs, with no welfare benefits, dependent on their earnings and the whims of the masters, and threatened by the trend of recklessly hiring apprentices. Within a few years, the journeymen decided to turn to the Consulate in search of a remedy for their disastrous situation, proposing the foundation of a journeymen's guild, formally dedicated to collecting alms to assist members in difficulty.

After receiving the approval of the University of Master Silk Stocking Makers, and with royal approval, the *Università dei lavoranti calzettai in seta* (University of Silk Stocking Journeymen) was founded on April 1, 1737 (Lis et al. 1994; Romero Marín and von Briesen 2024). From the first sentences of the document, it is evident that the statute proposed by the journeymen focused on their working conditions, which were precarious due to the lack of funds allocated to them by the University of Master Silk Stocking Makers in times of need (Duboin 1848, 875—April 1, 1737). As early as 1738, a year after the foundation of the University of Silk Stocking Journeymen, the members submitted a new petition to Carlo Emanuele III, denouncing the long-standing custom of masters resorting to the underpaid labor of apprentices.[14] After conducting the necessary checks, the Consulate of Commerce Council confirmed the truth of their claims. The inspection revealed that of 52 workshops, there were a total of 336 looms (302 active and 34 idle) but only 154 journeymen and as many as 87 apprentices (1 apprentice for every 2 journeymen). Furthermore, in many cases, masters with four looms had four apprentices and no journeymen, which, according to the journeymen, directly damaged the profession's reputation by allowing the introduction of mediocre products to the market.

Recalling the solutions found in the case of silk weavers with the restriction on the number of looms, the members of the Consulate of Commerce decided to introduce a similar measure by regulating the number of apprentices masters could have in their workshops. Thus, silk stocking masters with fewer than three looms could not have any apprentices, those with between three and six looms could have one, and those with more than six could have two. Transgressors would be punished with a heavy fine of 50 gold *scudi* (Duboin 1849, 888–889—June 7, 1738).

The mandatory hiring of journeymen soon caused a boom in employment, and "lacking fertile ground for new journeymen,"[15] in 1745 the king granted silk stocking masters the right to employ a number of apprentices equal to half the number of their looms, though never more than four, even if they had more than eight looms. Faced with new complaints promptly raised by the journeymen, who found themselves thrust back into the pre-1738 conditions, the master craftsmen were prepared. After denouncing the journeymen's behavior toward apprentices, they managed to demonstrate the inconsistency of their claims—prompting the Consulate to conclude that the lack of work for the journeymen stemmed from their

[14] AST, C, *Materie economiche,* Cat. IV, m. 8, fasc. 2, March 10 and May 20, 1738.

[15] AST, C, *Materie economiche*, Cat. IV, m. 8, fasc. 2, March 10, 1738.

own prejudicial behavior toward the proper management of the workshops by the masters, their lack of professionalism, and their corrupting influence on the apprentices.[16]

The wave of complaints did not subside, and in 1748, the silk stocking masters submitted a request to the Consulate, asking for permission to hire an apprentice even if they had only one frame. It did not take long for the journeymen to respond, firmly oppose the proposed measure, and reiterate the reasons given 10 years earlier. However, after conducting a new survey of the workshops and the workforce, the Consulate concluded that the situation would not change, as there were enough looms to provide work for everyone.[17] The status of the journeymen, therefore, despite the statutes, remained extremely precarious (Marucco 1998). Similar tensions between masters, apprentices, and journeymen were common in other European guild systems (Epstein 1993; Moioli 2004), where the regulation of training and entry barriers served to preserve skill transmission and product standards; yet only in a few cases—such as in Piedmont—did journeymen succeed in obtaining formal recognition by establishing a legally sanctioned guild with its own statute.

4 The Genesis of a Paradigm: the April 8, 1724 Manifesto

The Consulate and the guilds were not the only aspects of state economic policy that posed challenges to the institutional innovations linked to the silk production sector. To ensure economic growth for the duchy through the silk industry, a redesign of the practical framework regulating the sector was required: the legislative apparatus. The existing jumble of laws, edicts, and patents governing silk production was disorganized and difficult to implement effectively. With the May 17, 1687 Manifesto, the young Duke Vittorio Amedeo II took the first step by consolidating all laws concerning the various stages of silk processing into one single edict. Yet, the result was little more than a compilation, clearly in need of further refinement. Even after the edict's publication, the circumstances remained unchanged, as individual laws continued to appear in the Savoyard legal framework, largely disconnected from the edict (Duboin 1848, 514—April 28, 1701; 156—June 11, 1711).

[16] AST, C, *Materie economiche*, Cat. IV, m. 8, fasc. 30, May 24, 1746.
[17] AST, C, *Materie economiche*, Cat. IV, m. 9, fasc. 4, September 24, 1748.

Thanks to the inspections conducted by members of the Chamber of Accounts and specialists in the countryside (Picco 1992; Rosso 1992; Chicco 1995; Grassi 2023), the quality of Piedmontese silk steadily improved. Year by year, its reputation grew across Europe, enabling the Savoyard economy to secure a prominent position in the international trade of raw and semi-finished silk. At the same time, Piedmont began laying the foundations for developing the silk weaving phase—a sector that had already taken root in France and England. By the late seventeenth century, French looms, which traditionally relied on silk from Messina, Milan, and other northern Italian hubs, increasingly turned to Piedmont, a rising force on the commercial stage. Throughout the early modern period, a continuous exchange of goods, capital, and skilled labor defined the relationship between France and Piedmont. This dynamic forged, particularly between the seventeenth and eighteenth centuries, a complex interplay of rivalry and interdependence—a relationship rooted in mutual economic reliance yet marked by a fierce desire for independence (Tolaini 2002). The nuanced nature of eighteenth-century ties between these two powers cannot be reduced to a simple portrayal of Piedmont's subordination to France's dominant commercial hubs. Instead, the relationship was one of uneasy coexistence—a challenging but essential partnership for both regions. Within the two silk-producing regions, conflicting interests, diverging priorities, and state economic ambitions often clashed. For example, at the end of the seventeenth century, quality standards were dictated by Turin's merchants. It was nearly impossible for Lyonnais merchants to set terms for a product of such incomparable quality, unmatched anywhere else in Europe, including France. This is clearly demonstrated by the extensive correspondence between the Lyon *Chambre de Commerce* (Chamber of Commerce) and Louis XIV during the 1706 siege of Turin, which reveals how Jean Anisson (1642?–1721), *Député de Lyon au Conseil du commerce* (Lyon Council of Commerce's representative), successfully persuaded the Sun King to ensure that silk produced in the Duchy of Savoy continued to supply Lyon. This decision prevented Piedmontese merchants from shifting their focus toward Geneva—a vigorous, neighboring, and formidable commercial competitor to France (Tolaini 2002). Furthermore, by the late seventeenth century, some French merchants had already recognized the increasing value of Piedmontese silk production and begun relocating some of their operations south of the Alps, to the territories of the House of Savoy (Chicco 1995).

While the Lyonnais artisans and merchants continued to rely on the production of raw silk from Piedmont, the English, facing a significant rise in the cost of maritime silk imports due to their conflict with France, decided to implement policies aimed at achieving self-sufficiency in thread production for weaving (Chaloner 1963; Chicco 1995). Following a tradition that is still largely to be reconstructed, the Lombe brothers were the first to propose the installation of hydraulic spinning machines in England (Moioli 1988; Chicco 1995). Whether John Lombe actually traveled to Piedmont remains uncertain (Chicco 1995), but around 1717, the small town of Derby saw the establishment of a hydraulic spinning mill *alla piemontese* for which the Lombe brothers sought a patent and exclusive rights (Chaloner 1963). The potential loss of a major customer like England, which imported both high-quality raw silk—vital for sustaining the relentless pace of the hydraulic spinning mill—and organzine for the Spitalfields looms, would have been a severe blow to the Savoyard trade, depriving it of a significant portion of its market.

It is unclear how much of this development was due to the new technological competition and how much to the actual scarcity of cocoons.[18] But what is certain is that on June 20, 1722, Vittorio Amedeo II issued a decree prohibiting the extraction of cocoons and raw silk from his territories (Duboin 1848, 451—June 20, 1722) until further notice, imposing heavy fines on anyone caught smuggling (Hafter 2007; Macleod et al. 2023; Montenach 2024). After a brief period in which the first Hanoverian King, George I (1660–1727), saw his kingdom enter European silk trade, the Piedmontese export ban on raw materials forced the monarch to confront reality: the new hydraulic spinning mill technology was heavily reliant on raw silk from Piedmont. The English complaints reached the Turin court soon after. In August, Secretary of State Lord John Carteret (1690–1763) sent a formal complaint to the King of Sardinia through the Piedmontese ambassador to the English court, Tommaso Ercole Roero, Marquis of Cortanze (1661–1747). Carteret's strategy was to avoid informing Vittorio Amedeo II of the potential damage the ban could inflict on the emerging English silk industry. On the one hand, he emphasized that "England abounds in both raw and processed silks from various regions of Italy,"[19] but on the other hand complained about the

[18] The poor cocoon harvest had already led to the annual suspension of raw silk exports abroad in 1697, 1698, and 1700 (Duboin 1848, 446–447).

[19] "L'Angleterre abbonde de soies crües, et travaillées de divers êtats de toute l'Italie."

trade ban on Piedmontese silks, especially those stemming from the Monferrato area.[20] A thorough investigation was required to assess the benefits of reaching an agreement with Carteret, and the technical expertise of Count Galleani[21] and merchants Gioanetti, Albertino, Villanis, and Bosso was sought. In particular, probably because he had recently returned from England, Bosso's report convinced the experts of the necessity to suspend the supply of raw silk to England, where, following the establishment of a silk weaving factory ten years earlier, numerous hydraulic silk mills had already been set up. The English were unable to produce their own silk because they could not farm silkworms, meaning they had to import it. The silk required to supply the hydraulic spinning mills had to come from Piedmont, as silks from Turkey, China, and other parts of Italy did not have the same qualities. After receiving reassurance from the experts that the threatened British embargo on wool supplies would not cause significant damage to his territories, and being warned that resuming raw silk exports to Great Britain would lead to the replacement of Piedmontese organzine with English products, Vittorio Amedeo II composed and sent his response to Carteret in September. Without revealing too much, the king justified his decision by pointing out firstly that the poor cocoon harvest that year would not provide enough raw silk even for the needs of Piedmont's own spinning mills. Secondly, he expressed his desire to align with broader foreign monopoly policies. Just two months later, John Lombe passed away, leaving his brother Thomas in charge of the industry. He soon had to contend with the monopolistic choices of the King of Sardinia: the attempts to replace Piedmontese raw silks with Levantine silks, of poor quality, or Chinese silks, of good quality but too expensive, had proven ineffective (Chaloner 1963; Chicco 1995). The English government's only way of breaking this impasse was by developing sericulture in the new American colonies, a project awash with challenges (Chicco 1995).

This negotiation, which did not conclude in 1722 but continued with further developments in the following years (Chicco 1995), fits perfectly within the broader vision for the silk industry championed by Vittorio Amedeo II. Through carefully crafted legislation in the final decades of the seventeenth century and the early years of the eighteenth, he guided the

[20] AST, C, *Materie economiche*, Cat. IV, m. 7, fasc. 20, 1722.

[21] Gio Girolamo, son of Gio Francesco Galleani, founder of the first hydraulic spinning mills in Piedmont.

steady growth of Piedmont's silk manufacturing, laying the foundation for its success. At the start of the eighteenth century, the king's unwavering confidence allowed Piedmont to stand firm against both England and France. He was fully convinced that throughout Europe's "fashionable" regions, Piedmontese organzine was without equal, and that anyone wishing to work with hydraulic spinning mills would, sooner or later, need to rely on Piedmontese raw silk.

The economic dispute between Vittorio Amedeo II of Savoy and George I of Hannover[22] clearly strengthened the commercial power of the Kingdom of Sardinia, enabling the king to aim even higher. In 1724, he charged the Consulate with drafting "a new regulation, which, by defining the duties of workers involved in the spinning and dyeing of silk, as well as the master weavers of silk fabrics, set out the precise methods for carrying out the spinning, dyeing, and fabric production processes" (Duboin 1848, 166—April 8, 1724). The extensive correspondence between the king and the Council of Commerce clearly highlights the growing importance of the silk industry for Savoy trade. The dream of achieving production independence was becoming reality, making the establishment of an appropriate legislative framework crucial.

The first draft of the law was presented to the king on February 19, the result of a collaborative effort between the Consulate and a commission of experts, which included some of the leading figures in Turin's silk industry. The documents clearly show that despite the confusion surrounding the regulations in the previous century, what was required was not a complete reform but rather a synthesis achieved by selecting and revising existing laws. The new edict was therefore modeled on the 1687 one, clarifying ambiguities, adding specific guidelines on machinery sizes, silk reeling mills, and increasing the penalties for violations. The law reaffirmed the general rules for each profession, which had largely remained unchanged, and introduced technical details on the quantity and quality of dyeing materials for dye baths, soap types, and the dimensions of fabric—based on the June 11, 1711 edict (Duboin 1848, 156—June 11, 1711). The importance of monitoring activities and ensuring the suitability of workshops was also stressed, with mandatory inspections. In particular, it was proposed that the Consulate's officials themselves would carry out inspections for dyers and weavers. The former lacked a formal guild statute while

[22] AST, C, *Materie economiche*, Cat. IV, m. 7, fasc. 23, March 7, 1724; fasc. 26, May 16, 1724.

the latter might resist due to the role innovation played in the industry, particularly with regard to the risk of new weaving patterns being copied between different workshops. The negotiations to finalize the manifesto continued for another month. The final draft of the law reached City Hall on March 21, and a week later, it was sent to the Chambéry *Chambre de Commerce* (Chamber of Commerce), coming into force across the entire Kingdom of Sardinia on April 8, 1724. Unlike previous laws on the silk industry, the new manifesto was, in effect, a state reform.[23]

April 8, 1724, thus marks the culmination of a complex legislative development process and the point at which an innovative productive paradigm was solidified—a paradigm that would be fervently defended within the kingdom and eagerly sought by competitors in the years to come. The royal order was a comprehensive, finally refined version of the numerous previous ducal orders, becoming the *exemplum legis* for the other silk-related edicts published throughout the eighteenth century in the kingdom. The Piedmontese silk industry at last had a technical and legislative framework for the sector, the result of collaboration between institutions and merchants, capable of encompassing all aspects of the industry and ensuring the production of thread of a quality superior to any made elsewhere in Europe.

5 Conclusions

A decade after the Foscarini embassy in Turin, Zaccaria Betti, a Veronese member of the *Accademia dei Georgofili* (Georgophiles Academy), published the poem *Il baco da seta* (The Silkworm), inspired by Tesauro's *La Sereide*. In the historical dissertation that accompanies the poem, the author dedicates a few lines to the work of Vittorio Amedeo II, highlighting how his contemporaries saw the legislative actions of the government institution as a key element for the success of the industry. Betti writes:

> Vittorio Amedeo awakened the natural readiness of the inhabitants and brought the silk industry to its highest level of perfection. Even today, we must acknowledge that this region (Piedmont) embodies the highest degree of diligence in taking advantage of the gifts of the climate, and all the efforts made to apply the knowledge of the craft. Who would not admire a principality fully focused on the advancements of silk, that forms councils to over-

[23] AST, C, *Materie economiche*, Cat. IV, m. 7, fasc. 24, March 27, 1724.

> see it, and issues general instructions for the proper training of silk workers and the reeling of cocoons? What wise regulations came from this, balancing the interests of individuals with the benefits of the homeland and the rights of the principality, which became models for the most astute nations in Europe, who annually turn to Turin to seek material for their finest fabrics?[24] (Betti 1765, 242)

This is just one example of similar praise found in the works of other prominent eighteenth-century writers, such as Griselini, Gemelli, Muratori, and Zanon. Historians differ about the significance of Vittorio Amedeo II's reformism (Prato 1908; Quazza 1957; Bulferetti 1963; Stumpo 1979; Symcox 1983; Rosso 1992, 2018). But an examination of the phases from his reign's early years, which led to the publication of the manifesto on April 8, 1724, and the foundation of the guilds in the 1730s, requires engaging with a broad economic and social project. This endeavor aimed at positioning Piedmont in the international trade arena to outpace rival powers by harnessing the institutional, legal, and civil structure of the state (Symcox 1983, 2002; Hupfel 2019).

The resulting institutional model established a fundamentally monolithic foundation for the industry's structure, reflecting its origins as a product of monarchy. But the constitutive elements of this totem—namely, the social apparatus made up of people, families, and guilds, in turn keepers of techniques and technologies, knowledge and skills, socially expected roles, and aspirations—could change. The result would be a reshaping of the internal organization of the industry according to the needs of an international market in which Piedmontese silk played a significant role (Sabel and Zeitlin 1997). Each of these elements plays a specific part in defining not only the existence of the silk industry itself but also of the state, the market, and each artisan. In this context, the role of merchants, producers, and workers changed rapidly due to the constant reorganization of the institutions that represent, at different times, their social, economic, and political power. In this context, the guilds are tools that define social roles, at least superficially. The success of the representational role,

[24] "Vittorio Amedeo svegliò la naturale prontezza degli abitanti, e fece arrivare il setificio fino alla maggior perfezione; dovendosi anche in oggi riconoscere in quella Nazione (Piedmont) il sommo della diligenza per approfittarsi de' doni del clima, e tutto lo sforzo per impiegarci il sapere dell'arte. Chi non ammirerà un Principato tutto rivolto ai progressi della seta, che forma Consigli che vi preseggano, e bandisce generali istruzioni per la buona educazione de' filugelli, e per la filatura de' bozzoli?" (Betti 1765, 242).

in fact, is not guaranteed—especially when it clashes with socially and economically stronger powers.

Ultimately, the success of Piedmontese silk resulted from a top-down strategy. The introduction of a new tribunal, the application of new laws, and the structuring of a system of representation through the guilds actively contributed to defining the characteristics of the basic production units: the artisans. Bound by laws and institutions, they developed a unique embodied expertise that transcended the link between the mind, eye, and body in the creative act, revealing its essence as context dependent. However, as repositories of expertise, artisans were an integral part of the material structure of technology. As human beings, they acted within a social context governed by institutions and laws. Their lived experience and social life therefore shaped not only their personalities and character, but also their knowledge, skills, and labor (Epstein 2013). If the authorities wished to foster forms of artisanal expertise capable of serving their economic policies, they had to recognize the fundamental role of workers as individuals whose skills had been developed through direct experience. In a specific institutional context such as Piedmont—where laws encouraged the acquisition of a specific artisanal intelligence, refined through the work itself—observation and direct contact with materials and machinery allowed artisans to attain a level of professionalization that made them irreplaceable and challenging to transfer (Bertucci 2021).

Bibliography

Abrate, Mario. 1960. Lineamenti di storia economica del Piemonte. In *Storia del Piemonte*, vol. I, 565–637. Turin: Casanova & C.

Acemoglu, Daron, and James A. Robinson. 2012. *Why nations fail: The origins of power, prosperity, and poverty*. New York: Crown Business.

Ago, Renata. 1998. *Economia barocca. Mercato e istituzioni nella Roma del Seicento*. Rome: Donzelli.

Allegra, Luciano. 1987. *La città verticale. Usurai, mercanti e tessitori nella Chieri del Cinquecento*. Milan: FrancoAngeli.

Arnaldi di Balme, Clelia, and Maria Paola Ruffino. 2019. Madame Reali. Cultura e potere da Parigi a Torino. In *Cristina di Francia e Giovanna Battista di Savoia Nemours*, 1619–1724. Genoa: SAGE.

Banaji, Jairus. 2019. *A brief history of commercial capitalism*. Chicago: Haymarket Books.

Bellavitis, Anna. 2018. *Women's work and rights in early modern urban Europe*. Cham: Palgrave Macmillan.

Bertucci, Paola. 2021. Spinners' hands, imperial minds: Migrant labour, embodied expertise, and the failed transfer of silk technology across the Atlantic. *Technology and Culture* 62 (4): 1003–1031.

Betti, Zaccaria. 1765. *Del Baco da Seta. Canti IV. Con annotazioni.* Verona: Andreoni.

Boissonade, Prosper. 1932. *Colbert, le triomphe de l'étatisme: la fondation de la suprématie industrielle de la France, la dictature du travail (1661–1683).* Paris: Rivière.

Borelli, Giovanni Battista. 1681. *Editti antichi e nuovi de' Sovrani Prencipi della Real Casa di Savoia, delle loro Tutrici, e de' Magistrati di qua da' Monti.* Turin: Zappata.

Borelli, Giorgio. 1999. Per una lettura del rapporto tra città, mestieri produttivi e corporazioni nell'Italia moderna. In *Corporazioni e gruppi professionali nell'Italia moderna*, ed. Alberto Guenzi, Paola Massa, and Angelo Moioli, 31–43. Milan: FrancoAngeli.

Bulferetti, Luigi. 1963. *Agricoltura, industria e commercio in Piemonte nel secolo XVIII.* Turin: Istituto per la storia del Risorgimento.

Burnham, Dorothy K. 1980. *Warp and weft. A textile terminology.* Toronto: Royal Ontario Museum.

Caligaris, Giacomina. 1999. Arti, manifatture e privilegio economico nel Regno di Sardegna durante il XVIII secolo. In *Corporazioni e gruppi professionali nell'Italia moderna*, ed. Alberto Guenzi, Paola Massa, and Angelo Moioli, 171–200. Milan: FrancoAngeli.

Caligaris, Giacomina. 2001. Il grande affare della seta e la formazione professionale a Torino nel Settecento. *Bollettino Storico-Bibliografico Subalpino* 99 (1): 61–103.

Cerutti, Simona. 1992. *Mestieri e Privilegi. Nascita delle corporazioni a Torino (secoli XVII - XVIII).* Turin: Einaudi.

Cerutti, Simona. 2003. *Giustizia sommaria. Pratiche e ideali di giustizia in una società d'Ancien Régime (Torino, XVIII secolo).* Milan: Feltrinelli.

Chaloner, William Henry. 1963. *People and industries.* London: Frank Cass & Co.

Chicco, Giuseppe. 1995. *La seta in Piemonte 1650–1800. Un sistema industriale d'ancien régime.* Milan: FrancoAngeli.

Cibrario, Luigi. 1830. *Relazioni dello Stato di Savoia negli anni 1574, 1670, 1743 scritte dagli Ambasciatori veneti Molini, Bellegno e Foscarini con note e illustrazioni del N.U. Luigi Cibrario.* Turin: Alliana.

Cole, Charles W. 1931. *French mercantilist doctrines before Colbert.* New York: Smith.

De Goey, Ferry, and Jan Willem Veluwenkamp. 2002. *Entrepreneurs and institutions in Europe and Asia 1500–2000.* Amsterdam: Aksant.

De Munck, Bert. 2022. Shared skills and technologies of community formation. Artisanal epistemologies, secrecy and governmentality in long-term context. In

The republic of skill. Artisan mobility, innovation, and the circulation of knowledge in premodern Europe, ed. David Garrioch, 35–64. Leiden: Brill.

Della Valentina, Marcello. 1999. Da artigiani a mercanti: carriere e conflitti nell'Arte della seta a Venezia tra '600 e 700'. In *Corporazioni e gruppi professionali nell'Italia moderna*, ed. Alberto Guenzi, Paola Massa, and Angelo Moioli, 645–665. Milan: FrancoAngeli.

Dessert, Daniel. 2019. *Colbert ou le mythe de l'absolutisme*. Paris: Fayard.

Devoti, Chiara, ed. 2021. *Maria Giovanna Battista di Savoia-Nemours. Stato, capitale, architettura*. Florence: Olschki.

Duboin, Felice Amato. 1848. *Raccolta per ordine di materie delle leggi cioè editti, patenti, manifesti, ecc. emanate negli stati di terraferma sino all'8 dicembre 1798 dai sovrani della real casa di Savoja, t. 15, v. 17*. Turin: Baricco ed Arnaldi.

Duboin, Felice Amato. 1849. *Raccolta per ordine di materie delle leggi cioè editti, patenti, manifesti, ecc. emanate negli stati di terraferma sino all'8 dicembre 1798 dai sovrani della real casa di Savoja, t. 16, v. 18*. Turin: Baricco ed Arnaldi.

Engerman, Stanley L. 1994. The big picture: How (and when and why) the west grew rich. *Research Policy* 23 (5): 547–559.

Epstein, Stephan R. 1998. Craft guilds, apprenticeship, and technological change in pre-industrial Europe. *The Journal of Economic History* 58 (3): 684–731.

Epstein, Stephan R. 2013. Transferring technical knowledge and innovating in Europe, c. 1200-c. 1800. In *Technology, skills and the pre-modern economy in the east and the west*, ed. Maarten Prak and Jan Luiten Van Zanden, 25–67. Leiden-Boston: Brill.

Firpo, Luigi. 1983. *Relazioni di ambasciatori veneti al senato. Tratte delle migliori edizioni disponibili e ordinate cronologicamente*. Vol. 11. Turin: Bottega d'Erasmo.

Franceschi, Franco. 2020. Big business for firms and states: Silk manufacturing in Renaissance Italy. *Business History Review* 94 (1): 95–123.

Garden, Maurice. 1970. *Lyon et les Lyonnais au XVIIIe siècle*. Paris: Les Belles Lettres.

Grassi, Mario. 2023. Quando la qualità non basta. Luci e ombre del primato serico piemontese tra Sei e Settecento. *RiSES - Ricerche di storia economica e sociale* 9 (1–2): 47–72.

Guardamagna, Laura. 2021. La seta nel Piemonte della seconda Reggenza: una questione produttiva, economica e di prestigio. In *Maria Giovanna Battista di Savoia-Nemours. Stato, capitale, architettura*, ed. Chiara Devoti, 207–226. Florence: Olschki.

Guenzi, Alberto, Paola Massa, and Angelo Moioli, eds. 1999. *Corporazioni e gruppi professionali nell'Italia moderna*. Milan: FrancoAngeli.

Hafter, Daryl M. 2007. Stratégies pour un emploi: travail féminin et corporations à Rouen et à Lyon, 1650–1791. *Revue d'histoire Moderne et Contemporaine* 54 (1): 98–115.

Holmström, Mark. 2002. History and social justice. In *Entrepreneurs and institutions in Europe and Asia 1500–2000*, ed. Ferry De Goey and Jan Willem Veluwenkamp, 32–52. Amsterdam: Aksant.

Hupfel, Simon. 2019. *L'Économie politique des soieries. Les manufactures de Lyon et de Londres de leur origine à 1848.* Paris: Classiques Garnier.

Lanaro, Paola. 1999. Gli Statuti delle Arti in età moderna tra norma e pratiche. Primi appunti dal caso veneto. In *Corporazioni e gruppi professionali nell'Italia moderna*, ed. Alberto Guenzi, Paola Massa, and Angelo Moioli, 327–346. Milan: FrancoAngeli.

Lis, Catharina, Hugo Soly, and Lee Mitzman. 1994. "An irresistible phalanx": Journeymen associations in Western Europe, 1300-1800. *International Review of Social History* 39 (2): 11–52.

Macleod, Catriona, Alexandra Shepard, and Maria Ågren, eds. 2023. *The whole economy: Work and gender in early modern Europe.* Cambridge: Cambridge University Press.

Marucco, Giuseppe. 1998. Le associazioni di mutuo soccorso. In *Milleottocentoquarantotto. Torino, l'Italia, l'Europa*, ed. Umberto Levra and Rosanna Roccia, 149–154. Turin: Archivio Storico della Città di Torino.

Massa, Paola, and Angelo Moioli. 2004. *Dalla Corporazione al mutuo soccorso.* Milan: FrancoAngeli.

Mazzarella, Ferdinando. 2020. The Italian historiography on commercial law. Old tendencies and new perspectives. In *Pour une histoire européenne du droit des affaires: comparaisons méthodologiques et bilans historiographiques*, ed. Luisa Brunori, Olivier Descamps, and Xavier Prévost, 17–65. Toulouse: Presses de l'Université Toulouse Capitole.

Merlin, Pierpaolo. 1992. Emanuele Filiberto e la nascita di una capitale. In *Storia illustrata di Torino II*, ed. Valerio Castronovo, 341–360. Milan: Sellino.

Merlin, Pierpaolo. 1995. *Emanuele Filiberto. Un principe tra il Piemonte e l'Europa.* Turin: SEI.

Merlin, Pierpaolo. 1998. Amministrazione e politica tra Cinque e Seicento: Torino da Emanuele Filiberto a Carlo Emanuele I. In *Storia di Torino III*, ed. Giuseppe Ricuperati, 111–169. Turin: Einaudi.

Merlin, Pierpaolo. 2021. Potere e regalità dei Duchi di Savoia nella prima età moderna: la testimonianza degli ambasciatori veneti. *Studi Piemontesi* 50:77–85.

Minard, Philippe. 1997. L'inspection des manufactures en France, de Colbert à la révolution. *Annales Historiques de La Révolution Française* 309:483–491.

Minard, Philippe. 1998. *La Fortune du colbertisme. État et industrie dans la France des Lumières.* Paris: Fayard.

Minard, Philippe. 2000. Colbertism continued? The inspectorate of manufactures and strategies of exchange in eighteenth-century France. *French Historical Studies* 23 (3): 477–496.

Minard, Philippe. 2008. The market economy and the French state: Myths and legends around Colbertism. *L'Économie Politique* 37 (1): 77–94.
Mira, Giuseppe. 1964. La dottrina economica mercantilista. In *Città, mercanti, dottrine nell'economia europea dal IV al XVIII secolo. Saggi in memoria di Gino Luzzatto*, ed. Amintore Fanfani, 207–251. Milan: Giuffrè.
Mitchell, William. 1904. *An essay on the early history of the law merchant.* Cambridge: St. Catherine's College.
Moioli, Angelo. 1988. Assetti manifatturieri nella Lombardia politicamente divisa. In *Storia dell'industria lombarda*, ed. Sergio Zaninelli, 1–102. Milan: Polifilo.
Monestarolo, Giorgio. 2006. Negozianti e imprenditori nel Piemonte d'antico regime. In *La cultura economica di Ignazio Donaudi delle Mallere (1744–1795).* Florence: Olschki.
Montenach, Anne. 2024. *Gender, space and illicit economies in eighteenth-century Europe uncontrolled crossings.* London: Routledge.
Mozzarelli, Cesare, ed. 1988. *Economia e corporazioni: il governo degli interessi nella storia d'Italia dal Medioevo all'età contemporanea.* Milan: Giuffrè.
Muzzarelli, Maria Giuseppina. 2020. *Le regole del lusso. Apparenza e vita quotidiana dal Medioevo all'età moderna.* Bologna: Il Mulino.
Naldi, Carlo, Elena Gianasso, and Costanza Roggero. 2011. *Maria Giovanna Battista di Savoia Nemours. Memorie della Reggenza.* Turin: Centro Studi Piemontesi.
Navire, Federico. 2008. *Torino come centro di sviluppo culturale: un contributo agli studi della civiltà italiana.* Frankfurt: Peter Lang.
North, Douglass C. 1989. Institutions and economic growth: An historical introduction. *World Development* 17 (9): 1319–1332.
North, Douglass C. 1990. *Institutions, institutional change and economic performance.* New York: Cambridge University Press.
North, Douglass C. 2000. Understanding institutions. In *Institutions, contracts and organizations: Perspectives from new institutional economics*, ed. Claude Ménard, 7–10. Cheltenham: Elgar.
North, Douglass C., and Robert Paul Thomas. 1973. *The rise of the Western world: A new economic history.* New York: Cambridge University Press.
Ogilvie, Sheilagh. 2019. *The European guilds: An economic analysis.* Princeton: Princeton University Press.
Pfister, Ulrich. 2008. Craft guilds, the theory of the firm, and early modern proto-industry. In *Guilds, innovation and the European economy, 1400–1800*, ed. Stephan R. Epstein and Maarten Prak, 25–51. Cambridge: Cambridge University Press.
Picco, Leila. 1992. Il Settecento: l'affermazione della seta. In *Torino sul filo della seta*, ed. Giuseppe Bracco, 67–118. Turin: Archivio Storico della Città di Torino.
Prak, Maarten, and Jan Luiten Van Zanden, eds. 2013. *Technology, skills and the pre-modern economy in the east and the west.* Leiden: Brill.

Prato, Giuseppe. 1908. *La vita economica in Piemonte a mezzo il secolo XVIII*. Turin: Società Tipografico-Editrice Nazionale.

Prato, Giuseppe. 1920. Le ambizioni commerciali e marittime di un ministro piemontese del secolo XVIII. *Miscellanea di Studi Storici in Onore di Giovanni Sforza* 2:11–23.

Quaglioni, Diego. 1998. Corpus, universitas, pluralità di corpi: alle radici di un archetipo giuridico-istituzionale. In *Corpi, fraternità, mestieri nella storia della società europea*, ed. Danilo Zardin, 39–49. Rome: Bulzoni.

Quazza, Guido. 1957. *Le riforme in Piemonte nella prima metà del Settecento*. Modena: Società Tipografica Editrice Modense.

Raviola, Blythe Alice. 2015. Genova per noi. Feudatari, nobili, banchieri e altri liguri nel Piemonte della prima età moderna. In *Genova e Torino. Quattro secoli di incontri e scontri. Nel bicentenario dell'annessione della Liguria al Regno di Sardegna*, ed. Giovanni Assereto, Carlo Bitossi, and Pierpaolo Merlin, 121–142. Genoa: Società Ligure di Storia Patria.

Romero Marín, Juanjo, and Brendan J. von Briesen. 2024. Asociacionismo artesano: Gremios, cofradías y hermandades durante la transición al régimen liberal (Barcelona, 1784-1839). In *Artesanos: Una historia social en España (siglos XVI-XIX)*, ed. Francisco Hidalgo Fernández and José Antolín Nieto Sánchez, 361–393. Ciudad Real: Ediciones de la Universidad de Castilla-La Mancha.

Rosenberg, Nathan, and Luther E. Birdzell. 1986. *How the West Grew Rich*. New York: Basic Books.

Rosso, Claudio. 1992. Dal gelso all'organzino: nascita e sviluppo di un'industria trainante. In *Torino sul filo della seta*, ed. Giuseppe Bracco, 39–66. Turin: Archivio Storico della Città di Torino.

Rosso, Claudio. 2018. Il Seicento ritrovato: società, istituzioni, economia nel secolo barocco. In *Gli spazi sabaudi. Percorsi e prospettive della storiografia*, ed. Blythe Alice Raviola, Claudio Rosso, and Franca Varallo, 113–124. Rome: Carocci.

Sabel, Charles, and Jonathan Zeitlin, eds. 1997. *World of possibilities. Flexibility and mass production in Western industrialization*. Cambridge: Cambridge University Press.

Sacco, Italo Mario. 1930. Professioni, Arti e Commerci nelle Costituzioni di Carlo Emanuele I per il Piemonte e per il porto di Nizza. *Biblioteca della Società Storica Subalpina* 121:1–29.

Sewell, William H. 1980. *Work and revolution in France. The language of labor from the old regime to 1848*. Cambridge: Cambridge University Press.

Stumpo, Enrico. 1979. *Finanza e stato moderno nel Piemonte del Seicento*. Rome: Istituto Storico Italiano per l'età moderna e contemporanea.

Symcox, Geoffrey. 1983. *Victor Amadeus II. Absolutism in the Savoyard state 1675–1730*. Berkeley: University of California Press.

Symcox, Geoffrey. 2002. La trasformazione dello Stato e il riflesso del potere. In *Storia di Torino IV*, ed. Giuseppe Ricuperati, 719–867. Turin: Einaudi.
Tolaini, Roberto. 2002. Un rapporto di dipendenza? L'evoluzione delle relazioni seriche Lione-Torino tra Seicento e Ottocento. *Società e Storia* 25 (98): 725–759.
Valsecchi, Franco. 1959. *L'Italia nel Settecento*. Milan: Mondadori.
Venturi, Franco. 1969. *Settecento riformatore. Da Muratori a Beccaria*. Turin: Einaudi.
Venturi, Franco. 1970. *Utopia e riforma nell'Illuminismo*. Turin: Einaudi.
VV. 1986. *La Cappella dei Mercanti. Storia e immagini per una ricca Congregazione*. Turin: Mariogros/Tomasone.

CHAPTER 5

Innovation and Entrepreneurship: The Rise of Industrial Capitalism in Piedmont's Silk Economy

1 Introduction

"A ruler cannot lack wealth when the richest men are under his rule"[1] (Donaudi delle Mallere 1776, I). This precept, drawn from advice given in the fifteenth century to Eleonora of Aragon by her Neapolitan tutor, Count Diomede Carafa, opens the *Saggio di Economia Civile* published in 1776 by Count Ignazio Donaudi delle Mallere. A precept with a long history (Cusumano 1870), it expresses the core ideals of the Piedmontese author, whose family, originally silk traders, had only lately entered the ranks of the nobility (Jannaccone 1903; Ricuperati 1994; Monestarolo 2006a). This essay, the only work published by Donaudi, was often interpreted as a strategic attempt to secure a position within the trade magistracies of the Savoyard state. Yet, a more nuanced reading reveals that Donaudi's decision to open his essay with this precept reflects a deeper principle: the prosperity of a state does not lie simply in the accumulation of wealth but in the intricate relationship between power and the management of economic resources (Monestarolo 2006a; Sorella 2007). It is plausible, then, that when Donaudi chose this phrase to preface his work, he had a particular group of ***ditissimi homines*** in mind: the body of skilled traders who had bolstered Savoyard commerce by producing and trading

[1] "Neque enim Rex inopis esse potest, cujus Imperio ditissimi homines subjiciuntur" (Donaudi delle Mallere 1776, I).

M. Grassi, *The Silk Industry in Early Modern Piedmont*, Labour in History and Society,
https://doi.org/10.1007/978-3-032-15353-1_5

silk (Monestarolo 2006a, b). But who were these traders? Answering this question requires moving beyond a top-down perspective and adopting a step-by-step analysis of the social factors that defined their roles within the silk industry. In a state like the Kingdom of Sardinia, where the government's mercantilist ambitions were reshaping the economic landscape, traders played a pivotal role—serving as both instruments and directors in a symphony composed around the chords of economic development.

This chapter examines the interaction between capitalism, mercantilism, and enterprise through a prosopographical study of traders. The dynamics of credit, manufactories' management, and labor organization are first reconstructed to contextualize the environment in which traders operated in early modern Piedmont. This framework highlights how the commerce-production link developed profoundly innovative features. Through a process that was anything but linear, these dynamics redefined the economic and social roles of traders, allowing the nebulous figure of the "merchant-entrepreneur" to evolve. This transformation expanded their spheres of action and laid the groundwork for the emergence of the entrepreneur *tout court*. Rather than following a straightforward transition from mercantile to industrial capitalism, this process should be understood as the coexistence of multiple capitalist forms within early modern economies. In this context, commercial capitalism can be read as a distinct and fully developed form of accumulation, in which merchants directly organized and controlled production (Banaji 2019). From this perspective, the Piedmontese experience provides a particularly revealing example of how commercial and industrial logics could intersect within the same economic ecosystem, giving rise to hybrid entrepreneurial forms sustained by both private and state capital (Franceschi 2020). Taken together, these dynamics invite a reinterpretation of capitalist development—one that moves beyond a teleological narrative of progress and instead embraces a plural history of practices, where traders, manufacturers, and state agents interacted through intertwined economic structures.

Central to this discussion is the sociolinguistic issue of professional labels. The extensive studies on trade and entrepreneurship in the early modern period have, over time, created a stratification of concepts, ideas, and positions—often deeply contradictory (Prak 2001). This conceptual complexity hinders a clear understanding of the historical role of traders and their relations with entrepreneurship (Cavaciocchi 1991; Amatori 2006; Lanaro 2007; Caracausi 2007; Casson and Casson 2013). In response, this chapter revisits this theme by consulting the "dictionary" of primary sources (Cerutti 2006). The focus is on how historical actors in this specific time and place adopted certain terms, which mirror socially and economically constructed categorizations. This approach enables a reexamination of entrepreneurs within their historical context, emphasizing their role in the transition from mercantile capitalism to industrial capitalism.

Among the key figures shaping these economic dynamics, the state emerges once again as a leading force—the "main entrepreneur" of the modern era (Stumpo 1979, 367). Early modern governments' mercantilist ambitions were often realized through state-funded initiatives aimed at expanding both productive and commercial sectors. At a time when few possessed the means to independently establish large industrial-scale manufactories, the state played a central role in mobilizing capital and directing enterprises (Symcox 1983). However, far from representing a simple partnership between rulers and merchants, this system was characterized by a constant interplay of collaboration and control (Banaji 2019; Franceschi 2020). Within this framework, the Savoyard model appears as a state-managed form of commercial capitalism, in which political authority and private enterprise were deeply intertwined. Through financing mechanisms that would, in theory, allow merchants engaged in these ventures eventually to reimburse the state, Royal Manufactories began to take shape in Piedmont following the model of those in France. In this arrangement, the state and traders collaborated in establishing factories, and managing their operations. A further dimension of this state entrepreneurship involved the exploitation of workshops within charitable institutions, where the underpaid labor of the poor and of children helped to offset production costs.

As will be discussed, the entrepreneurial state relied on its *ditissimi homines* to implement its economic strategies, using its legislative power to expand production, organize labor, and stimulate trade. The transition of traders toward entrepreneurship, the stratification of productive and commercial roles, and the involvement of the entrepreneurial state in financing large manufactories highlight how the role of the traders within the mercantilist framework is far from straightforward. Both indispensable and dangerous, this period's traders are one of the faces of "otherness" (Magnusson 1994; Cerutti 2003; Roncaglia 2005; Ruggiero 2013; Rössner 2015, 2016). According to Donaudi, these *ditissimi homines* of silk were those who operated in the international trade arena and had the potential to strengthen Piedmont's economic position. However, he points out that they were a particularly unstable social category on which to base the success of the state's economy and needed to be treated with caution. Traders, who cultivated relationships with foreign trade professionals as part of their job, often became reliant on foreign markets and lost sight of the "public happiness" of their home state. Donaudi believed that traders were, in this historical context, to be regarded as true enemies of the homeland—an attitude that made them, despite being natives, strangers to the nation (Monestarolo 2006a). Upon closer inspection, traders emerge as having a somewhat split personality—being progressive and conservative, depending on the circumstances. As Sabel and Zeitlin (1997) suggest, they take a rational approach to the reality around them, grounded in their experience and needs. This allows them to pursue what seems to be the best possible alternative at any given moment, even if it appears harmful in the short or long term. Traders are a crucial part of this historical narrative—an ambiguous social class (Baumol 1968; Toninelli 2004, 2006; Isenmann 2016; Rössner 2016) that, despite extensive study, remains as resilient as the Lernaean Hydra. Every time a head is cut off—as if the theme had reached its final resolution—a new one springs forth, bringing fresh questions to the surface.

2 Reeling Mills, Spinning Mills, and Looms: the Development of a Piedmontese Silk Economic System

Between the seventeenth and eighteenth centuries, silk production in Piedmont underwent significant transformations—closely intertwined with changes in the role of the trader, making the two processes virtually inseparable.

As recorded in the *Registro di visita e delli atti per il regolamento della fabrica delle sette* (Register of Inspections and Proceedings for the Regulation of the Silk Manufacture) compiled by Galleani in 1667, at that time, there were only a few modestly sized silk reeling mills in the Racconigi area. Here several female reelers were already proficient in the new reeling method *alla piemontese*.[2] Silk reeling continued to be a predominantly domestic activity, carried out by peasant women linked by birth or marriage to families overseeing the entire raw silk production chain. This

[2] AST, SR, *Camerale Piemonte*, art. 539 consegne bigatti e semenze d'essi, fasc. 5, June 16, 1667.

included not only the creation of raw silk but also mulberry cultivation, leaf selection, silkworm farming, and cocoon sorting. In the 1660s, silk production in Piedmont was still fundamentally a rural endeavor. The number of reeling machines was limited, with most being described as "old-fashioned." Farmers purchased silkworm eggs, cultivated mulberry trees, raised silkworms, and harvested cocoons. They either sold the cocoons or reeled raw silk, which was then purchased by those handling the subsequent phases of production. Yet, within a few years, this traditional system would change profoundly. As later inspections demonstrate, most traditional machinery had been replaced within a few years by equipment *alla piemontese*.[3]

At the same time, new regulations on production oversight integrated silk reeling mills into expanding commercial networks. This shift required larger spaces, greater reliance on salaried labor, and the ability to secure enough cocoons to ensure competitive output of raw silk on the market. During this period, a new production model emerged. While exceptions cannot be ruled out, historical records suggest that traders typically went into debt to finance the initial capital for their businesses (Chicco 1992, 1995; Caligaris 2001). This financial pressure compelled them to bring their products to market quickly, repay their loans, and generate sufficient profits to sustain and expand their businesses in the following years. The rising costs of oversight and the increasing economic significance of high-quality raw silk production encouraged the centralization of reeling machinery, accelerating the shift from predominantly domestic production to large-scale *filande* (silk reeling mills) (Chicco 1992).[4] The Piedmontese *filanda*, as both an architectural and organizational paradigm, spread rapidly and kept many of its defining characteristics well into the twentieth century, both within Piedmont and beyond (Bracco 1992; Chierici 1992; Chierici and Palmucci Quaglino 1993).

During this period, the first attempts to integrate the reeling and twisting processes within a single facility began to take place in Piedmont. This

[3] AST, SR, *Camerale Piemonte*, art. 539 consegne bigatti e semenze d'essi, fasc. 8.1, 1668.

[4] The ideal silk reeling mill would be nothing more than a structure consisting of tall and spacious porticoes that "have neither vaults nor flat ceilings above them and are simply covered by their roof, arranged in a straight line or in a courtyard-like arrangement. Inside, the reeling machines should be placed at a proper distance from each other to prevent the condensation of fumes resulting from the boiling water in the basins and to allow the reelers to move easily. Additionally, the floor should be inclined to ensure better drainage of the water" (Turbini 1778, 23).

innovation enhanced control over the production of raw silk destined for spinning, significantly improving both the productivity of the operation and the quality of the twisted yarn (Chicco 1995; Battistini 1998). At the same time, it reduced production costs for the two phases and minimized waste (Tolaini 1997). What was emerging was a system of large-scale silk spinning mills managed by experienced traders who oversaw every aspect of capital investment and labor organization. A notable example of this integrated approach can be found in the estate of the Count of Sordevolo in Abbadia di Stura. The manor housed a large silk reeling mill with 52 reeling machines, a silk spinning mill, a warehouse, and worker dormitories—all within the same establishment (Lanaro 2006; Caracausi 2021).[5]

These organizational changes not only redefined roles within silk production but also introduced new operational challenges for traders. The first and most critical issue was sourcing the cocoons, which could be achieved in several ways. Some traders owned land where peasants managed mulberry and silkworm farming, thereby gaining direct access to the cocoons. Advance contracts with farmers were made before the season began or through brokers specializing in the buying and selling of cocoons, known as *sensali* (Legnani Annichini 2013, 2021). Moreover, some traders traveled to the markets of major Piedmontese towns, negotiating cocoon purchases after inspecting samples. In all cases, however, without cocoons, there could be no *filanda*. The second challenge was finding an appropriate location for silk reeling mills. The need for large spaces to house multiple reeling machines, combined with the desire to minimize the number of supervisors and offset transportation costs for raw materials from rural areas, led traders to rent farmhouses, castles outbuildings, or country estates. Finally, with the new method of reeling, selecting skilled labor became an even more delicate and crucial task. Traders, either directly or with the help of trusted staff, sought out the best reelers, approaching them in public spaces or at home, and offering them positions at the silk reeling mills (Grassi 2026). These new operational demands, in a rapidly changing environment, required substantial investments—without even accounting for additional costs such as firewood, maintenance, and unforeseen issues. Such rising expenses were indicative of a broader shift: the silk reeling mills began to move away from traditional rural management and embrace a capitalist model, with traders

[5] AST, SR, *Consolato di Commercio*, Costituti (NSI), m. 110, *Causa Audifreddi/Monier, Moris & Co.*, September 25, 1736 (Lanaro 2005; Caracausi 2021).

assuming control of production and gradually diminishing the role of peasant labor.

Even artisans employed in the later stages of production were not spared from these winds of change. Previously, they were responsible for overseeing both production and commercialization, purchasing machinery and yarn, organizing production through the commission system, and selling the finished goods directly to merchants (Berengo 1965). However, once traders took charge of raw silk production, their growing influence led them to gradually take over other sectors of the production process, expanding their authority on multiple fronts. They took control of artisans' work, exclusively handling commissions and allocating tasks to the artisans. They increasingly organized the whole production chain, eventually assuming direct responsibility for transferring semi-finished goods between production stages. Clearly, this was not a sudden transformation; instead, it developed progressively over the eighteenth century, gaining strength and becoming firmly established by the middle decades.

According to records stating that master spinners were required to submit to the *Consolato di Commercio* (Consulate of Commerce) when setting up a new spinning mill, preserved from 1739 to 1786, it appears that only about 60 spinning mills were owned by artisans, while the majority belonged to traders and companies. For example, in 1739, 42 spinning mills were owned and managed by artisans, while 119 were either owned or leased by traders and companies. A comparison with the 1742 commercial census of artisans and merchants in Turin reveals that nearly half of the 48 "bankers and traders" listed—some in partnership, others individually—were also owners of spinning mills in 1739, alongside the nobility, doctors, and lawyers.[6] Among them were traders involved in both the silk and fashion, sectors, such as the Gioanetti family. This overlap of surnames across various professional categories within the textile world likely suggests family involvement in businesses related to the sector (Monestarolo 2006b).

[6] The document includes over 260 business declarations. AST, SR, *Consolato di Commercio*, m. 60, 1739–1786.

3 A Matter of Terminology: Merchants, Traders, Entrepreneurs

The people who have thus far been referred to as "traders" in early modern Piedmont were identified by various titles that reflected specific socio-economic expectations—which underwent significant transformations between the seventeenth and eighteenth centuries. As a matter of fact, the definition of professions involved in the silk trade was already a matter of debate in the eighteenth century. Even members of the Consulate of Commerce questioned who should be considered a trader—a controversy that emerged in relation to tax legislation for the establishment of silk reeling mills. At the heart of the issue was the definition of "trader" itself and, by extension, the obligation to pay the relevant professional tax.[7] As the Consulate of Commerce highlighted, not all individuals who established a silk reeling mill qualified as traders, and many were unable to sustain such an operation for more than one or two consecutive years. The Chamber wanted to prevent ownership of silk reeling mills from becoming a monopoly controlled by a small group of traders—excluding, on the one hand, occasional silk reeling mills, and on the other, aristocratic owners of silk reeling mills. Therefore, it recommended not applying the traders' tax universally to everyone who established silk reeling mills. This matter was ultimately resolved by a Royal Decree, which clarified that people who engaged in silk reeling without pursuing any other commercial activity were not to be classified as merchants and therefore exempt from the tax. This measure ensured that the tax applied exclusively to those who operated silk reeling mills as part of their own commercial enterprises or, more specifically, those producing silk intended for further processing into semi-finished or finished textiles within their own businesses.[8]

The production of raw silk was, in fact, inherently volatile. Year by year, the number of silk reeling mills, reeling machines, and traders involved in raw silk production could fluctuate dramatically, as it was directly tied to the cocoon harvest (Arese 1922; Chicco 1995). To prepare for the opening of a silk reeling mill in the spring, traders had to cover substantial expenses upfront, often taking on debt. In many cases, this meant that the loans contracted for the new season also served to repay outstanding debts from the previous year. This pattern is evident in the intermittent

[7] *Leggi e Costituzioni di Sua Maestà*. 1729. Turin: Accademia Reale.

[8] AST, C, *Materie economiche,* Cat. IV, m. 7, fasc. 29, n.d. (but 1723–1724).

appearances of certain merchants, such as Barberis and Maggia, in the fiscal records in which silk reeling mill owners formally declared their intent to set up operations. Each year, these manufactories were required to report to the Consulate of Commerce, providing details on their operating period, the location of their facility, and the number of reeling machines they intended to operate. This series of records has been preserved continuously from 1759 to 1788. At times, merchants had to pause their activities to rebuild their financial reserves before re-entering the silk trade by purchasing cocoons and restarting raw silk production. For example, in 1777, during one of the most serious crises in the sector, only three applications for raw silk production in the Turin area were submitted to the Consulate of Commerce (Ranza 1777; Chicco 2002). Yet just 2 years later, in 1779, the same area reached an unprecedented peak for the whole century, with 34 silk reeling mills operating a combined total of more than 650 reeling machines.[9]

Although the fiscal definition of "trader" had been established, ambiguities surrounding the term persisted, as it remained inherently multifaceted. Donaudi, in his *Saggio di Economia Politica e Pratica sovra lo Stato Presente delle Finanze e Commercio del Re di Sardegna* (Essay on Political and Practical Economy on the Present State of the Finances and Commerce of the King of Sardinia), sought to clarify the significant transformations underway by proposing a hierarchy of roles within the commercial world. He argued that the evolution of the trader's title was marked by distinct phases, shaped by the political and commercial strategies of the traders themselves. When new silk-processing techniques and technologies were introduced from the late seventeenth century to the first half of the eighteenth century—traders, despite their institutionally ambiguous status (as illustrated by debates over their inclusion or exclusion from the Consulate of Commerce), were primarily considered bankers and money changers (Cerutti 1992; Monestarolo 2006a). According to Donaudi, during this time, Lyonnais traders would travel to Turin to negotiate the prices of Piedmontese silk, directly engaging with local artisans. By the 1740s, however, Piedmontese traders had successfully positioned themselves as intermediaries between the local artisans and the Lyonnais traders. This shift marked a significant turning point in the local silk trade, and a few years later, in 1755, Minister Bogino's monetary reform fundamentally altered the landscape (Quazza 1957; Balani 1987; Monestarolo 2006a).

[9] AST, SR, *Consolato di Commercio*, m. 62 consegne delle filature, 1759–1788.

By introducing fixed exchange rates, the reform eliminated the possibility of speculating on currency as a commodity, reshaping the dynamics of the trade (Monestarolo 2006a). According to Donaudi, this growing interference by traders in the silk industry led to the establishment of an unexpected and rigid tripartite hierarchy. Traders and bankers were at the top of the pyramid, followed by merchants, and finally artisans.

Traders and bankers were among the few people capable of raising and lending the capital required to purchase raw materials, tools, and properties. This financial leverage allowed them to fund the endeavors of merchants or even directly manage silk production enterprises. Merchants, in turn, occupied an ambiguous position. They could engage in wholesale or retail trade and sometimes even in production. Yet, according to Donaudi, they were often more focused on quick profits, indiscriminately selling both foreign and domestic fabrics at similar prices. In doing so, they harmed their own long-term profitability. At the lowest level of the hierarchy were the artisans—formerly independent craftsmen who accepted commissions, produced fabrics, and sold their goods. Still, with the new role assumed by traders, they now found themselves increasingly dependent on those higher up in the commercial hierarchy.

The involvement of traders in production stages has often been interpreted as the boundary between medieval merchant capitalism and the early stages of industrial capitalism (Braudel 1949; Hilton 1952; Dobb 1963; Day 1999). This perspective aligns well with the example of Piedmontese entrepreneurship, which seems to transcend the traditional definition of the "merchant-entrepreneur." This term is frequently used, albeit with some conceptual challenges (Prak 2001; De Vivo 2017), to describe the economic relations of the early modern period. Piedmontese entrepreneurs were not merely involved shipping raw materials and goods, or in their commercialization, nor in financing production; in fact, they directly shaped its structure and operations. They fostered the concentration of numerous machines and laborers in single buildings, sometimes integrating various production stages, taking control of the workshops, and reorganizing the entire silk supply chain under their power. As highlighted in Donaudi's work, by the 1770s, the interference of commercial interests in the organization of labor within factories had become a well-established fact. The entrepreneurs' role increasingly resembled that of capitalist industrial entrepreneurs: they organized production by amassing capital whether their own or others', gathering the labor force, selecting the best site for operations, choosing production techniques, negotiating for raw materials, and finding outlets for the finished products (Flinn 1966; Berta 2006; Lanaro 2007).

However, the case of the Piedmontese silk industry suggests that this type of economic actor had already emerged by the early eighteenth century, as merchants increasingly assumed direct control over production. Archival evidence supports this view: a 1702 report on the state of the silk industry lists 28 individuals explicitly described as *imprenditori* (entrepreneurs), together with the number of looms they operated. Although historiography has generally identified the 1770s as the period when the term first appeared in economic vocabulary (Cortelazzo et al. 2004, 567), this earlier occurrence indicates that the concept—and its language—was already circulating in Piedmont. Such linguistic evidence shows how practice often preceded theory, anticipating later analytical categories and revealing an early awareness of entrepreneurial agency (Berta 2006; Lanaro 2007). The document further reveals that fixed capital was not the determining criterion for being considered an *imprenditore*: while some had many looms in operation (the Sclopis & Tempia society, with its 77 looms, was the leading silk fabric producer in Turin), others only owned one or two looms (such as the entrepreneur Dupuy).[10]

Although the terminology is insufficient to fully define the characteristics of the profession, further research supports this interpretation. A nominal search of the *imprenditori* of 1702 in the 1705 census of the Turin population uncovered information on around 20 of them, including 2 widows who, after their husband's death, took over the business. Yet, since entrepreneurs did not constitute a distinct professional category, they were recorded as *mercanti* (merchants), *mercanti da seta* (silk merchants), or *mercanti da panno* (cloth merchants). A glance at records of elections for representatives of the silk merchants' professional category from the late seventeenth century, who had not yet formed an official guild separate from the weavers, is quite enlightening. These records show that while all the entrepreneurs from 1702 were listed among the silk merchants, not all silk merchants were considered entrepreneurs. In fact, the records also include several names of artisan master silk weavers. Thus, the vague distinction between entrepreneurs and silk merchants at the beginning of the century can be understood as the ability of the former—and the helplessness of the latter—to manage and provide capital for multiple stages of production. This interpretation aligns with Monestarolo's

[10] AST, C, *Materie economiche,* Cat. IV, m. 7, fasc. 7, 1702.

reconstruction of the merchant's *cursus honorum*: a path that began with commercial activity (buying and selling fabrics, acquiring looms) and, through capital accumulation and expanding their scope, could lead the aspiring merchant to rent or purchase silk spinning and silk reeling mills.

As can be expected, these processes effectively excluded artisans from engaging in market dynamics, leading to the formation of a deeply endogamous society of local traders (Monestarolo 2006b). A study of the residential settings of these entrepreneurs through the 1705 census of the population revealed a recurring pattern of family members working together in trade,[11] suggesting the importance of keeping the business within the family. The underlying reasons were the significant capital required, the commercial network carefully established with correspondents in European and global markets, and, at least in part, the fixed capital involved (Monestarolo 2006a, b).

4 The State as Entrepreneur: Royal Manufactories and Trade Companies

When discussing entrepreneurs, it is difficult to overlook what has often been called the main entrepreneur of the early modern period: the state (Braudel 1949; Stumpo 1979). The growing recognition of Piedmontese silk abroad, driven by the collaboration between institutions and the merchant class, prompted the central government not only to legislate but also to fund state projects for the establishment of privileged manufactories. The duke's desire to establish large, state-subsidized factories in Piedmont—capable of strengthening the House of Savoy's position on the European landscape through centralized production—likely stems from the success of French *Manufactures* and the mercantilist ideas of the Duchy of Savoy's finance ministers, Giovanni Battista Truchi di Levaldigi and Antonio Garagno (Chicco 1992; Merlin 2021; Grassi 2024). However, unlike the French case, the privilege granted to Piedmontese manufactories to carry the "royal" title, while it involved public intervention by the duke, did not directly require financial contributions to create risk capital (Picco 1992). The ducal intervention in Piedmont was limited to granting privileges and, at most, providing loans to initiate the manufactories (Gonzalez Enciso 1980).

[11] Notably, the households of the three widow entrepreneurs followed the same pattern.

As a matter of fact, government participation in production activities was not a novelty, as demonstrated by the case of the Albergo di Virtù, a charitable institution for indigent youth. Since its foundation in 1580, the Albergo di Virtù played a unique role in the development of silk fabric production in Turin. Like other charitable institutions of the early modern period (Cavallo 1980, 1995; Moody 2001; Garbellotti 2013; Zucca Micheletto 2013; Ferrando 2018, 2020; Agua de la Roza 2018, 2020), the Albergo hosted workshops managed by skilled artisans, but it stood out for its explicit goal of training a highly skilled class of silk weavers.[12] Established with the funds and will of the *Compagnia di San Paolo* (Saint Paul Company), the institution saw Duke Carlo Emanuele I contribute financially in 1587. It was managed by the *Ufficio delle Finanze* (Finance Office), granted royal status, and provided with an annual income of 600 gold *scudi*. From that year onward, the Council mandated that the institution accommodate 60 poor children, both boys and girls, and grant workshops to experienced artisans who could train them in a profession—preferably silk weaving. To be admitted, they had to meet specific requirements: according to the institution's rules, boys had to be between 9 and 14 years old, while girls could be accepted only after turning 7 and before reaching 13—even though these rules were often disregarded.[13] They were also required to provide a guarantor to cover any potential costs arising from damage or escape.[14] By the seventeenth century, the training offered by the masters silk weavers at the Albergo di Virtù was considered among the best in the city (Borelli 1681, 223 - January 7, 1667). By the eighteenth century, it had become one of the main hubs of silk production in Turin.[15]

From 1746 onward, however, female apprentices were formally excluded, and the regulations were reformed. Pupils had to be at least 12 years old, healthy, have a guarantor, and possess basic reading and

[12] AST, C, *Materie ecclesiastiche*, Luoghi pii di qua dai monti, m. 16 d'addizione, fasc. 3, 1747.

[13] As evidenced by the *Ordinati* of the Institute, which recorded inspections of the female pupils, the girls often remained in the Albergo well beyond the established age. AST, SR, *Regio Albergo di virtù*, Ordinati, m. 52, 1704–1719

[14] Often, the escape of the pupils meant the loss of the clothing provided at the expense of the institution.

[15] In the 1720s, a spinning mill was set up, while silk-stocking workshops were established over the century.

writing skills.[16] Throughout the eighteenth century, over a hundred masters, mostly silk weavers, rotated in managing the workshops. Between January 1751 and May 1799, 1197 pupils were admitted, but only a third completed the apprenticeship; the rest either fled, died, or were expelled. The matriculation book of the University of Master Weavers of Gold, Silver, and Silk of Turin reveals that between 1678 and 1798, about 150 Albergo pupils became masters in Turin, making up 12.5% of the total number of enrolled masters.

While government involvement in manufacturing is already evident in this case, the Albergo manufactory also had to meet other goals such as supporting indigent youth. Nevertheless, with the success of the Piedmontese silk industry gaining international recognition, projects for royal manufactories *à la Colbert* began to take shape. Although there are reports of a proposal for a silk fabric factory in 1700, as well as occasional details about the *Fabrica delle stoffe del Magazeno Reale* (Fabrics Manufacture of the Royal Storehouse), located within the *Ospedale di Carità* (Hospital of Charity),[17] it was not until 1710 that clearer information about the privileged manufactories emerged. That year, the project to establish a royal silk factory in French style took off, with the establishment of the *Fabbrica Reale di Stoffe in Oro, Argento e Seta* (Royal Manufacture of Gold, Silver, and Silk Fabrics) by merchants Giacomo Matteo Gariglio and Michel Charbonet.[18] The plan was to equip the factory with 100 looms and provide dormitories and services for the workers. Vittorio Amedeo II readily accepted the proposal, granting them numerous privileges and exemptions. However, the factory faced significant financial troubles right from the beginning: by 1711, additional capital was already sought from some bankers, but even these funds proved insufficient.[19] The breaking point came in 1715 with the death of Louis XIV, the beginning of the Regency of Philip II of Orléans (1674–1723), and the new financial system based on fiat money introduced by John Law (1671–1729) (Cussen 2023). Law was the *Contrôleur Général des Finances du Royaume de France* (French General Controller of Finances) who

[16] AST, SR, *Regio Albergo di Virtù*, Ordinati, m. 53, August 24, 1746.

[17] AST, C, *Materie economiche*, Cat. IV, m. 22 di II addizione, March 29, 1700; AST, SR, *Consolato di Commercio*, Costituti, m. 106, *Causa Graneri/Fabrica delle stoffe del Magazeno Reale*, November 19, 1705; Costituti, m. 107, *Causa Ganna/Sighino*, January 21, 1707.

[18] AST, C, *Materie economiche*, Cat. IV, m. 7, fasc. 8, January 19, 1710.

[19] AST, SR, *Consolato di Commercio*, Costituti, m. 108, *Causa Barili/Gariglio e Charbonet*, September 11, 1711.

transformed the European economic landscape—leaving the Royal Manufacture in Turin struggling and forcing Gariglio and Charbonet to once again turn to the government. In 1716, a congress was convened with representatives from the government, finance, and commerce to address the issue. While they confirmed the factory's importance, they pointed out the financial problems resulting from insufficient investment, despite royal exemptions. To avoid reducing the number of looms, which would result in fewer workers and limited production, the congress decided to find a new partner. They opted for banker Giuseppe Antonio Costeis, who, along with his son Francesco, promised to become a partner for 10 years and to contribute 200,000 *lire*. Yet, by early 1718, the Royal Manufacture was on the brink of collapse: the Costeis had neither fulfilled their promises nor contributed any funds. A year later, the process to liquidate the Royal Factory began due to the Costeis' bankruptcy, and to escape secular justice, they sought refuge in a church. After a lengthy series of investigations, the Royal Manufacture was handed over in November 1719 to Gaspare Antonio Vergnasco. In the 1720s, he completed the full liquidation of the capital, effectively bringing an end to the failed venture of the Royal Manufacture of Gold, Silver, and Silk Fabrics (Picco 1992; Bulferetti 1963; Caligaris 2004).[20]

In contrast to the establishment of the Royal Silk Manufacture, the project for a *Tintoria Reale* (Royal Dyehouse) only started to develop in the 1760s (Picco 1986). In 1761, Carlo Emanuele III extended an invitation to a craftsman named Costa from Avignon to come to Turin. By August of that year, Costa had set up his dyeing workshop near the castle of Venaria Reale. He had promised to create a fully integrated manufactory—including a silk spinning mill, dye workshop, weaving manufacture, and a retail shop. However, the 1764–1765 reports show that the factory had no more than 40 looms and a dyeing workshop. Shortly after, the French master was dismissed, and the factory faced imminent closure. Its survival was ensured by Carlo Francesco Vanetto, a silk weaver who proposed taking over the business.[21] Vanetto had been a master at the Regio Albergo di Virtù for over 20 years, and in partnership with the

[20] AST, C, *Materie economiche*, Cat. IV, m. 6 d'addizione, fasc. *Pareri, relazioni, lettere, memoriali ed altre scritture relative (...) la Fabbrica Reale di sete esercita dalli Garriglio e Charbonet, alli quali erano poi stati associati li padre e figlio Costeis*, 1716–1719.

[21] APSA, *Università dei mastri vellutai*, v. 4, f. 50v, *Iscrizione matricolare di Carlo Francesco Vanetto*, 1729.

charitable institution, he successfully took over the Venaria manufactory, appointing Lorenzo Coriasso as the master dyer.[22] This partnership, set to last 25 years, was a joint venture, with both parties contributing 50,000 *lire* equally in funds and fixed capital, with government support.[23] Despite this backing, problems arose almost immediately. By 1767, Count San Martino d'Agliè's annual report revealed a profit of just 56 *lire* and 4 *soldi* (Picco 1986). The shortcomings were attributed to the limited volume of silk sent for dyeing and the frequent illnesses among workers, likely due to the unhealthy air near the Ceronda stream that ran through the area.[24] This prompted the idea to separate fabric manufacturing (which remained under the Vanetto-Regio Albergo partnership until 1777) from dyeing. Count Giuseppe San Martino d'Agliè identified a critical issue, namely, that the dyeing facility's location was remote and far from Turin, the central hub for silk production and trade. With the king's approval, the count personally took charge of finding a better location in Turin and worked closely with Vanetto. They eventually selected Casa Oliva in the *borgo di Po* district. Relocating the facility took over a year. Once completed, the new Royal Dyehouse featured a large workshop with 13 dyeing vats, worker accommodations, and other necessary facilities (Picco 1986). Despite these improvements, its scale remained modest, with a relatively small number of workers.[25] The main differences lay in the volume of commissions, the availability of dyes, and the funds at its disposal—although in some months the facility only processed minor orders.[26] In the end, even this royal initiative ended in failure. On March 18, 1777, the Royal Dyehouse was officially granted, via royal patent, to master Coriasso, who managed it as his own until his death.[27]

Beyond these manufactories, the Consulate of Commerce, acting on royal orders, drafted plans to establish a trading company, the purpose of

[22] AST, SR, *Regio Albergo di Virtù*, Ordinati, m. 54, December 15, 1765.

[23] AST, SR, *Regio Albergo di Virtù*, Ordinati, m. 54, December 15, 1765; January 14, 1766.

[24] AST, SR, *Ufficio Generale delle Finanze*, I archiviazione, *Commercio*, m. 4, *Ricevute delle spese fatte da Lorenzo Coriasso deputato per la Tintoria Reale al Borgo di Po della città di Torino*, 1767.

[25] AST, C, *Materie economiche*, Cat. IV, m. 11, fasc. 23, April 14, 1768.

[26] AST, SR, *Ufficio Generale delle Finanze*, I archiviazione, Commercio, m. 3, *Libro di Cassa Tintoria Reale 1767–1774*.

[27] AST, SR, *Regio Albergo di Virtù*, Convenzioni, liti, transazioni di liti, b. 5, 1777. After Coriasso's death, his widow would take care of the dyeing business in the nineteenth century.

which was to significantly boost the production and trade of Turin's textiles. The seventeenth century in Europe had seen numerous state-backed ventures rise and fall, such as the *Compagnia di commercio genovese con le Indie Orientali* (Genoese East India Trading Company) in 1644 or the *Compagnia di Commercio per le compravendite tra i dominii sabaudi e il Portogallo* (Trading Company for exchanges between the Savoyard territories and Portugal) in 1681. Perhaps influenced by a recent Venetian initiative, a proposal for a new trading company in Turin was presented to the king on March 3, 1729.[28] The purpose of the company project was to supply Savoy, Italy, and Germany with Piedmontese goods, establish trade links with Spain and Portugal by acquiring ships, and help develop the ports of Villafranca and Oneglia (Monestarolo 2013).[29] However, the project was abandoned, and no further attempts to found a trading company in Turin were made until the 1750s.

The collapse of one of Turin's most prominent banks, Monier, Moris & Co., in 1751 probably reignited interest in the idea, leading to the actual foundation of a trading company within one year (Caligaris 1998, 1999, 2004). The *Compagnia Reale del Piemonte per le Opere e Negozi in Seta* (Royal Company of Piedmont for Silk Production and Trade), effectively a joint-stock company, was established with a twenty-year agreement and launched in May 1752 (Picture 5.1). Over the first three years, it sold 71 shares at 5000 *lire* each, raising a total of 355,000 *lire*.[30] With these funds, the company established a new factory, initially known as *Fabbrica della Carità* (Charity Factory), which was soon renamed *Fabbrica Reale del Piemonte* (Royal Factory of Piedmont). Despite high hopes, the company's fortunes were checkered, and it continued to operate until 1792. A detailed report from that year revealed that the factory, much like the other royal initiatives, was facing severe difficulties due to a lack of shareholders, insufficient funding, and persistent accounting and liquidity problems. The Royal Company, which had survived for over 40 years, was replaced the following year by the *Associazione Reale per le Manifatture in Seta* (Royal Association for Silk Manufacturing). Its goals were virtually

[28] AST, C, *Materie economiche*, Cat. III, m. 1, fasc. 36, August 17, 1720.

[29] AST, C, *Materie economiche*, Cat. III, m. 1 da ordinare, fasc. *Idea e progetto d'una Compagnia di Commercio compilato dal Consiglio di Commercio d'ordine di S.M.*, March 3, 1729.

[30] AST, C, *Materie economiche*, Cat. IV, m. 11 d'addizione, fasc. 6, 1792.

Picture 5.1 Coat of arms of the Royal Company of Piedmont for silk production and trade in Turin. Anonymous copper engraving (*Source:* ASCT, *Coll. Simeom*, C 4158. Courtesy of the Historical Archive of the City of Turin)

identical to those of the former Royal Company, with the notable exception that its shares were now valued at 500 *lire* each.[31]

5 Conclusions

The dynamic evolution of the Piedmontese silk industry attracted significant attention, sparking discussions on the economic and social implications of a manufacturing sector that, through the integration of agriculture and commerce, was increasingly regarded as a key pillar of the state's prosperity. A prominent contribution to these debates was made through the works of Donaudi. Although often confined to the relative obscurity typical of Piedmontese writings of the time, his treatises are actually some of

[31] AST, C, *Materie economiche,* Cat. IV, m. 11 d'addizione, fasc. *Azioni nella società della manifattura delle sete,* 1793.

the most significant pre-Smithian economic works in Italy, alongside those of Genovesi, Beccaria, Verri, and Ortes (Cossa 1878; Jannaccone 1903). In his *Saggio di Economia Civile*, after thoroughly exploring the roles of agriculture and manufacturing, Donaudi begins the final chapter, entitled *Del rapporto, che ha il commercio colle Finanze* (On the Relationship Between Commerce and Finances), as follows:

> There is a close connection between finances and commerce: everything that benefits commerce strengthens finances, and everything that harms commerce also damages finances. (...) When a state neglects the cultivation of its lands and the development of trade, the prince's finances will struggle to thrive, for they are essentially a share of the products of agriculture and commerce. (Donaudi delle Mallere 1776, 138)

This statement offers a suitable conclusion to the broader argument that Donaudi develops throughout the essay, mirroring the precept of Count Carafa. However, a more original and realistic idea of Donaudi's thinking can be found in his *Saggio di Economia Politica*, where he focuses on the state's role in managing the economy (Jannaccone 1903; Monestarolo 2006a). In the latter treatise, Donaudi emphasizes the precarious political situation of the social class to which his family belonged: the traders, particularly those involved in the silk trade. By this time, the process of consolidating raw silk production activities into a few large factories was well advanced. A century after Galleani's visit in 1667, the once prevalent small-scale silk reeling mills throughout the Piedmontese countryside had almost disappeared, replaced by industrial-scale facilities (Arese 1922; Chicco 1995). These operations dominated production and reshaped its practices, creating significant opportunities to amass wealth. Piedmont's rigid social structure, marked by aristocratic control, hampered a smooth transition to more open trade practices. According to Donaudi, the land ownership system dominated by the nobility had two major negative effects. Firstly, it drastically limited the land's economic potential, hindering growth and innovation in both agriculture and manufacturing, failing to capitalize on the innovative drive of traders. Secondly, it concentrated access to public office—a privilege reserved for the nobility—in the hands of a select few, creating a closed power structure that restricted the exchange of ideas and resources (Amatori 2006). Donaudi argued that this system not only suppressed the country's economic vitality but also reinforced harmful stagnation in social and political relations. In stark contrast to the aristocracy—who were prohibited from engaging in trade (Merlotti 2000; Merlotti and di Netro 2002; Mola di Nomaglio 2006)—stood the capitalist traders who, despite their economic influence, were excluded from political decision-making.

Under these circumstances, Donaudi believed that traders' wealth could neither translate into nor justify political power. Even though he himself came from that very milieu, he believed that traders should be denied social mobility due to their ambiguous status, their extensive foreign networks, and their now absolute control over the Kingdom of Sardinia's most important productive sector: silk. The risk of Piedmont's state-driven silk economy falling entirely into the hands of foreign traders—and thereby making the country dependent on other states—was tangible, as the evidence showed. For example, it is significant that the crown and government had endeavored to transform Piedmont into a producer of silk fabrics through state incentives, comprehensive legislation, and by establishing royal manufactories. Nevertheless, the kingdom's main export to global markets remained a semi-finished product, impossible to replicate elsewhere with the same characteristics, unlike textiles, which remained under the dominance of Lyon's industry. Indeed, the *alla piemontese* organzine was of exceptional quality—the finest on the European market—but it was still a semi-finished product. Once exported and turned into fabric by foreign artisans, its value multiplied. These finished goods were then sold as foreign products, even within Piedmont itself, and made foreign traders rich. In the process, they strengthened foreign economies while undermining the Kingdom of Sardinia's economic development plans. In Donaudi's view, the only solution was to reform the state's foundational structure. More specifically, he suggested reconciling the rigid divide between the nobility, who could not engage in trade, and the merchant class, who had no access to political decision-making to perhaps pave the way to genuine economic progress.

Moreover, while the relationship between the nobility and traders required reform on the one hand, on the other, it was essential for the state to better recognize their crucial role as drivers of innovation and economic growth, supporting their choices and positions accordingly. In fact, the relationship between the state and the trading class, when examined alongside the history of the Piedmontese silk industry, reveals a deep ambivalence. On the one hand, government institutions created laws aimed at shaping a specific model of manufacturing organization and characterized by a legislative framework that sought to align with European guild traditions. On the other hand, the crown funded initiatives that, in the pursuit of market expansion, ended up supporting the ambitions of traders. Essentially, granting statutes and privileges to guilds and supporting royal factories were two sides of the same coin—a coin stamped with the image of the King of Sardinia (Monestarolo 2006a, b, 2013). However, the mercantilist government had conflicting interests. It had to balance the success of the silk threads sold by traders, which brought clear advantages to the state, with the growing desire of this commercial class for greater freedom. In this context, the traders seized every opportunity to circumvent the legal control of guilds. For example, they sought privileges to hire apprentices and journeymen outside the guild system or made artisans reliant on their commissions.

Although studying these figures in "flesh and blood" (Clarkson 1991, 295) remains challenging, traders—those "strange beasts" that historiography never seems to tire of—were, in their transition toward industrial entrepreneurship, perceived by both the state and much of society as embodiments of the "other" (Cerutti 1992, 2003; Ruggiero 2013; Rössner 2016). In the collective mindset, this "otherness" was seen as acting against the national interest for personal gain. Even so, it was equally regarded as a necessary evil and crucial in maintaining the state's budget, settling foreign debts, and funding military expenses (Bulferetti 1963; Stumpo 1979). Traders, then, were players whom it was impossible to reject outright but who needed to be carefully managed. They had to be transformed into *ditissimi homines*, key economic and social actors, in order to prevent the Piedmontese economy from falling into the hands of rival states.

In conclusion, the dynamics of the eighteenth-century Piedmontese silk industry reveal not a simple shift but the coexistence—and gradual interweaving—of mercantile and industrial forms of capitalism. Within this hybrid system, entrepreneurs emerged as both agents and products of a state-managed economy, embodying a new synthesis between trade, production, and power.

Bibliography

Agua de la Roza, Jesús. 2018. El trabajo forzado infantil en las instituciones asistenciales madrileñas: proyecto ilustrado, manufactura y disciplinamiento (1750-1800). In *Palacios, plazas, patíbulos: la sociedad española moderna entre el cambio y las resistencias*, ed. James S. Amelang, Fernando Andrés Robres, Rafael Benítez Sánchez-Blanco, Ricardo Franch Benavent, and Mirian Galante Becerril, 181–194. Valencia: Tirant lo Blanch.

Agua de la Roza, Jesús. 2020. Manufacturas, caridad y salario en la red asistencial madrileña del Setecientos. *Mediterranea* 17 (48): 143–170.

Amatori, Franco. 2006. Entrepreneurship. *Imprese e Storia* 34:233–267.
Arese, Giovanni. 1922. *L'industria serica piemontese dal secolo XVII alla metà del XIX*. Turin: Bona.
Balani, Donatella. 1987. *Il vicario tra città e Stato: l'ordine pubblico e l'annona nella Torino del Settecento*. Turin: Deputazione Subalpina di Storia Patria.
Banaji, Jairus. 2019. *A brief history of commercial capitalism*. Chicago: Haymarket Books.
Battistini, Francesco. 1998. *Gelsi, bozzoli, caldaie. L'industria della seta in Toscana tra città, borghi e campagne (secc. XVI-XVIII)*. Florence: Olschki.
Baumol, William J. 1968. Entrepreneurship in economic theory. *American Economic Review* 58 (2): 64–71.
Berengo, Marino. 1965. *Nobili e mercanti nella Lucca del Cinquecento*. Turin: Einaudi.
Berta, Giuseppe. 2006. *L'enigma dell'imprenditore (e il destino dell'impresa)*. Bologna: Il Mulino.
Borelli, Giovanni Battista. 1681. *Editti antichi e nuovi de' Sovrani Prencipi della Real Casa di Savoia, delle loro Tutrici, e de' Magistrati di qua da' Monti*. Turin: Zappata.
Bracco, Giuseppe. 1992. L'Ottocento: dalla seta alla finanza. In *Torino sul filo della seta*, ed. Giuseppe Bracco, 119–148. Turin: Archivio Storico della Città di Torino.
Braudel, Fernand. 1949. *La Méditerranée et le monde méditerranéen à l'époque de Philippe II*. Paris: Colin.
Bulferetti, Luigi. 1963. *Agricoltura, industria e commercio in Piemonte nel secolo XVIII*. Turin: Istituto per la Storia del Risorgimento.
Caligaris, Giacomina. 1998. Trade guilds, manufacturing and economic privilege in the kingdom of Sardinia during the eighteenth century. In *Guilds, markets, and work regulations in Italy, 16th–19th centuries*, ed. Alberto Guenzi, Paola Massa, and Fausto Piola Caselli, 56–81. Aldershot: Ashgate.
Caligaris, Giacomina. 1999. Arti, manifatture e privilegio economico nel Regno di Sardegna durante il XVIII secolo. In *Corporazioni e gruppi professionali nell'Italia moderna*, ed. Alberto Guenzi, Paola Massa, and Angelo Moioli, 171–200. Milan: FrancoAngeli.
Caligaris, Giacomina. 2001. Il grande affare della seta e la formazione professionale a Torino nel Settecento. *Bollettino Storico-Bibliografico Subalpino* 99 (1): 61–103.
Caligaris, Giacomina. 2004. Successi e fallimenti del lavoro corporato: i prodotti del tessile seta a Torino nel Settecento. In *Dalla corporazione al mutuo soccorso. Organizzazione e tutela del lavoro tra XVI e XX secolo*, ed. Paola Massa and Angelo Moioli, 347–379. Milan: FrancoAngeli.
Caracausi, Andrea. 2007. Capitali e mercanti-imprenditori in età moderna (Italia settentrionale, secc. XVII-XVIII). *Annali di Storia dell'impresa* 18:283–299.

Caracausi, Andrea. 2021. Una compagnia di cordelle di seta nella seconda metà del Seicento: la "Eredi Giupponi & C." di Padova. *OS. Opificio Della Storia* 2 (2): 8–21.

Casson, Mark, and Catherine Casson. 2013. *The entrepreneur in history: From medieval merchant to modern business leader*. Cham: Palgrave Macmillan.

Cavaciocchi, Simonetta, ed. 1991. *L'impresa, industria, commercio, banca, secc. XIII-XVIII*. Florence: Le Monnier.

Cavallo, Sandra. 1980. Assistenza femminile e tutela dell'onore nella Torino del XVIII secolo. *Annali della Fondazione L. Einaudi* 14:127–155.

Cavallo, Sandra. 1995. *Charity and power in early modern Italy. Benefactors and their motives in Turin, 1541–1789*. Cambridge: Cambridge University Press.

Cerutti, Simona. 1992. *Mestieri e Privilegi. Nascita delle corporazioni a Torino (secoli XVII-XVIII)*. Turin: Einaudi.

Cerutti, Simona. 2003. *Giustizia sommaria. Pratiche e ideali di giustizia in una società d'Ancien Régime (Torino, XVIII secolo)*. Milan: Feltrinelli.

Cerutti, Simona. 2006. Processo ed esperienza. La nascita dei corpi di mestiere a Torino tra Sei e Settecento. In *Giochi di Scala. La microstoria alla prova dell'esperienza*, ed. Jacques Revel, 171–200. Rome: Viella.

Chicco, Giuseppe. 1992. L'innovazione tecnologica nella lavorazione della seta in Piemonte a metà Seicento. *Studi Storici* 33:195–215.

Chicco, Giuseppe. 1995. *La seta in Piemonte 1650–1800. Un sistema industriale d'ancien régime*. Milan: FrancoAngeli.

Chicco, Giuseppe. 2002. Alla periferia del sistema moda. In *Storia di Torino IV*, ed. Giuseppe Ricuperati, 911–935. Turin: Einaudi.

Chierici, Patrizia. 1992. Da Torino tutt'intorno: le "fabbriche da seta" dell'antico regime. In *Torino sul filo della seta*, ed. Giuseppe Bracco, 177–202. Turin: Archivio Storico della Città di Torino.

Chierici, Patrizia, and Laura Palmucci Quaglino, eds. 1993. *Le Fabbriche Magnifiche. La seta in provincia di Cuneo tra Seicento e Ottocento*. Cuneo: L'arciere.

Clarkson, Leslie A. 1991. The pro-industrial entrepreneur. In *L'impresa. Industria, commercio, banca, secc. XIII-XVIII*, ed. Simonetta Cavaciocchi, 295–312. Florence: Le Monnier.

Cortelazzo, Manlio, Michele A. Cortelazzo, and Paolo Zolli. 2004. *L'etimologico minore. Dizionario etimologico della lingua italiana*. Bologna: Zanichelli.

Cossa, Luigi. 1878. *Guida allo studio dell'economia politica*. Milan: Hoepli.

Cussen, Oliver. 2023. Empire and enlightenment after John Law: Merchant capitalism and political economy in the French East India Company. *The Journal of Modern History* 95 (3): 519–556.

Cusumano, Vito. 1870. Diomede Caraffa, economista italiano del secolo XV. *Archivio Giuridico* 6:481–495.

Day, John. 1999. *Money and finance in the age of merchant capitalism*. Oxford: Blackwell.

De Vivo, Paola. 2017. *L'impresa come istituzione sociale*. Bologna: Il Mulino.
Dobb, Maurice. 1963. *Economic growth and underdeveloped countries*. New York: International Publishers.
Donaudi delle Mallere, Ignazio. 1776. *Saggio di economia civile*. Turin: Avondo.
Ferrando, Francesca. 2018. Tra arbaggi e vareghi. Le manifatture tessili dell'Albergo dei poveri di Genova all'inizio del Settecento. *Storia Urbana* 40 (156–157): 163–185.
Ferrando, Francesca. 2020. "Acciò la gente stii occupata". Le manifatture dell'Albergo dei poveri di Genova. *Storia Economica* 23 (1): 41–72.
Flinn, Michael W. 1966. *Origins of the industrial revolution*. London: Barnes & Noble.
Franceschi, Franco. 2020. Big business for firms and states: Silk manufacturing in Renaissance Italy. *Business History Review* 94 (1): 95–123.
Garbellotti, Marina. 2013. *Per carità: poveri e politiche assistenziali nell'Italia moderna*. Rome: Carocci.
González Enciso, Agustín. 1980. *Estado e Industria en el Siglo XVIII: La Fábrica de Guadalajara*. Madrid: Fundación Universitaria Española.
Grassi, Mario. 2024. A delicate equilibrium: State projects, guild dynamics, and personal interests in silk weaving in ancient regime (Turin, eighteenth century). In *A global history of silk. Trade and production from the 16th to the mid-20th century*, ed. Manuela Martini, Pierre Vernus, and Tomoko Hashino, 97–118. Cham: Springer.
Grassi, Mario. 2026. The Main Purpose: Bargaining, Wages, and Gender in the Eighteenth-Century Piedmontese Silk Manufacture. In *A Historical Casebook of Wage Formation Wage Determination and Wage Bargains, 1500–1950*, ed. Giulio Ongaro, Judy Z. Stephenson, and Luca Mocarelli. Cham: Palgrave Macmillan.
Hilton, Rodney H. 1952. Capitalism. What's in a name? *Past and Present* 1:32–43.
Isenmann, Moritz. 2016. From privilege to economic law. Vested interests and the origins of free trade theory in France (1687–1701). In *Economic growth and the origins of modern political economy: Economic reasons of state*, ed. Philipp R. Rössner, 105–121. London: Routledge.
Jannaccone, Pasquale. 1903. Di un economista piemontese del secolo XVIII (D. delle M.). *Atti della Regia Accademia delle Scienze di Torino* 38:352–377.
Lanaro, Paola. 2005. Il contesto economico e territoriale nei secoli XV-XVIII. In *Andrea Palladio e la villa veneta da Petrarca a Carlo Scarpa*, ed. Guido Beltramini and Howard Burns, 148–152. Venice: Marsilio.
Lanaro, Paola, ed. 2006. *At the Centre of the Old World. Trade and manufacturing in Venice and on the Venetian mainland (1400–1800)*. Toronto: Centre for Reformation and Renaissance Studies.
Lanaro, Paola. 2007. Il mercante e l'imprenditore. L'evoluzione storica attraverso il lessico. *Annali di storia dell'impresa* 18:209–216.
Legnani Annichini, Alessia. 2013. *Proxeneta est in tractando. La professione ingrata del mediatore di commercio (secc. XII-XVI)*. Bologna: BUP.

Legnani Annichini, Alessia. 2021. Il mediatore di commercio tra professione privata e pubblico ufficio (secc. XVI-XVIII). In *Italia-Francia allers-retours: influenze, adattamenti, porosità*, ed. Luisa Brunori and Cristina Ciancio, 31–44. Rome: Historia et ius.

Magnusson, Lars. 1994. *Mercantilism. The shaping of an economic language.* London: Routledge.

Merlin, Pierpaolo. 2021. Sviluppo economico e mobilità sociale nel Piemonte della seconda reggenza: gli ufficiali della Camera dei conti di Piemonte. In *Maria Giovanna Battista di Savoia-Nemours. Stato, capitale, architettura*, ed. Chiara Devoti, 187–205. Florence: Olschki.

Merlotti, Andrea. 2000. *L'enigma delle nobiltà Stato e ceti dirigenti nel Piemonte del Settecento.* Florence: Olschki.

Merlotti, Andrea, and Tomaso Ricardi di Netro. 2002. Nobiltà e borghesia. Armi e commercio. In *Famiglie nobili e borghesi. Dall'arsenale a nuovi mestieri*, ed. Francesco Gianazzo di Pamparato, 233–256. Turin: Piemonte Cultura.

Mola di Nomaglio, Gustavo. 2006. *Feudi e nobiltà negli stati dei Savoia: materiali, spunti, spigolature bibliografiche per una storia, con la cronologia feudale delle Valli di Lanzo.* Lanzo Torinese: Società Storica delle Valli di Lanzo.

Monestarolo, Giorgio. 2006a. Negozianti e imprenditori nel Piemonte d'antico regime. In *La cultura economica di Ignazio Donaudi delle Mallere (1744–1795).* Florence: Olschki.

Monestarolo, Giorgio. 2006b. Una chiusa élite? I negozianti-banchieri di Torino attraverso i censimenti fiscali (1734-1797). *Società e Storia* 113:469–518.

Monestarolo, Giorgio. 2013. *Dare e Avere. Commercio e politica delle riforme nel Piemonte del XVIII secolo.* Turin: Kaplan.

Moody, Margaret J. 2001. *The royal poorhouse in 18th-century Turin, Italy: The king and the paupers.* Lewiston: Edwin Mellen Press.

Picco, Leila. 1986. Colori e sete sulla riva di un fiume. La Regia Tintoria di sete al Borgo di Po a Torino nel Settecento. *Studi in Memoria di Mario Abrate* 2:915–940.

Picco, Leila. 1992. Il Settecento: l'affermazione della seta. In *Torino sul filo della seta*, ed. Giuseppe Bracco, 67–118. Turin: Archivio Storico della Città di Torino.

Prak, Maarten, ed. 2001. *Early modern capitalism: Economic and social change in Europe, 1400–1800.* London: Routledge.

Quazza, Guido. 1957. *Le riforme in Piemonte nella prima metà del Settecento.* Modena: Società Tipografica Editrice Modense.

Ranza, Giannantonio. 1777. *Della Sereide d'Alessandro Tessauro.* Vercelli: Tipografia Patria.

Ricuperati, Giuseppe. 1994. Il Settecento. In *Storia d'Italia. Il Piemonte sabaudo. Stato e territori in età moderna*, ed. Pierpaolo Merlin, Claudio Rosso, Geoffrey Symcox, and Giuseppe Ricuperati, 439–834. Turin: UTET.

Roncaglia, Alessandro. 2005. *The wealth of ideas: A history of economic thought.* Cambridge: Cambridge University Press.

Rössner, Philipp R. 2015. Heckscher reloaded? Mercantilism, the state and Europe's transition to industrialization (1600–1900). *The Historical Journal* 58 (2): 663–683.
Rössner, Philipp R., ed. 2016. *Economic growth and the origins of modern political economy. Economic reasons of state 1500–2000.* London: Routledge.
Ruggiero, Vincenzo. 2013. *The crimes of the economy. A criminological analysis of economic thought.* London: Routledge.
Sabel, Charles, and Jonathan Zeitlin, eds. 1997. *World of possibilities. Flexibility and mass production in Western industrialization.* Cambridge: Cambridge University Press.
Sorella, Vincenzo. 2007. Mallere, Ignazio Donaudi conte delle. *Dizionario Biografico degli Italiani* 68.
Stumpo, Enrico. 1979. *Finanza e stato moderno nel Piemonte del Seicento.* Rome: Istituto Storico Italiano per l'età moderna e contemporanea.
Symcox, Geoffrey. 1983. *Victor Amadeus II. Absolutism in the Savoyard state 1675–1730.* Berkeley: University of California Press.
Tolaini, Roberto. 1997. Filande, mercato e innovazioni nell'industria serica italiana. In *Gli Scoti di Pescia (1750–1860).* Florence: Olschki.
Toninelli, Pier Angelo. 2004. Una nota sulla storia del concetto di imprenditore. In *Studi in onore di Giovanni Miccoli*, ed. Liliana Ferrari, 459–478. Trieste: Edizioni dell'Università di Trieste.
Toninelli, Pier Angelo. 2006. *Storia d'impresa.* Bologna: Il Mulino.
Turbini, Gaspare Antonio. 1778. *L'economia per la filatura delle sete e descrizione di tutte le fabbriche ad essa appartenenti perfino all'uscita delle stoffe lavorate.* Brescia: Vescovi.
Zucca Micheletto, Beatrice. 2013. Family solidarity vs institutional relief? Interaction and complementarity between different survival strategies in 18th-century Turin. In *Assistenza e solidarietà in Europa sec. XIII-XVIII*, ed. Francesco Ammannati, 521–531. Florence: Firenze University Press.

CHAPTER 6

Silk Work, Silk Workers: Crafting Expertise Through Migration, Training, and Gender

1 Introduction

To drive economic growth, the entrepreneurial state, traders, and machinery all depended—willingly or not—on the skilled hands of men and women who could produce goods with specific characteristics. The artisanal society, briefly mentioned in earlier chapters, now takes center stage. The following pages explore its defining traits and position the world of labor in the Piedmontese silk industry within a broader historiographical current that has reexamined the pre-industrial economy—challenging the conventional view of early modern work as entangled in a dense web of guild regulations, and revealing instead how loose and permeable that fabric could be (Sewell 1980; Kaplan and Koepp 1986; Sonenscher 1989; Cerutti and Poni 1990; Ago 1998; Rosenband 1999; Trivellato 2000; Allegra 2004, 2005; Sarti et al. 2018).

This analysis unfolds through the multifaceted story of Anna Maria Pajsio, whose experience exposes the complexities of professional life under the ancien régime. The choice of this case study is not accidental: in 1746, Anna Maria was one of the master silk weavers at the Albergo di Virtù, a prestigious charitable institution that had been a cornerstone of Piedmontese silk production since the late sixteenth century (Borelli 1681, 223—January 7, 1667). For over a century, all the masters had been men, responsible for training male apprentices. Yet because the institution also housed girls, their instruction was usually limited to winding,

M. Grassi, *The Silk Industry in Early Modern Piedmont*, Labour in History and Society,
https://doi.org/10.1007/978-3-032-15353-1_6

under female supervision.[1] The only exception was the widow Ponzia's workshop, founded in 1719 to teach silk-gauze weaving[2]—an initiative designed to offer the institute's female apprentices training in a specialized craft (Cenedella and Fumi 2015; Schalk 2017; Caracausi and Maitte 2020). However, in 1746, the Albergo di Virtù underwent a drastic change: it excluded female apprentices altogether. Why, then, was Anna Maria Pajsio admitted to the ranks of the masters in that very year? By conducting a meticulous microhistorical reconstruction, which traces how Anna Maria's trajectory intersected with those of other men and women navigating the dynamics of professional training, power, and survival in eighteenth-century Turin, it is possible to reveal overlooked facets of professional life in the ancien régime.

The story of Anna Maria and her silk-weaving skills has deep roots, in both time and space, tracing back to long before her birth. The first part of this chapter focuses on Pierre Millori—Anna Maria's future father-in-law and one of many French weavers who settled in Turin during the seventeenth century. The growth of Piedmont's silk industry was fueled by the influx of artisans and experts who recognized Turin as an ideal hub for their crafts and trades. While the Piedmontese case remains intertwined with well-known social dynamics of migration—such as poverty, war, or exclusion due to factors like religion—it also brings to light another possible key motivation: personal aspiration. In this context, these artisans' decision to migrate, whatever the distance, appears to be deliberate and driven by the growing reputation of Piedmontese silk products in Europe by the late seventeenth century. Yet, the lives of Pierre and Anna Maria would never have intersected if not for the birth of Pietro Millori, who would later become Anna Maria's second husband. Unlike Pierre, Pietro was born in Turin and followed traditional steps to enter the guild system. The dynamics that defined guilds and their relationship with the mercantile world will be addressed, along with the factors influencing the transmission of professions related to high-quality craftsmanship and the social dynamics shaping this context. Finally, the focus will shift to Anna Maria's life and professional experience. By examining the social factors that shaped the life of this silk-weaving craftswoman, it becomes possible to uncover the intricacies of a world formally excluded from the guild system.

[1] AST, C, *Materie ecclesiastiche,* Luoghi pii di qua dai monti, m. 16 d'addizione, fasc. 2.
[2] AST, SR, *Regio Albergo di Virtù*, Ordinati, m. 52, December 10, 1719.

Seen from a bottom-up perspective, the reconstruction of Anna Maria's role, career, and experiences—together with those of her fellow artisans—reveals once again the gap between norms and practice, between formal and informal institutions, and between inherited views of the ancien régime and the realities found in the archives, echoing recent historiographical efforts to reassess labor and its social worlds in the past (Allegra 2005; Laudani 2006).

2 Pierre. The Migrant Origins of Expertise

Anna Maria Francesca Adelaide Pajsio was born on May 11, 1712, in Turin, the daughter of Pietro Michele and Margarita.[3] Around the age of 14, Anna Maria was promised in marriage to her cousin, Gio Michele Muratore.[4] Their marriage lasted only a few years, due to the premature passing of Gio Michele. In 1732, shortly after reaching adulthood, Anna Maria remarried Pietro Millori, whose father, Pierre, was a silk weaver from Tours. This marriage marks the beginning of our story: the union between Anna Maria and Pietro would profoundly shape the course of her life. To understand how, however, it is necessary to take a step back and consider the broader context in which their lives unfolded.

The success of the Piedmontese silk industry was shaped by multiple factors, with one standing out: the emigrant artisan. Historiography has often linked the expulsion of Huguenots from the Kingdom of France following the revocation of the Edict of Nantes in 1685 to the rise of silk production centers in England and the Netherlands, thereby implicitly framing silk weaving skills as religion-dependent (Dupâquier 1994; Pettegree 1994; Kershen 2005; Treasure 2013; Carpanetto 2014; Stanwood 2020; Murdoch 2021). The migration of French craftsmen to the House of Savoy's Piedmontese territories has also been interpreted through this lens (Prato 1908; Pascal 1937; Romagnani 2002, 2021).

[3] "Fidem facio, siccuti in libris baptisatorum metropolitane S. Joannis reperitur descriptum, prout seguitur videlicet, Francesca Anna Maria Adelaida filia di Pietro Michele et Margarita giugali Pajsio nata li 11 e battesata li 12 maggio 1712 cura S. Marco Padrini Gio Michele Villatti et Anna Maria Bonina" (I hereby certify that the following entry appears in the baptismal registers of the Metropolitan Church of St. John: Francesca Anna Maria Adelaida, daughter of Pietro Michele and Margarita, lawful spouses Pajsio, was born on May 11 and baptized on May 12, 1712, in the Parish of St. Mark. Godparents: Gio Michele Villatti and Anna Maria Bonina). AST, SR, *Insinuazione Torino*, 1733, v. 1, c. 853.

[4] AST, SR, *Insinuazione Torino*, 1726, v. 6, c. 1077.

Nevertheless, the preservation of two registers titled *Rollo dei francesi* (Roll of the French), dated 1690 and 1704, raises doubts about this assumption. The two censuses of French-born residents reveal a remarkably heterogeneous sample, including individuals of different backgrounds, genders, professions, and ages—many of whom had arrived at various times throughout the seventeenth century. Why would Protestants flee persecution in France only to encounter new dangers in Piedmont, especially after the infamous Piedmontese Easter of 1655, during which many people of the same faith were brutally massacred in the Piedmontese valleys (Kolrud 2014; Fratini 2021)?[5] How can the limited number of silk weavers among the Protestants listed in the preserved *Rolli dei religionari* (Rolls of Protestants) from the 1720s onward be explained (Pascal 1927, 1937; Romagnani 2002, 2021, 2023)? And finally, why were none of the silk weavers identified as *religionario* in these censuses, unlike other French migrants?[6] Historiography has also frequently highlighted the pivotal role of governments in pursuing industrial espionage and implementing policies to "attract" skilled labor (Dolza 2007; Schulz 2007; Davids and De Munck 2014; Henrich and Simpson 2019; Garrioch 2022; Consterdine 2018). These measures often included granting privileges to artisans specialized in certain trades who were willing to relocate. In both the case of the Huguenots and that of individually privileged migrants, however, caution is required (Hilaire-Pérez and Verna 2006). As recent historiography on migratory movements has demonstrated, treating artisan mobility as an undifferentiated flow is problematic, as it risks obscuring the diversity of actors, motivations, and institutional frameworks involved. For this reason, migration cannot be reduced to the simple push-and-pull dynamics of poverty or state incentives. In many cases, mobility itself became an economic resource, mediated through the agency of local elites who acted as entrepreneurs of labor—organizing, directing, and profiting from the circulation of skilled workers (Fontaine 2005; Ehmer 2011).

[5] Reports of the tragic massacre of the Waldensians in the Piedmontese valleys quickly spread across Europe (Tron 2005; Fratini 2021).

[6] For example, the journeyman pot maker Luigi Aglande, originally from Languedoc. AST, C, *Paesi per A e per B*, Provincia di Torino, m. 4, fasc. 20.

This perspective, however, risks overstating the power of elites and state policies, overlooking how artisans actively navigated, adapted to, or resisted these structures in pursuit of their own goals and futures. In doing so, it tends to oversimplify the complex phenomenon of migration—obscuring the migrants themselves and the personal motivations, choices, and aspirations that shaped their trajectories (Richards 2018; Gietel-Basten 2020; De Haas 2021). Recent social science studies have shown that migration decisions are shaped by individual, rational choices (Carling and Collins 2018). This shift in perspective has led to a reconceptualization of the migrant figure, whose migration experience is now seen as an ongoing process of subjective becoming (Collins 2018). This new perspective humanizes migration, enabling a transition beyond rigid categorizations and stereotypes that have long influenced the debate on the topic. What has further revitalized research in this area is the recent emphasis on migrants' aspirations—a valuable interpretative lens that has offered significant insights into the field (Seiger et al. 2020; Salazar 2023). Through this perspective, the subjectivity and identity of migrants can be understood as perpetually evolving, shaped neither solely by their place of origin nor by the manner of their arrival, but by a complex interplay of factors that traditional frameworks often fail to capture (Erdal and Oeppen 2018; Carling and Collins 2018).

The arrival of small groups of foreign experts in Turin during the seventeenth century, employed in the silk industry, reveals the significant role of aspiration in early modern migration—despite the relatively limited numbers involved. These foreign silk weavers seem to have been motivated more by the opportunity to take advantage of recent Piedmontese innovations in the sector than by the need to escape social hardship or religious persecution (Lodigiani 2008; Filipović et al. 2012; Hornung 2014; Nicholson and Gillain 2025). By this time, Piedmont's potential in the silk sector was already widely recognized across Europe. In his *L'Italia regnante o vero nova descritione dello stato presente de tutti Principati, e Republiche d'Italia* (Italy Reigning, or a New Account of the Current State of All the Principalities and Republics of Italy), published in Geneva in 1675, the cosmopolitan intellectual Gregorio Leti painted a captivating picture of the Duchy of Savoy. Leti referred to Piedmont as Cockaigne (*Paese di Coccagna*) (65) and true Eden ("vero luogo d'Adamo et Eva nello stato dell'Innocenza") (211). He enhanced his descriptions with detailed accounts of its local products—including its prized silks, which had recently achieved renown.[7] He also highlighted the presence of skilled merchants, while lamenting that the Piedmontese failed to fully capitalize on their region's abundant resources.[8] In short, Piedmont, with its rich but underexploited resources and the production of the highly sought-after *organzino*, was an appealing destination for ambitious individuals eager to profit from its potential.[9]

By the late seventeenth century, records show that Turin was home to approximately 100 French silk weavers, whose families and households brought the total to around 300 individuals.[10] Although the 1690 census does not reveal where these people originally came from, the 1704 census identifies Tours, Lyon, and Avignon as the main places of origin. These relocations often involved considerable distances. Tours, for instance, is 700 kilometers from Turin, while Lyon and Avignon, though closer, are still over 300 kilometers away—not to mention the challenges posed by crossing the Alps (Cavaciocchi 1994; Viazzo and Cerri 2009). One of these migrants was Michel Bon[11] from Tours, France, who in 1689 received a patent for "having made the decision 22 years ago to come to this city of Turin, along with his wife Maddalena, to engage in the production of brocades and other silk fabrics, and to teach others this craft."[12] A subsequent patent from 1704 recounts that "40 years ago, he decided to move his residence from said city (Tours) to this one (Turin), where he has always remained dedicated to the production of brocades, damasks, and other silk fabrics, being among the first to introduce and teach this craft in

[7] "In the state of Piedmont, goods of all kinds are produced; (...) Carmagnola is a place where a fair is held every Wednesday, attracting a large crowd from Piedmont and the Republic of Genoa, with a great abundance of merchandise. Here, as well as in Saviano, the finest silks are produced and then sent to Lyon, Geneva, Flanders, and other places (...). In short, all of Piedmont is, so to speak, a land of Cockaigne, or at least of such abundance that the Piedmontese are content to wander and turn within this wealth, without troubling themselves with anything else" (Leti 1675, 64–65).

[8] Leti's accounts stemmed from his personal experiences during his time at the Savoyard court. His work gained significant recognition and, according to Tiraboschi, became a cornerstone of Italian historiography of the era—despite criticism of his verbosity and inclination to flatter the ruling monarchs (Tiraboschi 1780, 258–259).

[9] A dynamic that closely mirrors the one observed in the Venetian glass industry (McCray 1999; Maitte 2009).

[10] AST, C, *Paesi per A e per B*, Provincia di Torino, m. 4, fasc. 20; m. 5, fasc. *Rollo dei Francesi habitanti in Torino nell'Anno 1704*.

[11] Identifiable in documents as Michele Bon, Michele Bono, Michele Buono, or Michelle Lebon.

[12] AST, SR, *Camerale Piemonte*, *Patenti*, m. 108, f. 148, May 21, 1689.

Piedmont."[13] These documents highlight Michel's individuality in his decision to relocate to Turin due to personal aspiration. This fact remains unchanged even if his arrival was influenced by any potential Savoy government incentives. Moreover, the sources show that most of these migrations appear to have been permanent and in some cases helped foster the emergence of artisan dynasties associated with silk weaving, such as the cases of the Colombo, Gottiè, Roland, and Vanet families.[14]

Guild records further illustrate the diversity of those involved in silk weaving, highlighting the artisans' different origins and the significant contribution of migration to the development of the Piedmontese silk industry. The guild admission register, which documented the names and origins of most master weavers accepted between 1678 and 1795, offers a clear and detailed insight into this aspect. In the guild's founding year, 1678, there were 167 registered masters, 148 of whose origins are known. Strikingly, the majority were not native to the capital. Turin-born weavers were only one-third of the total, while the remaining two-thirds came from the Ligurian Riviera (1), the Milanese area (4), Savoy (5), the Kingdom of France (23), and, most prominently, other parts of Piedmont (70).[15] However, it is worth noting that in the following years French weavers kept appearing in the guild's admission register records in Turin, with entries continuing up to 1790. Through guilds, foreign artisans were able to transform professional skill into social capital (Fontaine 2005; Garrioch 2022).

From the guild register, another form of mobility toward Turin during the same period emerges. This time, it covered a short distance—just 15 kilometers—but was crucial to the development of the silk weaving industry. Among the 70 Piedmontese weavers listed as early guild members, 20 came from Chieri but resided in Turin, while another 14 lived there permanently—yet remained affiliated with the capital's guild. In essence, half of the Piedmontese weavers came from Chieri, also known as the "city of fustian." A historic center for producing mixed cotton-wool and cotton-linen fabrics, Chieri had been one of the first Piedmontese cities to establish a formal guild, with statutes dating back to 1482 (Cerutti 1992; Mazzaoui 1981). Over the years, artisans from Lombardy, Genoa, and France had settled in the city, contributing—albeit amid tensions—to the

[13] AST, SR, *Camerale Piemonte, Patenti*, m. 135, f. 84, March 22, 1704.

[14] APSA, *Università dei mastri vellutai*, v. 4, 1677–1795.

[15] APSA, *Università dei mastri vellutai*, v. 4, 1677–1795.

production and trade network that brought Chieri renown across Europe (Allegra, 1987; Comba 1988; Mazzaoui 1981). The wars and plagues of the seventeenth century, along with the centralizing policies of the House of Savoy, reshaped the landscape. A demographic shift increasingly favored Turin, where new institutions, banks, and economic opportunities were concentrated (Levi 1985; Rosso 2002). This shift likely explains why 20 artisans from Chieri migrated to Turin, while the 14 guild members who remained in Chieri may have continued to combine their roles as both weavers and agricultural laborers (Allegra 1987).

In the silk weaving sector, the convergence of French and Chieri textile traditions appears to have played a key role in Turin's burgeoning industry. This convergence led the Savoy government to develop ambitious plans for expanding manufacturing, confident in the future success of Piedmontese fabrics (Grassi 2024). A 1702 report on the silk industry lends further credibility to these accounts. Based on information from the guild, the report reveals that while only 18 of the 187 master weavers were French, there was near parity in the number of local and foreign laborers: 121 Piedmontese workers compared to 110 foreigners, of whom 101 were French.[16]

This is the context in which the story of Pierre Millori takes shape. Pierre was Anna Maria Pajsio's father-in-law and the father of Pietro, her second husband. Pierre's life story illustrates how aspiration in the migratory context serves as an interpretative lens that, situated at the intersection of individuality, collectivity, and institutions, functions as the "social grounding of individual desire" (Ray 2006). Born in the 1650s in Tours, Pierre was a 30-year-old bachelor when he arrived in Turin in the 1680s with 500 *lire* and his expertise as a weaver and fabric designer. After achieving his goal of completing the training required to become a master weaver in the Piedmontese capital in 1697, he married Giovanna. They had two children, Caterina and Pietro. By 1702, Pierre was one of the 18 French master weavers recorded in the census. His son Pietro followed in his footsteps, becoming a master in 1730, just two years before marrying Anna Maria. Pierre's aspiration to establish himself in the Savoyard capital was fulfilled. From his first year as a master, he actively participated in guild meetings, using his membership in the professional association as a key means of social integration. His story reveals a deep intertwining of migratory and personal ambitions, enabling him to transform his skills into a

[16] AST, C, *Materie economiche*, Cat. IV, m. 7, fasc. 7, 1702.

means of achieving full integration into the new city, gaining professional recognition, and becoming part of its social fabric.[17]

Silk weavers like Pierre, however, were not the only ones pursuing these types of migratory paths. During the same period, while many French weavers crossed the Alps and Piedmontese artisans passed over the rolling hills surrounding Turin, spinners, dyers, and stocking makers from other regions followed similar routes. Francesco Ballabin, a silk spinner from Bellagio on Lake Como, settled in Turin and became a leading figure among spinners of hand-operated spinning mills. For many years, he served as a representative of the Spinners' Guild and as a member of the board of the Confraternity of the *Santissima Annunziata*.[18] His journey mirrors those of the Carrera brothers, Milanese owners of some of Turin's major production facilities, or Eusebio Chiapusso, originally from Avignon.[19] These names frequently appear in the Consulate of Commerce records. Even in this case, there were Piedmontese who had relocated to the capital. They did so although there was a spinning guild in Racconigi and the opportunity to work in spinning mills throughout Piedmont—not just in Turin, as was the case with weavers—a difference that shaped patterns of migration. The 1690 Roll of French already highlighted significant differences between migrating weavers and spinners: only four French spinners appeared in the document, and this trend nearly disappeared by 1704, as no French spinners were recorded in that year's Roll of French. Unlike weavers, spinners' reluctance to migrate to Piedmont seems particularly indicative when viewed against the backdrop of migratory aspirations. If by the 1660s, Piedmont had earned a reputation for excellence in yarn production, this was not the case for France. For French spinners—many of whom came from Avignon, Nîmes, or Montpellier—moving to Piedmont would not have been another chapter in their professional journey. Instead, it would have meant starting from scratch in a place where they lacked citizenship rights, social connections, and the technical expertise required to meet the demands of a competitive market with increasingly specific quality standards. The inability to transport essential machinery further compounded the difficulty of such a move.

[17] However, stability was not always the ultimate goal of artisans, as historiographical research has shown (Maitte 2009; Maitte and Rygiel 2017; Caracausi et al. 2018; Zucca Micheletto 2022).

[18] AST, SR, *Consolato di Commercio*, m. 51 Filatoristi da seta, 1724–1728; AST, SR, *Insinuazione Torino*, 1713, v. 1, c. 301.

[19] AST, C, *Materie economiche,* Cat. IV, m. 7, fasc. 1, 1708.

A similar pattern likely applied to silk dyers. Although records about this profession from the late seventeenth and early eighteenth centuries are scarce, the 1690 census lists seven French silk dyers residing in Turin, which dropped to just a couple by 1704. However, the government's decision in 1687 to limit silk dyeing to just five workshops—all operated by Piedmontese—forced many dyeing establishments to shift their focus to other textile products. Combined with the logistical challenges of setting up a workshop, such as acquiring equipment and gaining access to water (a crucial resource for dyeing), these restrictions likely discouraged migratory aspirations among silk dyers.

Lastly, the migration of stocking makers displays distinct and intriguing characteristics, setting it apart from other forms of migratory labor. According to the 1690 census, the first French stocking makers using the loom—after Hanford—arrived in the 1670s, just as Piedmontese silk was gaining international acclaim. This migration, though small, continued steadily into the early eighteenth century, as evidenced by comparisons between the French censuses of 1690 and 1704. In this regard, the 1705 population census provides a strikingly clear picture: all the master stocking makers active in Turin were of French origin, while most of the workers were Piedmontese, primarily from Turin (Balani et al. 2005).[20] The novelty of the profession, which for centuries had been carried out exclusively by hand throughout Europe, was a rare opportunity for those skilled in the production of stockings using the stocking frame. For these migrants, the aspiration to move abroad was not only driven by the economic value of exporting their machinery and techniques. It was also about seizing the opportunity to pioneer a craft in which they—or their parents—had already invested in their homeland, as was the case with Michel Bon. In this sector, the French became the sole masters with exclusive expertise, and the only ones capable of creating a professional class with broad productive and commercial ambitions. It is perhaps no coincidence that, even in the 1720s, documents on silk stocking production were still in French—a trend that gradually changed over time. By the late 1730s, a local class of silk stocking makers had emerged, strong enough to formally exclude foreigners from master positions through new guild statutes (Epstein 1991; Ogilvie 2011, 2019; Chase 2017; Di Bari 2019). The Clusels, Pollés, and Puechs who arrived in Turin from the Kingdom of

[20] The original documents are preserved in AST, SR, *Camerale Piemonte*, Art. 530, v. 2, 1705.

France in the late seventeenth century not only established themselves as skilled artisans but also fulfilled their aspirations for social recognition. Initially celebrated as master craftsmen, they laid the groundwork for future generations to become some of Turin's most prominent traders—sometimes achieving political positions also.[21] From the workshops of Tours to the guild halls of Turin, the paths of weavers like Pierre Millori traced a geography of skill and desire that linked distant worlds. Through their labor, these migrants transformed technical knowledge into social possibility, weaving together the material and symbolic threads of a new urban identity—one that prefigured the global dynamics of skilled-labor migration discussed in recent comparative labor histories (Ehmer and Lentz 2023).

3 Pietro: The Guild as a Training Ground

After the 1705 census, Pierre Millori disappears from the historical record—it is unclear whether this was because he died or for other reasons. On the contrary, the path of his son Pietro appears inseparable from his father's migratory ambitions, while also being deeply intertwined with the structure and practices of the craft guilds in early modern Turin. This trajectory, in turn, would profoundly reshape the life of his wife, Anna Maria, following Pietro's death.

The circumstances of how Pietro and Anna Maria met remain unknown, as does the extent of the connection between the Pajsio and Millori families—whether through neighborhood ties, kinship, professional relationships, or shared devotional practices. Nevertheless, in 1730, after completing the required training under the guild system, Pietro became a master silk weaver—qualified, however, only for fabrics with simple striped patterns known as *solie*, but not for more complex designs. Pietro's career appears to have followed a conventional path: born in Turin around 1703, he achieved master status at the age of 25 or 26. According to guild regulations, this implies that Pietro entered apprenticeship at around 15—although it is possible that, prior to his formal training, he may have spent some time working in his father's workshop.

The past few years have seen renewed interest in professional training in the early modern period, a long-standing focus of historiographical

[21] For example, in 1792, two members of the Clusel family held roles in the Consulate of Commerce (Duboin 1848, 67—March 28, 1792).

research (Prak and Wallis 2020; Bellavitis and Sapienza 2023; Schäfer et al. 2023; Hidalgo Fernández and Nieto Sánchez 2024). Scholars have explored how skills were transmitted, emphasizing how guilds enforced a rigid tripartite structure on professional training (Rainbird 1997; Farr 2000; Prak et al. 2006; Epstein and Prak 2008; Garrioch 2022; Schäfer et al. 2023). This institutional framework depended, in practice, on a wide range of variables, since participation in this guild model and actual skill were not necessarily directly proportional. The development of skills, in fact, involved elements such as an individual's exposure to artisanal techniques and technologies within the family, interactions with skilled artisans and laborers, the complexity of the machinery used, market demands, institutional expectations for learning, and, last but not least, the cognitive aptitude of the trainee (Bertucci 2021; Grassi 2026; De Munck 2022; Garrioch 2022). To grasp the discrepancies between institutional expectations and practical realities, it is essential to start with what is commonly referred to as the "guild paradigm"—a standardized model derived from the statutes of the trades (Hafter 2007; Nieto Sánchez and Zofío Llorente 2015; Ferrer-Alòs 2022). The silk trades in Piedmont developed within guilds that were formed at different times and in diverse ways. The establishment of the Consulate of Commerce in 1677 manifested the government's push for greater control over the silk professions. But it was not until 1687—with the founding of the University of Master Merchant Weavers of Gold, Silver, and Silk—that the framework for workforce training began to take shape, setting a precedent for the statutes of other professions in the silk sector. This is evident, for example, in the case of the *Università dei mastri filatoristi in seta* (University of Master Silk Spinners), where the training process was regulated exclusively by the April 8, 1724, Manifesto. The same was true for the *Università dei tintori in seta* (University of Silk Dyers)—despite the widespread disregard for training timelines, which led to the republication of the regulations for dyers in 1732 (Duboin 1849, 931—April 11, 1732). Finally, in 1734, the formation of the University of Master Silk Stocking Makers also led them to define their training period. There were variations in the years of training required, which different statutes outlined (ranging from a minimum of six years for taffeta weavers to a maximum of nine for spinners and weavers), along with the exams and fees necessary for guild membership. What stands out is the guild councils' endeavor to regulate both the transfer of skills and the gradual introduction of new masters into the competitive dynamics between workshops—even if, for example, apprenticeship terms were far from rigid. Exemptions, shortened contracts, and individual arrangements often undermined the formal statutes, revealing a high degree of flexibility in how training was actually organized (Prak and Wallis 2019, 2023; Zucca Micheletto 2019; Bellavitis and Sapienza 2023; Nieto 2025; Wallis 2025).

When interpreting these regulations, the masters' role stands out, as they were both workshop heads and trainers of highly skilled new labor. This role, in fact, is key to understanding how the guild system should be interpreted in the context of professional training. Not only did the statutes give masters institutional authorization to decide how long apprenticeships would last, but they also gave them the power to assess, through examinations, the skills of aspiring masters. As a result, they evaluated the entry of new workers into the guild system on a case-by-case basis. On the one hand, these criteria ensured that only adequately trained labor was admitted. On the other hand, it allowed masters to delay the admission of new masters purely at their discretion, which played a crucial role in the lives of aspiring masters. This becomes even clearer when considering the privileges granted to a master's family, such as the ability for sons to pay a reduced registration fee or, in the event of a father's death, sometimes to shorten the apprenticeship period (Hobsbawm 1984; Dambruyne 1998; Zucca Micheletto 2008; Manieri and Sciarretta 2011; Chilese 2012; Bellavitis 2018a; Wallis 2020). Overall, becoming a master in early modern society was not merely about acquiring the autonomy to produce goods. It also involved masters exercising authority over their profession's whole training system, while gaining access to exclusive rights for themselves and their families. Pietro Millori, for instance, as the son of a master, was able to join the guild by paying only 6 *lire*, a significantly lower fee than what a new master without familial ties to an enrolled master would have had to pay.[22]

Apprenticeship, however, went far beyond pure professional training as we understand it today. Among the Consulate of Commerce's surviving documents is a small collection of apprenticeship contracts. Although these are limited in number, they offer valuable insights into very

[22] In 1687, at the time of the guild's founding, the admission fee was 4 *lire* for masters who had been practicing the trade for years, 5–6 *lire* for the sons of registered masters (who sometimes also contributed donations to the guild), and 20 *lire* for newly admitted masters with no prior affiliation to the guild. With the new statute of 1739, the admission fee increased to 25 *lire* for the sons of masters and 50 *lire* for newcomers.

significant issues when studying professional training in the early modern period, and they extend beyond the boundaries of the specific profession itself (Zucca Micheletto 2020a, 2020b; Bellavitis and Sapienza 2023). According to the documents,[23] apprentices typically began their careers at a young age and were usually guided toward the trade by their parents, highlighting the need for mediation during the contracting process. Given the low literacy levels of the parties involved and the trust-based nature of their relationships, these agreements were sometimes made verbally, thus saving the cost of transcription (which was around 1–2 *lire*).[24] In any case, the apprenticeship contract was only finalized after a probationary period of varying length (typically between 7 and 15 days)[25] during which the master would assess whether it was worth training the apprentice. Yet, sometimes, a written contract—called *capitolazione*, due to its division into distinct chapters (*capitoli*) outlining the terms—was made. The key points open to negotiation typically centered on three main aspects: the duration of the apprenticeship, compensation, and the obligations of both parties.

One of the first elements requiring negotiations was the length of the apprenticeship. By law, this period varied depending on the profession—even though it did not require the training to be completed under a single master's supervision.[26] A crucial document for apprentices who switched masters was the *benservito*—a simple piece of ordinary paper on which masters, in their own handwriting and in just a few lines, confirmed that they had trained the apprentice (Picture 6.1).[27]

Remuneration was also a key aspect of the apprenticeship contract—a topic that has sparked considerable debate due to its complex and variable nature (Mocarelli 2018; Hatcher and Stephenson, 2018; Maitte 2021; Caracausi and Mocarelli 2022; Zucca Micheletto 2020b). While some apprentices received a wage, others were required to pay a fee to the master for the training they received. In the former case, there were generally two main types of remuneration: full payment in money and a reduced salary complemented by additional services. This system reflected the

[23] AST, SR, *Consolato di Commercio*, m. 67 Fabbricatori di taffetà lisci e rigati. 1754.

[24] AST, SR, *Consolato di Commercio,* Costituti, m. 3, *Causa Days/Porta,* August 25, 1723.

[25] AST, SR, *Consolato di Commercio*, Costituti, m. 107, *Causa Capua/Ravioletti,* May 18, 1709.

[26] AST, SR, *Consolato di Commercio,* Costituti, m. 3, *Causa Days/Porta,* August 25, 1723.

[27] AST, SR, *Consolato di Commercio*, m. 67 Fabbricatori di taffetà lisci e rigati, *sottomissione di Clara Anonati,* September 23, 1784.

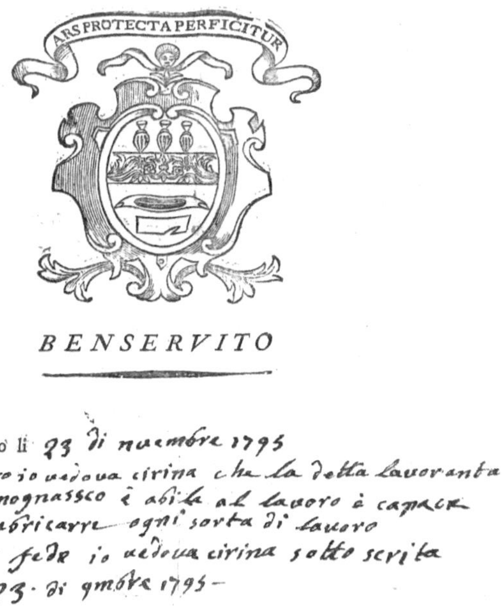
ARS PROTECTA PERFICITUR

BENSERVITO

Torino li 23 di novembre 1795
dichiaro io vedova cirina che la detta lavoranta
mariamognassco è abile al lavoro è capace
di fabricarre ogni sorta di lavoro
per fede io vedova cirina sotto scrita
li. 23. di 9mbre 1795 –

Picture 6.1 Example of a *benservito* in which the mistress weaver "widow Cirina" attests the skills of Maria Magnasco. (*Source*: AST, SR, *Consolato di Commercio*, m. 67 Fabbricatori di taffetà lisci e rigati, Benservito di Maria Magnasco, November 23, 1795. Courtesy of the State Archives of Turin)

apprentice's transition from learner to worker, not just through the training they received but also through their wage, which typically increased over time. Multiple factors influenced the wage, which could vary based on the supplementary services provided by the master, such as food, lodging, and clothing. When the apprentice's family was required to pay a training fee to the master, the situation becomes more ambiguous. This fact challenges the conventional belief that enrolling a child in an apprenticeship would alleviate the family's financial burden (Zucca Micheletto 2008; Bizzarri 2011; Bellavitis 2018b; Ehmer 2023). However, as the documents indicate, the guild often disapproved of this arrangement.[28]

[28] AST, SR, *Consolato di Commercio*, Costituti (NSI), m. 127, *Causa Vallino/Fornas*, January 24, 1779.

Another crucial aspect of the contract concerned the apprentice's duties, which varied depending on whether they lived with the master or returned home after work. Regardless of their living arrangements, all apprentices were bound by a strict duty of obedience to the master and expected to be diligent. Nevertheless, for those residing in the master's household, the apprentices were no longer under the custodianship of their biological fathers and mothers, but under the masters' instead. The master as a *buon padre di famiglia* (good father of the family) had authority over both the apprentices' professional and personal life (Morra and Bazzanella 2002).[29] This arrangement meant that the apprentice was strictly banned from leaving the master's house, whether on holidays or weekdays, without the master's explicit permission. What is more, the master typically required a guarantor to cover any potential damage or costs caused by the apprentice or, should they run away, the cost of replacing them. In fact, an apprentice disappearing was not a minor issue—especially financially—for the master. The sudden and deliberate departure of a worker could seriously hinder workshop operations, leaving machinery idle and work unfinished.[30] Furthermore, the requirement to live with the master could also lead to considerable hardships for young apprentices. As noted in various studies about apprenticeship in Europe (Lane 1996; Caracausi 2014; Franceschi and Molà 2018; Feci and Schettini 2017; Bellavitis and Sapienza 2023), in Turin it was also possible to find reports of masters using physical punishment on apprentices. Under the authority of the master, they could be beaten or chastised for "educational purposes" (Ruff 2001; Zucca Micheletto 2020b; Wallis 2025). Such practices, while troubling, were probably not particularly shocking at the time, as these episodes of violence were often cited as minor aggravating factors in broader cases, such as those arising from the early termination of work contracts.[31] Another important aspect of the contract concerned the apprentice potentially falling ill. Although the period of tolerance varied, it was rare for apprentices to remain in the master's house for more than eight days if they were ill. After this period, the apprentice was expected to

[29] If the apprentice was entrusted to the teachings of a female master, the phrase used would be "good mother of the family." AST, SR, *Consolato di Commercio*, m. 67 Fabbricatori di taffetà lisci e rigati, *Capitolazione di Teresa Maria Friotta*, October 13, 1754.

[30] AST, SR, *Consolato di Commercio*, Costituti, m. 107, *Causa Capua/Ravioletti*, May 18, 1709.

[31] AST, SR, *Consolato di Commercio*, Costituti (NSI), m. 110, *Causa Leger/Genova*, June 20, 1735.

either return home or be transferred to one of the city's hospitals (Newton 2012; Prak and Wallis 2020; Zucca Micheletto 2020b; Bellavitis and Sapienza 2023). In any case, the lost workdays were not considered wasted, as the apprentice was contractually obligated to make up for the missed time at the end of the apprenticeship. Finally, records reveal some more unusual and specific obligations, further illustrating the diverse range of terms found in an apprenticeship contract. These transcended workshop duties and could include assisting with household chores, caring for young or elderly family members, or even sharing any additional skills the apprentice possessed, such as teaching others how to play a musical instrument (Bellavitis and Sapienza 2023).[32]

Nonetheless, the relationship between master and apprentice was far from being fully defined by formal agreements. While these contracts provide a broad outline of the working relationship's characteristics, they do not capture its full complexity. For instance, some contracts included clauses prohibiting physical and verbal abuse, explicitly stating that the master must fulfill his teaching duties "without harsh words, and even less so through actions."[33] Moreover, the relationship between master and apprentice often extended beyond the household. Living under the master's roof came with certain expectations, such as accompanying him on business trips when needed.[34]

Once the contract—whether verbal or written—was finalized, the master was required to register the apprentice with the Consulate of Commerce. Following the model of records still preserved in numerous French archives, apprentices' names were entered into registries alongside the start date of their apprenticeship and the name of their master.[35] At the end of the six-year apprenticeship, the master was expected to issue a state-

[32] AST, SR, *Consolato di Commercio*, m. 67 Fabbricatori di taffetà lisci e rigati, *Capitolazione di Gio Domenico Terzaroglio*, October 11, 1755.

[33] AST, SR, *Consolato di Commercio*, m. 67 Fabbricatori di taffetà lisci e rigati, *Capitolazione di Anna Maria Gerardi*, February 24, 1755.

[34] AST, SR, *Consolato di Commercio*, Costituti, m. 3, *Causa Days/Porta*, August 25, 1723.

[35] However, the catastrophic events surrounding the history of the Consulate of Commerce's archives—which were meant to preserve the records of apprentices, journeymen, and masters under the oversight of the central administration—have made it impossible to gain a realistic understanding of either the numbers or the social composition of this broader class of subordinate workers. These records undoubtedly existed at the time, as they were frequently cited in legal cases with references to registration numbers and pages. Yet, the documents themselves have been lost.

ment confirming the apprentice's training, allowing them to advance to the next stage: the journeyman phase. To formalize their status as a journeyman, the apprentice (or their patrons) had to pay a fee of 2 *lire* to the guild's treasury. Upon payment, their name was added to the journeyman register, marking their progression toward becoming a master (Duboin 1848, 323—June 10–18, 1739). However, for many, the journeyman phase was not just a transitional stage between apprenticeship and mastery, but rather the peak of their career. While Savoyard legislation prescribed a minimum period of three years, for some this phase lasted much longer, and for others, it ended only due to illness, old age, or death.

Nevertheless, exceptions to this process did exist: through royal privilege, granted upon formal petition, some apprentices could shorten their apprenticeship or skip the journeyman phase entirely. While this privilege was occasionally granted in private workshops, it was the standard at the Albergo di Virtù. In this institution, royal privilege was conferred directly to the establishment, where apprentices, upon completing a six-year apprenticeship, were deemed sufficiently skilled to pass the master's examination and formally join the guild. Although it is difficult to determine the total number of apprentices trained throughout the century, the Albergo's admission register shows that 1197 apprentices were accepted into the institution between January 1751 and May 1799.[36] The Albergo di Virtù had a significant impact on Piedmontese silk production. It is perhaps no coincidence that some of the few surviving artifacts of eighteenth-century Piedmontese silk manufacturing are pieces created by the Albergo's workshops, now housed in the Metropolitan Museum of Art in New York (Pictures 6.2, 6.3, and 6.4).

Widowed again after the death of Pietro Millori, her second husband, it was precisely to the Albergo di Virtù that Anna Maria Pajsio turned in 1746, requesting admission as a master silk weaver. Her case illustrates the disparity between the idealized image of guilds and the reality of professional life under the ancien régime. But let us take it one step at a time.

[36] Date of the last pupil accepted before the end of the century: the first pupil admitted in the nineteenth century entered the Albergo di Virtù in December 1801.

Picture 6.2 Silk and metal thread fabric produced in the Albergo di Virtù of Turin, Italy. 1716–1719. (*Source:* Metropolitan Museum of Art, New York. Friedsam Collection, #32.100.396. https://www.metmuseum.org/art/collection/search/222572)

4 Anna Maria: Outside the Ranks, Inside the Workforce

On the night of December 16, 1732, at the home of Pietro Michele Pajsio, Anna Maria's father, the atmosphere was tense and eventful. Throughout the night, the apartment on *contrada di Po* saw a series of visitors come and go. The first to arrive, alongside notary Perdomo, were relatives of Anna Maria's late first husband, Muratore, who returned the dowry she had brought to their marriage years earlier, valued at 500 *lire*.[37] A few hours later, at four in the morning, Pietro Millori arrived to finalize a new dowry contract. On this occasion, the same 500 *lire* were handed to Pietro, who, as part of the *augumento obnubitiale* (a customary matrimonial endowment), not only assigned his future wife some jewelry gifted

[37] AST, SR, *Insinuazione Torino*, 1733, v. 1, c. 854.

Picture 6.3 Silk and metal thread fabric produced in the Albergo di Virtù of Turin, Italy. 1716–1719. (*Source:* Metropolitan Museum of Art, New York. Davis Collection, #30.95.67. https://www.metmuseum.org/art/collection/search/222357)

during their engagement, but also gave her a financial settlement of 256 *lire* as well as the trousseau (*fardello*).[38] Furthermore, he promised that, in the event of his premature death, she would inherit "all his present and future belongings, including (…) the tools of his trade as a silk weaver."

And that is precisely what happened. When Pietro Millori died unexpectedly in the autumn of 1746, the couple's financial situation was precarious. The *post-mortem* inventory, compiled a few months after Pietro's death, listed only a handful of furnishings, weaving tools, debt notes from moneylenders, and records of charitable donations of low-quality garments to the navy. Despite these modest belongings, Anna Maria

[38] Among them were also two "roetti per l'arte da vellutaio," a type of spinning wheel used to prepare bobbins for silk weaving. AST, SR, *Insinuazione Torino*, 1733, v. 1, c. 854.

Picture 6.4 Silk and metal thread fabric produced in the Albergo di Virtù of Turin, Italy. 1716–1719. (*Source*: Metropolitan Museum of Art, New York. Davis Collection, #30.95.64. https://www.metmuseum.org/art/collection/search/222356)

managed to seize control of her social and financial circumstances, turning her life into a story of personal emancipation and resilience. With five looms, shuttles, spinning wheels, and combs at her disposal, she continued to work as a silk weaver, benefiting from the "widow's privilege." This widespread practice within the guild systems allowed widows to take over managing their late husband's workshop, ensuring their livelihood and professional continuity (Klapisch-Zuber 1990; Ogilvie 2003; Della Valentina 2003, 2012; Bellavitis 2005; Birriel Salcedo 2008).[39]

For decades now, the interplay between gender and work has been at the forefront of historiographical research (Clark 1919; Boserup 1970; Tilly and Scott 1978). By merging labor history with gender studies, scholars have highlighted the complex dynamics shaping this relationship. They have uncovered numerous nuances and specificities, including concepts like recognition and value (Scott 1986; Sarti et al. 2018; Bellavitis and Martinat 2022; Montenach 2022; Zucca Micheletto 2022)—while inevitably considering the framework of guild systems within the context of the ancien régime (Angers 1991). Between "decline theory" (Clark 1919) and "golden age theory" (Pinchbeck 1930)—which interpreted women's exit from domestic labor as either a loss of status or a potential path to emancipation—Judith Bennett's influential voice emerged in the 1980s. She argued that between the twelfth and nineteenth centuries, women continued to be confined to "traditionally feminine" professions and were consistently underpaid (Bennett 1988). In particular, Angela Groppi (1990, 1996) criticized the tendency of excluding women from guild structures during the ancien régime (Bellavitis 2021). Drawing on evidence from archival sources, Groppi demonstrated that this phenomenon followed an "accordion pattern," alternating periods of exclusion with moments of inclusion. According to this interpretation, women were most often excluded from the outer reaches of the guilds during times of economic crisis in the sectors where they worked (Groppi 1996; Bellavitis 2016, 2018, 2021; Pescarolo 2019).

The study of women's relationship to labor is a complex one. A key challenge lies in the sporadic documentation of their presence by institutions and guilds (Humphries and Sarasúa 2012; Groppi 1990; Bellavitis 2018a; Sarti et al. 2018; Criado Perez 2019). Census and tax records typically refer to women as mothers, wives, or daughters of workers and rarely as professionals in their own right (Chabot 1990; Guenzi 1990; Panciera 1990; Simon-Muscheid 1990; Groppi 1996; Bellavitis 2018a). Even when women are mentioned in professional contexts, their involvement is often not defined by their profession but rather by their familial role, reflecting the ongoing "being vs. doing" debate recently highlighted in the studies (Bellavitis 2016; 2018). In the case of the guilds associated with the Piedmontese silk industry, the first use of female-specific terms appears in

[39] AST, SR, *Insinuazione Torino*, 1746, v. 2, c. 225.

the May 17, 1687, Manifesto (Duboin 1848, 37 – May 17, 1687) outlining regulations for the silk industry, referring specifically to silk spinners and weavers. In the context of weaving, women were not recognized as workers in their own right, but only in their roles as relatives of a master craftsman. The law stated that this familial connection allowed men who married the daughter or widow of a master to gain access to the guild by paying only 6 *lire*, like other privileged figures such as sons of masters, instead of the usual 20 *lire* (Duboin 1849, 41–42 – May 17, 1687; Bellavitis 2016). Despite their culturally alleged "social inferiority" and exclusion from the status of master, women were still deemed capable of giving their future husbands not only a significant financial advantage in entering the guild, but also technical skills. Consulate records reveal several cases of women running workshops as early as the first decades of the eighteenth century. However, granting a woman—whether married or unmarried—permission to manage a workshop was not a public recognition of her artisanal skills; rather, it was a privilege extended by the sovereign, typically as an act of charity (Cerutti 1992; Allegra 2004).[40] Nevertheless, the "widows' privilege" was rooted in long-standing custom, with the practice of passing workshops to widows to allow them to continue working after their husbands' deaths. This practice implicitly assumed that they had mastered their husbands' trade during their marriage. In Turin, guild masters frequently attempted to restrict the professional opportunities of widows, often reporting to the Consulate their alleged inability to properly train apprentices. In 1739, they succeeded in excluding them from teaching roles, relegating them to managing workshops on their own (Duboin 1849, 323—June 10, 1739). Even with this change reflected in the guild statutes, the deep-seated sexist prejudice against women's ability to manage workshops persisted. A few years later, the guild masters petitioned the Consulate again, questioning the competence of around 20 widows who were members of the silk weavers' guild at the time (Rodríguez Gonzálvez 2011).[41]

Yet, despite these challenges, women were far from absent in workshops. On the contrary, their roles—though often invisible in official records—were at times crucial to production management. A striking

[40] AST, C, *Materie economiche*, Cat. IV, m. 7, fasc. 50, January 29, 1731.
[41] AST, C, *Materie economiche*, Cat. IV, m. 8, fasc. 13, 1740–1744.

example is Ludovica Barili, the wife of a master spinner.[42] Her prominence is evident from three lawsuits in which she appeared before the Consulate of Commerce. These records clearly show that she, not her husband, handled their spinning mill's management and business operations, even though she did not appear in the guild's documents and was illiterate. Whether recovering funds lost to minor silk thefts by an employee[43] or denouncing the mismanagement of the Royal Manufacture of Gold, Silver, and Silk Fabrics by the privileged merchants Gariglio and Charbonet, Ludovica consistently played a major role in the testimonies. Her husband Lorenzo, by contrast, appears only sporadically—and always in a subordinate role. In short, even if they had no formal recognition in official records and were illiterate and subjected to merchants' demands, women could indeed run workshops—and did so without necessarily submitting to abusive colleagues or suppliers. While historiography has for some time emphasized women's co-management of workshops (Bellavitis 2018), their presence in court records, attested in notarial and judicial sources, as Ågren suggests, may reflect a pragmatic division of labor (Ågren 2017).[44]

In workshops, moreover, female apprentices and workers were by no means uncommon. On the contrary, masters often preferred to hire women because they could be paid less—an explicitly gendered form of discrimination. Excluded from the higher ranks of the guild, women also posed no threat of future competition. For example, a petition submitted to the Consulate in 1741 records the complaints of silk weavers' journeymen, who reported that masters preferred to hire "a few male apprentices but many female ones, who take our places to our disadvantage. Indeed, women, whether they marry a weaver or not, will no longer be in a position to work or run a workshop."[45] Whether this objection reflected reality is unclear. However, inspection reports from 1744 reveal that, in March, women made up around 35% of the 471 journeymen and 50% of the 257 apprentices in the craft. By August, there were ten more female apprentices

[42] AST, SR, *Consolato di Commercio,* Costituti, m. 108, *Causa Barili/Gariglio e Charbonet,* September 11, 1711.

[43] AST, SR, *Consolato di Commercio,* Costituti, m. 107, *Causa Barili/Barberis,* June 3, 1709; June 7, 1709.

[44] While Ågren's linguistic approach offers valuable tools to trace women's economic agency in early modern sources, its reliance on formal, male-authored records may inadvertently reproduce the very boundaries it seeks to challenge—those that confine women's labor to domestic or auxiliary roles (Ågren 2018; Sarti et al. 2018).

[45] AST, C, *Materie economiche,* Cat. IV, m. 8, fasc. 21, 1741.

than male ones. Nevertheless, the fact that women were identified in records as apprentices or journeymen did not suggest they had any real prospects of advancing their careers. In weavers' households, women were expected to contribute to the workshop, but not necessarily or always at the loom. Records suggest that many women, broadly labeled as "weavers," actually earned their living as silk unwinders (*davanere*) or warpers (*licciarole*). The *davanere* prepared the shuttles destined for the loom (Picture 6.5), while the *licciarole* were responsible for setting up the looms (Picture 6.6). Although these roles did not appear in official documentation, they were crucial in weaving workshops, saving weavers valuable time and allowing them to focus on the later stages of fabric production. It is highly likely that Anna Maria Pajsio performed similar tasks while her husband was alive. Yet, after Pietro's death, thanks to the "widow's privilege" and the inherited weaving equipment—though only a fraction of her original dowry—she made her way to the gates of the Albergo di Virtù. There, she applied for admission to the board of the charitable institution as a master craftswoman. Her petition was granted, and in November 1746,

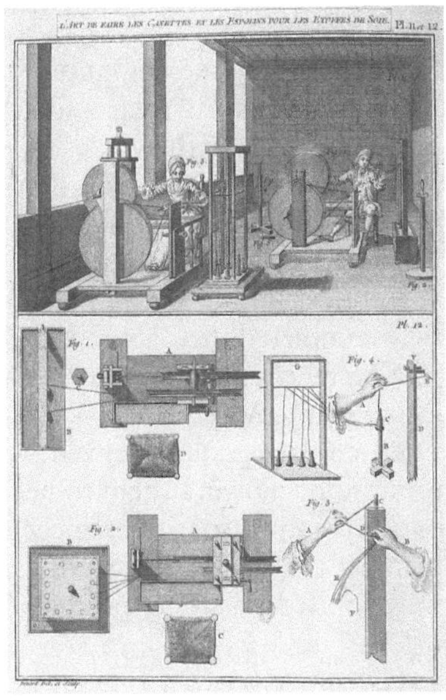

Picture 6.5 The work of the *davanera* and the perspective of the unwinding machine. (*Source*: Paulet 1773, *Planches* 11 and 12. Bibliothèque nationale de France. Gallica. https://gallica.bnf.fr/ark:/12148/bpt6k10671700)

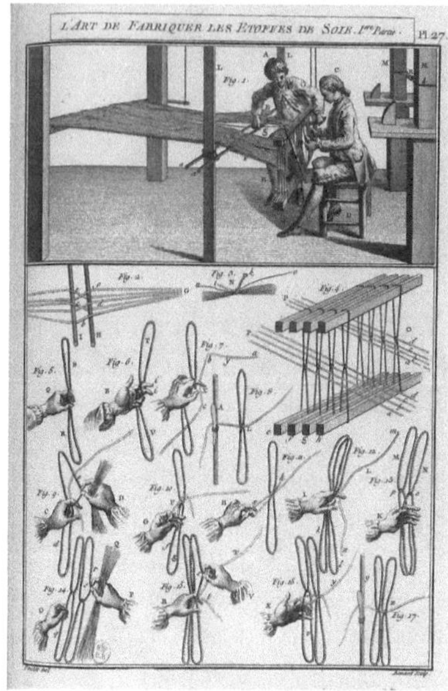

Picture 6.6 The work of the *licciarolo* and the necessary movements for the preparation of the heddles (*Source*: Paulet 1776, *Planche* 27. Bibliothèque nationale de France. Gallica. https://gallica.bnf.fr/ark:/12148/bpt6k1067192k)

Anna Maria was assigned two rooms within the charitable institution for life.[46] In return, she committed to training three apprentices in the art of silk weaving, paying each 4 soldi per day for the first five years and 5 soldi per day in the sixth, while also covering the maintenance costs of her accommodation. The workshop, referred to in all documents as "the widow Millori's workshop," officially opened in December 1746. Equipped with five looms and two apprentices, Anna Maria trained 13 apprentices during the first ten years. Of these, seven apprentices successfully completed their apprenticeships and advanced their careers.[47]

Nevertheless, Anna Maria's path took a new direction upon the publication of the May 17, 1754, edict (Duboin 1848, 844—May 17, 1754). The new law granted female weavers access to the highest rank in the profession, allowing them to become masters without needing to be widows or request special privileges. Although excluded from the management of the guild, they were granted teaching roles, even though these were limited to taffeta production. The purpose of this measure was to

[46] AST, SR, *Insinuazione Torino*, 1747, v. 2, c. 36.

[47] AST, SR, *Regio Albergo di Virtù*, Diari dei mastri, m. 218–219, 1746–1757; APSA, *Università dei mastri vellutai*, v. 4, 1677–1795.

boost the workforce dedicated to weaving silk taffeta, a fabric that was not only highly lucrative but also labor-intensive to produce uniformly (Molà 2000; Styles 2019; Groppi 2021). To achieve the rank of master, applicants had to be at least 18 years old, submit a formal request to the Consulate, provide a certificate of good moral conduct from their parish priest, prove they had completed at least three years of apprenticeship, and pass a professional examination. Once granted their printed license by the Consulate, they were officially recognized as master craftswomen.[48] Consequently, the second half of the eighteenth century marked a brand-new chapter in Anna Maria's life. From 1754 onward, her workshop welcomed not only the male weaving apprentices but also young female taffeta-weaving apprentices, as shown by the documents related to the examinations required to become master craftswomen—but not in records associated with the Albergo di Virtù.[49]

Moreover, through social connections likely related to her involvement with the charitable institution, Anna Maria met Vittorio Amedeo Boeri, a lieutenant in the army of the King of Sardinia. At the age of 47, she married him, making it her third marriage.[50] Over her decade of activity within the charitable institution, Anna Maria had managed to build a considerable personal fortune. This is evident from the substantial dowry of 15,000 *lire* that she "secured for herself, her heirs, and successors," a significant leap from the 500 *lire* her father had provided for her first two marriages.[51] Little is known about the couple's life together: both were widowed, and Boeri had a daughter from his previous marriage. Furthermore, by the 1770s, Anna Maria's life intersected with that of her niece, Rosa Orsola, the daughter of her brother Domenico Pajsio. Also a weaver, Domenico had fallen into poverty during the 1760s and entrusted his eight-year-old daughter to Anna Maria's care.[52] Consulate records reveal that Rosa Orsola worked with her aunt in taffeta production for five years, from

[48] APSA, *Università dei mastri vellutai*, v. 3, May 17, 1754; AST, SR, *Consolato di Commercio*, m. 66 Fabbricatori di taffetà lisci e rigati, 1754–1783; m. 67, 1783–1798.

[49] AST, SR, *Regio Albergo di Virtù*, Diari dei mastri, m. 218–224, 1746–1782.

[50] AST, SR, *Insinuazione Torino*, 1759, v. 10, c. 103.

[51] AST, SR, *Insinuazione Torino*, 1726, v. 6, c. 1077; 1733, v. 1, c. 854; 1759, v. 10, c. 103.

[52] ASCT, *Ospedale di Carità*, Libri delle informazioni, v. 13, c. 329, *Richiesta di Domenico Pajsio*, June 26, 1766.

Picture 6.7 Certificate of admission to the profession of silk taffeta weaver of Rosa Pajsio. The text states that Rosa worked in the workshop of the master silk weaver Mrs. Marianna Boeri—i.e., Anna Maria Pajsio. (Source: AST, SR, *Consolato di Commercio*, m. 66, Fabbricatori di taffetà lisci e rigati, *Patente di Rosa Pajsio*, April 27, 1781. Courtesy of the State Archives of Turin)

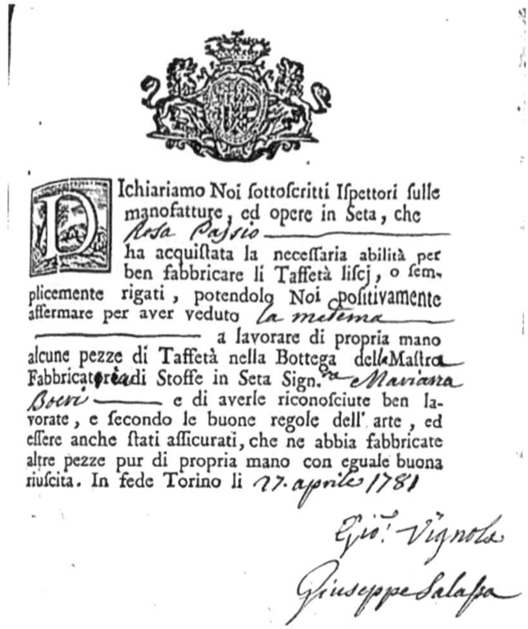

DIchiariamo Noi ſottoſcritti Iſpettori ſulle manofatture, ed opere in Seta, che Rosa Pajsio ha acquiſtata la neceſſaria abilità per ben fabbricare li Taffetà liſcj, o ſemplicemente rigati, potendolo Noi poſitivamente affermare per aver veduto la medema a lavorare di propria mano alcune pezze di Taffetà nella Bottega della Maſtra Fabbricatrice di Stoffe in Seta Sign.ra Marianna Boeri e di averle riconoſciute ben lavorate, e ſecondo le buone regole dell' arte, ed eſſere anche ſtati aſſicurati, che ne abbia fabbricate altre pezze pur di propria mano con eguale buona riuſcita. In fede Torino li 27. aprile 1781

Gio. Vignola

Giuseppe Salassa

approximately 1776 to 1781. That year, at the age of 19, she successfully entered the guild as a master craftswoman (Picture 6.7).[53]

5 Conclusions

The bond between aunt and niece, already strong during Rosa Orsola's childhood, deepened over the years through their constant collaboration in the workshop. This close relationship inspired Anna Maria to decide to bequeath her workshop to Rosa Orsola, hoping to help her niece secure a respectable dowry and a promising marriage.[54] Records of this decision reveal that, at its peak, Anna Maria's workshop had two looms for taffeta production (valued at 76 *lire*), two looms for satin (107 *lire*), a fifth unused loom (10 *lire*), a vertical warping machine (60 *lire*), and numerous other weaving tools (427 *lire*). The dowry, however, was to be disbursed

[53] AST, SR, *Consolato di Commercio*, m. 66 Fabbricatori di taffetà lisci e rigati, *Patente di Rosa Pajsio*, May 2, 1781.

[54] AST, SR, *Insinuazione Torino*, 1782, v. 6, c. 547; 1783, v. 1, c. 1603; 1789, v. 9, c. 1121.

only after Anna Maria's death and only if Rosa Orsola could cover the expenses of her aunt's burial (Grassi 2023).

Unfortunately, Anna Maria's plans did not come to fruition. The silk industry crisis between 1789 and 1792, her advancing age, and the financial strain caused by the need for treatments for her recurring illnesses forced her to rewrite her will. In this new version, she revoked the bequest of the workshop to her niece, named her husband as her sole heir, and significantly reduced the provisions for her burial and memorial.[55] While Rosa Orsola disappears from the historical record, Anna Maria's journey continued for a few more years. By 1794, at the age of 82, she was once again widowed and blind. In that year, she decided to name her stepdaughter Teresa as her universal heir before vanishing from the records altogether.[56]

Anna Maria's story is emblematic of pathways documented across Italian and European contexts. In its specificity, it challenges simplified pictures of labor under the ancien régime from multiple angles, making her one among countless untold narratives preserved in the dusty silence of the archives. Through the seamless intertwining of her private and professional lives, Anna Maria's mastery of silk weaving and leadership of a weaving workshop established her as a respected expert in her field. This expertise, likely coupled with considerable skills, enabled her acceptance into the Albergo di Virtù, one of the main luxury manufacturing institutions in ancien régime Turin.

The expertise Anna Maria acquired was not rooted in the traditional training paths characteristic of guild life during the ancien régime. Her knowledge was developed through unconventional paths, learned informally while working alongside her second husband. These skills were passed down by Pietro Millori. He was a second-generation immigrant who, thanks to the aspirations and technical expertise of his father Pierre—an ambitious French artisan—and the standardized training he received in Turin, managed to establish his own business. He successfully integrated into a social and economic system where loyalty in craftsmanship was a cornerstone for securing commissions—and, ultimately, work. Anna Maria's skills emerged in a unique production context to which, ultimately, she did not formally belong.

[55] AST, SR, *Insinuazione Torino*, 1792, v. 6, c. 1033.

[56] AST, SR, *Insinuazione Torino*, 1794, v. 10, c. 330.

Yet Anna Maria's expertise granted her access to exclusive privileges. It enabled her to train the next generation of master weavers—and, from the 1750s onward, female master weavers. These skills were woven into the warps of the looms she inherited from Millori and were meant, at least, to shape the future of her niece Rosa Orsola. In doing so, Anna Maria sought to replicate, in a feminine form, the dynamics traditionally associated with the "son of the trade," a cornerstone of the upper ranks of the guilds (De Munck 2017). While guilds in Turin, as in many other Italian and European cities, were formally closed and exclusionary, Anna Maria Pajsio's case demonstrates that within these rigid structures, certain spaces for freedom existed—albeit grounded in privilege.

In conclusion, Anna Maria's life experience calls for a reassessment of professional training during the ancien régime. The overlap between guild membership and the acquisition of know-how was, at best, partial—especially when considering the role of women in artisan workshops and their capacity to transfer knowledge, even without formal recognition as "masters" (Wallis 2019, 2025; De Munck 2022; Garrioch 2022; Hidalgo Fernández and Nieto Sánchez 2024). Even when women were eventually granted the title of master, they could still not access the same rights as their male counterparts. The transfer of know-how, in fact, transcended social variables such as gender or age. However, within the institutional framework of guilds, it became a tool of power. If productive labor for the market is seen as a social construct—designed by society to meet its own needs—it becomes clear that possessing or lacking professional skills was a decisive element. Whether kneading bread, planting a fruit tree, or weaving a luxurious brocade, these market-driven activities demanded specific expertise, from mastering techniques that reduced waste while maximizing raw material efficiency to performing complex tasks swiftly and skillfully (Quintini 2014; Brunello and Wruuck 2021; Deming and Silliman 2024). Those lacking such skills were inevitably subject to the authority of those who possessed them. This power dynamic could manifest itself in countless ways, often involving physical or psychological violence (Caracausi 2014; Zucca Micheletto 2020a, 2020b). During guild training, it also granted those imparting knowledge the ability to shape apprentices' opportunities or place restraints on them in the future, emphasizing how the study of guilds reveals them not merely as training-focused institutions, but rather as mechanisms for market control, power enforcement, and the perpetuation of social hierarchies.

Bibliography

Ago, Renata. 1998. *Economia barocca. Mercato e istituzioni nella Roma del Seicento.* Rome: Donzelli.

Ågren, Maria, ed. 2017. *Making a living, making a difference. Gender and work in early modern European society.* Oxford: Oxford University Press.

Ågren, Maria. 2018. The complexities of work: analyzing men's and women's work in the early modern world with the verb-oriented method. In *What is work? Gender at the crossroads of home, family, and business from the early modern era to the present*, ed. Raffaella Sarti, Anna Bellavitis, and Manuela Martini, 226–242. New York-Oxford: Berghahn.

Allegra, Luciano. 1987. *La città verticale. Usurai, mercanti e tessitori nella Chieri del Cinquecento.* Milan: FrancoAngeli.

Allegra, Luciano. 2004. Fra norma e deroga. Il mercato del lavoro a Torino nel Settecento. *Rivista storica italiana* 116:872–925.

Allegra, Luciano. 2005. Un modèle de mobilité sociale préindustrielle Turin à l'époque napoléonienne. *Annales. Histoire, Sciences Sociales* 60 (2): 443–474.

Angers, Denise. 1991. Le rôle de la famille et la place de la femme dans l'organisation du travail en Allemagne à la fin du Moyen Âge, bilan historiographique. In *Travail et travailleurs au Moyen Âge et au début des temps modernes*, ed. Claire Dolan, 63–78. Toronto: Pontifical Institute of Mediaeval Studies.

Balani, Donatella, Eric Monkkonen, and Geoffrey Symcox. 2005. *Census of Turin, Italy, 1705.* Inter-university Consortium for Political and Social Research, 2005-12-15.

Bellavitis, Anna. 2005. "Et vedoando sia donna et Madonna". Guardianship and remarriage in early modern Venice. In *Favoured and less favoured in law and legal practice: Gender, power and authority 12th–19th centuries*, ed. Grethe Jacobsen, Helle Vogt, Inger Dübeck, and Heide Wunder. Copenhagen: Royal Danish Library.

Bellavitis, Anna. 2016. *Il lavoro delle donne nelle città dell'Europa moderna.* Rome: Viella.

Bellavitis, Anna. 2018a. *Women's work and rights in early modern urban Europe.* Cham: Palgrave Macmillan.

Bellavitis, Anna. 2018b. Stepfamilies and inclusive families in early modern Venice. In *Stepfamilies in Europe, 1400–1800*, ed. Lyndan Warner, 56–72. London: Routledge.

Bellavitis, Anna. 2021. Arricchire i questionari: la storia del lavoro di Angela Groppi. *Genesis* 20 (2): 13–25.

Bellavitis, Anna, and Monica Martinat. 2022. Il valore delle donne. Saggio introduttivo. *Genesis* 21 (2): 7–14.

Bellavitis, Anna, and Valentina Sapienza, eds. 2023. *Apprenticeship, work, society in early modern Venice*. London-New York: Routledge.
Bennett, Judith M. 1988. "History that stands still": Women's work in the European past. *Feminist Studies* 14 (21): 269–283.
Bertucci, Paola. 2021. Spinners' hands, imperial minds: Migrant labour, embodied expertise, and the failed transfer of silk technology across the Atlantic. *Technology and Culture* 62 (4): 1003–1031.
Birriel Salcedo, Margarita M. 2008. Introducción. Sobrevivir al cónyuge: viudas y viudedad en la España Moderna. *Chronica nova: Revista de historia moderna de la Universidad de Granada* 34:7–12.
Bizzarri, Giulio. 2011. Un contratto di apprendistato/servitù domestica femminile di area lucchese della prima metà del secolo XIII. *Bullettino Storico Pistoiese* 113:177–190.
Borelli, Giovanni Battista. 1681. *Editti antichi e nuovi de' Sovrani Prencipi della Real Casa di Savoia, delle loro Tutrici, e de' Magistrati di qua da' Monti*. Turin: Zappata.
Boserup, Ester. 1970. *Women's role in economic development*. New York: St. Martin's Press.
Brunello, Giorgio, and Patricia Wruuck. 2021. Skill shortages and skill mismatch: A review of the literature. *Journal of Economic Surveys* 35 (4): 1145–1167.
Caracausi, Andrea. 2014. Beaten children and women's work in early modern Italy. *Past and Present* 222 (1): 95–128.
Caracausi, Andrea, and Corine Maitte. 2020. Les institutions charitables comme lieux de travail, XVe-XVIIIe siècle. *Mediterranea. Ricerche Storiche* 48:83–96.
Caracausi, Andrea, and Luca Mocarelli. 2022. Salari e standard di vita in età pre-industriale. *Economia & Lavoro* 56 (2): 31–43.
Caracausi, Andrea, Nicoletta Rolla, and Marco Schnyder, eds. 2018. *Travail et mobilité en Europe (XVIe-XIXe siècles)*. Villeneuve d'Ascq: Presses Universitaires du Septentrion.
Carling, Jørgen, and Francis Leo Collins. 2018. Aspiration, desire and drivers of migration. *Journal of Ethnic and Migration Studies* 44 (6): 909–926.
Carpanetto, Dino. 2014. *Nomadi della fede. Ugonotti, ribelli e profeti tra Sei e Settecento*. Turin: Claudiana.
Cavaciocchi, Simonetta, ed. 1994. *Le migrazioni in Europa secc. XIII-XVIII*. Florence: Le Monnier.
Cenedella, Cristina, and Gianpiero Fumi, eds. 2015. *Oltre l'assistenza: lavoro e formazione professionale negli istituti per l'infanzia irregolare in Italia tra Sette e Novecento*. Milan: Vita e Pensiero.
Cerutti, Simona. 1992. *Mestieri e Privilegi. Nascita delle corporazioni a Torino (secoli XVII-XVIII)*. Turin: Einaudi.
Cerutti, Simona, and Carlo Poni. 1990. Per un numero di Quaderni Storici sui conflitti nel mondo del lavoro. *Quaderni Storici* 25 (3): 983–985.

Chabot, Isabelle. 1990. La reconnaissance du travail des femmes dans la Florence du bas Moyen Âge: contexte idéologique et réalité. In *La donna nell'economia, secc. XIII-XVIII*, ed. Simonetta Cavaciocchi, 563–576. Florence: Le Monnier.

Chase, Malcolm. 2017. *Early trade unionism. Fraternity, skill and the politics of labour*. London-New York: Routledge.

Chilese, Valeria. 2012. *I mestieri e la città: le corporazioni veronesi tra XV e XVIII secolo*. Milan: FrancoAngeli.

Clark, Alice. 1919. *Working life of women in the seventeenth century*. London: Routledge.

Collins, Francis Leo. 2018. Desire as a theory for migration studies: Temporality, assemblage and becoming in the narratives of migrants. *Journal of Ethnic and Migration Studies* 44 (6): 964–980.

Comba, Rinaldo. 1988. *Contadini signori e mercanti nel Piemonte medievale*. Rome-Bari: Laterza.

Consterdine, Erica. 2018. *Labour's immigration policy*. Cham: Palgrave Macmillan.

Criado Perez, Caroline. 2019. *Invisible women: Exposing bias in a world designed for men*. London: Chatto and Windus.

Dambruyne, Johan. 1998. Guilds, social mobility and status in sixteenth-century Ghent. *International Review of Social History* 43 (1): 31–78.

Davids, Karel, and Bert De Munck, eds. 2014. *Innovation and creativity in late medieval and early modern European cities*. London-New York: Routledge.

De Haas, Hein. 2021. A theory of migration: The aspirations-capabilities framework. *Comparative Migration Studies* 9 (1): 8.

De Munck, Bert. 2017. *Guilds, labour and the urban body politic. Fabricating Community in the Southern Netherlands, 1300–1800*. London-New York: Routledge.

De Munck, Bert. 2022. Shared skills and Technologies of Community Formation. Artisanal Epistemologies, secrecy and governmentality in long-term context. In *The republic of skill. Artisan mobility, innovation, and the circulation of knowledge in Premodern Europe*, ed. David Garrioch, 35–64. Leiden-Boston: Brill.

Della Valentina, Marcello. 2003. *I tessitori di seta a Venezia nel Settecento*. Padua: Cleup.

Della Valentina, Marcello. 2012. "Parone": donne alla guida di una bottega artigiana a Venezia nel '700. In *Donne, lavoro, economia a Venezia e in Terraferma tra medioevo ed età moderna*, ed. Anna Bellavitis and Linda Guzzetti, 145–159. Venice: Deputazione di Storia Patria per le Venezie.

Deming, David J., & Mikko I. Silliman. 2024. Skills and human capital in the labour market. *NBER Working Paper* 32908

Di Bari, Aldo G. 2019. Inserimento ed esclusione dei forestieri negli statuti delle corporazioni bolognesi (secoli XIII-XV). *I quaderni del m.æ.s.* 17 (1): 70–102.
Dolza, Luisa. 2007. Utilitas et delectatio: libri di tecniche e teatri di macchine. In *Il Rinascimento italiano e l'Europa. Produzione e tecniche*, ed. Philippe Braunstein and Luca Molà, 115–144. Costabissara: Colla.
Duboin, Felice Amato. 1848. *Raccolta per ordine di materie delle leggi cioè editti, patenti, manifesti, ecc. emanate negli stati di terraferma sino all'8 dicembre 1798 dai sovrani della real casa di Savoja*, t. 15, v. 17. Turin: Baricco ed Arnaldi
Duboin, Felice Amato. 1849. *Raccolta per ordine di materie delle leggi cioè editti, patenti, manifesti, ecc. emanate negli stati di terraferma sino all'8 dicembre 1798 dai sovrani della real casa di Savoja*, t. 16, v. 18. Turin: Baricco ed Arnaldi
Dupâquier, Jacques. 1994. Macro-émigrations en Europe (xvie-xviiie siècle). In *Le migrazioni in Europa secc. XIII-XVIII*, ed. Simonetta Cavaciocchi, 67–90. Florence: Le Monnier.
Ehmer, Josef. 2011. Quantifying mobility in early modern Europe: The challenge of concepts and data. *Journal of Global History* 6 (2): 327–338.
Ehmer, Josef. 2023. Wage labour as a life phase: Life-cycle service and petty commodity production in early modern Europe. In *Life course, work, and labour in global history*, ed. Josef Ehmer and Carola Lentz, 359–388. De Gruyter Oldenbourg.
Ehmer, Josef, and Carola Lentz, eds. 2023. *Life course, work, and labour in global history*. Berlin/Boston: De Gruyter Oldenbourg.
Epstein, Steve A. 1991. *Wage labor and guilds in medieval Europe*. Chapel Hill-London: The University of North Carolina Press.
Epstein, Stephan R., and Maarten Prak, eds. 2008. *Guilds, innovation and the European economy, 1400–1800*. Cambridge: Cambridge University Press.
Erdal, Marta B., and Ceri Oeppen. 2018. Forced to leave? The discursive and analytical significance of describing migration as forced and voluntary. *Journal of Ethnic and Migration Studies* 44 (6): 981–998.
Farr, James R. 2000. *Artisans in Europe, 1300–1914*. Cambridge: Cambridge University Press.
Feci, Simona, and Laura Schettini, eds. 2017. *La violenza contro le donne nella storia. Contesti, linguaggi, politiche del diritto (secoli XV-XXI)*. Rome: Viella.
Ferrer-Alòs, Llorenç. 2022. El gremio cuando interesa. Producción y comercialización de pañuelos de seda en Manresa (Cataluña) en el siglo XVIII. *Studia Historica: Historia Moderna* 44 (1): 409–444.
Filipović, Jovan, Srečko Devjak, and Goran Putnik. 2012. Knowledge-based economy: The role of expert diaspora. *Panoeconomicus* 59 (3): 369–386.
Fontaine, Laurence. 2005. Montagnes et migrations de travail. Un essai de comparaison globale (XVe-XXe siècles). *Revue d'histoire moderne & contemporaine* 52 (2): 26–48.

Franceschi, Franco, and Luca Molà. 2018. Discriminazione, sopraffazione, violenza nel mondo del lavoro. In *Violenza alle donne. Una prospettiva medievale*, ed. Anna Esposito, Franco Franceschi, and Gabriella Piccinni, 57–84. Bologna: Il Mulino.

Fratini, Marco. 2021. Les vaudois dans la propagande visuelle des Provinces-Unies à la fin du XVIIe siècle. *Revue d'histoire du protestantisme* 6 (4): 401–440.

Garrioch, David, ed. 2022. *The republic of skill. Artisan mobility, innovation, and the circulation of knowledge in Premodern Europe*. Leiden-Boston: Brill.

Gietel-Basten, Stuart. 2020. Circular visualisation of historical migration in England in the long eighteenth-century. *Heliyon* 6 (11): e05490.

Grassi, Mario. 2023. "Nulla sendovi più certo che la morte". Lettura e interpretazione della vita artigianale nella Torino d'ancien régime attraverso i documenti del fondo Insinuazione. In *La vita in atto. Donazioni, lasciti, testamenti tra Torino e Italia settentrionale (secoli XVI-XVIII)*, ed. Anna Cantaluppi and Blythe Alice Raviola, 241–260. Florence: Olschki.

Grassi, Mario. 2024. A delicate equilibrium: State projects, guild dynamics, and personal interests in silk weaving in ancient regime (Turin, eighteenth century). In *A global history of silk. Trade and production from the 16th to the mid-20th century*, ed. Pierre Vernus, Manuela Martini, and Tomoko Hashino, 97–118. Cham: Springer.

Grassi, Mario. 2026. The Main Purpose: Bargaining, Wages, and Gender in the Eighteenth-Century Piedmontese Silk Manufacture. *A Historical Casebook of Wage Formation. Wage Determination and Wage Bargains, 1500–1950* eds. Giulio Ongaro, Judy Z. Stephenson, and Luca Mocarelli, 41–146. Cham: Palgrave Macmillan.

Groppi, Angela. 1990. Il lavoro delle donne: un questionario da arricchire. In *La donna nell'economia, secc. XIII-XVIII*, ed. Simonetta Cavaciocchi, 143–154. Florence: Le Monnier.

Groppi, Angela, ed. 1996. *Il lavoro delle donne*. Rome-Bari: Laterza.

Groppi, Angela. 2021. La transmission d'un métier et l'exercice d'un travail: limites et avantages de genre (Rome, XVIIe-XVIIIe siècle). *Clio. Femmes, Genre, Histoire* 54:233–245.

Guenzi, Alberto. 1990. La tessitura femminile tra città e campagna. Bologna, secoli XVII-XVIII. In *La donna nell'economia secc. XIII-XVIII*, ed. Simonetta Cavaciocchi, 248–259. Florence: Le Monnier.

Hafter, Daryl M. 2007. *Women at work in preindustrial France*. Philadelphia: University of Pennsylvania Press.

Hatcher, John, and Judy Z. Stephenson, eds. 2018. *Seven centuries of unreal wages. The unreliable data, sources and methods that have been used for measuring standards of living in the past*. Cham: Palgrave Macmillan.

Henrich, Eureka, and Julian M. Simpson, eds. 2019. *History, historians and the immigration debate. Going Back to where we came from*. Cham: Palgrave Macmillan.
Hidalgo Fernández, Francisco, and José Antolín Nieto Sánchez, eds. 2024. *Artesanos. Una historia social en España (siglos XVI-XIX)*. Ciudad Real: Ediciones de la Universidad de Castilla-La Mancha.
Hilaire-Pérez, Liliane, and Catherine Verna. 2006. Dissemination of technical knowledge in the Middle Ages and the early modern era: New approaches and methodological issues. *Technology and Culture* 47 (3): 536–565.
Hobsbawm, Eric J. 1984. Artisan or labour aristocrat? *The Economic History Review* 37 (3): 355–372.
Hornung, Erik. 2014. Immigration and the diffusion of technology: The Huguenot diaspora in Prussia. *American Economic Review* 104 (1): 84–122.
Humphries, Jane, and Carmen Sarasúa. 2012. Off the record: Reconstructing women's labor force participation in the European past. *Feminist Economics* 18 (4): 39–67.
Kaplan, Steve Laurence, and Cynthia J. Koepp, eds. 1986. *Work in France. Representations, meaning, organization, and practice*. Ithaca, NY: Cornell University Press.
Kershen, Anne. 2005. *Strangers, Aliens and Asians. Huguenots, Jews and Bangladeshis in Spitalfields 1666–2000*. London: Routledge.
Klapisch-Zuber, Christiane. 1990. La mère cruelle. Maternité, veuvage et dot. In *La maison et le nom. Stratégies et rituels dans l'Italie de la Renaissance edited by Christiane Klapisch-Zuber*, 249–261. Paris: Éditions de l'École des hautes études en sciences sociales.
Kolrud, Kristine. 2014. The Waldensians and the Piedmontese Easter of 1655. In *Iconoclasm from antiquity to modernity*, ed. Kristine Kolrud and Marina Prusac, 139–151. London-New York: Routledge.
Lane, Joan. 1996. *Apprenticeship in England, 1600–1914*. London: UCL Press.
Laudani, Simona. 2006. Apprenties ou jeunes salariées ? Parcours de formation dans les métiers de Catane (XVIIIe -XIXe siècles). *Histoire Urbaine* 15 (1): 13–25.
Leti, Gregorio. 1675. *L'Italia Regnante*. In *ò Vero Nova Descritione Dello Stato presente di tutti Prencipati, e Republiche d'Italia II*. Geneva: De la Pietra.
Levi, Giovanni. 1985. *Centro e periferia di uno Stato assoluto. Tre saggi su Piemonte e Liguria in età moderna*. Turin: Rosenberg & Sellier.
Lodigiani, Elisabetta. 2008. Diaspora externalities and technology diffusion. *Économie internationale* 115:43–64.
Maitte, Corine. 2009. *Les chemins de verre. Les migrations des verriers d'Altare et de Venise (XVIe-XIXe siècles)*. Rennes: Presses universitaires de Rennes.
Maitte, Corine. 2021. Rémunérer et compter le travail sur les chantiers Médicis (fin xvie siècle-début xviie siècle). *Histoire & Mesure* 36 (1): 3–36.

Maitte, Corine, and Philippe Rygiel. 2017. Mobilités et travail. *Historiens et géographes* 438:71–79.

Manieri, Flavio, and Luca Sciarretta. 2011. Mutamenti socioeconomici e variazioni normative dell'apprendistato. *Quaderni di Tecnostruttura* 43:7–11.

Mazzaoui, Fennel Maureen. 1981. *The italian cotton industry in the later Middle Ages. 1100–1600.* Cambridge: Cambridge University Press.

McCray, Patrick W. 1999. *Glassmaking in Renaissance Venice.* London-New York: Routledge.

Mocarelli, Luca. 2018. What is wrong with the history of wages: Or the divide in economic history—A reappraisal suggested by eighteenth-century Milan. In *Seven centuries of unreal wages. The unreliable data, sources and methods that have been used for measuring standards of living in the past*, ed. John Hatcher and Judy Z. Stephenson, 95–109. Cham: Palgrave Macmillan.

Molà, Luca. 2000. *The silk industry of Renaissance Venice.* Baltimore-London: Johns Hopkins University Press.

Montenach, Anne. 2022. Il valore del lavoro delle donne: conflitti sulle retribuzioni nella Grande Fabrique lionese nel XVIII secolo. *Genesis* 21 (2): 43–63.

Morra, Lucia, and Carla Bazzanella. 2002. Considerazioni sul buon padre di famiglia. *Rivista Critica del Diritto Privato* 20:529–563.

Murdoch, Tessa. 2021. *Europe divided: Huguenot refugee art and culture.* London: V&A Publishing.

Newton, Hannah. 2012. *The sick child in early modern England, 1580–1720.* Oxford: Oxford University Press.

Nicholson, Annalisa, and Christophe Gillain. 2025. Introduction: Exile and innovation. *Renaissance Studies* 39 (1): 8–25.

Nieto Sánchez, José Antolín. 2025. *La rama ignorada del saber: El aprendizaje artesano en Castilla durante el siglo XVI.* Ciudad Real: Ediciones de la Universidad de Castilla-La Mancha.

Nieto Sánchez, José Antolín, and Juan Carlos Zofío Llorente. 2015. Los gremios de Madrid durante la Edad Moderna: una revisión. *Áreas 34:47–61.*

Ogilvie, Sheilagh. 2003. *A bitter living: Women, markets, and social capital in early modern Germany.* Oxford: Oxford University Press.

Ogilvie, Sheilagh. 2011. *Institutions and European trade: Merchant guilds, 1000–1800.* Cambridge: Cambridge University Press.

Ogilvie, Sheilagh. 2019. *The European guilds: an economic analysis.* Princeton-Oxford: Princeton University Press.

Panciera, Walter. 1990. Emarginazione femminile tra politica salariale e modelli di organizzazione del lavoro nell'industria tessile veneta nel XVIII secolo. In *La donna nell'economia, secc. XIII-XVIII*, ed. Simonetta Cavaciocchi, 585–596. Florence: Le Monnier.

Pascal, Arturo. 1927. La tolleranza religiosa in Piemonte al tempo di Vittorio Amedeo II. *Bollettino della Società di Studi Valdesi* 50:99–131.

Pascal, Arturo. 1937. Notizie e documenti sulla Colonia Protestante di Torino nella prima metà del secolo XVIII. *Bollettino della Società di Studi Valdesi* 67:11–62.

Paulet, Jean. 1773. L'art du fabriquant d'étoffes de soie, section 3–4. Paris: Delatour

Paulet, Jean. 1776. L'art du fabriquant d'étoffes de soie, section 7, partie 1. Paris: Delatour

Pescarolo, Alessandra. 2019. *Il lavoro delle donne nell'Italia contemporanea.* Rome: Viella.

Pettegree, Andrew. 1994. Protestant migration during the early modern period. In *Le migrazioni in Europa secc. XIII-XVIII*, ed. Simonetta Cavaciocchi, 441–458. Florence: Le Monnier.

Pinchbeck, Ivy. 1930. *Work: Women workers and the industrial revolution, 1750–1850.* London: Routledge.

Prak, Maarten, and Patrick Wallis, eds. 2020. *Apprenticeship in early modern Europe.* Cambridge: Cambridge University Press.

Prak, Maarten, and Patrick Wallis. 2023. Transferring useful knowledge: Quality mechanisms in European apprenticeship. In *L'economia della conoscenza: Innovazione, produttività e crescita economica nei secoli XIII-XVIII*, ed. Giampiero Nigro, 177–192. Florence: Firenze University Press.

Prak, Maarten, Catharina Lis, Jan Lucassen, and Hugo Soly. 2006. *Craft guilds in the early modern low countries. Work, power, and representation.* Aldershot: Ashgate.

Prato, Giuseppe. 1908. *La vita economica in Piemonte a mezzo il secolo XVIII.* Turin: Società Tipografico-Editrice Nazionale.

Quintini, Glenda. 2014. Skills at work: How skills and their use matter in the labour market. *OECD Social, Employment and Migration Working Papers* 158:1–62.

Rainbird, Helen. 1997. The social construction of skill. In *Education and work in Great Britain, Germany and Italy*, ed. Annette Jobert, Catherine Marry, Helen Rainbird, and Lucie Tanguy, 177–189. London-New York: Routledge.

Ray, Debraj. 2006. Aspirations, poverty, and economic change. In *Understanding Poverty*, ed. Abhijit Vinayak Banerjee, Roland Bénabou, and Dilip Mookherjee, 409–421. Oxford: Oxford University Press.

Richards, Eric. 2018. *The genesis of international mass migration. The British case, 1750–1900.* Manchester: Manchester University Press.

Rodríguez Gonzálvez, Francisco Jorge. 2011. *Seda y Lógica Comunitaria: Evolución legal e institucional de los gremios sederos en Murcia durante los siglos XVI-XIX.* Murcia: EDITUM.

Romagnani, Gian Paolo. 2002. Presenze protestanti a Torino fra Sei e Settecento. In *Storia di Torino V*, ed. Giuseppe Ricuperati, 423–451. Turin: Einaudi.

Romagnani, Gian Paolo. 2021. *"Religionari". Protestanti e valdesi nel Piemonte del Settecento.* Turin: Claudiana.

Romagnani, Gian Paolo. 2023. La presenza dei protestanti in città e lo sviluppo imprenditoriale nel Settecento. *Studi Emigrazione* 60:573–589.

Rosenband, Leonard N. 1999. Social Capital in the Early Industrial Revolution. *Journal of Interdisciplinary History* 29 (3): 435–457.

Rosso, Claudio. 2002. Uomini e poteri nella Torino barocca (1630–1675). In *Storia di Torino IV. La città fra crisi e ripresa (1630–1730)*, ed. Giuseppe Ricuperati, 7–195. Turin: Einaudi.

Ruff, Julius R. 2001. *Violence in early modern Europe 1500–1800.* Cambridge: Cambridge University Press.

Salazar, Noel B. 2023. Mobile places and emplaced mobilities: Problematizing the place-mobility nexus. *Mobilities* 18 (4): 582–592.

Sarti, Raffaella, Anna Bellavitis, and Manuela Martini, eds. 2018. *What is work? Gender at the crossroads of home, family, and business from the early modern era to the present.* New York-Oxford: Berghahn.

Schäfer, Dagmar, Annapurna Mamidipudi, and Marius Burning, eds. 2023. *Ownership of knowledge: Beyond intellectual property.* Cambridge, Massachusetts: MIT Press.

Schalk, Ruben. 2017. From orphan to artisan: Apprenticeship careers and contract enforcement in the Netherlands before and after the guild abolition. *The Economic History Review* 70 (3): 730–757.

Schulz, Knut. 2007. La migrazione di tecnici, artigiani e artisti. In *Il Rinascimento italiano e l'Europa. Produzione e tecniche*, ed. Philippe Braunstein and Luca Molà, 89–114. Costabissara: Colla.

Scott, Joan W. 1986. Gender: A useful category of historical analysis. *The American Historical Review* 91 (5): 1053–1075.

Seiger, Fiona-Katharina, Christiane Timmerman, Noel B. Salazar, and Johan Wets, eds. 2020. *Migration at work: Aspirations, imaginaries & structures of mobility.* Leuven: Leuven University Press.

Sewell, William H. 1980. *Work and revolution in France. The language of labor from the old regime to 1848.* Cambridge: Cambridge University Press.

Simon-Muscheid, Katharina. 1990. La lutte des maîtres tisserands contre les tisserandes à Bâle. La condition féminine au XVe siècle. In *La donna nell'economia secc. XIII-XVIII*, ed. Simonetta Cavaciocchi, 383–389. Florence: Le Monnier.

Sonenscher, Michael. 1989. *Work and wages: Natural law, politics and the eighteenth-century French trades.* Cambridge: Cambridge University Press.

Stanwood, Owen. 2020. *The global refuge: Huguenots in an age of empire.* New York: Oxford University Press.

Styles, John. 2019. Fibres, fashion and marketing: Textile innovation in early modern Europe. In *Cotton in context. Manufacturing, marketing, and consuming textiles in the German-speaking world (1500–1900)*, ed. Kim Siebenhüner, John Jordan, and Gabi Schopf, 35–60. Göttingen: Vandenhoeck & Ruprecht.

Tilly, Louise A., and Joan W. Scott. 1978. *Women, work, and family*. New York: Holt, Rinehart, and Winston.

Tiraboschi, Girolamo. 1780. *Storia della Letteratura Italiana. VIII. Dall'anno MDC fino all'anno MDCC*. Modena: Società tipografica.

Treasure, Geoffrey R. R. 2013. *The Huguenots*. New Haven: Yale University Press.

Trivellato, Francesca. 2000. *Fondamenta dei vetrai. Lavoro, tecnologia e mercato a Venezia tra Sei e Settecento*. Rome: Donzelli.

Tron, Daniele. 2005. *Le "Pasque piemontesi" e l'internazionale protestante*. Turin: Claudiana.

Viazzo, Pier Paolo, and Riccardo Cerri. 2009. *Da montagna a montagna. Mobilità e migrazioni interne nelle Alpi italiane nei secoli XVII-XIX*. Magenta: Zeisciu.

Wallis, Patrick. 2019. Between apprenticeship and skill: Acquiring knowledge outside the academy in early modern England. *Science in Context* 32 (2): 155–170.

Wallis, Patrick. 2020. Apprenticeship in England. In *Apprenticeship in early modern Europe*, ed. Maarten Prak and Patrick Wallis, 247–281. Cambridge: Cambridge University Press.

Wallis, Patrick. 2025. *The market for skill. Apprenticeship and economic growth in early modern England*. Princeton: Princeton University Press.

Zucca Micheletto, Beatrice. 2008. Lavoro femminile, figli ed economia domestica nella Torino di Antico Regime. *Genesis* 8 (1–2): 165–192.

Zucca Micheletto, Beatrice. 2020a. Working in and for the charity institutions: Patterns of employment and actors in early modern Savoy-Piedmont State. *Mediterranea* 17 (48): 199–222.

Zucca Micheletto, Beatrice. 2020b. A large 'umbrella': Patterns of apprenticeship in eighteenth-century Turin. In *Apprenticeship in early modern Europe*, ed. Maarten Prak and Patrick Wallis, 78–105. Cambridge: Cambridge University Press.

Zucca Micheletto, Beatrice. 2022. Storia del lavoro, storia delle donne e di genere. Percorsi storiografici per l'Europa preindustriale. *Economia & Lavoro* 56 (2): 45–63.

CHAPTER 7

The Baroque Industrial District: Silk and the Urban Transformation of Turin

1 Introduction

"Towns are like electric transformers. They increase tensions, accelerate the rhythm of exchange and constantly recharge human life,"[1] wrote Braudel in his masterpiece *Civilisation Matérielle, Économie et Capitalisme* (1979, 421). An enduring perspective, considering that nearly two millennia previously Plutarch had argued that "a city, like a living thing, is a united and continuous whole": like a human being.[2] The terms of comparison may have changed, but the fundamental concept remains the same: the city, often seen as an inert mass of matter, is alive and dynamic. Despite being a human construction, the city helps define human experiences, convey political messages, shape culture, and delineate the very existence of people (LeCain 2017). Alongside individuals' contribution to Piedmont's silk industry, the city should also be considered an actor,

[1] "Les villes sont autant de transformateurs électriques: elles augmentent les tensions, elles précipitent les échanges, elles brassent sans fin la vie des hommes" (Braudel 1981, 479).

[2] "ὥσπερ ζῷον οὐκ ἐξιστάμενον αὑτοῦ." Plutarch then continues, stating, "This does not cease to be itself as it changes in growing older, nor does it become one thing after another with the lapse of time, but is always at one with its former self in feeling and identity, and must take all blame or credit for what it does or has done in its public character, so long as the association that creates it and binds it together with interwoven strands preserves it as a unity." Plutarch, *De Sera Numinis Vendicta*, Moralia, 559, 15 (De Lacy and Einarson 1959, 245).

M. Grassi, *The Silk Industry in Early Modern Piedmont*, Labour in History and Society,
https://doi.org/10.1007/978-3-032-15353-1_7

capable of both embracing and rejecting, aggregating, and dividing, creating communities, and generating unexpected issues. A consideration of the silk industry's spread in an urban setting by analyzing the city's evolution, its urban structure, streets, and buildings allows an examination of issues commonly perceived as contemporary, like zoning and environmental pollution (Cronon 1993; Rosen and Tarr 1994; Richards 2003; Schott 2004; Sinclair et al. 2010; Billen et al. 2012; Hanlon and Heblich 2022; Gindelsky and Jedwab 2023). This perspective challenges the stereotypical image of European "baroque" cities as utopian stages solely focused on central power representation and expands the discourse on the incongruities between political expectations and social reality (Zucker 1955; Cohen and Szabo 2008; Blunt and De Seta 2021). Institutional and regulatory needs for manufacturing, practical requirements in terms of sewage treatment and hydraulic energy supply channels, and families' daily needs frequently did not align and, in fact, usually conflicted with one another (Poni 1990; D'Amico 1994; Mocarelli 2001; Guenzi 2008; Barbot and Caracausi 2009; Boone 2012; Prak 2018; Ago 2023).

During the early modern era, the city of Turin underwent profound urban change and expanded in size three times between the sixteenth and eighteenth centuries (Comoli Mandracci 1983a; Rosso 2002; Navire 2008). The start of construction on the first two areas toward the south (*Città Nuova*) and east (*Città Nuova di Po*) coincided with a phase when the silk industry in Piedmont was flourishing (Bracco 1992; Chierici and Palmucci Quaglino 1993; Chicco 1995; Chierici 2004, 2007). These newly developed areas were earmarked as ideal places to establish artisanal workshops specializing in silk production. Thus, with the expansion of Turin's fortified perimeter (Picture 7.1), what was once beyond the city walls, out of sight of rulers, nobility, and residents, gradually became part of daily life. Furthermore, the new city walls redefined the city's outskirts, shifting them a few kilometers outward and transforming the two boroughs beyond the Dora and Po Rivers into suburban areas, which experienced continuous industrially driven growth during the early modern period (Calabi 2004; Greif et al. 2015). The physical transformations of the city and its environs had profound implications on both artisans and citizens, illustrating how the city effectively operates as a catalyst of economic development and shapes both urban and social dynamics. This chapter sheds light on a largely unexplored aspect of the Piedmontese silk industry, simultaneously demonstrating the inadequacy of traditional

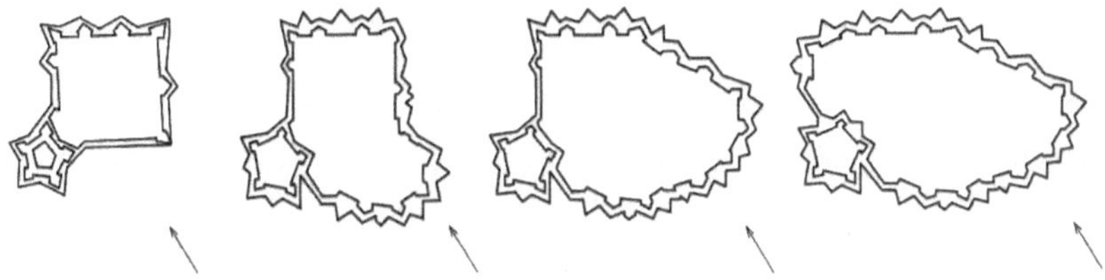

Picture 7.1 Expansion of the city perimeter of Turin between 1563 and the 1720s. From left to right: the original perimeter at the time of the construction of the defensive Citadel; the first extension of the walls with the addition of *Città Nuova*; the second expansion with *Città Nuova di Po*—both from the seventeenth century; and finally, the completion of the city's "almond-shaped" perimeter in the 1720s (*Source*: author's elaboration)

definitions used to describe pre-modern cities exclusively as "baroque stages" (Mayernik 2019).

Until 1563, Turin was merely the Italian peripheral court of the dukes of Savoy, whose capital was in Chambéry (Pollak 1991; Merlin 1998). The city had a typical grid-like structure inherited from Roman times, altered only slightly during the Middle Ages and the Renaissance (Romano 1990; Comba and Roccia 1993; Bonardi and Settia 1997; Pagella et al. 2006). After the Peace of Cateau-Cambrésis (1559) and considering the significance that the Italian peninsula's northwestern territories gained during the Italian Wars, Duke Emanuele Filiberto I decided to relocate the capital south of the Alps, in Turin (Comoli Mandracci 1998). During this period, while defensive and military fortification measures were implemented, resulting in the construction of the well-known Citadel (Claretta 1890; Scotti Tosini 1998), the city itself remained largely unchanged for decades (Ricuperati 1998), experiencing, as Comoli Mandracci stated, "half a century of quiet mediocrity" (1998, 201). Turin maintained its quadrangular shape while, just beyond the walls, inhabited centers developed over time, resembling proper villages. Notably, the Dora and Po boroughs stood out, emerging along the course of the two rivers and remaining physically separated from the city by the city walls.[3]

[3] The history of *borgo Dora* and *borgo di Po* remains understudied, particularly when viewed independently from the broader historical narrative on Turin (Bianchi 1991; Spallone 1999; Damieri and Pozzati 2016).

In the early seventeenth century, following conflicts for supremacy of Monferrato and adjacent territories, Duke Carlo Emanuele I decided to strengthen the layout of the new capital, which initiated a slow and evolving project for urban expansion with a defensive perspective (Pollak 1988). The first urban growth project, called *Città Nuova*, and its main square, *piazza San Carlo*, were inaugurated in 1620. This event coincided with the arrival of Maria Cristina of Bourbon-France (1606–1663) who had come to Turin to marry the future Duke Vittorio Amedeo I (1587–1637). However, this was just a part of the initial project. The undertaking stagnated for a long time due to the complex international political situation, a plague epidemic in northern Italy in the 1630s, and the intricate succession to the ducal throne, marked by the death of the first heir and the ensuing period of regency, which led to what is known as the Piedmont civil war (Merlin 1998).

Development only resumed in the second half of the seventeenth century, with the construction of the second area known as *Città Nuova di Po*. "I want the enlargement of Turin to be both political and economic," wrote Duke Carlo Emanuele II of Savoy in 1669 in his journal. While preparing a speech for his Privy Council, the sovereign noted that he wanted to propose the "creation of new spaces for people, who are already so numerous that they can no longer find a place in the city to live (…) wishing to ennoble the city by building academies, colleges for nobles, and many other public places, with the aim of attracting foreign artisans, shopkeepers and bankers (…) to make the city famous."[4] The duke's plan was clear, and required action on two fronts. The first one was political and representative, involving construction of new palaces and infrastructure capable of comfortably accommodating everyone participating in court life. The second one was economic, aimed at positioning the duchy among the great economic powers of the time via the development of the arts and manufacturing. Furthermore, the introduction of artisans and craftsmen, a venture initiated during Carlo Emanuele I's reign in the 1620s, was an integral part of his plan (Borelli 1681, 927–929—August 12, 1621; Rosso 1992a; Cerutti 1992, 2012; Stumpo 2002; Symcox

[4] "L'agrandimento di Torino che volio fare tanto politico come economico et di far la forteza più bona (…) per far logo al popolo che già è cresciuto in tanto numero che ora mai non capisce più nella presente città (…) per nobilitarla con la construsione di academie collegi di nobili et molti altri luoghi publici per l'esercizio delle virtù a fine d'atirarvi artefici negozianti banchieri et altri virtuosi forestieri rendendola celebre come spero mi reuscirà" (Claretta 1878, 69–70).

2002a, 2002b; Raviola 2015), precisely in the years in which the first hydraulic spinning mills had been installed in *borgo Dora* (Rosso 1992b, 2002).

The preserved plans for the city's expansion highlight the interpretation of Savoy expectations by the royal architects. In addition to fortifications, projects by Vitozzi, Negro di Sanfront, Castellamonte, Morello, and Valperga aimed to give the city a picturesque appearance by constructing squares, streets in straight lines, and arcades (Boggio 1895; Viglino Davico 2005a, 2005b, 2008). The plans placed particular emphasis on constructing a new square, *piazza Carlina*.[5] This space's purpose was to become the new royal square, reflecting the Savoy family's authority and dynastic continuity. However, the urban plan failed to account for the scale of needs of new citizens employed in silk manufacturing. Expectations soon had to yield to reality. With the ducal dispositions of August 22, 1678, it was already evident that the area, particularly the new square, would not assume a representation role. The municipality bore most of the expenses, disregarding the duke's original intentions, and transformed what was known as *Città Nuova di Po* into an urban space focused primarily on a specific purpose: the development of the local silk industry.

Moreover, Vittorio Amedeo II, under whose reign Piedmontese silk production reached its peak, reintroduced the initiative to attract foreign skilled labor. According to the edict of April 28, 1701, all artisans, whether subjects or foreigners, who established shops and workshops in *Città Nuova* or *Città Nuova di Po*, would be naturalized and exempt from paying taxes (Duboin 1827, 808—April 28, 1701). Thus, the policies aimed at attracting labor helped populate the new quarters of the city. The blocks between *contrada Nuova*, the axis of the southward expansion, and *contrada di Po*, the arterial road connecting the royal palace to the Po River, became the primary areas where silk workers lived.

What had been conceived as a baroque stage had to grapple with the socio-economic reality of Turin. In the context of constructing a *ville bien policée*, the development of the new urban area played a role in reinforcing the hierarchical order characteristic of the ancien régime, effectively shaping "social harmony" in accordance with the norms of that era (Gordon 1994; Roodenburg and Spierenburg 2004). Consequently, these expansions materialized as spaces of social constraint within the city walls. By the

[5] Not to be confused with *piazza San Carlo*, the epicenter of the southward expansion (Comoli Mandracci 1983b; Pollak 1989).

late seventeenth century, charitable institutions, monasteries, artisan workshops, and the Jewish ghetto had settled in the two expanding urban areas (Stumpo 2002; Symcox 2002a; Friedrichs 2014).

According to Berengo, craftsmanship was a predominant sensory element in cities of the past:

> One of the initial perceptions, and perhaps the foremost, upon entering a city that travelers and wayfarers likely experienced, was that of craftsmanship. It stood as an unmistakable element of urban life, presenting itself right from the initial houses in the villages. This intensity of craftsmanship persisted beyond the city gates, within the walls, and even beneath the loggias and porticoes of the central squares.[6] (Berengo 1999, 401)

This description most likely applies to those arriving in Turin in the early modern period. As the travelers approached the city—whether they hailed from Lombardy or the Ligurian Riviera—they would have had to enter either the Dora or Po borough and cross the gates of the walled perimeter before finally setting foot in Turin. Along these routes, and even within the city, they would have immersed themselves in a backdrop where the sight, sounds, and olfactory experiences would have undoubtedly converged, revealing the industrial nature of arts, crafts, and manufacturing, particularly those related to silk.

2 A Dual-Phase Industry: Hydraulic and Hand-Operated Silk Spinning Mills

A traveler coming to Turin from Milan most likely entered the city through *borgo Dora*, where the first *alla bolognese* hydraulic silk spinning mills of Piedmont were situated. Unlike Bologna, where a reorganization of the urban water network in the fifteenth century facilitated the spread of water-powered factories within the city walls (Guenzi and Poni 1987; Poni 1990, 2009; Martelli 2005; Righi 2016),[7] Turin's industrial infrastructure was primarily located in suburban areas. While the natural

[6] "Una delle prime percezioni (la prima forse) di star entrando in una città che doveva essere avvertita dai viandanti e dai viaggiatori, era quella del lavoro artigiano: era un elemento inconfondibile della vita urbana, che si manifestava sin dalle prime case dei borghi, e permaneva intenso al di là delle porte entro le mura, sin sotto le logge e i portici delle piazze centrali" (Berengo 1999, 401).

[7] Regarding the hydraulic system of Bologna, see Martelli (2005, 22–25).

waterfall near the bastions north of Turin had facilitated the operation of mills, which were powered by the abundant yet not excessively forceful flow of the Dora River since medieval times,[8] the urban layout of Turin precluded the establishment of water-powered factories within the city walls. This effectively constrained large-scale production to *borgo Dora* (Bracco 1988; Chierici 1992).

If the oldest hydraulic spinning mill in Turin belonged to Galleani,[9] twenty years later, in 1681, a second silk spinning mill known as "Pinardi"[10] was installed (Marchis 1992, 2016), overlooking the opposite bank of the canal *dei molini di Dora*. The two establishments represented significant advancements in organzine production. On the one hand, the Piedmontese silk industry was gaining prominence on the European scene for processing organzine in water-powered facilities in Turin's outskirts and in Piedmont's rural areas. On the other hand, the much older and more widespread practice in the city of Turin was working the silk thread with hand-operated spinning mills, many of which remained active throughout the eighteenth century. The gap between the sizes of the manufactories and the results of silk processing on hand-operated and water-powered silk spinning mills is evident in a report presented by the spinners' guild to the Consulate of Commerce on April 25, 1708. Count Galleani's hydraulic spinning mill, with its five machines and 80 employees, produced approximately 10,000 pounds of silk annually. In contrast, the Pinardi hydraulic spinning mill, with four machines and around 80 employees, produced 9000 pounds of silk. An observation of the data on the two largest hand-operated facilities within Turin's walls reveals a distinct disparity. The Ferraris brothers' and the Chiarbonello brothers' spinning mills, both with four machines and 50 employees, produced half the amount of thread.[11]

[8] Originally, it mainly concerned mills for grinding wheat, but over the centuries, other types of mills were introduced, such as those for crushing olives, processing metals, wood, wool, and hemp (Bonardi 1988; Chierici 1988).

[9] ASCT, *Ordinati (1661-1663)*, v. 194, c. 209r, October 13, 1663.

[10] As in the case of Galleani, the spinning mill was named after its founder, Girolamo Pinardi. The request to establish this spinning mill dates to 1681. ASCT, *Protocolli e minutari*, vol. 45, c. 10.

[11] Both the Ferraris brothers' and the Chiarbonello brothers' spinning mills produced 4500 pounds of silk each year. AST, C, *Materie economiche,* Cat. IV, m. 7, fasc. 1, April 25, 1708.

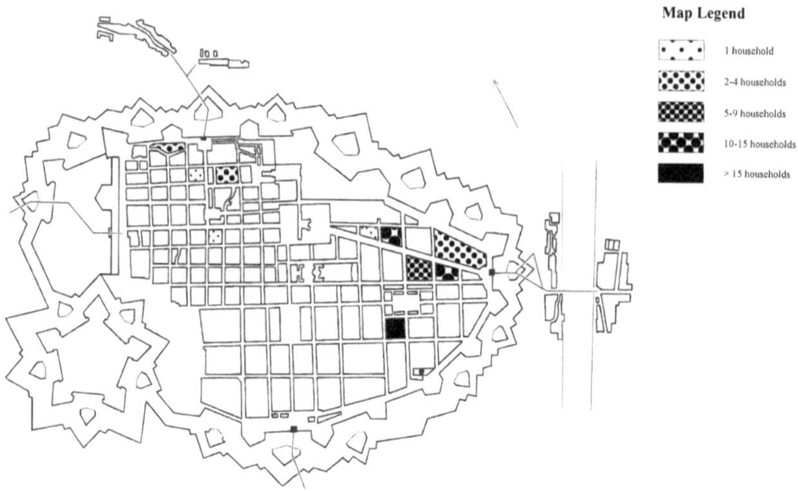

Map 7.1 Map of the urban distribution of silk spinners in 1705 (*Source*: author's elaboration based on the 1705 Census of the Population of Turin—AST, SR, *Camerale Piemonte*, Art. 530, v. 2, 1705)

As post-mortem inventories of spinners in the eighteenth century proved,[12] hand-operated spinning mills were typically located in the masters' homes. Turin's 1705 census showed that, with the exception of isolated spinner households near *piazza Castello*,[13] the majority of spinners' households were situated in *Città Nuova di Po*, along *contrada di Po* and around *piazza Carlina* (Map 7.1).

Moreover, an analysis of where spinners seeking assistance at the *Ospedale di Carità* between 1742 and 1800 lived provided an approximate understanding of the workforce engaged in both water-powered and hand-operated silk spinning mills in Turin for about 60 years.[14] *Borgo Dora* clearly stands out as the most densely populated area of spinners' households, even though a significant number of them resided in *Città Nuova di Po* (Map 7.2).

[12] AST, SR, *Consolato di Commercio*, Costituti, m. 1, *Atto e testimoniali di consegna di Gio Batta Cravosio*, April 28, 1714; m. 3, *Consegna presentata dal sig. Carlo Domenico Prina*, March 6, 1723; *Assicurazioni*, m. 152, *Assicurazione Monetti*, September 2, 1763.

[13] Among them, there was a resident in San Michele's block, likely engaged in producing silk yarns for the numerous ribbon makers residing in the area (Balani et al. 2005).

[14] ASCT, *Ospedale di Carità*, Libri delle informazioni, v. 7-26, April 1742–February 1802.

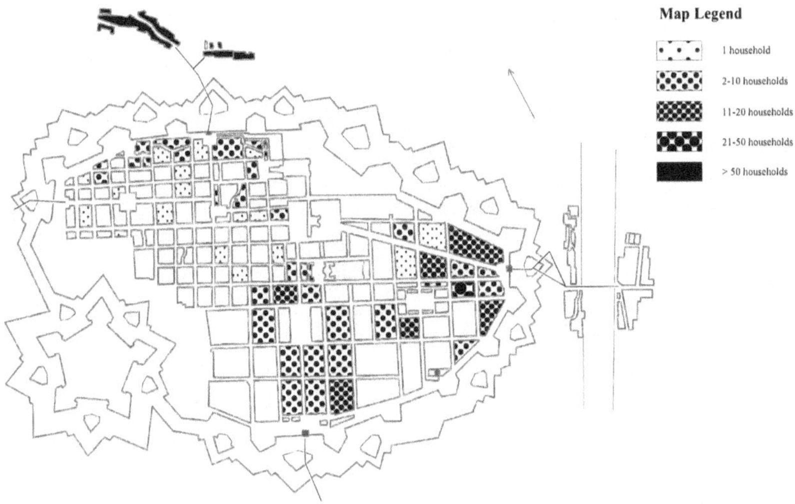

Map 7.2 Map of the urban distribution of silk spinners between 1742 and 1800 (*Source*: author's elaboration based on the *Libri delle Informazioni* of the Charity Hospital of Turin—ASCT, *Ospedale di Carità*, Libri delle informazioni, v. 7–26, April 1742–February 1802)

These data underscore the influence of residential proximity to the workplace on the demographic distribution of employees. However, the spinning mills had significant turnover of labor, which meant that individuals and households were constantly moving. Indeed, assistance requests reveal that children of spinners, born within a few years of each other, could have been baptized in different parishes,[15] indicating that entire families often relocated within the city's territory over a short period, likely motivated by work-related factors.[16] The remarkable mobility of spinner journeymen is further demonstrated by their applications to the guild to become masters. It was rare for apprentices to spend their entire training period—both as an apprentice and as a journeyman—at a single spinning mill. In such cases, family-related factors, such as mill

[15] An exception is made for children baptized in the Cathedral of Turin (parish of San Giovanni), where, during the Lenten season, children from impoverished families were baptized, even if they resided in other parishes.

[16] ASCT, *Ospedale di Carità*, Libri delle informazioni, v. 18, c. 377, *Richiesta di Giuseppe Ametto*, April 5, 1779; v. 21, c. 577, *Richiesta di Giuseppe Galliano*, September 2, 1787.

ownership by a relative or the presence of a family member working there, typically influenced this decision.

Nevertheless, once the journeyman training period concluded, cohabitation between masters and journeymen often evolved into a neighborly relationship. On the one hand, this arrangement minimizes the time journeymen took to reach the workplace, while on the other, it enabled masters to maintain active control over their workforce. The purpose of this dynamic is challenging to explain, except from the perspective of maximizing labor time, coupled with the masters' opportunity to employ both the journeymen and their families (Paolucci 1996; Maitte and Terrier 2014, 2020).

Indeed, employing journeymen's wives at the spinning mills was a common practice, as data from the Hospital of Charity's registers underscore. With the implementation of hydraulic silk spinning mills, the conventional practice of cohabitation between masters and journeymen acquires innovative characteristics. One crucial aspect was the size of the building, allowing for an internal organization in terms of space that exceeded the domestic room layout (Sarti 2002). These extensive hydraulic spinning mills sometimes included rooms and, less frequently, the construction of separate buildings nearby for workers and their families to live in.[17] Unfortunately, historical sources provide limited insights into the internal dynamics of hydraulic spinning mills, the early factories that incorporated living quarters within them in the capital of the House of Savoy's territories. The only available records that provide information on the living conditions of the spinners residing within the walls of the spinning mills in *borgo Dora* come from the Hospital of Charity archive. This aspect was documented in 30 requests to the hospital between 1742 and 1782.[18] Fourteen were single-person households, nine were small households with two to four individuals, and seven were larger households with five to eight members—all of whom belonged to the same family, with no external members present. In the majority of these multi-member households, both parents worked at the spinning mill, confirming that all occupants both lived and worked in these mills. These data suggest that owners of hydraulic spinning mills preferred hiring individuals without families,

[17] Consider the building adjacent to the *filatoio Rosso* in Caraglio (CN), purposefully constructed by the Galleani family to accommodate the workforce.

[18] After 1782, no individuals declaring residence in the spinning mills of *borgo Dora* are recorded.

encouraging them to reside in the accommodations provided. This arrangement reduced the distance between living quarters and workplaces, encouraging a seamless integration of private and professional life. The creation of an internal community within the factory would have limited workers' interactions with the outside world, thereby influencing their social relationships. Spinners employed by and living in *borgo Dora*'s spinning mills would have spent their daily lives in a community primarily consisting of fellow spinners and engaging in social activities with them. If they had not already been married when they were employed, it is likely that they would have chosen a spouse from those working at the spinning mill.

These factors probably contributed to a significant social divide between workers at the hydraulic spinning mills and those in city workshops or nearby. An analysis of requests submitted to the Hospital of Charity provides insight into the commonalities between these two categories of spinners and where they diverged. Notably, while the number of requests from spinners in the boroughs remained under 35 every ten years, requests from city-based spinners fell below 40 only in the decade 1790–1800. The data clearly emphasize a significant increase in requests made by spinners to the Hospital of Charity between 1760 and 1779. In the period analyzed, the disparity in the number of requests made by spinners from *borgo Dora* compared to those from Turin is evident. Even in the 1770s, a decade marked by the major crisis of 1777 (Chicco 1995), spinners from Turin seeking assistance from the charitable institution were considerably more numerous than those from *borgo Dora* (Table 7.1). In most cases, these requests were initiated by women, and in general, a significant number of workers employed at the spinning mill sought hospital admission due to either illness or old age. Furthermore, 15% of spinners from *borgo Dora* sought support from a wet nurse, whereas only 6% of Turin-based spinners made similar requests. Additionally, the ambiguous requests for *qualche soccorso* (any assistance)[19] among spinners in the borough amounted to 12%, which contrasts with the 25% observed for spinners living within the walls. Finally, while urban spinners frequently sought assistance from the hospital for minor ailments, only two spinners from *borgo Dora* requested "any assistance" due to illness—both cases were linked to their

[19] "*Qualche soccorso*," "any assistance," essentially meant that any aid provided by the Opera would be much appreciated.

Table 7.1 Requests to the *Ospedale di Carità* by men and women employed in hand-operated and hydraulic spinning mills between 1742 and 1800 (*Source:* author's elaboration based on the *Libri delle Informazioni* of the Charity Hospital of Turin—ASCT, *Ospedale di Carità*, Libri delle informazioni, v. 7–26, April 1742–February 1802)

	Borgo Dora, hydraulic spinning mills			*Turin, hand-operated spinning mills*		
	Men	*Women*	*Total*	*Men*	*Women*	*Total*
1740–1749	7	9	16	31	27	58
1750–1759	5	9	14	18	30	48
1760–1769	18	16	34	19	57	76
1770–1779	10	19	29	24	65	89
1780–1789	8	10	18	14	45	59
1790–1800	5	9	14	15	24	39
Total	53	72	125	121	248	369

spouses' health issues.[20] Based on this information, it is plausible that the economic stability of spinners in *borgo Dora* was more robust, enabling them to navigate challenging periods without needing to seek assistance from the charitable institutions—except for specific circumstances, like wet nursing.

The eighteenth century brought significant transformations to the spinning profession. However, an industry operating at different speeds persisted because, despite the silk crisis at the end of the century, hand spinners still worked within Turin's walled perimeter. In 1802,[21] besides the 33 households residing in *borgo Dora*, numerous spinner households remained concentrated in the southeastern part of the city. The only exception was the cluster of workers in San Michele's block, located near *Porta Palazzo* (the primary link between the city and *borgo Dora*) (Map 7.3).

[20] Pregnancy has been considered in the selected sample.

[21] The 1802 Napoleonic census has been fully cataloged by a group of students under the guidance of Maria Carla Lamberti and is digitally preserved at the Department of History, Economic History section, at the University of Turin. The original census records can be found in ASCT, *Coll. XII*, Censimento del 1802. I would like to express my gratitude to the Department of History at the University of Turin for providing me access to the database.

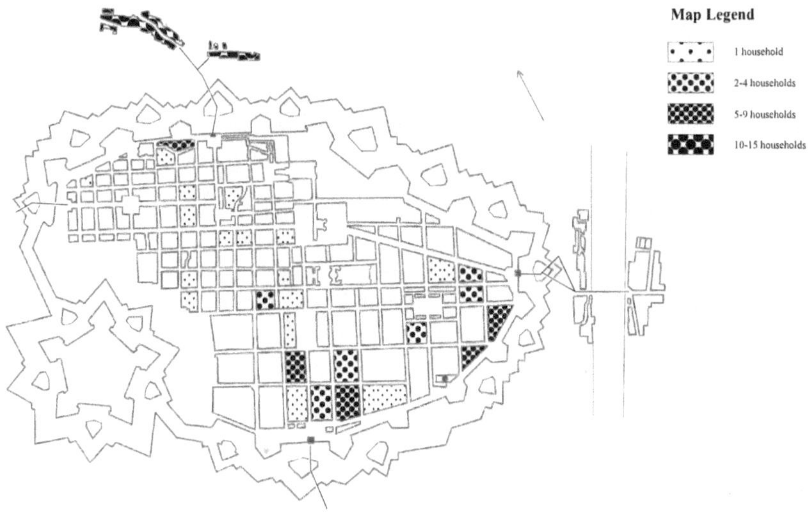

Map 7.3 Map of the urban distribution of silk spinners in 1802 (*Source*: author's elaboration based on the 1802 Census of the Population of Turin—ASCT, *Coll. XII*, Censimento del 1802)

3 From Urban Streets to the River's Edge: The Governance of Silk Dyeing

A traveler arriving in Turin from Genoa would most likely have entered the city from the southeast, first venturing through the narrow streets of *borgo di Po*. While *borgo Dora* had a long-standing association with manufacturing and mills, the swift currents of the Po River did not permit the eponymous borough to develop a comparable industrial profile. On the contrary, water transport, fishing, laundry, and probably some dyeing establishments were situated along the banks of the Po. Within the city walls, dyeing activities were concentrated in the street known as *contrada dei coriatori*. Situated on the periphery of the city even before its expansion, this street housed not only dyers but also tanners practicing their craft. Despite lacking proximity to canals or streams, historical sixteenth-century maps revealed the presence of flowing watercourses within the city, known as *doire*, into which dyers and tanners disposed of their processing waste (Picture 7.2).

Picture 7.2 The two watercourses that originated from *Porta di Susa* (top) and traversed the city before flowing into the Po River (bottom) are clearly visible on this map, which is modeled on the renowned map produced Jan Kraeck for Duke Emanuele Filiberto I in 1572. (*Source*: Valesio, Francesco, *Augusta Taurinorum in Sabaudie*, Copperplate engraving from *Raccolta di le più Illustri et Famose Città di tutto il Mondo*, n.d. but end of the seventeenth century. Bibliothèque nationale de France. Gallica. https://gallica.bnf.fr/ark:/12148/btv1b52503977t)

In the early 1600s, there is documented evidence of a modest number of silk dyers within the walls of Turin.[22] Although there were just a few of them, their presence was unfortunate for the capital city, considering the public health issues caused by contaminated wastewater and fumes generated by the dyeing processes. The first order for dyers to relocate from the city center and establish operations beyond the walls dates back to 1676. This coincided with the final phase of *Città Nuova* expansion and the ongoing construction of fortifications for *Città Nuova di Po*. The priority of the superintendent of police (known as the *Vicariato*) was to make the area more habitable for residents, given the significant demographic

[22] AST, SR, *Camerale Piemonte*, art. 271, *Cottizo de tutti li mercanti et artisti di qua da monti consignati*, March 15, 1619.

growth following the end of the major plague outbreak in the 1630s. Conversely, the Savoy family's primary objective was to construct a new urban area that would symbolize their political power.

The persistent emission of noxious fumes, both day and night, prompted government intervention, ordering dyers and tanners to relocate to the outskirts of the city. This decree underscored the two-fold advantages of relocating such facilities. Firstly, it improved environmental conditions for citizens. Secondly, artisans were able to access a more abundant water supply being closer to the rivers (Borelli 1681, 907—May 12, 1676). There is no detailed information on the process or on whether the relocation of dyeing establishments took place. However, the reissuance of the ordinance in 1683 is documented, albeit with a revised objective: to oversee the manufacturing process. The updated decree stipulated, "the precedent set by other cities in foreign states confirms that there is no alternative but to relocate all silk dye masters outside the city walls towards and along the banks of the Po River," allowing an expert appointed by the Crown to monitor the quality of the materials and dyes used (Duboin 1849, 955—June 20, 1683).

In pursuit of this objective, the *Torrette* basins (*fontane delle Torrette*) were constructed directly on the banks of the river Po during the final decades of the seventeenth century (Picture 7.3). What was intended to be a definitive solution turned out to be a source of numerous legal disputes. In 1722, for instance, the Consulate was asked whether wool dyers should be allowed to use the basins typically reserved for silk dyers. It required the intervention of Antonio Maria Lampo, the superintendent overseeing fortification works, to ensure that this decision did not compromise the purity of the water used by the silk dyers (Duboin 1849, 954—May 28, 1722). Disputes about the use of the basins also arose among silk dyers, as evidenced by a case in 1730. In that year, the guild's council had the *Torrette* basins fixed, requesting contributions from all dyers to cover the expenses. Nevertheless, only some of the city's dyers, residing by the Po, could actually "purge and wash their silks" at these basins. Meanwhile, those conducting their activities in other parts of the city "did not have the privilege to use the basins, opting for alternative locations (...) for which they paid private rent."[23]

[23] AST, SR, *Consolato di Commercio,* Costituti, m. 11, *Causa tintori opperari/Sindaci dell'Università de' mastri tintori,* September 26, 1730.

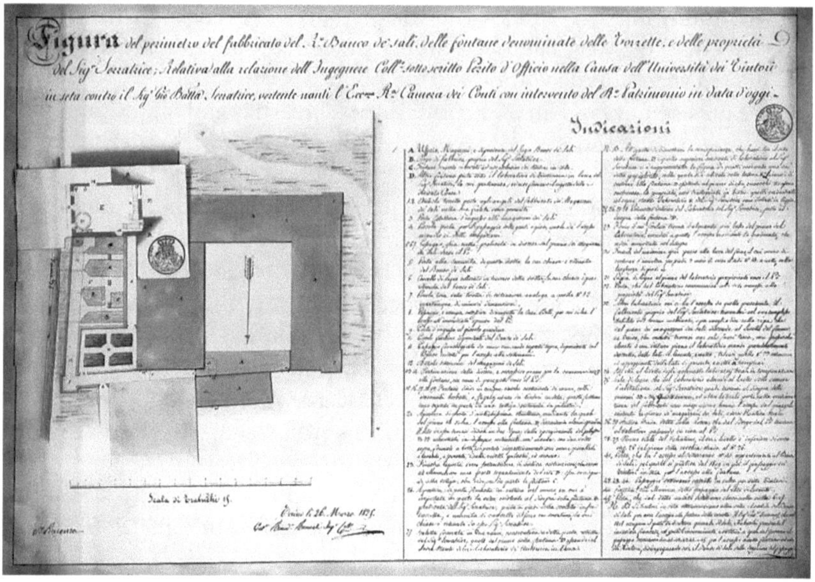

Picture 7.3 Plan of the Torrette fountains. On the left, the five basins and their respective drains of the dye workshop owned by Serratrice can be identified. (*Source*: Brunati, Benedetto, *Figura del perimetro del fabbricato del Regio Banco de' Sali delle fontane denominate delle Torrette e delle proprietà del Sig. Serratrice (…)*. March 26, 1825. AST, SR, *Tipi e disegni*, art. 663, n. 144. Courtesy of the State Archives of Turin)

This decree confirms that, indeed, some dyeing establishments had relocated to the Dora and Po boroughs, thereby leveraging the city's river flows. Conversely, despite both municipal and royal orders, some silk dyeing establishments continued to operate in *contrada dei coriatori*. The order to relocate dyeing establishments outside the walled perimeter was reissued during the 1750s. This decision was part of a broader urban modernization initiative. On the one hand, the increase in the city's population (which had reached 58,128 people by 1750), and on the other hand, issues related to urban rentals (that consistently provided tenants with income through subletting) prompted the House of Savoy to reconsider the city's urban layout (Roggero 2002). This initiative not only reiterated the removal of harmful manufactories but also involved the restoration and alignment of palace facades, the sanitization of specific areas, and the

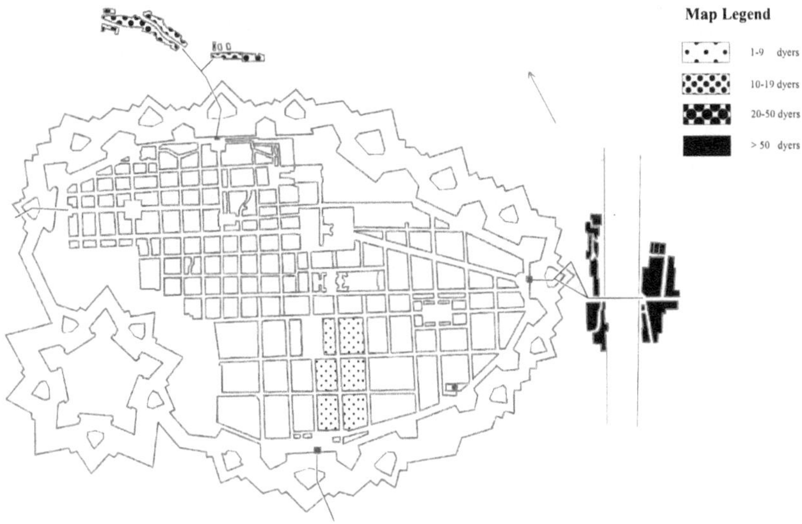

Map 7.4 Map of the urban distribution of silk dyers in 1768 (*Source*: author's elaboration based on the 1768 petition submitted by the dyers for the renovation of the *Torrette* basins—AST, C, *Materie economiche*, Cat. IV, m. 11, fasc. 23, April 14, 1768)

regularization of streets (Varallo 2002). In addition, another ordinance, published in 1755, mandated the relocation of all silk dyeing establishments to *borgo di Po* and all tanneries and hat-making workshops to *borgo Dora*, "deeming (the presence of these harmful manufacturing activities) unsuitable for this metropolis (…) in terms of cleanliness, air quality, and the risk of fire" (Duboin 1849, 944—January 22, 1755). More than a decade later, in 1768, *borgo di Po* housed only 13 dyeing establishments out of a total of 26. Seven were located in *borgo Dora*, while six remained within the walls, specifically in *contrada dei coriatori* (Map 7.4).[24]

Nevertheless, 20 years later the situation of dyeing workshops in the city had clearly changed. As highlighted by the sources, between 1768 and 1792, 50% of these businesses had either closed or changed management. However, 13 dyeing workshops not only remained under the ownership of the families that initially claimed them but had often not even been

[24] AST, C, *Materie economiche*, Cat. IV, m. 11, fasc. 23, April 14, 1768.

Map 7.5 Map of the urban distribution of silk dyers in 1792 (*Source*: author's elaboration based on the 1792 Trade Census—AST, C, *Materie economiche,* Cat. IV, m. 11 d'addizione, fasc. 6, 1792)

passed down from father to son. In 1792, *borgo di Po* also housed 14 dyeing workshops, and in *borgo Dora*, 5 were still in operation. At this point, only two silk dyeing workshops remained in the *contrada dei coriatori* (Map 7.5).

In the nineteenth century, the ambitious seventeenth-century plan to relocate dyeing establishments beyond the city walls was finally realized. During this period, the city primarily served as somewhere to live for some of the historical dyers' families, who could conveniently access their nearby dyeing facilities situated in *borgo di Po*.[25] In the end, the attempt to relocate the dyeing establishments away from *borgo Dora* proved to be unsuccessful. At least three silk dyeing workshops were still running there as late as 1802. Despite these exceptions, *borgo di Po* remained the central location for Turin's dyeing industry, benefiting from the continuous flow of the river and the *Torrette* basins. It housed approximately 20 silk dyeing workshops, employing around 65 workers, including masters and

[25] ASCT, *Coll. XII*, Censimento del 1802; AST, C, *Materie economiche*, Cat. I, m. 2 d'addizione, *Volume contenente li nomi, cognomi e patria de' mastri e padroni*, 1792.

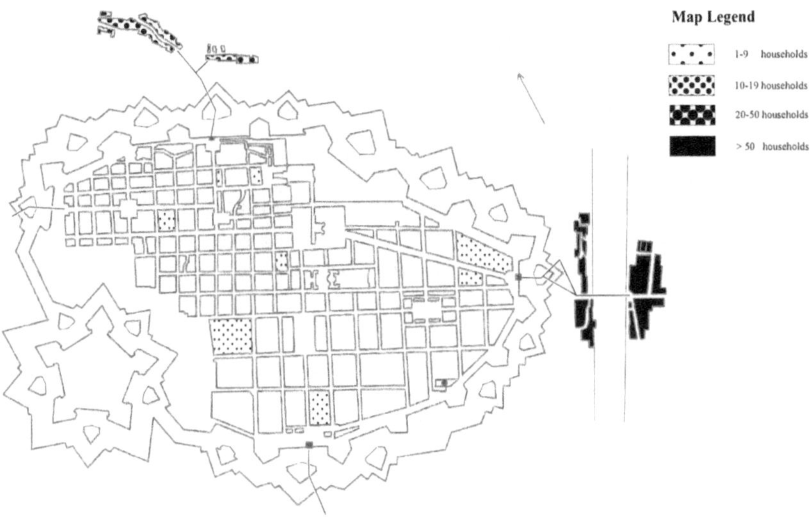

Map 7.6 Map of the urban distribution of silk dyers in 1802 (*Source*: author's elaboration based on the 1802 Census of the Population of Turin—ASCT, *Coll. XII*, Censimento del 1802)

journeymen (Map 7.6). In conclusion, *borgo di Po* was undeniably considered by the authorities as a significant urban resource, situated not far from the city walls and accommodating all those establishments that could potentially disrupt the peaceful life of the city's residents.

The presence of dyeing workshops in the Po borough persisted throughout the nineteenth century, particularly during the 1820s, when *Città Nuova di Po* expanded toward the banks of the Po. It is worth noting that during this period of urban development, marked by the construction of *piazza Vittorio*[26] and the neighboring districts, a street was called *contrada dei tintori* (literally "Dyers' street"—now the concluding section of via Maria Vittoria between via Plana and Lungo Po Diaz).

[26] Built after Napoleon's ousting and the reinstatement of the House of Savoy, the square was originally named after Vittorio Emanuele I in 1814. However, it quickly became known among the locals as *piazza Vittorio*, and following Italy's victory in the eponymous battle that concluded World War I, it was officially renamed *piazza Vittorio Veneto* in 1920 (Castelnuovo and Rosci 1980; Comoli Mandracci 1983a; Volpiano 2001).

4 The Rhythm of the Loom: Noise, Silk Weavers, and Housing Struggles

Upon entering the city, travelers continued their sensory journey, guided by the stimuli emanating from Turin's vibrant productive landscape. The sensory experience did not cease beyond the city gates; instead, it shifted from the gushing rivers to the rhythmic, mechanical sounds of weavers' looms. Since the early eighteenth century, there had been a noticeable concentration of weavers living in *Città Nuova di Po* (Balani et al. 2005), particularly in neighborhoods around *contrada di Po* and *piazza Carlina* (Map 7.7).

The second urban expansion was conceived as an area "reflecting royal resonance." The centerpiece of *Città Nuova di Po* was *piazza Carlina*, a newly designed royal square meant to symbolize Carlo Emanuele II's power, featuring a fountain, an equestrian sculpture, and arcades surrounding it (Comoli Mandracci 2002). Yet the colossal project was soon abandoned, due to both the duke's passing and the area's transformation into a preferred site for manufacturing facilities (Symcox 2002a). In fact,

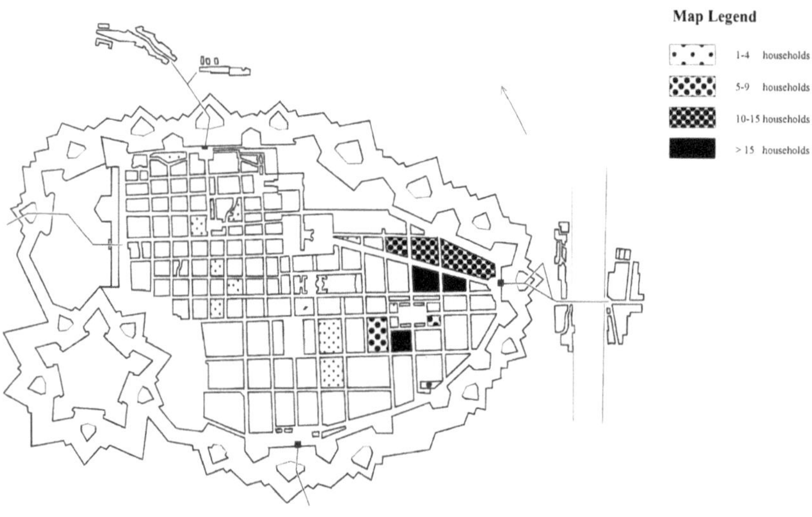

Map 7.7 Map of the urban distribution of silk weavers in 1705 (*Source*: author's elaboration based on the 1705 Census of the Population of Turin—AST, SR, Camerale Piemonte, Art. 530, v. 2, 1705)

just a few steps away there were the workshops of spinners and weavers and, a little further, the dyeing workshops of *contrada dei coriatori*. This pattern outlined the profile of an industrial district, its urban design significantly influenced by the privileges granted to craftsmen by the House of Savoy. Artisans relocating to *Città Nuova* and *Città Nuova di Po*, from foreign lands to establish their workshops enjoyed tax exemptions and other concessions. This was clearly in line with the Duke of Savoy's economic expansion plan. The area's new function becomes even more apparent on consideration of the position of the Royal Manufactories that were opened and closed within the city during the eighteenth century (Map 7.8). Therefore, over the course of the eighteenth century, *Città Nuova di Po* had become the main area where artisans engaged in weaving silk fabrics on looms lived (Map 7.9).

These new dynamics unveiled significant public order issues. The incessant noise caused by the looms irritated the people living in the area and landlords. As a result of the noise pollution caused by the machinery, tenants began vacating their rented houses, one after another, inflicting severe financial losses on property owners. Faced with these challenges, property

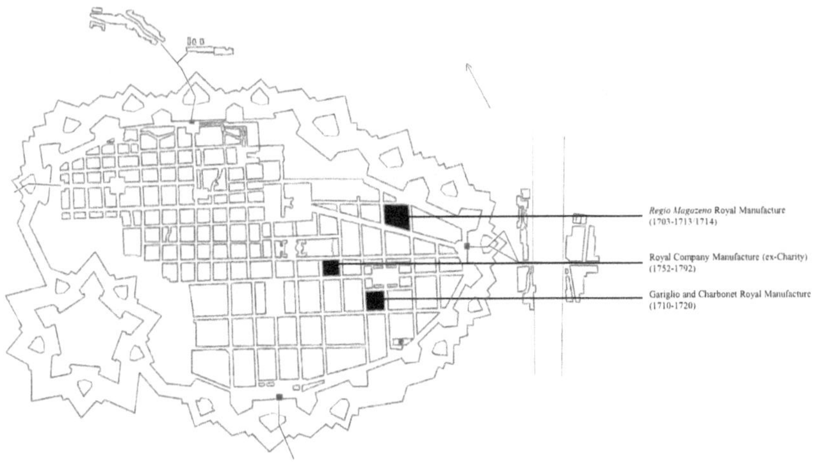

Map 7.8 Location of the Royal Manufactories in the city and period of activity. (*Source*: author's elaboration based on AST, SR, *Consolato di Commercio*, Costituti, m. 106; AST, C, *Materie economiche*, Cat. IV, m. 6 d'addizione; m. 7; m. 11 d'addizione)

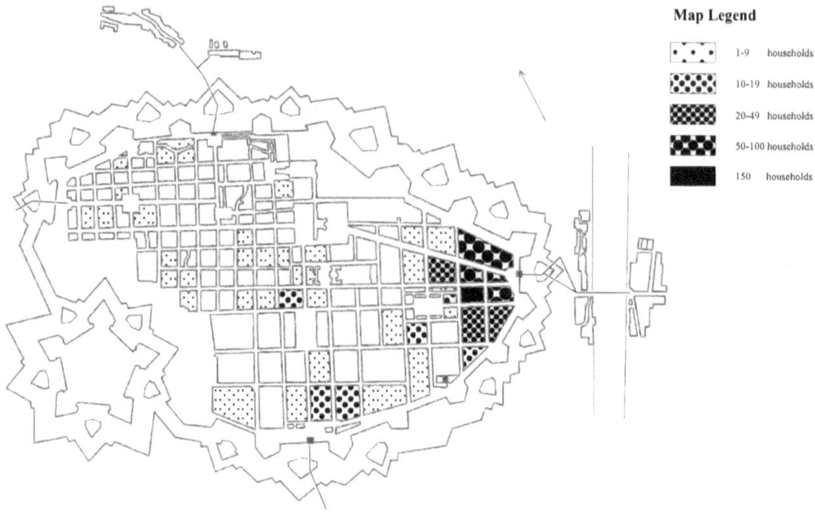

Map 7.9 Map of the urban distribution of silk weavers between 1742 and 1800 (*Source*: author's elaboration based on the *Libri delle Informazioni* of the Charity Hospital of Turin—ASCT, *Ospedale di Carità*, Libri delle informazioni, v. 7–26, April 1742–February 1802)

owners in *Città Nuova di Po* had no choice but to increase rental prices or opt not to renew rental contracts for silk weavers' households. In 1747, these weavers had to seek the king's help with securing suitable places to live and work more easily. The royal ministers were thus compelled to acknowledge that:

> It is not easy for some of the masters of the mentioned guild to find rental rooms. Many houses, extending from the Po borough to *piazza Carlina* and subsequently up to *Porta Nuova*, which are traditionally sought after and suitable for their craft, have been occupied for various purposes. The noise generated by the looms during their working hours discourages home-owners from renting rooms to these masters, favoring other, less disruptive individuals.[27]

[27] "Non è difficile che alcuni de' mastri di detta Università incontrino difficoltà nel ritrovare camere in affitto, poiché oltre di essere state occupate per diversi usi più case dalla contrada di Po verso Piazza Carlina, e successivamente sino a Porta Nuova ove sono sempre stati i quartieri più ricercati e convenevoli per l'arte di cui si tratta, il rumore che fanno i telaj,

The interests of the state and people of Turin appeared to find no common ground. The Superintendent of Police, guarantor of citizenship, made it clear that while the need to assist weavers was evident, there was the risk that owners, unable to find additional tenants, would soon be forced to implore the king for subsidies. The proposal made in the hope of addressing the housing issue for weavers became a recurring theme throughout the century. It was essential to identify sites exclusively designated for installing looms and establishing dwellings for the weavers and their families. However, these measures were never implemented, and the weavers' pleas did not achieve the desired effect, resulting in authorization granted by the king to the superintendent of police to intervene in cases of perceived problems between artisans and landlords.

Only eight years later, in 1755, the king made an attempt to facilitate the search for housing for silk weavers. Carlo Emanuele III designated Count Fontanella di Baldissero's house, near the Arsenal and the Citadel, as a dwelling "for the master weavers who could not find any accommodation in the city." However, even after the necessary repairs, Casa Fontanella could only accommodate 14 weaver households. Three years later, not a single weaver lived in the new royal house, likely due to the distance between Casa Fontanella and the central hub of silk fabric production in *Città Nuova di Po.* Consequently, the issue remained unresolved (Palmucci Quaglino 1992).

In 1777, the issue of housing for silk weavers resurfaced through a new plea sent to the king by master weavers and journeymen. Despite numerous "earnest requests" made by the artisans to the superintendent of police's office "to secure a stable lodging," the housing problem persisted. Weavers were still "frequently evicted by the property owners due to the deafening nature of their profession."[28] The proposal to "provide these indispensable workers for trade, advantageous to the country, with a stable residence" was made and suggested the construction of a new building "on the sites presently occupied by *baracconi* (shanties) in *piazza Carlina*" (Palmucci Quaglino 1992, 221–222). The king gave his approval, various projects concerning the dismantling of the shanties were presented, and

all'ora quando sono nell'attale lavoro, alliena gli proprietarj di dette case dall'accordare camere in affitto a suddetti mastri, amando meglio di preferire altre persone meno incomode." AST, C, *Materie economiche,* Cat. IV, m. 8, fasc. 32, March 16, 1747.

[28] ASCT, *Coll. X,* v. 1, *Registro del congresso degli Edili,* c. 21, November 1, 1777.

new blocks in *piazza Carlina* created.[29] However, the building was never constructed due to objections from residents and the request, made that same year by hatter Gaetano Martin, to establish a hat factory "near *Porta Nuova* (...) which could also be suitable for the weavers of this city."[30]

A solution was finally envisioned in the 1780s when the weavers' guild approached the king. This time, the intention was to purchase the entire San Pasquale's block—a peripheral block in the southeastern zone of the city, partly unbuilt and partly occupied by a charitable institution called *Casa di Correzione* (House of Correction). The value of the block, amounting to 53,775 *lire*, was to be paid over twenty years by the guild to the charitable institution, which could maintain its headquarters there. The building, constructed based on suggestions from silk technicians during the eighteenth century (Turbini 1778; Milizia 1781; Griselini 1783; Chierici and Palmucci 1987; Palmucci Quaglino 1992), was meant to feature "simple architecture and a layout adapted for the lodging of the workers," to accommodate approximately seventy households, each with six or seven looms. The process of constructing the weavers' lodging was overshadowed by economic difficulties that delayed completion. In 1784, the San Pasquale's block could only accommodate "ten families with sixty looms." During the same year, in an attempt to overcome the evident economic challenges faced by the guild, the *Trinitari Scalzi di San Michele* (Discalced Trinitarians of Saint Michael) came forward, proposing to purchase the entire block. They committed to completing the rebuilding of the block and, by constructing a church and a convent, providing "new residences for 40 families with 238 looms and 40 attics," at a good price. In the 1780s, therefore, there was a concentration of weaver households residing in the San Pasquale's block, although it is clear from the map that several households continued to live and work in the surrounding quarters of *contrada di Po*, *piazza Carlina*, and the neighborhoods near *Porta Nuova* (Map 7.10). But shortly afterward, the religious order also faced financial constraints. In the 1790s, the house had not yet been completed and, to cover expenses, the Trinitarians were compelled to offer the apartments, theoretically intended for weavers, to the highest bidder.[31] The

[29] AST, C, *Materie ecclesiastiche,* Luoghi pii di qua da' monti, m. 17, fasc. 3, 1743.

[30] ASCT, *Coll. X*, v. 1, *Registro del congresso degli Edili,* c. 35, June 29, 1780.

[31] The dwellings of San Pasquale's block accommodated a blacksmith, a locksmith, a cobbler, a mason, along with the *Scuole di Carità e Mendacità Sbandita* (Schools of Charity and Suppression of Beggary), a tavern, the warehouse for lard storage, the *Ufficio Generale del*

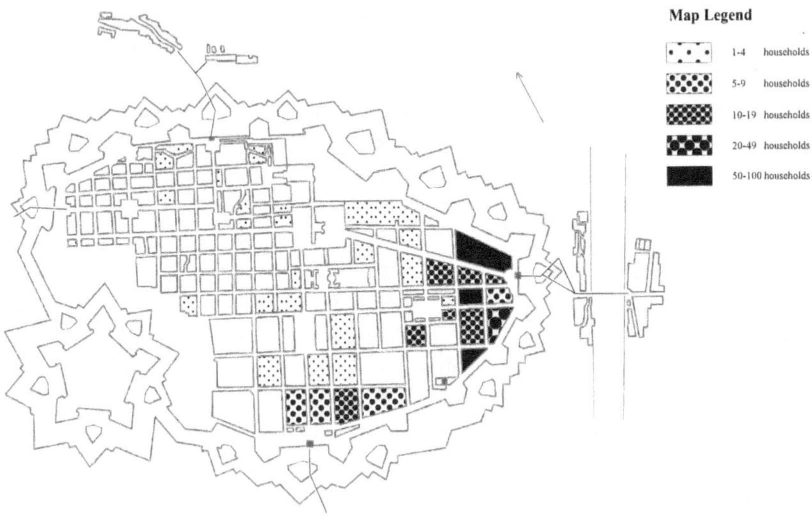

Map 7.10 Map of the urban distribution of silk weavers in 1802 (*Source*: author's elaboration based on the 1802 Census of the Population of Turin—ASCT, *Coll. XII*, Censimento del 1802)

French occupation in 1797 put an end to the troubled history of the San Pasquale's block, which had already been largely abandoned by the artisans for whom it had been destined for twenty years earlier. By 1802, the situation remained largely unchanged.[32]

Only after the Congress of Vienna and the restoration of the throne of the Kingdom of Sardinia to the House of Savoy did the weavers' guild reassert itself in the Consulate in 1820:

> The University of master weavers of silk, gold, and silver fabrics of the present City, humbly represents to Your Excellency that the property owners of the houses have dismissed a great portion of the aforementioned silk weavers, and already eighty looms have ceased their work in the old house of S. Paolo, *contrada delle Rosine* (...) as (...) another eighty in the house formerly Ceveris at *Rondeau di Po* (...) and the others in the houses nearby either dismissed or threatened to leave, and likewise in the house of the

Soldo (Central Bureau for Military Pay), and Austrian troops and lieutenants (Palmucci Quaglino 1992).

[32] ASCT, *Coll. XII*, Censimento del 1802.

Ritiro delle Rosine, under the pretext of repairs, but much more due to the tremendous disruptions and noises inherently associated with their craft.[33]

Therefore, nearly a century on, the issue of housing for silk weavers was far from being resolved, presenting characteristics strikingly similar to those of the 1740s in the nineteenth century.

5 Conclusions

The drastic urban transformations of early modern Turin exemplify how a city's physical structure shapes social dynamics. In the seventeenth century, the old city, following a grid structure, became primarily residential, while expansions to the south (*Città Nuova*) and east (*Città Nuova di Po*) facilitated the growth of manufacturing within the city walls, with the basic unit being the domestic-sized workshops (Becattini 1987; Poni 2001). By the late 1600s, an industrial district had emerged, composed of domestic-sized workshops near residential areas. However, this concentration caused significant inconvenience, including foul-smelling odors and noise, which altered the appearance of the new city. The incorporation of once-external neighborhoods within the fortified perimeter reshaped the urban layout, turning the boroughs beyond the rivers into areas on the outskirts.

The installation of hydraulic spinning mills in *borgo Dora* at the end of the seventeenth century further transformed the geography of the city's production facilities, as the need for continuous water flow displaced many hand-operated silk spinners. Some adapted by changing their products, relocating—often to *borgo Dora*—or abandoning their work altogether. Unlike spinners, whose activities depended on the Dora River's layout, dyers and weavers were primarily influenced by the city's growth in terms of space and government policies. In the seventeenth century, dyers operated within the city, particularly in *contrada dei coriatori*, benefiting from

[33] "L'Università de' mastri fabbricanti e mercanti di stoffe in seta, oro e argento della presente città, umilmente rappresenta all'E.V. che i proprietarj delle case hanno licenziato grandissima parte de' suddetti, e di già si contano ottanta telaj, che hanno cessato il loro lavoro nell'antica Casa di S. Paolo, contrada delle Rosine (...) come (...) altri ottanta nella casa già Ceveris al Rondeau di Po (...) e gli altri in dette case o licenziati o minacciati di sortirne, e così pure nella casa del Ritiro delle Rosie, nelle prime sotto pretesto di riparazioni ma molto più per i grandissimi disturbi e rumori che di necessità sono annessi alla loro arte." AST, C, *Materie economiche*, Cat. IV, m. 22 di II addizione, fasc. 18, 1820.

water access and drainage systems. With the second phase of urban expansion, authorities ordered their relocation to *borgo di Po*, where specialized facilities like the *Torrette* basins were established. The plan took nearly a century to be fully realized and only by the early nineteenth century had the city center been freed from dyeing-related pollution. Noise pollution from the proliferation of weaving workshops posed a different challenge. Public order concerns led to efforts to confine artisans to the southeastern part of the city, particularly in the San Pasquale's block. Even so, the plan yielded limited results, and issues surrounding weavers' living and working conditions persisted into the early nineteenth century.

The House of Savoy's ambition to expand Turin and establish a strong presence in European silk production played a pivotal role in these developments. The newly planned spaces had to accommodate population growth, the rise of silk manufacturing, and the resulting environmental and social challenges, all of which shaped the city's architecture and socioeconomic landscape. Despite these efforts, much of the new space became an outlying area for those marginalized in early modern society, housing the Jewish ghetto, charitable institutions, and artisans' workshops between *Città Nuova* and *Città Nuova di Po*. In conclusion, Turin's silk industry cannot be understood without considering the interplay between institutional, economic, and representational goals, urban planning, and technological advancements. These factors, along with physical changes to the city, machinery, and the tangible effects of industry—such as noise and pollution—profoundly shaped social dynamics. The city is not merely an object subject to what Winner (1980) defined as the "political use of urban space,"[34] but acts as a catalyst or a living organism, participating in shaping the society that resides, works, and governs within it.

Bibliography

Ago, Renata. 2023. *Roma barocca. Potere, arte e cultura nel Seicento*. Rome: Carocci.

Balani, Donatella, Eric Monkkonen, and Geoffrey Symcox. 2005. *Census of Turin, Italy, 1705*. Inter-University Consortium for Political and Social Research, 2005-12-15.

[34] "The issues that divide or unite people in society are settled not only in the institutions and practices of politics proper, but also, and less obviously, in tangible arrangements of steel and concrete, wires and transistors, nuts and bolts" (Winner 1980, 128).

Barbot, Michela, and Andrea Caracausi, eds. 2009. *Città in movimento (XV–XXI secolo). Cheiron*, 52(2).

Becattini, Giacomo. 1987. L'unità di indagine. In *Mercato e forze locali. Il distretto industriale*, ed. Giacomo Becattini, 35–48. Bologna: Il Mulino.

Berengo, Marino. 1999. *L'Europa delle città. Il volto della società urbana europea tra Medioevo ed età moderna*. Turin: Einaudi.

Bianchi, Cesare. 1991. *Porta Palazzo e il Balon. Storia e mito*. Turin: Il punto.

Billen, Gilles, Josette Garnier, and Sabine Barles. 2012. History of the urban environmental imprint: Introduction to a multidisciplinary approach to the long-term relationships between Western cities and their hinterland. *Regional Environmental Change* 12:249–253.

Blunt, Anthony, and Cesare De Seta. 2021. *La civiltà architettonica e le città del Barocco*. Naples: CLEAN.

Boggio, Camillo. 1895. Gli architetti Carlo ed Amedeo di Castellamonte e lo sviluppo edilizio di Torino nel secolo XVII. *Atti della Società degli Ingegneri e degli Architetti di Torino* 29 (1): 27–58.

Bonardi, Maria Teresa. 1988. Canali e macchine idrauliche nel paesaggio suburbano. In *Acque, ruote e mulini a Torino v. I*, ed. Giuseppe Bracco, 105–128. Turin: Archivio Storico della Città di Torino.

Bonardi, Maria Teresa, and Aldo A. Settia. 1997. La città e il suo territorio. In *Storia di Torino II*, ed. Rinaldo Comba, 7–96. Turin: Einaudi.

Boone, Marc. 2012. Cities in late medieval Europe: The promise and the curse of modernity. *Urban History* 39 (2): 329–349.

Borelli, Giovanni Battista. 1681. *Editti antichi e nuovi de' Sovrani Prencipi della Real Casa di Savoia, delle loro Tutrici, e de' Magistrati di qua da' Monti*. Turin: Zappata.

Bracco, Giuseppe, ed. 1988. *Acque, ruote e mulini a Torino v. I–II*. Turin: Archivio Storico della Città di Torino.

Bracco, Giuseppe, ed. 1992. *Torino sul filo della seta*. Turin: Archivio Storico della Città di Torino.

Braudel, Fernand. 1979. *Civilisation matérielle, économie et capitalisme*. Paris: Colin.

Braudel, Fernand. 1981. *Civilization and capitalism*, 15th–18th century, Translated by S. Reynolds. New York: Harper and Row

Calabi, Donatella. 2004. *The market and the city: Square, street and architecture in early modern Europe*. London: Routledge.

Castelnuovo, Enrico, and Marco Rosci, eds. 1980. *Cultura figurativa e architettonica negli Stati del Re di Sardegna, 1773–1861*. Turin: Stamperia artistica nazionale.

Cerutti, Simona. 1992. *Mestieri e Privilegi. Nascita delle corporazioni a Torino (secoli XVII–XVIII)*. Turin: Einaudi.

Cerutti, Simona. 2012. *Étrangers: Étude d'une condition d'incertitude dans une société d'Ancien Régime*. Paris: Bayard.
Chicco, Giuseppe. 1995. *La seta in Piemonte 1650–1800. Un sistema industriale d'ancien régime*. Milan: FrancoAngeli.
Chierici, Patrizia. 1988. Le strutture materiali dei mulini di Dora dal tardo medioevo alle soglie dell'Ottocento. In *Acque, ruote e mulini a Torino v. 1*, ed. Giuseppe Bracco, 273–299. Turin: Archivio Storico della Città di Torino.
Chierici, Patrizia. 1992. Da Torino tutt'intorno: le "fabbriche da seta" dell'antico regime. In *Torino sul filo della seta*, ed. Giuseppe Bracco, 177–202. Turin: Archivio Storico della Città di Torino.
Chierici, Patrizia. 2004. Racconigi: una città industriale d'antico regime tra fonti scritte e iconografiche. *Il tesoro delle città. Strenna dell'Associazione Storia della Città* 2:127–133.
Chierici, Patrizia, ed. 2007. *Un filo di seta, le fabbriche magnifiche in provincia di Cuneo*. Caraglio: Nerosubianco.
Chierici, Patrizia, and Laura Palmucci Quaglino. 1987. Per una storia del patrimonio industriale in Piemonte: il periodo napoleonico. *Publications de l'École française de Rome* 96:133–160.
Chierici, Patrizia, and Laura Palmucci Quaglino, eds. 1993. *Le Fabbriche Magnifiche. La seta in provincia di Cuneo tra Seicento e Ottocento*. Cuneo: L'arciere.
Claretta, Gaudenzio, ed. 1878. *Memoriale autografo di Carlo Emanuele II Duca di Savoia*. Genoa: Tipografia Regio Istituto Sordo-Muti.
Claretta, Gaudenzio. 1890. *L'edificazione della cittadella di Torino 1564–1573*. Turin: Stamperia Reale Paravia.
Cohen, Gary B., and Franz A. J. Szabo, eds. 2008. *Embodiments of power. Building Baroque cities in Europe*. New York-Oxford: Berghahn.
Comba, Rinaldo, and Rosanna Roccia, eds. 1993. *Torino fra Medioevo e Rinascimento. Dai catasti al paesaggio urbano e rurale*. Turin: Archivio storico della Città di Torino.
Comoli Mandracci, Vera. 1983a. *Torino*. Rome-Bari: Laterza.
Comoli Mandracci, Vera. 1983b. Analisi di un fatto urbano: piazza S. Carlo in Torino nel quadro della formazione e delle trasformazioni della "Città Nuova". In *La capitale per uno Stato*, ed. Vera Comoli Mandracci, 87–102. Turin: Celid.
Comoli Mandracci, Vera. 1998. Lo sviluppo urbanistico e l'assetto della città. In *Storia di Torino III*, ed. Giuseppe Ricuperati, 355–386. Turin: Einaudi.
Comoli Mandracci, Vera. 2002. L'urbanistica della città capitale e del territorio. In *Storia di Torino IV*, ed. Giuseppe Ricuperati, 431–461. Turin: Einaudi.
Cronon, William. 1993. The uses of environmental history. *Environmental History Review* 17 (3): 1–22.
D'Amico, Stefano. 1994. *Le contrade e la città. Sistema produttivo e spazio urbano a Milano fra Cinque e Seicento*. Milan: FrancoAngeli.

Dameri, Annalisa, and Alice Pozzati. 2016. Torino. Borgo Po: le architetture, il fiume e la collina. In *Delli aspetti de Paesi. Vecchi e nuovi media per l'immagine del paesaggio, v. 1, Costruzione, descrizione, identità storica*, ed. Annunziata Berrino and Alfredo Buccato, 1293–1302. Naples: Circe.

De Lacy, Phillip H., and Benedict Einarson, eds. 1959. *Plutarch's Moralia in fifteen volumes, VII*. Cambridge, MA: Harvard University Press.

Duboin, Felice Amato. 1827. *Raccolta per ordine di materie delle leggi cioè editti, patenti, manifesti, ecc. emanate negli stati di terraferma sino all'8 dicembre 1798 dai sovrani della real casa di Savoja*, t. 3, v. 2. Turin: Davico e Picco

Duboin, Felice Amato. 1849. *Raccolta per ordine di materie delle leggi cioè editti, patenti, manifesti, ecc. emanate negli stati di terraferma sino all'8 dicembre 1798 dai sovrani della real casa di Savoja*, t. 16, v. 18. Turin: Baricco ed Arnaldi

Friedrichs, Christopher R. 2014. *The early modern city 1450–1750*. London: Routledge.

Gindelsky, Marina, and Remi Jedwab. 2023. Killer cities and industrious cities? New data and evidence on 250 years of urban growth. *Journal of Economic Geography* 23 (1): 179–208.

Gordon, Daniel. 1994. *Citizens without sovereignty. Equality and sociability in French thought, 1670–1789*. Princeton: Princeton University Press.

Greif, Avner, Lynne Kiesling, and John V. C. Nye, eds. 2015. *Institutions, innovation and industrialization: Essays in economic history and development*. Princeton: Princeton University Press.

Griselini, Francesco. 1783. *Il setificio, ovvero memorie dodici sopra i diversi rami georgici e d'industria che lo costituiscono*. Verona: Moroni.

Guenzi, Alberto. 2008. L'identità industriale di una città e del suo territorio. In *Storia di Bologna. 3. Bologna nell'Età moderna*, ed. Adriano Prosperi, vol. 1, 449–524.

Guenzi, Alberto, and Carlo Poni. 1987. Sinergia di due innovazioni. Chiaviche e mulini da seta a Bologna. *Quaderni storici* 64:111–128.

Hanlon, W. Walker, and Stephan Heblich. 2022. History and urban economics. *Regional Science and Urban Economics* 94:103751.

LeCain, Timothy J. 2017. *The matter of history. How things create the past*. Cambridge: Cambridge University Press.

Maitte, Corine, and Didier Terrier, eds. 2014. *Les temps du travail. Normes, pratiques, évolutions (XIVe-XIXe siècles)*. Rennes: Presses universitaires de Rennes.

Maitte, Corine, and Didier Terrier, eds. 2020. *Les rythmes du labeur. Enquête sur le temps de travail en Europe occidentale, XIVe-XIXe siècle*. Paris: La Dispute.

Marchis, Vittorio. 1992. Le macchine della seta. In *Torino sul filo della seta*, ed. Giuseppe Bracco, 247–291. Turin: Archivio Storico della Città di Torino.

Marchis, Vittorio. 2016. *Storia delle macchine. Tre millenni di cultura tecnologica*. Rome-Bari: Laterza.

Martelli, Francesco. 2005. *Il viaggio in Europa di Pietro Guerrini (1682–1686). Edizione della corrispondenza e dei disegni di un inviato di Cosimo III dei Medici.* Florence: Olschki.

Mayernik, David. 2019. The Baroque city. In *The Oxford handbook of the Baroque*, ed. John D. Lyons, 211–237. Oxford: Oxford University Press.

Merlin, Pierpaolo. 1998. Amministrazione e politica tra Cinque e Seicento: Torino da Emanuele Filiberto a Carlo Emanuele I. In *Storia di Torino III*, ed. Giuseppe Ricuperati, 111–169. Turin: Einaudi.

Milizia, Francesco. 1781. *Principi di architettura civile.* Finale: De' Rossi.

Mocarelli, Luca. 2001. *Una realtà produttiva urbana nel secolo dei Lumi. Milano città atelier.* Brescia: Club.

Navire, Federico. 2008. *Torino come centro di sviluppo culturale: un contributo agli studi della civiltà italiana.* Frankfurt: Peter Lang.

Pagella, Enrica, Elena Rossetti Brezzi, and Enrico Castelnuovo, eds. 2006. *Corti e città: arte del Quattrocento nelle Alpi occidentali.* Milan: Skira.

Palmucci Quaglino, Laura. 1992. Lo spazio del lavoro: filatoi, filande e manifatture da seta a Torino tra Settecento e Ottocento. In *Torino sul filo della seta*, ed. Giuseppe Bracco, 203–246. Turin: Archivio Storico della Città di Torino.

Paolucci, Gabriella. 1996. The changing dynamics of working time. *Time and Society* 5 (2): 145–167.

Pollak, Martha D. 1988. From Castrum to capital: Autograph plans and planning studies of Turin, 1615–1673. *Journal of the Society of Architectural Historians* 47 (3): 263–280.

Pollak, Martha D. 1989. La Piazza Reale à Turin: du bastion à la place résidentielle. *Urbi* 11:LVI–LXX.

Pollak, Martha D. 1991. *Turin 1564–1680, urban design, military culture, and the creation of the absolutist capital.* Chicago: Chicago University Press.

Poni, Carlo. 1990. Per la storia del distretto industriale serico di Bologna (secoli XVI–XIX). *Quaderni storici* 25 (73): 93–167.

Poni, Carlo. 2001. Comparing two urban industrial districts: Bologna and Lyon in the early modern period. In *Knowledge, social institutions and the division of labour*, ed. Pier Luigi Porta, Roberto Scazzieri, and Andrew Skinner, 199–227. Cheltenham-Northampton: Edward Elgar Publishing.

Poni, Carlo. 2009. *La seta in Italia, una grande industria prima della rivoluzione industriale.* Bologna: Il Mulino.

Prak, Maarten. 2018. *Citizens without nations: Urban citizenship in Europe and the world, c. 1000–1789.* Cambridge: Cambridge University Press.

Raviola, Blythe Alice. 2015. Genova per noi. Feudatari, nobili, banchieri e altri liguri nel Piemonte della prima età moderna. In *Genova e Torino. Quattro secoli di incontri e scontri. Nel bicentenario dell'annessione della Liguria al Regno di Sardegna*, ed. Giovanni Assereto, Carlo Bitossi, and Pierpaolo Merlin, 121–142. Genoa: Società Ligure di Storia Patria.

Richards, John F. 2003. *The unending frontier. An environmental history of the early modern world*. Berkeley-Los Angeles: University of California Press.
Ricuperati, Giuseppe. 1998. Premessa. Capitale, municipalità, corte: i ruoli di una città complessa. In *Storia di Torino III*, ed. Giuseppe Ricuperati, XVII–XXXIII. Turin: Einaudi.
Righi, Laura. 2016. Produzione di seta e trasferimenti tecnologici tra legislazione e frodi: il caso di Bologna dal XIV al XVI secolo. *Archivio Storico Italiano* 174 (4): 639–668.
Roggero, Costanza. 2002. L'urbanistica nel secondo Settecento. In *Storia di Torino V*, ed. Giuseppe Ricuperati, 799–819. Turin: Einaudi.
Romano, Giovanni, ed. 1990. *Domenico della Rovere e il Duomo nuovo di Torino: Rinascimento a Roma e in Piemonte*. Turin: Cassa di risparmio di Torino.
Roodenburg, Herman, and Pieter Spierenburg, eds. 2004. *Social control in Europe 1500–1800*. Columbus: Ohio State University Press.
Rosen, Christine M., and Joel Arthur Tarr. 1994. The importance of an urban perspective in environmental history. *Journal of Urban History* 20 (3): 299–310.
Rosso, Claudio. 1992a. Dal gelso all'organzino: nascita e sviluppo di un'industria trainante. In *Torino sul filo della seta*, ed. Giuseppe Bracco, 39–66. Turin: Archivio Storico della Città di Torino.
Rosso, Claudio. 1992b. Seta e dintorni: lombardi e genovesi a Torino fra Cinque e Seicento. *Studi Storici* 33 (1): 175–193.
Rosso, Claudio. 2002. Uomini e poteri nella Torino barocca (1630–1675). In *Storia di Torino IV. La città fra crisi e ripresa (1630–1730)*, ed. Giuseppe Ricuperati, 7–195. Turin: Einaudi.
Sarti, Raffaella. 2002. *Europe at home. Family and material culture, 1500–1800*. New Haven: Yale University Press.
Schott, Dieter. 2004. Urban environmental history: What lessons are there to be learnt? *Boreal Environment Research* 9:519–528.
Scotti Tosini, Aurora. 1998. La cittadella. In *Storia di Torino III*, ed. Giuseppe Ricuperati, 414–450. Turin: Einaudi.
Sinclair, Paul J. J., Gullög Nordquist, Frands Herschend, and Christian Isendahl, eds. 2010. *The urban mind. Cultural and environmental dynamics*. Uppsala: Uppsala University Press.
Spallone, Roberta. 1999. Lettura e rappresentazione della trasformazione storica del borgo di Po a Torino dall'età neoclassica ad oggi. In *Borgo Po. Un'esperienza di rilievo della trasformazione*, ed. Secondino Coppo, Giuseppa Novello Massai, Leonardo Bisceglia, Pia Davico, and Roberta Spallone, 21–42. Turin: Levrotto & Bella.
Stumpo, Enrico. 2002. Economia urbana e gruppi sociali. In *Storia di Torino IV*, ed. Giuseppe Ricuperati, 247–272. Turin: Einaudi.
Symcox, Geoffrey. 2002a. La trasformazione dello Stato e il riflesso del potere. In *Storia di Torino IV*, ed. Giuseppe Ricuperati, 719–867. Turin: Einaudi.

Symcox, Geoffrey. 2002b. La reggenza della seconda madama reale (1675–1684). In *Storia di Torino IV*, ed. Giuseppe Ricuperati, 197–244. Turin: Einaudi.

Turbini, Gaspare Antonio. 1778. *L'economia per la filatura delle sete e descrizione di tutte le fabbriche ad essa appartenenti perfino all'uscita delle stoffe lavorate.* Brescia: Vescovi.

Varallo, Franca. 2002. Le feste da Vittorio Amedeo II a Vittorio Amedeo III. In *Storia di Torino V*, ed. Giuseppe Ricuperati, 821–839. Turin: Einaudi.

Viglino Davico, Micaela. 2005a. Autenticità e copia nei disegni di architettura militare. In *L'architettura degli ingegneri*, ed. Angela Marino, 9–26. Rome: Gangemi.

Viglino Davico, Micaela, ed. 2005b. *Fortezze "alla moderna" e ingegneri militari nel ducato sabaudo.* Turin: Celid.

Viglino Davico, Micaela, ed. 2008. *Architetti e ingegneri militari in Piemonte tra '500 e '700. Un repertorio biografico.* Turin: Omega.

Volpiano, Mauro. 2001. Una immensa piazza "per la venuta del re". In *Progettare la città. L'urbanistica di Torino tra storia e scelte alternative*, ed. Vera Comoli Mandracci and Rosanna Roccia, 217–222. Turin: Archivio Storico della Città di Torino.

Winner, Langdon. 1980. Do artifacts have politics? *Daedalus* 109 (1): 121–136.

Zucker, Paul. 1955. Space and movement in high Baroque city planning. *Journal of the Society of Architectural Historians* 14 (1): 8–13.

CHAPTER 8

External Pressures: Fashion, Cotton, and the Decline of Piedmont's Silk Industry

1 Introduction

The Piedmontese dialect used the word *teila*, which according to nineteenth-century Piedmontese-Italian dictionaries, referred to textile products made from vegetable fibers, particularly linen, hemp, and cotton. Its Italian counterpart, *tela* (cloth), as defined in the *Vocabolario degli Accademici della Crusca* (1691), does not specifically emphasize its association with vegetable fibers. Perhaps this is why, just below the main definition, the *Gran dizionario piemontese-italiano* of Vittorio Sant'Albino (1859) notes that the term *teila d'or o d'argent* existed—a type of fabric made of silk, gold, or silver. In pre-modern Italy, people selling *teile* were known as *mercanti da tela* (cloth merchants), a profession that had been well established in Piedmont since the Middle Ages. This trade proved highly lucrative, involving the export of locally produced textiles and the import of foreign goods for local consumption, as activities of merchants from Asti showed (Comba 1988). The early modern era saw a growing demand for silk products, prompting these merchants to concentrate on this profitable sector, selling imported fabrics both wholesale and retail. Over time, their offerings diversified, encompassing a wide range of goods—from cotton and silk fabrics to lace, ribbons, fans, caps, artificial flowers, and even silver or tortoiseshell snuff boxes. By the seventeenth century, these merchants had earned the title of *mercanti di moda* (fashion merchants). They were seen as arbiters of taste, introducing "diverse

M. Grassi, *The Silk Industry in Early Modern Piedmont*, Labour in History and Society,
https://doi.org/10.1007/978-3-032-15353-1_8

goods" and dictating "what is most appealing (...) shaping through their textiles, lace, and fashions what was considered beautiful, desirable, and useful by both ladies and gentlemen."[1] Essentially, *mercanti di moda* set the pace for avant-garde markets, stocking their shops and warehouses with Lyonnais drapes, Prussian crystals, and Flemish lace to cater to the exotic tastes of the noble-bourgeois elite *à la mode*. However, this approach did present challenges. For instance, merchants had to engage with extensive trade networks, adapt to unstable political and economic conditions, and manage markets shaped by global dynamics. All of these factors inevitably influenced the trade of goods, silk included.

This chapter examines how external pressures reshaped Piedmont's production and commerce, challenging in particular the development of the silk weaving sector. Yet this trajectory should not be seen in isolation but as one strand within a broader Italian and European reconfiguration of textile production between the late eighteenth and early nineteenth centuries, reflected in parallel developments across multiple regional centers. Building on the quantitative reconstructions of twentieth-century historians (Prato 1908; Bulferetti 1963; Chicco 1995), the chapter focuses on the underlying socio-economic shifts—from falling demand and changing production structures to labor mobility and state intervention—that defined this period of transition. Firstly, the chapter explores the emergence of seasonal fashion in Europe, a trend introduced by Lyonnais merchants in the seventeenth century. While Piedmont initially benefited from Lyon's success in the early eighteenth century, becoming a key supplier of yarns to the *Grande Fabrique*, the dominance of Lyonnais fabrics and growing competition soon made it clear that Piedmontese textiles could not compete with those from Lyon. Building on this, the chapter examines the role of fabric-lightening processes, shifting patterns of demand throughout the eighteenth century, and the appeal of Lyon as a weaving hub for foreign artisans. Alongside the rise of fashion, another major development reshaped European tastes and habits: the growing popularity of cotton fabrics, a shift with far-reaching socio-economic effects worldwide. The East India Companies played a crucial role in this transformation, importing lightweight cotton textiles that captivated Europeans with their practicality and exotic appeal. Two distinct responses emerged: on the one hand, efforts to stimulate the production of cotton fabrics on European soil, and on the other, the introduction of restrictive clothing

[1] AST, C, *Materie economiche*, Cat. IV, m. 8, fasc. 4, 1739.

laws aimed at curbing their production and consumption. By the early eighteenth century, cotton was perceived as a disruptive competitor to the lucrative silk industry. This chapter analyzes the elements that fueled cotton's rise, which, despite attempts to suppress its consumption, conquered legal barriers and became a staple across all social classes, establishing itself as the quintessential neoclassical fiber. This revolution extended beyond fabrics to accessories: by the mid-eighteenth century, the adaptation of the stocking frame for cotton challenged the traditional stocking industry. Finally, the chapter explores the impact of unpredictable climate changes on Piedmont's textile production, highlighting how these shifts dealt a decisive blow to the industry. In response, the government adopted countermeasures, merchants confronted the inherent limitations of the silk supply chain, and workers explored alternative paths to survive the crisis.

The merchants of fashion emerge as yet another key player among the many protagonists examined in this study. Although somewhat peripheral to the core Piedmontese silk industry, these traders wielded considerable influence, subtly shaping consumer preferences to their advantage. Their adaptability and extensive product offerings—far surpassing those of merchants dependent on silk—allowed them to carve out a distinctive role within the broader commercial ecosystem. In the 1730s, the Savoy government, confident in the success of its high-quality *organzino* across Europe, granted silk merchants exclusive rights to import foreign goods made from the prized thread. Despite this, fashion merchants repeatedly but unsuccessfully attempted to break into the foreign silk trade, forcing them to seek alternative avenues for their business. Nevertheless, their ability to navigate evolving trade dynamics proved vital. Their flexibility became crucial in navigating global market transformations, allowing them to stay competitive despite external pressures.

2 France's Golden Gateway: Lyon's Merchants and the Rise of Fashion

Although France had not succeeded in developing a fully integrated silk production chain, as early as the fifteenth century, it already featured a native class of artisans skilled in crafting certain highly sought-after plain fabrics.[2] This achievement was made possible not only by the introduction

[2] For example, the silk fabrics from Tours traded in Turin in 1637 were few compared to those from Venice, Genoa, or Lucca, but they were sold at the same price (Borelli 1681,

of foreign labor and the Lyon fairs' success—which attracted a multitude of merchants and silk products annually—but also via the imposition of strategic customs policies. Due to its geopolitical position, Lyon obtained significant privileges during the reign of Francis I, including the exclusive right to serve as the kingdom's sole entry point for foreign raw silk—an essential resource for sustaining the domestic silk industry. This solidified the position of Lyon's manufacturers, whose prominence on the international stage steadily increased over time. Colbert's appointment to court in the latter half of the seventeenth century, alongside the significant manufacturing reforms stemming from his mercantilist policies, enabled Lyon's silk industry to rapidly achieve enduring success. The city on the Rhône became the leading producer of silk fabrics in Europe. While silk manufacturing flourished in numerous French cities during the early modern period, Lyon stood out above all others, earning the title of "France's Golden Gateway" on the Italian side of the Alps (Zanon 1763, 164). As a result, the growing influx of silk fueled the expansion of the silk weaving profession in Lyon, with the number of weavers steadily rising throughout the period (Lequin et al. 1991).

This expansion empowered merchants to develop groundbreaking commercial strategies, emphasizing the production of luxurious fabrics tailored to the Parisian market and the sophisticated tastes of the royal court (Sewell 2010). A distinctive characteristic of Lyon's silk trade was the relatively swift evolution of fabric designs available to the public, effectively laying the foundation for what is now known as the fashion system. The strategic introduction of annual production variations by Lyonnais merchants played a pivotal role in the transition from luxury to elegance (Capuzzo 2006; Poni 2009). A key feature of this emerging fashion system was the regular modifications to both garment and fabric elements, prompting the nobility and the wealthy to abandon their old clothing in favor of new purchases (Belfanti 2008; Poni 2009; Riello 2012). Lyon's innovative production and commercial system presented significant challenges to rival industries, which struggled to produce *à la mode* fabrics quickly enough to compete. Through careful planning, Lyonnais merchants would introduce textiles with fresh, original patterns at high prices at the beginning of each season, attracting those eager to showcase their ability to wear the latest fashions (Poni 1993; Capuzzo 2006). By the end of the season, unsold stock would be heavily discounted. This aggressive

1016–1023—November 17, 1634).

market strategy was designed not only to outperform competitors but also to weaken and eliminate the production of foreign imitators (Poni 1993). While consumer preferences underwent a significant transformation during the eighteenth century, shaped by the new forms and colors introduced by Lyon's designers, recent studies indicate that annual innovations were, in fact, largely confined to specific patterned fabrics (Styles 2019).[3] The widespread use of silk fabrics and participation in the fashion system were privileges largely reserved for the wealthy and the nobility. Nonetheless, the market for second-hand silk garments, silk-blend textiles, and silk accessories had, in various ways, permeated even the lower social classes (Lemire 1988; Allegra 1996; Styles 2008; Riello 2012; Staples 2015; Jordan 2019; Trivellato 2021). As Lyon dictated the fast pace of fashion, the overall quality of fabrics began to decline. This was a reflection of a new disinterest in the durability of garments, which were increasingly seen as disposable items, to be replaced quickly in order to remain *à la mode*. However, this shift did not diminish the perceived excellence of these products. Instead, it redefined the very concept of quality, which departed from durability to focus instead on the refinement of the fabric and its visual impact (Dato 2023). This new interpretation of quality spread swiftly across Europe, but Lyonnais manufacturers remained unrivaled in setting the standard.

The success of Lyon's silk industry posed significant challenges for competing manufacturers, who faced declining orders and, consequently, the loss of jobs. Piedmont, one of the main suppliers of raw silk to what was known as the *Grande Fabrique lyonnaise*, was particularly affected. With France now largely self-sufficient, opportunities for Italian fabrics became increasingly limited—at least under their original branding. Several documented cases reveal that textiles produced in subalpine regions were, in fact, sold in France and Italy disguised as Lyonnais products (Hoshino 2001; Munro 2003; Poni 2009; Belfanti 2013). Given these circumstances, Piedmontese merchants were forced to rethink their strategies, shifting their focus to the production of lighter fabrics, which could be made more quickly and at lower cost, while requiring less silk. Unlike Lyonnais fabrics, these were primarily aimed at secondary markets, such as

[3] A significant shift occurred in the 1760s, marking the gradual transition from the Rococo style—characterized by floral bouquets and garlands—to more subdued motifs and plain-weave fabrics (Rothstein 1990; Poni 2009).

Germany and Eastern Europe, which were less influenced by the allure of French court-driven fashion trends (Poni 1993, 2001; Tolaini 1997).

Despite these adaptations, Turin's proximity to Lyon led many master weavers and workers to abandon the Piedmontese capital in favor of the French city. Records from the *Ospedale di Carità* document how the wives and children of silk weavers frequently sought assistance, reporting that they had been abandoned by the head of the household, who had emigrated to Lyon in search of work—leaving the family without any means of support (Cavallo 1995).

3 The Cotton Wave: Global Trade, Exoticism, and New Technologies

It would be misleading to assume that the attacks by Lyon's *Grande Fabrique* were the sole cause of the crisis in Piedmont's project to establish a full silk production chain through large-scale weaving and commercial distribution; equally significant was the gradual yet unstoppable spread of cotton across Europe (Mazzaoui 1981). While silk had dictated fashion trends since at least the sixteenth century, it soon faced competition from fabrics made of other materials that sought to replicate its luxurious appearance (Chorley 1993). Between the seventeenth and eighteenth centuries, the expansion of the East India Companies brought vast quantities of cotton textiles into Europe (Riello 2013a). During the early modern period, cotton fabrics secured a notable share of international trade thanks to their lightweight nature, affordability, and the allure of exotic garments and goods for European consumers (Mazzaoui 1981; Capuzzo 2006; Riello 2013a). In the Mediterranean area, *indiennes*—painted or printed cotton fabrics—became widely popular from the second half of the seventeenth century (Raveux 2004, 2008). The growing demand had significant consequences. As a French report from 1753 observed, the quality of imported cotton fabrics was steadily declining, while prices were rising rapidly (Riello 2013a). Alongside the flourishing production of colorful *indiennes*, the eighteenth century saw the rise of muslins and other white cotton fabrics, which gained widespread popularity, particularly in Great Britain and France. By the end of the century, these textiles had become wardrobe staples for the European nobility (Styles 2019). The Lyonnais fashion system also played a role in this process. Its success quickly encouraged producers of mixed and cotton textiles to capitalize on the trend by designing fabrics for the European market that featured colors and patterns inspired by French manufacturers (Styles 2000, 2019; Hohti 2025). While the incorporation of cotton into European fashion was a gradual process spanning centuries, it reached its peak in the eighteenth century. Initially embraced by the middle and upper classes, cotton eventually became common even among the lower classes (Mazzaoui 1981; Lemire 1991, 2018; Styles 2008; Lemire and Riello 2008; Richmond 2013; Hohti 2025). European states began to consider producing these sought-after textiles domestically, but they faced significant challenges, including securing raw materials and the lack of skilled labor necessary to establish an industry capable of competing with colonial production (Riello 2013a).

The decision to establish cotton textile manufacturing in Europe faced opposition in several states, which instead sought to prohibit its production, sale, and consumption (O'Brien et al. 1991; Riello 2013b). This was also the case in the Kingdom of Sardinia (Duboin 1849, 449—August 13, 1721). During the eighteenth century, after several failed attempts to set up manufacturing facilities for *indiennes* and mixed-cotton fabrics in Piedmont,[4] the unstoppable rise in cotton product consumption alarmed the Savoy government, prompting decisive measures (Levi Pisetzky 1969). The situation culminated at the end of the century with the issuance of the royal edict on November 13, 1792 (Duboin 1849, 783–784—November 13, 1792). On that occasion, Vittorio Amedeo III decreed a blanket ban on the use of cotton fabrics. Merchants were forbidden from trading these types of textiles and could only sell textiles they already had to buyers outside the state. Tailors faced strict bans not only from using cotton thread but also from accepting any work involving repairing or altering cotton garments. Equally stringent were the new regulations governing the public use of cotton clothing, which in some ways echoed the sumptuary laws widespread during the early modern period (Muzzarelli 2020). These belated efforts to impose top-down consumption regulations, however, proved unsuccessful. They underscore how, by the end of the century, the Savoyard political class had lost touch with the wave of mercantile innovation that had shaped the late seventeenth and early eighteenth centuries. Endeavors to create semi-autarchic economic structures, such as reducing exports of organzine (whose production continued to thrive) to encourage processing on a still-stagnating number of Piedmontese looms, fell short of the government's expectations. Preventing cotton consumption

[4] AST, SR, *Consolato di Commercio*, m. 19, 1724–1736; m. 19b, 1733–1818.

was clearly not a solution and laid bare the government's inability to take a holistic view of the industry and foresee the economic repercussions of its decisions.

The innovations related to cotton extended beyond clothing fabrics and soon encompassed the wide-ranging world of accessories, which enjoyed even broader appeal. Hosiery, in particular, provides a fascinating example. In the eighteenth century, Jedediah Strutt, a hosier from Derbyshire, applied his expertise to modify the silk stocking frame. In 1757, he patented what became known as the Derby Rib machine, capable of knitting ribbed stockings. Within a few years, and with minor modifications, the machine enabled the production of cotton knitwear on the frame. Despite facing numerous challenges—including accusations of plagiarism and protests from stocking makers—Strutt's innovations became widely adopted (Chapman 1974). In a decade, these machines had crossed the Channel, spreading rapidly across France, and reaching the Mediterranean coast. With the advances brought to the industry by inventors like Hargreaves, Arkwright, and Strutt, cotton was enjoying a period of extraordinary success (Belfanti 2005; Mutos Xicola 2026). Moreover, adapting the costly silk stocking frame for cotton stocking production enabled craftsmen with this type of machinery to maintain their trade and remain competitive against rival manufacturers—a practice particularly widespread among Genoese artisans. An industrial survey from 1787 reveals that over 900 frames were operating in Genoa and its surroundings, spread across 310 workshops. Furthermore, the active trade between Genoa and the Iberian Peninsula enabled Genoese stockings to maintain a solid presence in the markets of Spain, Portugal, and, albeit more modestly, the American colonies. The success of Genoese cotton stockings, as Belfanti hypothesizes, likely explains the decline of silk stocking production in the Kingdom of Sardinia. At the same time, however, Piedmont experienced significant growth in the wool industry and its related products, including stockings. By the 1750s, some Piedmontese merchants had already succeeded in producing wool stockings on frames, establishing workshops in the Biella region—a key hub for Piedmont's wool production (Zucca Micheletto 2020; Monestarolo 2013).

Nevertheless, while the Piedmontese silk stocking exports were struggling under the weight of shifting fashions, technological advancements, and socio-political changes, the quality of these products continued to enjoy a prestigious reputation across Europe. This is evident, for example, in the writings of Vincenzo Tonarini, a Bolognese author from the 1780s.

In his *Ragguaglio dei cambj, pesi e misure delle più mercantili piazze di Europa* (Reports on the Exchange Rates, Weights and Measures of the Principal Trading Cities of Europe) he described the Turin market, emphasizing that "silk stockings, patterned stockings, and organzine are the most essential trade items" (1780, 153). Similarly, Neapolitan historian Giuseppe Sigismondo, in his praise of the products made by the Casa del Salvatore—a renowned workshop in Naples—claimed that it produced "silk stockings on frames equal to those of Turin" (1788, 175). In 1799, Jacques Peuchet's *Dictionnaire universel de la géographie commerçante* (Universal Dictionary of Commercial Geography) further confirmed the prestige of Turin's silk stockings, noting that the Piedmontese capital produced "finer, superior in quality, and more affordable stockings than those produced in Paris, Lyon, and Nîmes"[5] (1799, 685). These dynamics reveal a dual reality: on the one hand, actual consumption patterns, and on the other, the reputation and prestige carefully cultivated around the local manufacturing industry (Picture 8.1).

4 Threads of Crisis: Climate, Unemployment, and the Challenges of a Changing World

Industry has the potential to shape the environment, influencing its structure and function. However, silk production—a sector heavily dependent on natural elements such as mulberry leaves, silkworm cocoons, and water flow—was particularly susceptible to unexpected climate changes. As a result, the environment itself played a crucial role in reshaping production, industry, and the market. As early as the first decades of the eighteenth century, for example, Giovanni Ruffino, the director of the Pinardi silk mill, appealed to the government for subsidies. Winter frosts had prevented the mill from operating, bringing production to a standstill (Symcox 2002).[6] Similar incidents recurred throughout the century, such as during the crisis of 1749. Despite these challenges, the impact on production and support for unemployed workers remained relatively limited (Cavallo 1995; Chicco 1995).

This pattern persisted until 1777 when an unusually harsh spring and a late frost seriously hindered the growth of mulberry buds, drastically

[5] "Bas de soie plus beaux, meilleurs en qualité, et ò meilleur compte que nos bas de Paris, Lyon et Nimes" (Peuchet 1799, 685).

[6] ASCT, *Comune di Torino*, Carte Sciolte 3909, 1710.

Picture 8.1 Visiting card of the "Manufacture of Stockings, Pants, and Gloves in Silk and Cotton," located in Rome, belonging to Stanislao Bosisio, a stocking maker from Turin. (*Source*: ASCT, *Coll. Simeom*, C 4156. Courtesy of the Historical Archive of the City of Turin)

reducing leaf production and cocoon development. The poor harvest was cautiously acknowledged in an edict issued on June 16, 1777, in which the Consulate advised farmers to carefully select cocoons for breeding the following year, stating that "this year's season has not been very favorable."[7]

[7] Giannantonio Ranza, in the reprint of *Della Sereide* by Alessandro Tesauro, includes his own *Memoria* on the method of preserving silkworm eggs, both to restore the first harvest in case of failure—such as in 1777—and to secure a second, more reliable harvest. The text skillfully describes various experiments in sericulture, attempting to provide scientific expla-

The reality, however, must have been much more serious: in 1777, only three requests were submitted to the Consulate of Commerce to begin processing raw silk in the Turin area.[8]

Far worse was the crisis of 1787—a catastrophic event that introduced significant new challenges. While the root causes—adverse weather conditions—remained consistent with previous crises, the measures adopted to address the problem were markedly different. A comparison of harvest reports from 1786 and 1787 revealed the stark reality: over 450,000 *rubbi* of cocoons were lost between the two years.[9] Most of the numerous silk mills in Piedmont would exhaust the limited supply of raw silk produced by spring 1787, well before the end of the year. Exports would face significant restrictions, and the production of organzine and other silk threads would barely meet the demands of local looms.

In light of the poor harvest, Count Petitti, then Chief President of the Consulate of Commerce, drafted a memorandum for the king, expressing deep concern for the immediate survival of the workforce employed in the sector. The document reported: "(In Turin's spinning mills, there are) 500 workers; most of the spinning mills are closed, leaving workers without any means of income. A total of 223 have been reported unemployed; among these, according to the mayors, there are 49 men and 174 women, none of whom are in a position to earn their daily bread." The situation was no better in the rest of Piedmont. Petitti continued: "(In Piedmont), there are 272 spinning mills employing 16,097 workers. Of these, 9373 still have work this year, while 6724 are already without employment. By January, apart from the 900 to 1000 workers who might remain employed until the next harvest, we will see 15,097 workers completely out of work." These figures represented only the obvious share of the industry. Petitti informed the king that "the actual number of workers employed in the mills is undoubtedly much higher, as many masters, fearing that their reports might lead to higher taxation, have significantly underreported. This is particularly evident in the community of Venaria Reale, where two mills operated by the Royal Company claimed to employ only 110 workers, while in fact there are 240. (...) From this, it can be estimated that the

nations for the poor yield of 1777 and suggesting that a second annual cocoon harvest could not only mitigate crises or crop failures but, in favorable conditions, significantly benefit the industry (Ranza 1777).

[8] AST, SR, *Consolato di Commercio*, m. 62 Consegne delle filature, 1759–1788.

[9] AST, C, *Materie economiche*, Cat. IV, m. 10 d'addizione, fasc. 13, 1788.

total number of people employed in the mills is closer to 25,000, a figure that aligns with the views of several experienced merchants who own mills." Finally, acknowledging that "most male and female workers employed in the silk sector sustain their families through the income they earn at the mills,"[10] it was estimated that by January 1788, the number of people left without any way of surviving due to the crisis would reach approximately 62,500. The gravity of the crisis is evident not only from the data mentioned above but also from the clear concern shown by the king and state authorities. The silk sector was under serious threat, endangering both the livelihoods of many workers and the reputation of Piedmontese organzine. After careful consideration, the government decided to entrust aid for unemployed silk workers to a newly established charitable institution, the *Ritiro degli Oziosi e Vagabondi* (Shelter for the Idle and Vagrants). Originally known as the *Casa di Correzione* (House of Correction), this institution was established in Turin to create, much like similar efforts in Rome, Paris, and Amsterdam,[11] a penitentiary for beggars.[12] It was part of the broader and lively debate on poverty that, during those years, engaged intellectuals and economists across Europe.[13] A significant boost came from the testamentary legacy of Count Gio Antonio Baratta of Fossano in December 1749, aimed at founding a charitable institution in his name. This initiative soon led to the opening of the House of Correction. Nonetheless, the process faced considerable obstacles. As the count resided in Rome, he had to appoint a local fiduciary heir. The choice fell on Giuseppe Moris, one of the major bankers in Turin, who just two years later would gain notoriety for the catastrophic collapse of his banking house (Caligaris 1988). The king's intervention was ultimately required to advance the project. The result was a partial revision of the institution's original mission—rehabilitating young people through

[10] AST, C, *Materie economiche,* Cat. IV, m. 9 d'addizione, fasc. 7, 1787.

[11] Information was gathered on correctional facilities established in the major European capitals to serve as a model for what would later become the House of Correction in Turin. AST, C, *Materie ecclesiastiche,* Luoghi pii di qua dai monti, m. 19, fasc. 10, June 25, 1750.

[12] AST, C, *Materie ecclesiastiche,* Luoghi pii di qua dai monti, m. 19, fasc. 2, n.d. (but 1755).

[13] "Au XVIe siècle, on soigne et on nourrit le mendiant étranger avant de l'expulser. Au début du XVIIe siècle, on le rase. Plus tard, on le fouette, et, à la fin du siècle, le dernier mot de la répression en fait un forçat." "In the sixteenth century, the foreign beggar is cared for and fed before being expelled. At the beginning of the seventeenth century, he is shaved. Later, he is whipped, and by the end of the century, the ultimate form of repression turns him into a convict" (Roupnel 1922, 98).

labor and the study of arithmetic and the humanities—by introducing apprenticeships in wool carding for about a dozen poor youth each year. The institution was renamed *Opera di Pietà* (House of Mercy), although it retained the popular nickname *Casa di Correzione*, setting aside plans to establish a correctional facility based on the European model. The situation remained unchanged until the 1780s, when renewed efforts to establish a detention facility for the poor prompted the conversion of the *Opera di Pietà* into the *Ritiro degli Oziosi e Vagabondi*. The underlying principle was that proper governance could not tolerate certain members of society remaining idle and failing to contribute to the well-being of the city and state (Geremek 1970, 1973; Lonni 1979; Maldini 1979). It was deemed essential to establish a workshop where what was then described as the "poisonous weeds" of society—comprising the poor, prostitutes, and beggars—could learn a trade and therefore contribute to the common good.[14] But which trade should be taught? While textiles were quickly identified as the preferred sector, significant debate arose over the choice of raw materials. Opinions were divided: some advocated for wool, others for silk, and still others for hemp. The high costs of acquiring wool and silk, combined with the technical challenges of weaving silk fabrics, ultimately narrowed the focus to hemp. Soon after, silk waste was also introduced into the production process. The workshop was entrusted to Carlo Ghiglione, a master silk weaver enrolled in the guilds of both Lyon and Turin. Ghiglione, who had previously directed the workshop of the *Ospedale di Carità* in Mondovì,[15] where fabrics made of silk floss and raw silk were produced, enthusiastically supported working with silk waste. He argued that this approach not only avoided wasting precious raw materials but also provided inmates with practical skills, equipping them for meaningful employment in the future.[16]

Thus, in 1788, the charitable institution was deemed the ideal place to support the numerous workers in the silk sector who, almost overnight, found themselves unemployed and with no immediate prospects for new employment. Fortunately, the cocoon harvest in 1788 was significantly

[14] AST, C, *Materie ecclesiastiche*, Luoghi pii di qua dai monti, m. 17 d'addizione, fasc. 2, n.d. (*post* 1755).

[15] AST, SR, *Consolato di Commercio*, m. 67 Fabbricatori di taffetà lisci e rigati, *sottomissione di Michele Binaj*, September 29, 1789.

[16] AST, C, *Materie ecclesiastiche*, Luoghi pii di qua dai monti, m. 17 d'addizione, fasc. 16, n.d. (but 1787–1788).

better, recording an increase of 366,933 *rubbi* compared to 1787 (Table 8.1).

The year 1787 marked the onset of an unavoidable downturn: the Piedmontese silk industry was in decline, setting off a chain reaction that impacted all production sectors connected to the precious fiber. As Senator Ghiliossi wrote in 1792, in addition to the shortage of raw materials, innovative and unexpected commercial dynamics had emerged over the previous decades. Despite an adequate silk supply in Piedmont that year, there was no demand for it.[17]

By the end of the century, European imports of silk from the East India Companies had risen sharply, particularly from Bengal (Federico 1994; Tolaini 1997; Hutkova 2019; Davini 2024). For instance, while England's raw silk imports before 1770 did not exceed 100,000 pounds, by 1780 they had doubled. This trend continued, reaching 500,000 pounds by 1800 and far surpassing imports from Italy and the Levant (Hertz 1909).

The widespread adoption of the *alla piemontese* reeling method, promoted by many European governments, had yielded some results, turning former loyal buyers into fierce competitors (Davini 2014), even if research

Table 8.1 Annual report on the cocoon harvest in 1788 compared to that of 1787: the findings show that in 1788 the harvest was more than double (*Source*: author's elaboration based on AST, C, *Materie economiche*, Cat. IV, m. 10 d'addizione, fasc. 13, 1788)

Subalpine Territories of the House of Savoy	*1787*	*1788*	*More than the previous year*	*Less than the previous year*
Piedmont	154,934 *rubbi*	406,010 *rubbi*	251,076 *rubbi*	–
Monferrato	24,317 *rubbi*	61,518 *rubbi*	37,201 *rubbi*	–
Alessandria and Lomellina	11,005 *rubbi*	49,520 *rubbi*	38,515 *rubbi*	–
Novara, Vigevano and Lake Maggiore	21,652 *rubbi*	48,164 *rubbi*	26,512 *rubbi*	–
Oltrepò and Tortona	6,774 *rubbi*	20,403 *rubbi*	13,629 *rubbi*	–
Total	218,682 *rubbi*	585,615 *rubbi*	366,933 *rubbi*	–

[17] AST, C, *Materie economiche,* Cat. IV, m. 21 di II addizione, fasc. 37, March 3, 1789.

suggests that the quality of this silk still did not match that of Piedmont (Chicco 1995). Yet, the English Crown had more tricks up its sleeve: the American colonies seemed to offer ideal conditions for developing raw silk production destined for England. As early as the early 1600s, James I had attempted to establish silk production in Virginia—a venture that soon failed (Craven 1949; Levy Peck 2005; Hutkova 2019; Davini 2024). However, following the installation of the spinning mill in Derby in 1720 and the blockade of Piedmontese silk, securing a reliable supply to sustain the Spitalfields industry became an urgent priority.

King George II saw a solution in transforming the new American colony—tellingly named Georgia—into a manufacturing hub for producing Piedmontese-style raw silk. The colony's history, under the leadership of Sir Oglethorpe, and its largely unsuccessful attempts to establish Piedmontese-style factories with a Piedmontese workforce, including high skilled reelers such as Gioanna Camosso, soon faced the challenge of the independence ideals fueling the American Revolution (Marsh 2020; Bertucci 2021). Yet the New World was far from Great Britain's only colonial asset. Attention turned to India, particularly Bengal, where the East India Company sought to establish Piedmontese-style factories. Once again, Piedmontese expertise proved essential: while the initial plan involved bringing high-skilled workers from southern France and northern Italy, much of the workforce came from Piedmont. Among them, Giacomo Wiss, a native of Novi, played a pivotal role. Nevertheless, the raw silk produced in Bengal did not match the quality of Piedmontese silk, even though it arrived in substantial quantities in Great Britain. It accounted for 40% of imports between 1773 and 1789—and kept English spinning mills and looms operational (Hutkova 2019).

It is interesting to note that the transfer of reeling expertise to Bengal seems to have been an exclusively male endeavor. To date, there is no evidence of any Piedmontese women among the dozen or so individuals (entrepreneurs and technicians) who contributed to establishing silk reeling mills in Bengal during the 1770s. Even so, their presence cannot be ruled out, as they may simply not appear in the records available. In Piedmontese silk reeling mills, practical activities were almost entirely the domain of women. While male involvement in the active phases of the reeling process cannot be completely dismissed, for now it remains undocumented. While male supervisors were present in the silk reeling mills, and male merchants were skilled at discerning high- and low-quality silk, production itself was another matter. The lack of hands-on experience with production techniques—combined with the challenges of adapting machinery to a different climate—could probably explain why modifications were necessary for the reeling machinery installed in Bengal. Even so, the resulting silk was of modest quality, comparable only to the raw silk produced in Calabria and Spain (Rey 2011; Davini 2014).

Great Britain was not the only state eager to appropriate Piedmontese innovations, as other European powers had also set their sights on acquiring its tightly controlled expertise. Vaucanson, Nollet, and Soumille are just a few of the most prominent figures who, in the latter half of the century, undertook "intelligent travels" (Bertucci 2013), meticulous studies, and numerous experiments to replicate silk production *alla piemontese* in France (Chicco 1995; Tolaini 1997). Treatises and ordinances published in Languedoc during the pre-revolutionary period are filled with plans for reeling devices, advancements in mechanisms, and equipment designed to eliminate thread defects (Teisseyre-Sallmann 1995; Bertucci 2013). Piedmontese silk was viewed as a model of excellence by France. Despite the country's relentless efforts, it was unable to be self-sufficient in producing high-quality silk and free itself from reliance on the organzine manufactured beyond the Alps.[18]

Piedmontese expertise also captured the attention of the Spanish and Portuguese crowns (Miguel López 1999; Miralles Martínez 2002; Olivares Galvañ 2005; Santos Vaquero 2010; Franch Benavent and Navarro Espinach 2017). Toward the end of the eighteenth century, Piedmontese silk specialists Fernando Gasparro and Pietro Palmerini arrived in Murcia, where, under a royal privilege, they founded the *Fábrica de Hilar y Torcer*

[18] This endeavor was subtly mocked by the authors of the "soie" entry in the *Encyclopédie*. "The Piedmont machine alone works this miracle—that is the point to be proven. But before going any further, it's worth noting that the inventors of these new machines in France don't claim they outperform the one from Piedmont—which is already telling—but only that they match it. That's something, at least. Yet, if that were true, it would be reason enough to dismiss them, since they cost more than the Piedmont machine. The real task, however, is to prove that these new machines fall far short of the Piedmont machine's perfection—and therefore, that they don't even measure up" ("Or la machine de Piémont seule opere cette merveille; c'est ce qu'il s'agit de démontrer: mais avant de passer outre, il est bon d'observer que les inventeurs de ces nouvelles machines en France, ne prétendent pas qu'elles prévalent à celle de Piémont: c'est déja un grand point, mais seulement qu'elles l'égalent; c'est encore quelque chose: car en supposant le fait, c'en est assez pour proscrire leur usage, parce qu'elles coutent plus cher que la machine de Piémont; mais il faut prouver que ces nouvelles machines n'approchent point de la perfection de celle de Piémont, & par conséquent qu'elles ne l'égalent pas") (Diderot and D'Alembert 1765, 274).

Seda al Estilo de Piamonte (Silk-Spinning and Twisting Manufactory Based on the Piedmontese Method). They were accompanied by a group of Piedmontese workers, including Ottavio Quattropani, Margarita Rosa, and Teresa—silk spinners and reelers who were supposed to teach their crafts to the local workforce (Olivares Galvañ 2005; Solà Parera 2010). Nevertheless, the enterprise led by Italians was short-lived and soon left the emigrant merchants and artisans in financial ruin (Robles Fernández and Navarro 1998, 2005; Sáiz González 1999; Olivares Galvañ 2005). A similar initiative emerged in Barcelona with Maria Margarita Bertot's arrival in the 1780s. She suggested and was soon granted permission to teach local girls and young women the art of silk reeling *alla piemontese* to the *Junta Particular de Comercio de Barcelona* (Local Board of Commerce of Barcelona). In July 1784, the *Escuela de Enseñanza de Hilatura de Seda según el Método de Piamonte* (Silk Spinning School taught according to the Piedmontese method) opened its doors. Yet within just three years, Bertot's endeavor failed to meet the Board's expectations. Following fiscal and technical inspections, the *Escuela* was closed in 1787 (Nogues-Marco 2023). The Piedmontese Arnaud family—bankers and former owners of a large silk factory in Venaria Reale that went bankrupt in the 1780s (Lopes Cordeiro 1992; Chicco 1995)—set up a spinning mill and a school to teach silk reeling *alla piemontese* during the same period in Chacim, a small town in Portugal's Trás-os-Montes region. The Arnauds' relocation to Trás-os-Montes was driven by a combination of the Portuguese government's skilled labor recruitment policies, personal aspirations, and a desire for rehabilitation after their bankruptcy (De Sousa 2001). However, there was significant opposition from the resident population, many of whom were already employed in the established local silk industry (Sequeira 2022). Most of the production, which saw little local consumption, was destined for the coasts of South America, particularly Brazil. Nevertheless, the establishment of the factory did not eliminate the need for Italian silk imports for weaving workshops; the silk produced in Trás-os-Montes was still too coarse to serve as weft in luxury fabrics (De Sousa 2005, 2017).

The attempts to introduce the Piedmontese method in southern Italy were particularly noteworthy. From the *Reale Scuola Serica* (Royal Silk School) of Villa San Giovanni to the *Scuola Reale* (Royal School) of Reggio in Calabria, the 1780s provided fertile ground for the adoption of this technique. This was especially true after a successful experiment in Genoa, where both Piedmontese and Calabrian silk were reeled using a

Piedmontese-style machine (Lamberti 1994; Chicco 1995; Parisi 2003; Ciccolella 2003). Both initiatives ultimately proved unsuccessful and soon faded into obscurity. According to Francesco Bal, a Piedmontese silk spinner and merchant whose recently unearthed autobiography sheds light on the matter, this failure was largely due to the incompetence of the reeling and spinning manufactories' directors, who lacked any technical knowledge or expertise (Lamberti 1994). The final blow came with the devastating earthquake of 1783. This disaster merely sealed the fate of an already faltering project—hampered by the absence of hydraulic spinning mills and the inadequate training of the workforce (Parisi 2003). These efforts unfolded alongside the far more renowned history of the monumental *Real Colonia* (Royal Colony) of San Leucio, near Caserta. Despite its brief period in operation, this complex remains one of the most remarkable examples of an integrated factory under the Italian ancien régime. Governed by a unique set of statutes—unparalleled within the landscape of early modern production regulations—the colony housed silk reeling and spinning mills, as well as weaving and dyeing workshops. Yet, the political upheavals that shook Europe at the close of the century brought even this ambitious silk enterprise to a halt, which would only be revived in a new form after the Congress of Vienna (Tescione 1932; Ciccolella 2003; Parisi 2003; Ragosta 2009).

Even in countries traditionally lacking raw materials for silk production, such as those in northeastern Europe, the idea of achieving self-sufficiency in the silk industry was beginning to take hold. Prussia was no exception: Frederick the Great, in collaboration with the renowned merchant Gotzkowsky, (unsuccessfully) established manufacturing facilities to compete with other European powers (Henderson 1959; Blanning 2016). The trend even reached Stockholm, where Queen Louisa Ulrika, the Prussian monarch's sister, invested in a project to create a silk manufacturing district symbolically called Kanton. Mulberry trees were planted, and Jean Meaurin, a silk manufacturing expert, was hired to oversee the initiative. This enabled Sweden to attain some modest yet limited success in the silk sector (Barton 1977; Johansson Åbonde 2010; Marsh 2020; Nyberg and Jakobsson 2021). Remarkably, even Russia sought to develop its own silk industry in the eighteenth century (Blackwell 1968; Bartlett 1979; Kahan 1985; Hellie 1999; Khodarkovsky 2002; Ruane 2009). It followed the example of other European monarchies by enlisting the expertise of Italians such as Parma and Notara, who were requested to promote sericulture and establish production facilities (Bartlett 1979).

Step by step, and despite setbacks, the growing success of the East India Companies, coupled with rising competition among European states, was beginning to yield tangible results. The introduction of Piedmontese innovations abroad spurred on the development of production and processing techniques. These methods, although unable to match the quality of Piedmontese silk, supplied threads that weakened Piedmont's dominant position in the silk industry by fueling the looms of textile-exporting manufacturers. Ultimately, by the end of the eighteenth century, Piedmont's silk industry faced threats on multiple fronts, as did the artisans and merchants who had depended on it throughout the century, signaling the gradual decline of what had once been a pillar of Piedmont's economy.

The convergence of global competition, climatic shocks, and shifting patterns of consumption exposed the fragility of an economic model long sustained by state coordination and protection. What unfolded was not an abrupt collapse but a slow and uneven transformation that eroded Piedmont's long-standing centrality in the European silk economy. The pressures of the international market, combined with the limits of state-managed production, revealed how vulnerable this system had become to external change. By the end of the century, the Piedmontese silk industry still embodied a legacy of technical excellence and institutional control—but one increasingly out of step with the broader dynamics of a globalizing world.

5 Conclusions

Granting official statutes to the University of Silk Merchants in 1738 reshaped the whole landscape of Piedmont's silk textile industry, notably by excluding fashion merchants from the silk trade and making them dependent on silk merchants for the import of costly fabrics produced abroad. However, the balance between global and local production was shifting rapidly, redefining supply and demand dynamics and, in turn, reshaping the ambitions, practices, and needs of both silk merchants and workers. The struggles of the global silk industry created increasing challenges for Piedmont in producing silk fabrics for international markets. In their ivory tower of privilege, silk merchants faced mounting difficulties that often led them to diversify, while *mercanti di moda* remained largely unaffected by this decline—continuing to hold a prominent role in a brand-new commercial world driven by fashion.

In late eighteenth-century societies, fashion merchants emerged as core figures. Their skills and expertise elevated their clients from merely covering their nudity to embodying elegance as refined gentlemen and ladies, ready to be admired in society. If artisans were the builders of the social "edifice" of man, fashion merchants were its architects and decorators (Belfanti 2008). The success of the Lyonnais fashion system and the rise of Indian-style cotton fabrics—both major impediments to the growth of Piedmont's textile sector—highlight the rapid transformation of European consumption patterns. Throughout the eighteenth century, the preference for lighter silk fabrics and the steady yet unstoppable rise of cotton in European wardrobes reshaped the dynamics of the textile trade, challenging established industries and redefining market demands. In this shifting landscape, Piedmontese silk weaving—once a major economic priority for the House of Savoy—found itself increasingly marginalized. Despite this decline, the superior quality of Piedmontese silk thread, perfected by the late seventeenth century and consistently maintained throughout the eighteenth, remained highly sought after by competing industries. Unfortunately, in an era where successful economic policies required a keen awareness of global trends, traditional markers of quality, such as durability, were no longer sufficient to sustain the Savoyard ambition of expanding their international commercial reach. As a result, Piedmont's silk industry, unable to fully adapt to the new demands of the global market, became confined to the thriving yet secondary role of producing semi-finished goods.

The already fragile Piedmontese silk industry faced mounting challenges with the climate crises of 1777 and 1787, which triggered major shortages of raw materials. While the scarcity of silk posed an immediate threat to artisans who depended on it, the more pressing, long-term issue was the steady decline in demand for finished Piedmontese silk goods. A good cocoon harvest in the following years might have mitigated the shortage, but the industry's damaged reputation on international markets posed a far greater risk. The decline in orders, driven by political uncertainty and increasing competition from European powers, threatened to permanently weaken silk production in the Kingdom of Sardinia. As is often the case, the greatest burden fell on the workers who, left jobless and with limited means, were forced to rely on urban charity. This critical situation prompted the Savoy government to seek a solution beyond mere handouts. Indeed, in the final decades of the century, silk workers repeatedly faced the specter of poverty during alternating years of crisis. The assistance initiatives of the late eighteenth century represented a significant departure from earlier welfare measures implemented during the numerous crises that had afflicted Turin's silk industry since the 1720s. Before 1787, Savoyard welfare primarily involved providing aid to impoverished workers through city institutions such as the Hospital of Charity. The scale of the 1787 crisis forced the king and the government to acknowledge the need for a new form of targeted assistance. This approach sought not only to address the immediate needs of unemployed workers but also to ensure continuity in employment, training, and income. By enabling unemployed workers to contribute modest earnings to their families' sustenance, this solution aimed at reducing reliance on direct aid. This initiative's objective was to retain highly skilled workers and prevent them from leaving or being driven into penury. However, it also signaled a growing recognition that the recurring unemployment crises in the silk sector no longer commanded the same level of attention from the central authorities. Other threats emerged on the horizon, and for the government, these dangers overshadowed the hardships of destitute workers.

In addition to seasonal fashions, shifting consumer trends, and raw material shortages, revolutionary ideals further disrupted the status quo, rapidly transforming the neighboring Kingdom of France. Contrary to the old adage that "the habit does not make the monk," in ancien régime Europe, whether you were a monk, king, noble, servant, merchant, or beggar, clothes quite literally "maketh the man." Revolutionary ideas of equality and fraternity sought to erase distinctions based on clothes, yet they also acknowledged the deep-rooted association between the old nobility and silk garments (Belfanti 2008). The economic situation was undergoing profound change. Long-standing buyers of Piedmontese organzine began sourcing silk from Asian markets, gradually abandoning Piedmontese hubs. Heavy gold-and-silk draperies were replaced by lighter cotton fabrics or silk-blended textiles, while the ostentatious luxury of the eighteenth century gave way to a preference for new forms of simplicity, whether genuine or merely simulated.

The global market was clearly transforming—and at an unprecedented pace. Its speed was dictated by the English, Dutch, and French, all of whom had been quick to embrace globally inspired innovations. Each of them in their own way was redefining the traditional methods of producing, trading, and distributing yarns and fabrics. They were reshaping societies that had already experienced the thrill of evocative concepts such as fashion, exoticism, and the revolutionary ideas of social equality.

Bibliography

Accademia della Crusca. 1691. *Vocabolario degli accademici della Crusca, 3rd edition*. Florence: Dizionario degli Accademici della Crusca. Florence: Stamperia dell'Accademia della Crusca.

Allegra, Luciano. 1996. *Identità in bilico: Il ghetto ebraico di Torino nel Settecento*. Turin: Zamorani.

Bartlett, Roger P. 1979. *The settlement of foreigners in Russia, 1762–1804*. Cambridge: Cambridge University Press.

Barton, H. Arnold. 1977. Canton at Drottningholm: A model manufacturing community from the mid-eighteenth century. *Scandinavian Studies* 49 (1): 81–98.

Belfanti, Carlo Marco. 2005. *Calze e maglie. Moda e innovazione nell'industria italiana della maglieria dal Rinascimento a oggi*. Mantua: Tre Lune.

Belfanti, Carlo Marco. 2008. *Civiltà della moda*. Bologna: Il Mulino.

Belfanti, Carlo Marco. 2013. *Contraffazione e cambiamento economico. Marche, imprese, consumatori*. Milan: Egea.

Bertucci, Paola. 2013. Enlightened secrets. Silk, intelligent travel, and industrial espionage in eighteenth-century France. *Technology and Culture* 54 (4): 820–852.

Bertucci, Paola. 2021. Spinners' hands, Imperial minds: Migrant labour, embodied expertise, and the failed transfer of silk technology across the Atlantic. *Technology and Culture* 62 (4): 1003–1031.

Blackwell, William L. 1968. *The beginnings of Russian industrialization, 1800–1860*. Princeton: Princeton University Press.

Blanning, Timothy C. W. 2016. *Frederick the Great: King of Prussia*. London: Allen Lane.

Borelli, Giovanni Battista. 1681. *Editti antichi e nuovi de' Sovrani Prencipi della Real Casa di Savoia, delle loro Tutrici, e de' Magistrati di qua da' Monti*. Turin: Zappata.

Bulferetti, Luigi. 1963. *Agricoltura, industria e commercio in Piemonte nel secolo XVIII*. Turin: Istituto per la storia del Risorgimento.

Caligaris, Giacomina. 1988. Crisi bancaria a Torino: il fallimento della Casa Monier, Moris & Co. (metà XVIII secolo). *Bollettino storico bibliografico subalpino* 86:523–591.

Capuzzo, Paolo. 2006. *Culture del consumo*. Bologna: Il Mulino.

Cavallo, Sandra. 1995. *Charity and power in early modern Italy. Benefactors and their motives in Turin, 1541–1789*. Cambridge: Cambridge University Press.

Chapman, Stanley D. 1974. Enterprise and innovation in the British hosiery industry, 1750–1850. *Textile History* 5 (1): 14–37.

Chicco, Giuseppe. 1995. *La seta in Piemonte 1650–1800. Un sistema industriale d'ancien régime*. Milan: FrancoAngeli.

Chorley, Patrick. 1993. The “draperies légères” of Lille, Arras, Tournai, Valenciennes: New materials for new markets? In *La draperie ancienne des Pays-Bas, débouchés de survie (14e-16e siècles)*, ed. Marc Boone and Walter Prevenier, 151–166. Louvain: Garant.
Ciccolella, Daniela. 2003. *La seta nel Regno di Napoli nel XVIII secolo.* Naples: Edizioni Scientifiche Italiane.
Comba, Rinaldo. 1988. *Contadini signori e mercanti nel Piemonte medievale.* Rome-Bari: Laterza.
Craven, Wesley F. 1949. *A history of the south: The southern colonies in the seventeenth century, 1607–1689.* Baton Rouge: Louisiana State University Press.
Dato, Moïra. 2023. Quality, novelty and price: The holy trinity of the Lyonnais silk fabrics in the 18th century. *RiSES—Ricerche di storia economica e sociale* 9 (1–2): 13–45.
Davini, Roberto. 2014. A global supremacy: The worldwide hegemony of the Piedmontese reeling technologies, 1720s–1830s. *History of Technology* 32:87–104.
Davini, Roberto. 2024. Global connections of raw silk production in 18th and 19th-century Bengal. *Oxford Research Encyclopedia of Asian History.*
De Sousa, Fernando. 2001. A fábrica das sedas de Chacim e a família Arnaud (1786–1790). *Biblos: Revista da Faculdade de Letras da Universidade de Coimbra* 77:209–226.
De Sousa, Fernando. 2005. The silk industry in Trás-os-Montes during the Ancient Regime. *E-Journal of Portuguese History* 3 (2): 1–14.
De Sousa, Fernando. 2017. A seda na região de Trás-os-Montes durante o Antigo Regime (séculos XV-XVIII). In *Las rutas de la seda en la historia de España y Portugal*, ed. Ricardo Franch Benavent and Germán Navarro Espinach, 401–432. Valencia: Universitat de València.
Diderot, Denis, and Jean Le Rond D’Alembert, eds. 1765. *Encyclopédie, ou dictionnaire raisonné des sciences, des arts et des métiers*, v. 15. Neuchâtel: Samuel Faulche & Co.
Federico, Giovanni. 1994. *Il filo d’oro: L’industria mondiale della seta dalla restaurazione alla grande crisi.* Venice: Marsilio.
Franch Benavent, Ricardo, and Germán Navarro Espinach, eds. 2017. *Las rutas de la seda en la historia de España y Portugal.* Valencia: Universitat de València.
Geremek, Bronisław. 1970. La lutte contre le vagabondage à Paris aux XIVe et XVe siècles. *Ricerche storiche ed economiche in memoria di Corrado Barbagallo* 2:211–236.
Geremek, Bronisław. 1973. Il pauperismo in età preindustriale (secoli XIV-XVIII). In *Storia d’Italia V*, ed. Ruggiero Romano and Corrado Vivanti, 669–698. Turin: Einaudi.
Hellie, Richard. 1999. *The economy and material culture of Russia, 1600–1725.* Chicago: University of Chicago Press.

Henderson, William O. 1959. The rise of the Berlin silk and Porcelain industries. *Business History* 1 (2): 84–98.

Hertz, Gerald B. 1909. The English silk industry in the eighteenth century. *The English Historical Review* 24 (96): 710–727.

Hohti, Paula, ed. 2025. *Refashioning the Renaissance. Everyday dress in Europe, 1500–1650.* Manchester: Manchester University Press.

Hoshino, Hidetoshi. 2001. *Industria tessile e commercio internazionale nella Firenze del Tardo Medioevo.* Florence: Olschki.

Hutkova, Karolina. 2019. *The English East India Company's silk enterprise in Bengal, 1750–1850: Economy, empire and business.* Woodbridge, Boydell & Brewer.

Johansson Åbonde, Anders. 2010. *Drömmen Om Svenskt Silke: Silkesodlingens Historia i Sverige 1735–1920.* Thesis: Swedish University of Agricultural Sciences, Alnarp.

Jordan, John. 2019. The non-revolutionary fabric: The consumption, chronology, and use of cotton in early modern Bern. In *Cotton in context. Manufacturing, marketing, and consuming textiles in the German-speaking world (1500–1900)*, ed. Kim Siebenhüner, John Jordan, and Gabi Schopf, 385–410. Göttingen: Vandenhoeck & Ruprecht.

Kahan, Arcadius. 1985. *The plow, the Hammer and the Knout: An economic history of eighteenth-century Russia.* Chicago: University of Chicago Press.

Khodarkovsky, Michael. 2002. *Russia's Steppe Frontier. The making of a Colonial Empire, 1500–1800.* Bloomington–Indianapolis: Indiana University Press.

Lamberti, Maria Carla. 1994. *Vita di Francesco Bal scritta da lui medesimo.* Milan: FrancoAngeli.

Lemire, Beverly. 1988. Consumerism in preindustrial and early industrial England: The trade in Secondhand clothes. *Journal of British Studies* 27 (1): 1–24.

Lemire, Beverly. 1991. *Fashion's favourite: The cotton trade and the consumer in Britain, 1660–1800.* Oxford: Oxford University Press.

Lemire, Beverly. 2018. *Global trade and the transformation of consumer cultures: The material world remade, c. 1500–1820.* Cambridge: Cambridge University Press.

Lemire, Beverly, and Giorgio Riello. 2008. East & West: Textiles and fashion in early modern Europe. *Journal of Social History* 41:887–916.

Lequin, Yves, Françoise Bayard, and Mathilde Dubesset. 1991. Un monde de soie: les siècles d'or des fabriques lyonnaises et stéphanoises (XVIIIe-XIXe siècles). In *Rhône-Alpes 500 années lumière: mémoire industrielle*, ed. Yves Lequin, 84–129. Paris: Plon.

Levi Pisetzky, Rosita. 1969. *Storia del costume in Italia.* Milan: Istituto editoriale italiano.

Lonni, Ada. 1979. Controllo sociale e repressione di polizia delle classi subalterne da Vittorio Amedeo II a Carlo Alberto. In *Storia del movimento operaio del socialismo e delle lotte sociali in Piemonte I*, ed. Aldo Agosti and Gian Mario Bravo, 143–184. Bari: De Donato.

Lopes Cordeiro, José Manuel. 1992. A technology transfer in Portugal's late eighteenth century: The royal silk twisting mill of Chacim. *Textile History* 23 (2): 177–188.

Maldini, Daniela. 1979. Classi dirigenti, governo e pauperismo (1800–1850). In *Storia del movimento operaio del socialismo e delle lotte sociali in Piemonte I*, ed. Aldo Agosti and Gian Mario Bravo, 185–218. Bari: De Donato.

Marsh, Ben. 2020. *Unravelled dreams: Silk and the Atlantic world 1500–1840.* Cambridge: Cambridge University Press.

Mazzaoui, Fennel Maureen. 1981. *The Italian cotton industry in the later Middle Ages. 1100–1600.* Cambridge: Cambridge University Press.

Miguel López, Isabel. 1999. *Perspicaz mirada sobre la industria del reino. El censo de manufacturas de 1784.* Valladolid: Ediciones Universidad de Valladolid.

Miralles Martínez, Pedro. 2002. *La sociedad de la seda: comercio, manufactura y relaciones sociales en Murcia durante el siglo XVII.* Murcia: EDITUM.

Monestarolo, Giorgio. 2013. *Dare e Avere. Commercio e politica delle riforme nel Piemonte del XVIII secolo.* Turin: Kaplan.

Munro, John H. 2003. Medieval woollens: The Western European woollen industries and their struggles for international markets, c. 1000–1500. In *The Cambridge history of Western textiles I*, ed. David Jenkins, 228–232. Cambridge: Cambridge University Press.

Mutos Xicola, Céline. 2026. A forgotten industry: hosiery in Occitania and Catalonia. Labour organisation, wages and gender (1700–1850). In: *Women in Textiles Remuneration, Labour Relations, and Gender in Europe during Industrialization (Eighteenth to Early Twentieth Centuries)*, ed. Manuela Martini, 141–153. Turnhout: Brepols.

Muzzarelli, Maria Giuseppina. 2020. *Le regole del lusso. Apparenza e vita quotidiana dal Medioevo all'età moderna.* Bologna: Il Mulino.

Nogués-Marco, Pilar. 2023. Quality, technology, and dexterity. Female silk-spinning manufacture in Barcelona at the end of the Old Regime. *RiSES—Ricerche di storia economica e sociale* 9 (1–2): 73–122.

Nyberg, Klas, and Håkan Jakobsson, eds. 2021. *Luxury, fashion and the early modern idea of credit.* London: Routledge.

O'Brien, Patrick, Trevor Griffiths, and Philip Hunt. 1991. Political components of the industrial revolution: Parliament and the English cotton textile industry, 1660–1774. *Economic History Review* 44 (3): 395–423.

Olivares Galvañ, Pedro. 2005. *Historia de la seda en Murcia.* Murcia: Editora Regional de Murcia.

Parisi, Roberto. 2003. La seta nell'Italia del Sud. Architettura e tecniche per la produzione serica tra Sette e Ottocento. *Meridiana* 47–48:245–274.

Peuchet, Jacques. 1799. *Dictionnaire Universel de la Géographie Commerçante*. Paris: Blanchon.

Poni, Carlo. 1993. Moda e innovazione: le strategie dei mercanti di seta in Lione nel secolo XVIII. In *La seta in Europa. Secc. XIII-XX*, ed. Simonetta Cavaciocchi, 17–55. Florence: Le Monnier.

Poni, Carlo. 2001. Standards, trust and civil discourse: Measuring the thickness and quality of silk thread. *History of Technology* 23:1–16.

Poni, Carlo. 2009. *La seta in Italia, una grande industria prima della rivoluzione industriale*. Bologna: Il Mulino.

Prato, Giuseppe. 1908. *La vita economica in Piemonte a mezzo il secolo XVIII*. Turin: Società Tipografico-Editrice Nazionale.

Ragosta, Rosalba. 2009. *Napoli, città della seta. Produzione e mercato in età moderna*. Rome: Donzelli.

Ranza, Giannantonio. 1777. *Della Sereide d'Alessandro Tessauro*. Vercelli: Tipografia Patria.

Raveux, Olivier. 2004. Espaces et technologies dans la France méridionale d'ancien régime: l'exemple de l'indiennage marseillais (1648–1793). *Annales du Midi* 116 (246): 155–170.

Raveux, Olivier. 2008. "À la façon du Levant et de Perse": Marseille et la naissance de l'indiennage européen (1648–1689). *Rives nord-méditerranéennes* 29:37–51.

Rey, Indrajit. 2011. *Bengal industries and the British industrial revolution (1757–1857)*. London: Routledge.

Richmond, Vivienne. 2013. *Clothing the poor in nineteenth century England*. Cambridge: Cambridge University Press.

Riello, Giorgio. 2012. *La moda. Una storia dal medioevo a oggi*. Rome-Bari: Laterza.

Riello, Giorgio. 2013a. *Cotton. The fabric that made the modern world*. Cambridge: Cambridge University Press.

Riello, Giorgio. 2013b. *When cotton was banned. Indian cotton textiles in early modern England*. Accessed July 10, 2024. https://cambridgeblog.org/2013/05/when-cotton-was-banned-indian-cotton-textiles-in-early-modern-england

Robles Fernández, Alfonso, and Elvira Navarro. 1998. Un molino hidráulico de la Ilustración: la real fábrica de seda al modo piamontés de Murcia. In *Actes II Jornades de Molinologia*, 385–395. Lleida: Fundació Pública Institut d'Estudis Ilerdencs.

Robles Fernández, Alfonso, and Elvira Navarro. 2005. La Real Fábrica de sedas a la Piamontesa de Murcia. Historia y tecnología de un molino hidráulico de la Ilustración. *Studi Piemontesi* 34 (1): 67–86.

Rothstein, Natalie. 1990. *Silk designs in the eighteenth century: In the collection of the Victoria and Albert Museum of London*. London: Thames & Hudson.

Roupnel, Gaston. 1922. *La Ville et la Campagne au XVIIe siècle, étude sur les populations du pays dijonnais*. Paris: Leroux.

Ruane, Christine. 2009. *The empire's new clothes: A history of the Russian fashion industry, 1700–1917*. New Haven: Yale University Press.

Sáiz González, Patricio J. 1999. *Invención, patentes e innovación en la España contemporánea*. Madrid: Oficina Española de Patentes y Marcas.

Sant'Albino, Vittorio. 1859. *Gran dizionario piemontese-italiano*. Turin: L'Unione tipografico-editrice.

Santos Vaquero, Ángel. 2010. *La industria textil sedera de Toledo*. Ciudad Real: EUCM.

Sequeira, Joana. 2022. Flax, wool and silk: Textile industries in medieval Portugal. In *Textiles of Medieval Iberia. Cloth and clothing in a multi-cultural context*, ed. Gale R. Owen, María Barrigón Crocker, Nahum Ben-Yehuda, and Joana Sequeira, 141–164. Woodbridge: The Boydell Press.

Sewell, William H. 2010. The empire of fashion and the rise of capitalism in eighteenth-century France. *Past and Present* 206 (1): 81–120.

Sigismondo, Giuseppe. 1788. *Descrizione della città di Napoli e suoi borghi*. Naples: F.lli Terres.

Solà Parera, Àngels. 2010. Silk technology in Spain, 1683–1800. *History of Technology* 30:111–120.

Staples, Kate K. 2015. The significance of the secondhand trade in Europe, 1200–1600. *History Compass* 13 (6): 297–309.

Styles, John. 2000. Product innovation in early modern London. *Past and Present* 168 (1): 124–169.

Styles, John. 2008. *The dress of the people: Everyday fashion in eighteenth-century England*. New Haven: Yale University Press.

Styles, John. 2019. Fibres, fashion and marketing: Textile innovation in early modern europe. In *Cotton in context. Manufacturing, marketing, and consuming textiles in the German-speaking world (1500–1900)*, ed. Kim Siebenhüner, John Jordan, and Gabi Schopf, 35–60. Göttingen: Vandenhoeck & Ruprecht.

Symcox, Geoffrey. 2002. La trasformazione dello Stato e il riflesso del potere. In *Storia di Torino IV*, ed. Giuseppe Ricuperati, 719–867. Turin: Einaudi.

Teisseyre-Sallmann, Line. 1995. *L'industrie de la soie en Bas-Languedoc XVIIe-XVIIIe siècles*. Paris: École nationale des chartes.

Tescione, Giovanni. 1932. *L'arte della seta a Napoli e la colonia di S. Leucio*. Naples: SIEM.

Tolaini, Roberto. 1997. *Filande, mercato e innovazioni nell'industria serica italiana*. In *Gli Scoti di Pescia (1750–1860)*. Florence: Olschki.

Tonarini, Vincenzo. 1780. *Ragguaglio dei cambj, pesi e misure delle più mercantili piazze di Europa*. Bologna: S. Tommaso d'Aquino.

Trivellato, Francesca. 2021. *Ebrei e capitalismo. Storia di una leggenda dimenticata*. Rome-Bari: Laterza.

Zanon, Antonio. 1763. *Dell'Agricoltura, dell'Arti e del Commercio in quanto unite contribuiscono alla felicità degli Stati. Lettere di Antonio Zanon.* Venice: Fenzo.

Zucca Micheletto, Beatrice. 2020. Working in and for the charity institutions: Patterns of employment and actors in early modern Savoy-Piedmont state. *Mediterranea* 17 (48): 199–222.

CHAPTER 9

Broken Threads: Silk, Power, and the Collapse of the Ancien Régime in Piedmont

1 Introduction

Nearly a month after their wedding in Versailles on September 6, 1775, the carriage with the newly wedded Carlo Emanuele IV (1751–1819) of Savoy and Maria Clotilde of Bourbon-France (1759–1802), King Louis XVI's younger sister, arrived in Turin. The royal couple passed through *Porta di Susa* (and beneath the triumphal arch erected for the occasion). As happened 50 years earlier to Carlo Emanuele's grandfather and namesake (Cerutti 1992), they were greeted on their way to the royal palace along the straight *contrada di Dora Grossa*, by the vibrant and multifaceted commercial and productive world of the capital. The silk weavers wore gray cloth with gold-trimmed shirts, satin stockings, and hats adorned with blue cockades. The stocking makers were dressed in crimson wool, while the hosiers donned blue cloth with golden satin shirts and stockings, resembling the garments of cobblers and leatherworkers, who wore chamois-colored shirts and stockings. The *acquavitai* (brandy makers and sellers) were dressed in coffee-colored cloth, but with white satin shirts and stockings. Tanners were clad in leather suits and trousers, with green carbine belts; barbers dressed in gray cloth with light blue shirts; tailors wore scarlet cloth with white shirts and stockings. Finally,

M. Grassi, *The Silk Industry in Early Modern Piedmont*, Labour in History and Society,
https://doi.org/10.1007/978-3-032-15353-1_9

goldsmiths were attired in blue cloth adorned with silver[1] (Ricuperati and Prestia 2002).

However, under the surface of this display of opulence, the reality of economic hardship was far less glamorous. Within two years, the crisis of 1777 took hold, followed ten years later by the 1787 crisis. And just 12 years after that, the winds of the French Revolution began to stir. The silk weavers, dressed in their golden-trimmed shirts, were not immune to the effects of these crises. The Piedmontese silk industry struggled to keep pace with the rapidly changing world, and the social instability among its workers grew at an alarming rate. The coronation of Carlo Emanuele IV and the exile of the Savoy family, driven by the French revolutionary troops, were imminent. Once again, the history of Piedmont and the history of the Kingdom of France were intertwined.

This chapter will explore how the events of the French Revolution and the subsequent, seemingly stable, Napoleonic period impacted the Piedmontese silk industry. An overview of the commercial and industrial landscape, as documented in the commercial censuses of the 1790s—following serious raw material shortages at the century's end—will serve as a starting point for examining the local repercussions of the Revolution. In a Piedmont where the common people seemed deeply bound to the Savoyard and Catholic crosses, the *arbres de la liberté* (trees of liberty) barely took root (Bronzini 2002; Pederzani 2016). Within months, the *Carmagnola* was overshadowed by the *Te Deum*. Workers and peasants, armed with pitchforks, perceived the arrival of the French revolutionary troops as an invasion, awaiting the Austrian and Russian forces in the hope of liberation (Vaccarino 1965; Levra 1990; Roccia 1990; Notario 1993; Rao 1999). The countryside was in flames, and the city barely held out. Although the monarchy was briefly and formally restored in 1799, Piedmont remained under the rule of a provisional Austrian government. Yet, the differences between the revolutionary French forces and the Austrian-Russian contingents were almost imperceptible: the people continued to starve (Vaccarino 1989; Allio 1990). Just one year after the "liberation" of Turin, Napoleon's victory at Marengo—arriving in Turin only ten days later—swiftly changed the course of events. There were no Cossacks on the horizon, no pitchforks in the hands of peasants and

[1] ASCT, *Ordinati*, v. 304, c. 74, October 14, 1774 and, in the appendix, c. 120, *Relazione di quanto si è operato all'occasione della pubblicazione e successiva celebrazione del matrimonio di S. A. R. il principe di Piemonte colla reale principessa Clotilde di Francia nell'anno 1775.*

workers. Piedmont was incorporated into the territories governed by the French *Consulat* and, in just a few years, became part of the First French Empire.

With the advent of the nineteenth century, the Savoyard monarchical institutions fall, formal inequalities collapse, and apparent hierarchies crumble. The institutional structure that had shaped eighteenth-century Turin was dismantled, piece by piece. Geopolitical boundaries vanished, customs barriers with France disappeared, transforming Piedmontese silk, in every sense, into French silk—and as such, it was shipped abroad. After the halt of production caused by the French Revolution, in Lyon—the only possible market for Piedmontese organzine—the looms resume their work again, striking the 4/4 beat of *Veillons au salut de l'Empire*. A brief sense of stability filled the young French Empire, though it lasted only a short time. The harsh climate of 1810–1811 curbed initial optimism (Labasse 1957). As in previous years, mulberry trees and silkworms proved to be unpredictable companions, capable of bringing quick profits or destroying all hopes in a single harvest, leaving entire families stuck between prosperity and penury. On the one hand, it was a tempting opportunity, while, on the other, an imminent threat. Raw silk was again scarce everywhere, including Piedmont (Woolf 1986; Henderson 2013; Mikaberidze 2020). The looms in Lyon, those that still worked, were processing old silk, following the 6/8 rhythm of *Le conscrit de Languedoc*. Three years later, Napoleon's defeat at Leipzig would once again turn the tables.

Finally, on May 9, 1814, the port of Genoa became the backdrop for the return of the ancien régime in Piedmont. It was a Piedmont where, during the French period, discontent had spread, and little had actually changed. The "ORDO POPULUSQUE TAURINUS OB ADVENTUM REGIS"[2] inscription would soon dominate the façade of the Church of the Gran Madre di Dio, the only church in Turin built at the Municipality's expense to celebrate the restored monarchy (Nada 1993; Comoli Mandracci 1983; Tuninetti and Stella 2000). With the 1814 Treaty of Fontainebleau, the allied powers of the Sixth Coalition returned what had been taken from the House of Savoy. The French territories of Nice and Savoy, along with Piedmont, were restored to the Kingdom of Sardinia, which was also granted access to the Ligurian Sea. The ancien régime had returned. After two decades of inactivity, the guilds were revived, but they

[2] "The Nobility and the People of Turin for the Return of the King."

now had to adapt to the new institutions established by the French government.

Recovery was slow, especially with the rise of new, nearby competitors. As times changed, so too did the entire social, economic, and political order, both in Europe and beyond. Though the Piedmontese silk industry, once declared doomed, experienced a resurgence over the following decades, it was no longer the dominant force it had once been. Instead, it had become just one of many silk producers in Italy.

2 The Mulberry Tree and the Tree of Liberty: Silk and the French Revolution in Piedmont

The silk crisis of 1787 was not resolved quickly. In the following years, the doors of the Shelter for the Idle and Vagrants were reopened, offering accommodation, food, and work for silk industry employees (Prato 1908; Cavallo 1995; Chicco 1995). The administrative turmoil in the capital during 1791–1792 further fueled discontent, often led by students, who made it clear to the government that greater control over the groups shaping the state was necessary—especially in a European context of growing instability (Carpanetto 2002; Ricuperati 2002; Delpiano 2009). In response to this turbulent climate, a royal order was issued to the Consulate of Commerce in the spring of 1792, requesting a detailed list of all manufacturing activities in the city, including information about workers.[3] The resulting document provides a crucial overview of the professional landscape in Turin at the end of the eighteenth century (Gozzini 2000a, 2000b). It is neither a guild report nor a comprehensive survey of the workforce. Instead, it focuses on workshops and manufactories. It is an invaluable resource for understanding Turin's manufacturing structure at the end of the ancien régime—although its representativeness has been questioned on several occasions (Allegra 2004; Zucca Micheletto 2014). The census recorded 19 spinning workshops (including the two spinning mills in *borgo Dora*), 22 silk dyeing workshops, 227 silk weaving workshops (17 of which operated within the Albergo di Virtù), and 35 silk stocking workshops.

After the major crisis of 1787, manual silk twisting seemed to recover in the city, with numbers slightly below those recorded in the early decades

[3]ASCT, *Coll. XII*, Censimento del 1802; AST, C, *Materie economiche*, Cat. I, m. 2 d'addizione, *Volume contenente li nomi, cognomi e patria de' mastri e padroni*, 1792.

of the eighteenth century. Except for the two hydraulic spinning mills (employing 101 workers at the former Pinardi mill and 88 at the former Galleani mill), most establishments employed between five and nine workers. By contrast, spinning mills with over ten workers were rare—except for the spinning mill operated by Giuseppe Carrera, which reached a peak of 28 workers. While previous studies on this document have often emphasized the low number of female workers (Allegra 2004; Zucca Micheletto 2014), the silk spinning sector presents a very different picture. In every spinning mill, women accounted for at least 60% of the workforce and often much more: of a total of 365 workers, 266 were women, with slightly more than 100 men. Furthermore, in smaller spinning mills such as those operated by Francesco Oliviero and the Calleri brothers, the workforce was exclusively female. This trend, as can be observed, stands in sharp contrast to the composition of the workforce in other silk-related workshops recorded in the census. In the 22 silk dyeing workshops, employing a total of 89 workers, the average workforce ranged from one to five workers per establishment. Only five dyeing workshops exceeded this occupational "standard." Between 1768 and 1792, the total number of workers in this sector increased by 22%. However, there were virtually no women in the workforce: only two workshops were run by female owners (who benefited from the widows' privilege), and none were employed as workers. Among the city's most prominent trades, as documented in the 1740s,[4] silk weaving remained dominant. In 1792 Turin had 210 weaving workshops, employing a total of 613 workers, in addition to 17 within the Albergo di Virtù, where 136 apprentices were trained. Over half of the master craftsmen employed between one and five workers, while 63 workshops had more than six employees. Only two workshops employed more than ten workers, while 33 were managed by a single master craftsman. Notable exceptions included 20 women managing their own workshops and a total of only 35 female workers employed. Lastly, 35 silk stocking makers' workshops were documented in Turin that year, employing a total of 231 workers. Among them, six workshops had been active since the mercantile census of 1742, passed down through generations and operating for over 50 years. On average, in 1742, master silk stocking makers employed between four and ten workers, with only four workshops exceeding that number. It is worth noting that the workshops of Giuseppe Ghione & Sons and Teghillo & Silva stood out, employing 27

[4] AST, SR, *Ufficio Generale delle Finanze*, I archiviazione, *Commercio*, m. 1, fasc. 23, 1742.

and 24 workers, respectively. Once again, as observed among dyers, no women were recorded in the workforce.

As other studies on this source have also pointed out, the data on female participation in workshops are clearly unreliable, as are the figures for workers in general (Allegra 2004; Zucca Micheletto 2014). The document depicts an almost exclusively male production system, where women's roles, though essential, remained absent from official records, shaped by dynamics governed by informal institutions such as the family (Groppi 1990; Humphries and Sarasúa 2012; Toffanin 2016; Sarti et al. 2018; Pescarolo 2019; Bellavitis 2021). Contemporary records from the weavers' guild, for instance, show that in 1795 there were 560 male workers, including 235 male apprentices, and 443 female workers, 198 of whom were female apprentices. In 1796, the total rose to 596 male workers, 224 of whom were apprentices, and 400 female workers, including 189 apprentices.[5] However, these were not the first recorded instances of female workers. For example, in 1788, there were 344 male workers, including 155 apprentices, and 200 female workers, of whom 68 were apprentices.[6]

The years that followed, shaped by the advance of revolutionary troops, the gradual French takeover of Piedmont, and the resulting political and institutional upheavals, brought widespread instability. King Vittorio Amedeo III (1726–1796) died in the final months of 1796—just after losing Savoy and Nice under the Armistice of Cherasco (April 28, 1796)—leaving behind a kingdom in economic ruin. It was therefore his son, Carlo Emanuele IV, known for his frail health, fervent religious devotion, and limited aptitude for political and military affairs, who acceded the throne (Broers 1996; Ricuperati and Prestia 2002). At the same time, 25-year-old Napoleon Bonaparte (1769–1821) assumed command of the Italian Campaigns, further exacerbating the already precarious situation of the Savoyard government (Ruggiero 1974). Within just two years, on December 6, 1798, Carlo Emanuele IV handed over the remaining Piedmontese territories to France. Two days later, he was exiled in Sardinia, his last remaining dominion, and subsequently embarked on a long pilgrimage between Italian courts (Ruggiero 1974; Merlotti 2012).

During the French Revolution, it was not only the monarchy but also its symbols that were condemned to the guillotine. Silk was one such

[5] AST, C, *Materie economiche*, Cat. IV, m. 21 di II addizione, fasc. *Elenchi de' fabbricanti nastri, e d'altri manifatturieri in seta*, 1794–1822.

[6] AST, C, *Materie economiche*, Cat. IV, m. 10 d'addizione, fasc. 6, 1788.

symbol. It epitomized the myth of Baroque luxury and, even at the end of the eighteenth century, remained a clear indicator of social status. For France, silk represented the Bourbons, Versailles, and the aristocracy—everything that the sans-culottes and Jacobins sought to eradicate (Higonnet 1998; Jennings 2007; Belfanti 2008; Riello 2012; Carnino 2014). By contrast, most Piedmontese perceived silk in an entirely different way. A good cocoon harvest meant farming families' survival, a substantial commission ensured bread on the weaver's table, and an active commercial network boosted the public purse. As rapid transformations reshaped the landscape, Piedmontese silk lost its main market. Lyon, seriously affected during the Reign of Terror (Longfellow 1981; Hanson 2003; Steinberg 2019), began a slow recovery only under the *Directoire* period. However, this revival was further hindered by the harsh conditions in the countryside of occupied Piedmont because during the Jacobin invasions in Piedmont, many plants, including mulberries, were destroyed (Bulferetti 1966), while the little silk produced remained largely unsold in Turin's warehouses. The severity of the crisis was emphasized by the 1798 report from the University of Master Weavers: for every three looms, two were idle. While the number of masters remained almost unchanged—due solely to guild regulations—the number of workers and apprentices had drastically decreased. Male workers numbered just 91 (with 167 male apprentices), while there were 85 female workers (and 85 female apprentices).[7]

The struggle endured in the years that followed. Northern Italy remained an open battlefield. Even what is imagined as the "liberation" by Austro-Russian forces in 1799, which had raised Piedmontese hopes for a return to an idealized past lost amid shifting regimes, soon proved to be an illusion. While the Jacobins had ruthlessly drained the already exhausted resources of subalpine communities, the arrival of Austro-Russian troops offered no relief. Contemporary accounts describe soldiers feeding their horses with corn and oats requisitioned from a population already weakened by a major food crisis (Labrousse 1948; Berger and Spoerer 2001). Piedmont was isolated, having lost its aristocratic network of international alliances due to the king's cession of his territories to France during exile (Bocca 2002; Riberi 2019; Pinto 2022). At the same time, neither the

[7] AST, C, *Materie economiche*, Cat. IV, m. 21 di II addizione, fasc. *Elenchi de' fabbricanti nastri, e d'altri manifatturieri in seta*, 1794–1822.

revolutionary forces nor the Austro-Russian troops provided a reliable ally (Vaccarino 1953; Zaghi 1986; Ricuperati 1992; Griseri 1997).

A few months later, Napoleon returned from Egypt and decisively defeated the Habsburg army at Marengo. This victory ended Austria's brief rule over the city of Turin and led to the creation of the "Subalpine Republic," which, like its neighbors—the Ligurian and Cisalpine Republics—was designed to enjoy formal autonomy. However, the situation was still highly precarious. Piedmont was struggling to recover from years of war and insurrection, economic stagnation, forced requisitions, famine, and livestock epidemics (Bulferetti 1966; Picco 1978). The Austrians' withdrawal from northern Italy, formalized by the Treaty of Lunéville in 1801, opened up new opportunities for the French *Consulat.* The Savoyard army was soon integrated into the French Republic's 27th military division. Shortly afterward, a new and entirely artificial border was drawn between Piedmont, with the Sesia River as its boundary, and the Kingdom of Italy (Ambrosini 2000). This caused significant disruption for a population that had long considered Novara and Vigevano as integral parts of the Kingdom of Sardinia, and thus subject to specific commercial and governmental dynamics (Bulferetti 1966).

The wrangling over French control of Piedmont was far from over. The measured strains of *La Marseillaise* now gave way to the more heroic and majestic echoes of the *Chant du Départ.* On August 2, 1802, Napoleon was granted the title of *Consul* for life (Zaghi 1986; Broers 1996).

3 Napoleonic Piedmont: From Kingdom to French Colony

A little over a month later, on September 21, 1802, a large crowd gathered at the *Teatro Nazionale* (National Theater)—formerly and still commonly known as the *Teatro Regio* (Royal Theater)—for a performance. During the event, General Jourdan declared the annexation of Piedmont to France, officially confirming what had already been a *de facto* reality for over a year (Ruggiero 1974; Romeo 2014). Prolonged economic uncertainty and political instability had exhausted all levels of Piedmontese society, so the announcement was greeted with lukewarm acceptance. Even peasants and workers who had taken up arms against the French invader in 1798 now yearned for nothing more than peace (Vaccarino 1989, 1990). Piedmont therefore vanished from maps as a distinct entity, and the once-separate subalpine and transalpine regions became more interconnected than ever. As the conflict in Piedmont drew to an end, it was time to rebuild the newly revolutionized French Republic and restore its institutions and commerce (Broers 1996).

The most immediate change was the abolition of customs duties between Piedmont and France, allowing Piedmont's prized semi-finished silk goods to enter Lyon and Paris duty-free, where they were refined into high-quality fabrics (La Macchia 2014; Ambrosini 2000). At the same time, Alpine infrastructure saw significant improvements, most notably with the opening of the Mont Cenis road, which connected Turin to Lyon via the Susa Valley (Blanchard 1920; Corino and Dezzani 1986; Trinchero 2009). Moreover, this period also saw the creation of new trade oversight institutions, including the *Chambre de Commerce* (Chamber of Commerce), the *Bourse* (Stock Exchange), and the *Tribunal de Commerce* (Commercial Court), which complemented the work of the Committee established after the dissolution of the Consulate of Commerce in 1799 (Allio 1990; Broers 1996). A new public silk-drying facility, the *Condition publique*, was also founded to replace the one lost in the devastating 1789 fire. The blaze had left the once-thriving silk depot partially destroyed and heavily looted (Allio 1990).

Furthermore, in keeping with the revolutionary spirit of the time (Root 1994; Fitzsimmons 2003, 2010; Ogilvie 2019), local trade guilds were abolished. The idea of dismantling corporate institutions, however, was not entirely new—Savoy officials had debated it as early as the 1750s in Consulate of Commerce meetings.[8] Yet, with guilds now effectively dissolved, entering a trade required obtaining a license and paying the necessary fees, while shopkeepers needed municipal approval, and those founding joint-stock companies required authorization from the Minister of the Interior (Levi 2000). This radical change in institutional and bureaucratic structures, though significant, ultimately failed to reinvigorate Piedmont's key manufacturing sectors, particularly luxury goods (Allio 1990). Nevertheless, by abolishing guilds, the once-rigid hierarchy of apprentice, journeyman, and master was replaced with a simpler owner-employee framework (Agosti and Bravo 1979; Papa 1976; Cottereau 1997). This shift became especially clear with the introduction of the *libretti degli operai* (employment booklets), mandatory work permits that

[8] AST, C, *Materie economiche*, Cat. III, m. 1 da ordinare, fasc. *Parere del Consiglio del Commercio per la soppressione delle corporazioni*, 1757.

workers had to submit to their workshop owners, who kept them throughout their contracts. Without them, they were unable to seek employment elsewhere. This system granted employers much stricter control over their workforce (Bravo 1968; De Fort 1979; Gozzini 2000a, 2000b).

The collapse of the guild system and the institutionalized division of social roles are vividly illustrated by one of the most telling documents of Napoleonic Turin: the 1802 population census (Muttini Conti 1951; Melano 1961; Lamberti 2002; Zucca Micheletto 2012).[9] Throughout the city and its suburbs, fewer than 200 individuals were officially registered as working in silk spinning—just one master, five apprentices, eight spinners, and over 170 other workers. A similar pattern can be observed among silk weavers: based solely on the census, it would appear that there were only four master weavers—an unrealistically low number. However, a detailed reconstruction, cross-referencing the census with other sources such as the guild admission register, the 1792 trade census, and late-century guild inspection records, enabled identification of 102 households in 1802 with at least one individual who had previously belonged to the guild as a "master."[10] The same trend was evident among stocking makers, where a clear distinction had once existed between masters and journeymen, each belonging to separate guilds (Caligaris 2002). The Napoleonic census explicitly recorded the role of craftsmen in only seven cases, grouping all other workers under the generic term "stocking maker." With the dissolution of guilds, the traditional language of trade and hierarchy faded. Job titles like spinner, silk weaver, and stocking maker acquired broader meanings, while apprentice, journeyman, and master gradually vanished. Under Napoleon, distinctions in skill and experience no longer defined people's place in the industry—ownership did. The divide was now between those who controlled capital and those who labored for them. During this period, the ability to own workshops and machinery outweighed the skills needed to operate and repair them or teach the mechanics. In this context, the capitalist entrepreneur emerged as a dominant figure, no longer tied to a specific guild structure. He speculated on property, acquired machinery, traded finished goods, assembled his workforce, and oversaw the

[9] ASCT, *Coll. XII*, Censimento del 1802.

[10] APSA, *Università dei mastri vellutai*, v. 4, 1677–1795; ASCT, *Coll. XII*, Censimento del 1802; AST, C, *Materie economiche*, Cat. I, m. 2 d'addizione, *Volume contenente li nomi, cognomi e patria de' mastri e padroni*, 1792; AST, SR, *Consolato di Commercio*, Congreghe, m. 30, 1789–1793; m. 31, 1794–1799.

entire production cycle—from the first spark beneath a silk-reeling basin to the final beat of the loom (Angeli 1982; Toninelli 2006; De Vivo 2017). The new relevance of their role became particularly evident in the robust resistance of Piedmont's commercial institutions to decisions imposed by the French central government. One of the most notable decisions was in 1803, when export duty on silk thread to foreign markets, in other words, anywhere outside the French Republic, was abruptly doubled from 3 to 6 francs per kilogram. The price hike made selling organzine abroad nearly impossible, inflicting serious damage on Piedmont's silk industry (Labasse 1957; Chierici and Palmucci 1987; Biagioli 1990). Piedmontese authorities, particularly members of the Chamber of Commerce—many of whom were silk entrepreneurs—repeatedly denounced the enormous economic and social damage caused by the *Consulat*'s policies (Allio 1990; La Macchia 2014). Even so, their protests went unheard. The days when the Savoyard administration actively supported the textile industry were a distant memory; for the Republic, Lyon's silk production was sufficient—nothing more was needed. Nevertheless, the French were well aware that the quality of silk produced in the Subalpine territories had to remain high. To ensure this was the case, the renowned April 8, 1724, Manifesto, which had long benefited Piedmont's silk industry, continued to be enforced year after year. The annual registration of silk reeling mills, strict oversight of operations, and daily wages for reelers—rules established nearly a century earlier—were still regarded as fundamental to maintaining superior production standards (Bulferetti 1957).

The fragile balance between England and France—established following French victories at Marengo and Hohenlinden and formalized through the Treaty of Lunéville (February 9, 1801) and the Peace of Amiens (March 25, 1802)—was soon shattered. France's aggressive interference in the political affairs of Batavia and Northern Italy, combined with repeated breaches of the peace treaty, left the French Republic increasingly isolated from the rest of Europe (Lieven 2015). The situation deteriorated in December 1804, when Bonaparte was crowned *Empereur des Français* at Notre-Dame, followed by his coronation as *Re d'Italia* in Milan's Duomo in May 1805 (Pagano 2007). The resistance of neighboring powers proved ineffective: the military successes of the *Grande Armée* had allowed the French Empire to dominate much of Western and Central Europe, either directly or indirectly (Woolf 2002; Broers 2014).

While the crushing defeat at Trafalgar marked the end of French naval ambitions over the oceans, Napoleon's dominance on land remained unchallenged (Adkins 2005; Juhász 2018). The victory at Austerlitz cemented France's supremacy in Europe, and with the triumph at Jena and his triumphant entry into Berlin in 1806, the war against Great Britain escalated to a new level. Unable to challenge Great Britain's transoceanic commercial supremacy, Bonaparte enacted what became known as the *Blocus continental* (Continental Blockade). Through the Berlin Decree, Napoleon effectively shut most European markets off from colonial goods, forcing the Empire's territories—and, by extension, its allied states—to develop a self-sufficient economic system. In Piedmont, this led to significant efforts to cultivate, for example, dye plants and extract natural colorants, experiments that would yield some success in the years to come (Abbri 1989; Marchis 1990; Dolza 2000).

During this period, the Piedmontese silk industry was caught in a web of contradictions. On the one hand, the imperial government pushed for modernization. For instance, it introduced steam-powered factories to boost production and lower the cost of silk fabrics, given the impossibility of importing cotton and colonial textiles (Allio 2008). The French administration also removed national tolls, transit fees, and monopoly privileges, encouraging free-market competition. On the other hand, the new borders between France and Piedmont were very artificial, and rising customs duties, along with the increasing difficulty of exporting Piedmontese silk, led many farmers to abandon mulberry cultivation in favor of other crops. This discouraged entrepreneurial investment in the silk industry. The imperial project for the silk industry was clear: Lyon's supremacy in the silk trade was unquestionable, and every regulation imposed across the French-controlled territories served to preserve its dominance (Bulferetti 1957). Under Napoleonic rule, Piedmont was, in effect, a colony of the French Empire—exploited for its resources yet never fully part of it. Its role was clear: to produce raw and thrown silk destined for the looms of Lyon, which left local entrepreneurs, artisans, and farmers trapped between the fading memory of prosperity and the harsh reality of French domination. Furthermore, when it did occur, innovation in Piedmont during this period was not aimed at advancing local manufacturing but rather at accelerating extraction and boosting supply (Bulferetti 1957).

These policies on silk production allowed Lyon to restore much of its former prestige, with artisan employment and production levels nearing pre-revolutionary figures (Labasse 1957). By this point, however, the conflict between the French Empire and its adversaries had expanded beyond the battlefield and had turned into a trade war. During the war against the Fourth Coalition (1806–1807), Lyon's textile trade stagnated, only recovering after the Treaty of Tilsit in July 1807. The agreement brought unexpected success, as French silks flourished at the prestigious Leipzig fairs, attracting buyers from Prussia, Sweden, and Russia, where fashion trends were spreading rapidly (Labasse 1957).

Then, the spring of 1810 arrived. Early that year, traders and merchants eagerly spread rumors of an exceptional silk harvest, triggering a rush to sell off the previous year's stock. Nevertheless, these optimistic expectations were soon shattered by unexpected frosts, fungal diseases affecting mulberry trees, and sudden silkworm die-offs. And it was not an isolated phenomenon—it struck every corner of the Empire. The crisis was so critical that the government rushed to respond, launching extensive inquiries and compiling statistical reports on production (Biagioli 1990). That said, gathering information is one thing—finding a solution is another. In the dynamics of supply and demand, time proves to be a ruthless adversary. By imperial decree, massive quantities of silk were sent to Turin from every Italian department. Yet, much of it remained unsold due to exorbitant prices, while Lyon's producers, secure in their monopoly, relentlessly pushed to drive costs down. Meanwhile, many Lyonnais merchants had bypassed Piedmont entirely, sourcing silk directly from the Kingdom of Italy and bringing the region's silk sector to a standstill. Despite decades of turmoil, Piedmont remained one of the leading producers of high-quality silk threads (Marchis 1990; Bracco 1992). But the Continental Blockade had become a double-edged sword. By now, Piedmontese entrepreneurs, artisans, and farmers could no longer ignore the inevitable: the golden age of the "great Piedmontese silk trade" was over. With no access to foreign markets, warehouses overflowed, and production came to a standstill. Any effort to circumvent the Continental Blockade proved futile; the silk industry, in both Piedmont and France, had become a burdensome relic—the emblem of the deepening economic and social collapse. This crisis would soon be overshadowed by Napoleon's most catastrophic defeats: the disastrous Russian campaign, the decisive rout at Leipzig, and the humiliating invasion of France by the Austro-Prussian-Russian alliance (February 10–15, 1814) (Hartley et al. 2015). Finally, he was exiled to Portoferraio (May 4, 1814). The French Empire was collapsing, and with it, twenty years of relentless hardship for Piedmont.

Picture 9.1 On the left, just on the other side of the bridge, the Pantheon-like Gran Madre di Dio Church. (*Source:* Brogi, Giacomo (attributed). *View of the Po and the Gran Madre di Dio in Turin, Italy.* 1864–1881. Photograph. Rijksmuseum, Amsterdam. https://www.rijksmuseum.nl/en/collection/RP-F-00-416)

On May 20, 1814, the hopeful citizens of Turin celebrated the triumphant return of King Vittorio Emanuele I (1759–1824). He entered the city by crossing the stone bridge over the Po River—commissioned by Napoleon himself—just steps away from the square where the Church of the Gran Madre di Dio (Great Mother of God) would later be built to commemorate the House of Savoy's restoration, as decreed by the municipality (Guardamagna 2001; Dameri and Pozzati 2016) (Picture 9.1).

Despite his sharply contrasting political opinions, the moderate liberal politician Massimo D'Azeglio (1798–1866) offers a singular account of that day in his memoirs *I miei ricordi* (1867/1868):

> At last, on the twentieth of May, the beloved and long-expected king arrived. I was under arms in *piazza Castello*, and I well remember the group formed

> by the king and his staff. Got up in the old-fashioned style, with powdered hair, bags and pig-tails, and wonderful cocked-hats *à la* Frederick II, they presented on the whole a somewhat comical appearance.[11] (D'Azeglio 1868, 177–178)

Although the king was mocked by the intellectual as comical and outdated, D'Azeglio also admits that,

> to me, however, and to every one else, it all looked very grand, and quite *en règle*; the usual *cris mille fois répétés* greeted the good prince, with such enthusiasm as to remove all doubt of the affection and sympathy of his faithful Turinese. (…) In this coach sat the good king, with his kind face, which though, it must be owned, not over-intellectual, was that of a thoroughly honest man (as was proved in 1821), and till one o'clock in the morning he drove slowly up and down the streets of Turin, amid the huzzas of the crowd, distributing smiles and salutations right and left.[12] (D'Azeglio 1868, 177–178)

When the monarchy was restored, along with the ancien régime, there was widespread hope for a period of stability, even though the ambitions of the Habsburg-Lorraine dynasty for Piedmont were already looming on the horizon (Talamo 2000). Yet the ancien régime world that gathered at the negotiating table during the Congress of Vienna no longer resembled the one once sumptuously represented by the French kings—that ancien régime that had made the opulence of Versailles, with its fine glassware, silk garments, and powdered wigs, a symbol of its rule.

[11] "Il venti di maggio finalmente arrivò questo re tanto annunziato e benedetto. Io mi trovavo in parata in piazza Castello, ed ho presente benissimo il gruppo del re col suo stato maggiore. Vestiti all'uso antico colla cipria, il codino e certi cappelli alla Federico II, tutt'insieme erano figure abbastanza buffe" (D'Azeglio 1867, 181).

[12] "Che però a me, come a tutti, parvero bellissime ed in piena regola; ed i soliti *cris mille fois répétés* accolsero questo buon principe in modo, da togliergli ogni dubbio sull'affetto e le simpatie dei suoi fedelissimi Torinesi. (…) In questo cocchio il buon re con quella sua faccia, via diciamolo, un po' di babbeo ma altrettanto di galantuomo (e si vide nel ventuno), girò fino al tocco dopo mezzanotte passo passo le vie di Torino, fra gli evviva della folla, distribuendo sorrisi e saluti a dritta e a sinistra" (D'Azeglio 1867, 181–182).

4 Apparent Death? The Rise, Fall, and Revival of Piedmont's Silk Industry in the Nineteenth Century

On May 21, 1814—just one day after returning to the capital—Vittorio Emanuele I signed an edict aimed at erasing 15 years of exile at one fell swoop. The ancien régime was brought back, restoring the institutional system outlined in the *Regie Costituzioni*, which had last been republished in 1770 by Carlo Emanuele III (Gozzini 2000a, 2000b). But what did the return of the monarchy mean for Piedmontese silk workers? Their world was suddenly catapulted back in time. This new era was marked by the revival of guilds and commercial institutions that had once defined their golden age, along with a new customs system that reopened foreign trade after the isolationist policies imposed during French rule (Levi 1999). These events—and the period as a whole—have been largely interpreted negatively. By the late nineteenth century, moderate political voices—including that of D'Azeglio—heavily criticized these measures. These people sought to highlight their own role in steering Piedmont and Italy toward a unified, modern, and constitutional state (Fubini Leuzzi 1978; De Rosa and Traniello 1996; Castronovo 2001). For example, Cesare Balbo, in his *Della Storia d'Italia dalle origini fino ai nostri tempi* (On the History of Italy from Its Origins to Our Times), wrote of this period:

> Every (European country) restored the old absolute structures; the good Piedmontese king did so even more than the others. Few advances were made, or as we later called them, few reforms; and even fewer were actually implemented at first. Those first twenty years must be counted among the darkest and most foolish Italy had ever experienced.[13] (Balbo 1849, 402–403)

However, this view must probably be reconsidered: restoring the ancien régime proved far more challenging than the King of Sardinia had envisioned (Montaldo 1995). The changes brought about during the French period—the growing influence of the bourgeoisie, experiments in economic self-sufficiency under Napoleon, and the decline of guild solidarity—had fundamentally reshaped the playing field. Consequently, it was

[13] "Tutti restaurarono le forme antiche, assolute; il buon re piemontese peggio che gli altri. Promossero pochi progressi, o, come le chiamammo poi, poche riforme; ne effettuarono anche più poche da principio, per tutti que' primi vent'anni, che furono, bisogna dirlo, de' più oscuri o più sciocchi vissuti mai in Italia" (Balbo 1849, 402–403).

much more difficult to implement the nostalgic decisions of "the good king" Vittorio Emanuele I. The Piedmontese silk industry, in particular, increasingly resisted the traditional structures that had once contributed to its eighteenth-century success. For too long, government institutions had failed to address the sector's struggles, paving the way for a production and commercial system that grew ever more reliant on private capital (Bulferetti and Luraghi 1966; Bracco 1992; Montaldo 1995). As a result, labor relations became more impersonal, while economic conditions drove a shift toward alternative textile industries such as wool and cotton (Castronovo 1964, 1965; Bulferetti and Luraghi 1966; Bassignana 1998a, 1998b). During the Napoleonic era, these industries had already undergone significant mechanization, attracting substantial foreign investment. Yet, counterbalancing the instability of French rule was the restoration of an idealized pre-1798 order (Meriggi 2000). The *Consolato di Commercio* resumed its role, swiftly dismantling the *Tribunal de Commerce*, the *Bourse*, and the *Chambre de Commerce*—institutions that were remnants of the *Consulat* period and would, ironically, reappear in Turin within a few decades (Levi 2000). Alongside the Consulate of Commerce, trade guilds, their statutes and masterworks, and the tripartite guild system (apprentice-journeyman-master) were also reinstated, once again shackling Piedmontese production to a system of privileges. Amid this broader return to the past, one institutional innovation from the French period was preserved: the employment booklets. These tools served as a way of overseeing labor and controlling worker mobility (Bravo 1968; Gozzini 2000b).

Technological innovations met a similar fate. A prime example is the Jacquard loom, patented in Lyon in 1801 (Poncelet 1857; Godart 1899; Dunham 1953). In the early Napoleonic years, its adoption in Piedmont had been deliberately hindered to prevent competition, given the significant reduction in labor it required. However, by the time of the 1811 crisis, some Jacquard-like machines had probably already reached Turin. Yet even by 1820, only 36 such looms were in operation in the Savoyard capital, all owned by commercial enterprises (Montaldo 1995). The collapse of the French Empire might have paved the way for a broader adoption of these innovations. Still, the revival of the guild system reestablished traditional mechanisms for preserving knowledge and reproducing the workforce. In weaving, this was less about secrecy and more about maintaining privileges designed to ensure a fair distribution of commissions among artisans (Jütte 2015). Even so, innovation was not completely suppressed. Between 1814 and 1834, 71 privilege requests were submitted to the Consulate of Commerce for the textile sector, although most pertained to wool production and processing of plant-based fibers (Dolza et al. 1992).

Finally, customs barriers and duties were reinstated—measures aimed at encouraging the economic revival of Piedmontese silk products. Protectionist policies for raw silk were reintroduced after the Napoleonic era, even as smuggling persisted unabated (Bracco 1992). Given the difficulties Piedmontese manufacturers faced in supplying the domestic market, import duties functioned more as a fiscal levy on consumption than a safeguard for local production (Prato 1920). The world had changed—fashions had shifted, purchasing power had evolved, and market expectations were no longer the same (Tolaini 2023). In this shifting landscape, Piedmont struggled to remain competitive. Only ribbons and hosiery found modest success abroad, while Lyon retained its undisputed dominance in fabric production. *Organzini*, long renowned for their superior quality, were still produced according to guidelines established in the late seventeenth century and reaffirmed in 1724. Nevertheless, production had also advanced elsewhere: in Bengal, for example, it significantly eroded the share of the London market once dominated by Piedmontese entrepreneurs (Angeli 1982).

Meanwhile, a formidable—and nearby—competitor was emerging: the Lombard textile industry. With the Restoration, the Lombardo-Venetian region came under Austrian rule, a power that had long defended the ancien régime against revolutionary France (Meriggi 1987, 2000). Following the Congress of Vienna and the Habsburgs' reacquisition of northern Italian territories, Lombardy's silk industry began a revival that, within a few decades, would make it the primary competitor of Lyon's *Fabrique* (Caizzi 1957; Zaninelli 1988; Tolaini 1997a, 1997b; Avellino 2023). Step by step, Lombard industry mirrored Piedmont's trajectory—most notably in the adoption of steam-powered silk-reeling basins, called the "Gensoul's Apparatus," patented in Lyon by Joseph Ferdinand Gensoul (Cayez 1979; Marsh 2020). These were introduced in Piedmont in 1806, in Lombardy in 1815, and only after the 1820s in the rest of Italy (Federico 1994). The adoption of new technologies, combined with the rapid economic shifts of the early nineteenth century, enabled the Lombard-Venetian market to carve out a strong international presence

(Bassignana 1998a, 1998b). Unlike Piedmont, this region had long enjoyed a more diversified commercial network, trading with both France and Central and Northern Europe, including England (Tolaini 1997b)—markets that, under Napoleon, had been closed to Piedmontese commerce. Further undermining Piedmont's position was a persistent customs dispute with the Austrian Empire, which, as early as 1817, had enacted tariff measures that effectively blocked the transit of Piedmontese goods through Lombardy (Nada 1993).

The 1820s was a turbulent decade, marked by the recovery from the economic crisis of 1816–1817 (Nada 1993), the Spanish-inspired anti-absolutist uprising (Gil Novales 2020), and the complex succession following the abdication of King Vittorio Emanuele I from the throne of Sardinia in 1821 (Nada 1993). It was in this context that the young Prince Carlo Alberto of Carignano (1798–1849) began to emerge. Influenced by revolutionary France, and still in his early twenties, he initially embraced the liberal ideas championed by the conspirators who ultimately forced his uncle to abdicate (Romeo 1974; Nada 1993). Despite a modest economic recovery, discontent was growing regarding the old protectionist mentality, which remained tied to group interests (Bulferetti and Luraghi 1966; De Fort 1979). As in neighboring Lombardy, the debate had taken on a whole new dimension and focused on the internal organization of manufacturing structures and the roles of employers and employees—in other words, labor relations. At the same time, a pre-liberal economic perspective was emerging, reducing the power of the centralized absolutist state over manufacturing in favor of private enterprise (Caizzi 1957; De Fort 1979). During these years, doubts about the guild system's usefulness resurfaced, with voices across different sectors calling for privileges to circumvent guild restrictions, reforms in apprenticeship rules, and changes that, if ignored, could destabilize the already fragile restored monarchy. The system of privileges was showing signs of weakness, especially as countries like England and France had long moved away from guild-based structures (De Fort 1979; Levra 2000).

In 1826, the central government itself called for reforms in the industrial and commercial sectors, making these issues impossible to ignore. However, the system of privileges remained largely intact: under Carlo Felice (1765–1831), Piedmont was stuck in outdated passivity, further reinforced by the prevailing belief that labor needed strict oversight. This reluctance became even more evident whenever initiatives for liberal reform were proposed (De Fort 1979). A notable example was the introduction of mandatory employment booklets in 1829, which extended beyond Turin's guild system to include apprentices and women. For the conservative Savoy government, guilds continued to serve as a crucial instrument of social control, safeguarding citizens while excluding outsiders (De Fort 1979). Yet, the guild system—designed to grant collective privileges to master craftsmen—could not keep pace with the rising trend of awarding individual exemptions from key fees and registration taxes. Within its ranks, the guilds were gradually disintegrating. Alongside established masters, a growing number of skilled workers operated outside the guild system—often preferred by employers. Informal mutual aid associations also emerged, prioritizing welfare over professional training. Meanwhile, as the guilds' budgets contracted, masters maintained policies that excluded workers from mutual benefits (Papa 1976; Lisanti 1979; Gheza Fabbri 1996; Bertini 2004). By this point, the downfall of the guild system was widely seen as inevitable.

When Carlo Alberto ascended the throne in 1831, his previously liberal sympathies soon proved short-lived. Once in power, he aligned with his predecessors in defending protectionist policies and the Restoration status quo—for example, one of his first actions was to impose new tariffs on imports and exports (Meriggi 2000). However, maintaining the ban on raw silk trade and imposing expensive tariffs had by then become relics of the past. Since at least 1826, the silk industry had been recovering, fueled by rising demand and increasing competition from Lombardy (Bracco 1992). While Carlo Alberto hesitated, likely fearing a loss of control over the revitalized silk industry, his State Council saw things differently. In 1834, after much debate, the king was finally persuaded to lift the ban on raw silk trading the following year. The move proved successful: raw silk trade flourished, while the market for thrown silk remained stable (Bracco 1992). Nevertheless, the swan song of the Piedmontese guild system was fast approaching (Levi 1999). Mounting social pressure from workers living in precarity, the continuous refusal to recognize mutual aid associations, and increasing normalization of exemptions from guild obligations led first to the abolition of the masterpiece requirement in 1838 and, finally, on August 14, 1844, to the complete dissolution of the guilds and their centuries-old privileges (Gozzini 2000a, 2000b). To fully understand these decisions, they must be viewed through the perspective of the growing need for capitalist development. This was not about freeing labor from dependency—dynamics that had already altered, and in some cases intensified, since the late eighteenth century—but about tightening control over the rapidly expanding extra-guild labor associations (Lisanti 1979). As the guild system steadily declined, it left a void that was filled by structural insecurity, informal worker networks, and growing reliance on charitable aid (Gozzini 2000b; Plataroti 2000). In response, the state sought to absorb and regulate these emerging forms of worker solidarity within the framework of mutual aid associations (Bravo 1968; Lisanti 1979; Marucco 1998).

5 Conclusions

Just one month after the abolition of the Piedmontese guilds, Milan hosted the *Sesta Riunione degli Scienziati Italiani* (Sixth Congress of Italian Scientists), an event that drew over a thousand experts from various scientific disciplines (Hortis 1922). The agronomy section devoted significant attention to silk, with discussions that underscored the thread's economic and industrial relevance. Among the attendees was Felice Maggiore Vicino, a member of the *Accademia Tiberina* (Tiberine Academy) and the recently founded *Associazione Agraria Subalpina* (Subalpine Agrarian Association) of Turin.[14] The following year, the Milan congress's prominence and the widespread interest in silk led Vicino to compose and publish a didactic poem entitled *Il baco da seta* (The Silkworm)—echoing a tradition that had included works by Tesauro and Betti in previous centuries. His poem—excessively academic and of modest literary quality—was dedicated to Carlo Alberto of Savoy, a ruler who, at that time, was enacting major institutional reforms that would soon transform the future of Piedmont and the Italian peninsula.

[14] *Atti della sesta riunione degli scienziati italiani*. 1848. Milan: Pirola.

E tu, Sabaudo Sire, Dall'alto seggio, a cui splendon d'intorno Le bilance d'Astrea, di Marte il brando, Di Minerva l'olivo, e il caducèo Dell'alipede Atlàntide, e novello Traggon dal senno tuo nobile vanto	And you, Savoy sire, From your exalted seat surrounded by The scales of Astraea, Mars's gleaming sword, Minerva's olive branch, and the winged sandals Of Atlantis, draw forth a fresh, Brilliant pride from your noble mind,
D'eccelso onor, tu generoso, o Alberto, Volgimi un guardo animator: d'Augusto Al nobil atto lusinghiero un vate igral D'estro s'accese, e con più ardite penne Il volo aderse al memorando canto.	O generous Alberto, of high renown, Inspire me with a single glance - as a poet is to Augustus, A bard moved by noble deeds Fired by genius, whose courageous feathers Take flight to join that timeless hymn.

Canto I, vv. 30–40

Although the dedication's ornate language had been outdated for at least a century and a half, the decision to depict Carlo Alberto seated on a throne—surrounded by symbols of justice (Astrea's scales), war (Mars's sword), wisdom (Minerva's olive branch), and commerce (Atlantis' winged sandals)—remains particularly revealing. It encapsulates his achievements up to that point, with silk playing a pivotal role. By lifting the ban on raw silk trade, in fact, he concluded a long-standing process that effectively opened Piedmont to the global market (Bracco 1992).

However, silk was just one aspect of his broader political vision. By 1845, the wave of anti-absolutist uprisings that had shaken Europe throughout the Restoration era was about to culminate in what is known as the "Springtime of the Peoples." This revolutionary movement would soon reach Piedmont, culminating on January 1, 1848, in the unequivocal end of absolute monarchy and the establishment of a constitutional regime via the granting of the *Statuto Albertino* (Levra and Roccia 1998; Levra 1999). In many ways, the collapse of Savoyard absolutism was only the final, formal step in a transformation that had long been underway—a process clearly evidenced by the rapid changes in the silk industry too. The old monopolies had disappeared, the guilds disbanded, and even Piedmont's once-unrivaled supremacy in silk production had waned (Bassignana 1998a, 1998b). By the late nineteenth century, Piedmont had become one of many silk-producing regions in Italy, alongside, among others, Lombardy, Veneto, and the Marche region. Yet, well into the twentieth century, silk remained a major economic sector for both Piedmont and Italy as a whole. Even today, memories of silkworm farming in the rural homes of grandparents and relatives persist. This final phase of

Piedmont's silk industry represents just one chapter in the broader history of the trade, which, in the decades to come, would extend across the entire Italian peninsula, evolving within a radically different social, economic, and political landscape from that of the early modern silk industry.

Bibliography

Abbri, Ferdinando. 1989. De utilitate chemiae in oeconomia reipublicae. La rivoluzione chimica nel Piemonte dell'antico regime. *Studi storici* 30 (2): 401–434.

Adkins, Roy. 2005. The world after Trafalgar. *New England Review* 26 (3): 151–169.

Agosti, Aldo, and Gian Mario Bravo. 1979. *Storia del movimento operaio del socialismo e delle lotte sociali in Piemonte I.* Bari: De Donato.

Allegra, Luciano. 2004. Fra norma e deroga. Il mercato del lavoro a Torino nel Settecento. *Rivista Storica Italiana* 116:872–913.

Allio, Renata. 1990. Le istituzioni economiche: progetti e realizzazioni. In *Ville de Turin, 1798–1814, I*, ed. Giuseppe Bracco, 119–146. Turin: Archivio Storico della Città di Torino.

Allio, Renata, ed. 2008. *Il Piemonte e la frontiera. Percorsi di storia economica dal Settecento al Novecento.* Turin: Centro Studi Piemontesi.

Ambrosini, Filippo. 2000. *Piemonte giacobino e napoleonico.* Milan: Bompiani.

Angeli, Stefano. 1982. *Proprietari, commercianti e filandieri a Milano nel primo Ottocento. Il mercato delle sete.* Milan: FrancoAngeli.

Avellino, Lorenzo. 2023. "They have no property to lose": The impasse of free labour in Lombard silk manufactures (1760–1810). *International Review of Social History* 68 (S31): 135–155.

Balbo, Cesare. 1849. *Della Storia d'Italia dalle origini ai tempi anno 1848. Sommario.* Lausanne: Bonamici e Boncompagni.

Bassignana, Pier Luigi. 1998a. Officine e manifatture. In *Milleottocentoquarantotto. Torino, l'Italia, l'Europa*, eds. Umberto Levra and Rosanna Roccia, 23–30. Turin: Archivio Storico della Città di Torino

Bassignana, Pier Luigi. 1998b. Il sistema manifatturiero. In *Milleottocentoquarantotto. Torino, l'Italia, l'Europa*, ed. Umberto Levra and Rosanna Roccia, 345–360. Turin: Archivio Storico della Città di Torino

Belfanti, Carlo Marco. 2008. *Civiltà della moda.* Bologna: Il Mulino.

Bellavitis, Anna. 2021. Arricchire i questionari: la storia del lavoro di Angela Groppi. *Genesis* 20 (2): 13–25.

Berger, Helge, and Mark Spoerer. 2001. Economic crises and the European revolutions of 1848. *The Journal of Economic History* 61 (2): 293–326.

Bertini, Fabio. 2004. *Le parti e le controparti. Le organizzazioni del lavoro dal Risorgimento alla liberazione.* Milan: FrancoAngeli.

Biagioli, Giuliana. 1990. Soie et soieries nell'Impero napoleonico. *Quaderni storici* 73 (1): 55–91.

Blanchard, Marcel. 1920. *Les routes des Alpes occidentales à l'époque napoléonienne (1796–1815). Essai d'étude historique sur un groupe de voies de communication.* Grenoble: Allier.

Bocca, Claudio. 2002. *I Savoia: le vicende di una casa regnante che, da un piccolo stato tra le montagne, ha saputo districarsi tra le grandi potenze europee, portando a compimento l'unificazione d'Italia.* Rome: Newton and Compton.

Bracco, Giuseppe. 1992. L'Ottocento: dalla seta alla finanza. In *Torino sul filo della seta*, ed. Giuseppe Bracco, 119–148. Turin: Archivio Storico della Città di Torino.

Bravo, Gian Mario. 1968. *Torino operaia. Mondo del lavoro e idee sociali nell'età di Carlo Alberto.* Turin: Fondazione Luigi Einaudi.

Broers, Michael. 1996. *Europe after Napoleon: Revolution, reaction and romanticism, 1814–1848.* Manchester: Manchester University Press.

Broers, Michael. 2014. Un empire des lois ? Les peuples de l'Empire et l'ordre juridique napoléonien. In *L'Empire napoléonien. Une expérience européenne?* ed. François Antoine, Jean-Pierre Jessenne, Annie Jourdan, and Hervé Leuwers, 261–280. Paris: Colin.

Bronzini, Giovanni Battista. 2002. L'albero della libertà e l'albero della fecondità. *Lares* 68 (3): 427–438.

Bulferetti, Luigi. 1957. *L'economia del Piemonte nel periodo napoleonico.* Rome: Istituto poligrafico dello Stato.

Bulferetti, Luigi. 1966. *Agricoltura industria e commercio in Piemonte dal 1790 al 1814.* Turin: Istituto per la storia del Risorgimento.

Bulferetti, Luigi, and Raimondo Luraghi. 1966. *Agricoltura industria e commercio in Piemonte dal 1814 al 1848.* Turin: Istituto per la storia del Risorgimento.

Caizzi, Bruno. 1957. *Storia del setificio comasco I, L'economia.* Como: Centro lariano per gli studi economici.

Caligaris, Giacomina. 2002. Processi di qualificazione e de-qualificazione del lavoro a Torino nell'età dell'assolutismo accentratore. In *Il lavoro come fattore produttivo e come risorsa nella storia economica italiana*, ed. Sergio Zaninelli and Mario Taccolini, 31–72. Milan: Vita e pensiero.

Carnino, Cecilia. 2014. *Lusso e benessere nell'Italia del Settecento.* Milan: FrancoAngeli.

Carpanetto, Dino. 2002. L'università nel XVIII secolo. In *Storia di Torino V*, ed. Giuseppe Ricuperati, 187–231. Turin: Einaudi.

Castronovo, Valeria. 1964. *L'industria laniera in Piemonte. Nel Secolo XIX.* Turin: ILTE.

Castronovo, Valeria. 1965. *L'industria cotoniera in Piemonte nel secolo XIX.* Turin: ILTE.

Castronovo, Valerio. 2001. *Il pensiero liberale nell'età del Risorgimento*. Rome: Istituto poligrafico e Zecca dello Stato.

Cavallo, Sandra. 1995. *Charity and power in early modern Italy. Benefactors and their motives in Turin, 1541–1789*. Cambridge: Cambridge University Press.

Cayez, Pierre. 1979. *L'industrialisation lyonnaise au XIXème siècle: du grand commerce à la grande industrie*. Lille: Université de Lille.

Cerutti, Simona. 1992. *Mestieri e Privilegi. Nascita delle corporazioni a Torino (secoli XVII–XVIII)*. Turin: Einaudi.

Chicco, Giuseppe. 1995. *La seta in Piemonte 1650–1800. Un sistema industriale d'ancien régime*. Milan: FrancoAngeli.

Chierici, Patrizia, and Laura Palmucci Quaglino. 1987. Per una storia del patrimonio industriale in Piemonte: il periodo napoleonico. *Publications de l'École française de Rome* 96:133–160.

Comoli Mandracci, Vera. 1983. *Torino*. Rome-Bari: Laterza.

Corino, Pier Giorgio, and Livio Dezzani. 1986. *Una strada per il Moncenisio. Da Vittorio Amedeo II a Napoleone I Bonaparte*. Susa: Melli.

Cottereau, Alain. 1997. The fate of collective manufactures in the industrial world: The silk industries of Lyons and London, 1800–1850. In *World of possibilities. Flexibility and mass production in Western industrialization*, ed. Charles Sabel and Jonathan Zeitlin, 75–152. Cambridge: Cambridge University Press.

D'Azeglio, Massimo. 1867. *I miei ricordi*. Edited by Alessandrina Ricci D'Azeglio. Florence: Barbera.

D'Azeglio, Massimo. 1868. *Recollections of Massimo D'Azeglio*, Translated with notes and an Introduction by Count Maffei. London: Chapman and Hall.

Dameri, Annalisa, and Alice Pozzati. 2016. Torino. Borgo Po: le architetture, il fiume e la collina. In *Delli aspetti de Paesi. Vecchi e nuovi media per l'immagine del paesaggio, v. 1, Costruzione, descrizione, identità storica*, ed. Annunziata Berrino and Alfredo Buccato, 1293–1302. Naples: Circe.

De Fort, Ester. 1979. Mastri e lavoranti nelle università di mestiere fra Settecento e Ottocento. In *Storia del movimento operaio del socialismo e delle lotte sociali in Piemonte I*, ed. Aldo Agosti and Gian Mario Bravo, 89–142. Bari: De Donato.

De Rosa, Gabriele, and Francesco Traniello, eds. 1996. *Cesare Balbo alle origini del cattolicesimo liberale*. Rome-Bari: Laterza.

De Vivo, Paola. 2017. *L'impresa come istituzione sociale*. Bologna: Il Mulino.

Delpiano, Patrizia. 2009. *Il trono e la cattedra. Istruzione e formazione dell'élite nel Piemonte del Settecento*. Turin: Deputazione subalpina di Storia Patria.

Dolza, Luisa. 2000. Utilitas o utilitarismo? Il ruolo sociale della scienza nell'Accademia delle Scienze di Torino. In *Il ruolo sociale della scienza (1789–1830)*, ed. Ferdinando Abbri and Marco Segala, 17–35. Florence: Olschki.

Dolza, Luisa, Vittorio Marchis, and Michelangelo Vasta. 1992. *I privilegi industriali come specchio dell'innovazione nel Piemonte preunitario (1814–1855)*. Turin: La Rosa.

Dunham, Arthur Louis. 1953. *La révolution industrielle en France (1815–1848)*. Paris: Marcel Rivière et Cie.

Federico, Giovanni. 1994. *Il filo d'oro: L'industria mondiale della seta dalla restaurazione alla grande crisi*. Venice: Marsilio.

Fitzsimmons, Michael P. 2003. *The night the old regime ended: August 4, 1789, and the French Revolution*. University Park: Pennsylvania State University Press.

Fitzsimmons, Michael P. 2010. *From artisan to worker: Guilds, the French state, and the organization of labor, 1776–1821*. Cambridge: Cambridge University Press.

Fubini Leuzzi, Maria. 1978. Contributi e discussioni su alcuni aspetti del pensiero storiografico di Cesare Balbo. *Rivista storica italiana* 90:834–854.

Gheza Fabbri, Lia. 1996. *Solidarismo in Italia fra XIX e XX secolo: le società di mutuo soccorso e le casse rurali*. Turin: Giappichelli.

Gil Novales, Alberto. 2020. *El Trienio Liberal*. Zaragoza: Prensas de la Universidad de Zaragoza.

Godart, Justin. 1899. *L'Ouvrier en soie. Monographie du tisseur lyonnais. Étude historique, économique et sociale*. Paris: Rousseau.

Gozzini, Giovanni. 2000a. Ceti e gruppi sociali nella Torino napoleonica. In *Storia di Torino*, ed. Umberto Levra, vol. VI, 21–44. Turin: Einaudi.

Gozzini, Giovanni. 2000b. Sviluppo demografico e classi sociali tra la Restaurazione e l'Unità. In *Storia di Torino*, ed. Umberto Levra, vol. VI, 279–340. Turin: Einaudi.

Griseri, Giuseppe. 1997. Introduzione storica. In *Napoleone in Italia: 1795, 1796 e 1800; il manoscritto Saluzzo 248 della Biblioteca Reale di Torino e l'opera grafica di Giuseppe Pietro Bagetti*, ed. Giuseppe Pietro Bagetti and Joseph François Marie Martinel, 9–10. Turin: B.L.U.

Groppi, Angela. 1990. Il lavoro delle donne: un questionario da arricchire. In *La donna nell'economia, secc. XIII–XVIII*, ed. Simonetta Cavaciocchi, 143–154. Florence: Le Monnier

Guardamagna, Laura. 2001. Molte proposte per la Gran Madre. In *Progettare la città. L'urbanistica a Torino tra storia e scelte alternative*, ed. Vera Comoli Mandracci and Rosanna Roccia, 223–230. Turin: Archivio Storico della Città di Torino.

Hanson, Paul R. 2003. *The Jacobin Republic under fire. The federalist revolt in the French revolution*. University Park: The Pennsylvania State University Press.

Hartley, Janet M., Paul Keenan, and Dominic Lieven, eds. 2015. *Russia and the Napoleonic wars. War, culture and society, 1750–1850*. London: Palgrave Macmillan.

Henderson, William O. 2013. *Industrial revolution on the continent. Germany, France, Russia 1800–1914*. London-New York: Routledge.

Higonnet, Patrice. 1998. *Goodness beyond virtue: Jacobins during the French revolution*. Cambridge, MA: Harvard University Press.

Hortis, Attilio. 1922. *Le riunioni degli scienziati italiani prima delle guerre dell'indipendenza 1839–1847*. Città di Castello: Leonardo da Vinci.
Humphries, Jane, and Carmen Sarasúa. 2012. Off the record: Reconstructing women's labor force participation in the European past. *Feminist Economics* 18 (4): 39–67.
Jennings, Jeremy. 2007. The debate about luxury in eighteenth- and nineteenth-century French political thought. *Journal of the History of Ideas* 68 (1): 79–105.
Juhász, Réka. 2018. Temporary protection and technology adoption: Evidence from the Napoleonic Blockade. *American Economic Review* 108 (11): 3339–3376.
Jütte, Daniel. 2015. *The age of secrecy: Jews, Christians, and the economy of secrets, 1400–1800*. New Haven: Yale University Press.
La Macchia, Angela. 2014. *La competitività dell'industria francese e il mercato sardo nella prima metà dell'Ottocento*. Milan: FrancoAngeli.
Labasse, Jean. 1957. *Le commerce des soies à Lyon sous Napoléon et la crise de 1811*. Lyon, Grenoble, Paris: P.U.F.
Labrousse, Ernest. 1948. *Le mouvement ouvrier et les idées sociales en France: de 1815 à la fin du XIXe siècle*. Paris: Centre de documentation universitaire.
Lamberti, Maria Carla. 2002. Una fonte "vecchia" per nuovi problemi: i censimenti per lo studio della mobilità in età preindustriale. *Quaderni Storici* 37 (2): 545–552.
Levi, Fabio. 1999. Il quadro economico d'insieme. In *Il Piemonte alle soglie del 1848*, ed. Umberto Levra, 23–40. Rome: Carocci.
Levi, Fabio. 2000. La vita economica tra il 1790 e il 1864 nel contesto piemontese e internazionale. In *Storia di Torino VI*, ed. Umberto Levra, 47–93. Turin: Einaudi.
Levra, Umberto, ed. 1999. *Il Piemonte alle soglie del 1848*. Rome: Carocci.
Levra, Umberto. 2000. Da una modernizzazione passiva a una modernizzazione attiva. In *Storia di Torino VI*, ed. Umberto Levra, XXI–CLX. Turin: Einaudi.
Levra, Umberto, and Rosanna Roccia, eds. 1998. *Milleottocentoquarantotto. Torino, l'Italia, l'Europa*. Turin: Archivio Storico della Città di Torino
Lieven, Dominic. 2015. International relations in the Napoleonic era: The long view. In *Russia and the Napoleonic wars. War, culture and society, 1750–1850*, ed. Janet M. Hartley, Paul Keenan, and Dominic Lieven, 12–27. London: Palgrave Macmillan.
Lisanti, Nicola. 1979. La nascita del movimento operaio (1815–1860). In *Storia del movimento operaio del socialismo e delle lotte sociali in Piemonte I*, ed. Aldo Agosti and Gian Mario Bravo, 219–268. Bari: De Donato.
Longfellow, David L. 1981. Silk weavers and the social struggle in Lyon during the French revolution, 1789–1794. *French Historical Studies* 12:1–40.

Marchis, Vittorio. 1990. Scienza e tecnica: innovazione e tradizione. In *Ville de Turin, 1798–1814, II*, ed. Giuseppe Bracco, 225–280. Turin: Archivio Storico della Città di Torino.

Marsh, Ben. 2020. *Unravelled dreams: Silk and the Atlantic world 1500–1840*. Cambridge: Cambridge University Press.

Marucco, Dora. 1998. Le associazioni di mutuo soccorso. In *Milleottocentoquarantotto. Torino, l'Italia, l'Europa*, eds. Umberto Levra and Rosanna Roccia, 149–154. Turin: Archivio Storico della Città di Torino

Melano, Giuseppe. 1961. *La popolazione di Torino e del Piemonte nel secolo XIX*. Turin: Museo nazionale del Risorgimento.

Meriggi, Marco. 1987. *Il regno Lombardo Veneto*. Turin: UTET.

Meriggi, Marco. 2000. State and society in the post-Napoleonic Italy. In *Napoleon's legacy: Problems of government in restoration Europe*, ed. David Laven and Lucy Riall, 49–63. Oxford: Berg.

Merlotti, Andrea. 2012. Una corte itinerante. Tempi e luoghi della corte sabauda da Vittorio Amedeo II a Carlo Alberto (1713–1831). In *Architettura e città negli Stati sabaudi*, ed. Filippo De Pieri and Edoardo Piccoli, 59–83. Macerata: Quodlibet.

Mikaberidze, Alexander. 2020. *Les guerres napoléoniennes. Une histoire globale*. Paris: Flammarion.

Montaldo, Silvano. 1995. *Manifatture, tecnologia, gruppi sociali a Torino nell'età della Restaurazione*. Turin: AMMA.

Muttini Conti, Germana. 1951. *Un censimento torinese nel 1802*. Turin: Giappichelli.

Nada, Narciso. 1993. L'età della Restaurazione (1814–1831). In *Il Piemonte sabaudo. Dal Periodo napoleonico al Risorgimento*, ed. Paola Notario and Narciso Nada, 97–475. Turin: UTET.

Notario, Paola. 1993. Il Piemonte nell'età napoleonica. In *Il Piemonte sabaudo. Dal Periodo napoleonico al Risorgimento*, ed. Paola Notario and Narciso Nada, 3–91. Turin: UTET.

Ogilvie, Sheilagh. 2019. *The European guilds: An economic analysis*. Princeton: Princeton University Press.

Pagano, Emanuele. 2007. *Enti locali e Stato in Italia sotto Napoleone. Repubblica e Regno d'Italia (1802–1814)*. Rome: Carocci.

Papa, Emilio Raffaele. 1976. *Origine delle società operaie in Piemonte. Da Carlo Alberto all'Unità*. Milan: Giuffrè.

Pederzani, Ivana. 2016. *Dall'albero della libertà alla croce sabauda: politica, società e salotti a Varese 1796–1861*. Milan: FrancoAngeli.

Pescarolo, Alessandra. 2019. *Il lavoro delle donne nell'Italia contemporanea*. Rome: Viella.

Picco, Leila. 1978. Le epizoozie dei bovini nel Piemonte del XVIII secolo. *Annali dell'Accademia di agricoltura di Torino* 120:241–266.

Pinto, Carmine. 2022. *Il brigante e il generale: La guerra di Carmine Crocco e Emilio Pallavicini di Priola*. Rome-Bari: Laterza.

Plataroti, Franco. 2000. *L'albero della povertà. L'assistenza nella Torino napoleonica*. Rome: Carocci.

Poncelet, Jean Victor. 1857. *Machines et outils appropriés aux arts textiles*. Paris: Imprimerie Impériale.

Prato, Giuseppe. 1908. *La vita economica in Piemonte a mezzo il secolo XVIII*. Turin: Società Tipografico-Editrice Nazionale.

Prato, Giuseppe. 1920. Giacomo Giovanetti e il protezionismo agrario nel Piemonte di Carlo Alberto. *Atti della Reale Accademia delle Scienze di Torino* 54:565–612.

Rao, Anna Maria, ed. 1999. *Folle controrivoluzionarie. Le insorgenze popolari nell'Italia rivoluzionaria e napoleonica*. Rome: Carocci.

Riberi, Mario. 2019. I Tapparelli d'Azeglio durante l'età napoleonica. In *"Une très-ancienne famille piémontaise". I Taparelli negli Stati sabaudi (XVII-XIX secolo). Raccolta di studi*, eds. Enrico Genta, Andrea Pennini, and Davide De Franco, 113–138. Milan: Ledizioni LediPublishing.

Ricuperati, Giuseppe. 1992. *Lo Stato sabaudo e la crisi dell'Ancien Régime*. Florence: Olschki.

Ricuperati, Giuseppe. 2002. Lo specchio degli ordinati. La città e lo Stato nel tempo di Carlo Emanuele III. In *Storia di Torino V*, ed. Giuseppe Ricuperati, 7–57. Turin: Einaudi.

Ricuperati, Giuseppe, and Luca Prestia. 2002. Lo specchio degli ordinati. La città e lo Stato dal tempo di Vittorio Amedeo III alla crisi definitiva dell'*Ancien Régime*. In *Storia di Torino V*, ed. Giuseppe Ricuperati, 477–594. Turin: Einaudi.

Riello, Giorgio. 2012. *La moda: Una storia dal Medioevo a oggi*. Rome-Bari: Laterza.

Roccia, Rosanna. 1990. Mutamenti istituzionali e uomini "nuovi" nell'amministrazione municipale. In *Ville de Turin, 1798–1814, I*, ed. Giuseppe Bracco, 15–49. Turin: Archivio Storico della Città di Torino.

Romeo, Rosario. 1974. *Dal Piemonte sabaudo all'Italia liberale*. Turin: Einaudi.

Romeo, Rosario. 2014. *Cavour e il suo tempo 1810–1842*. Rome-Bari: Laterza.

Root, Hilton L. 1994. *La Construction de l'État moderne en Europe: la France et l'Angleterre*. Paris: Presses universitaires de France.

Ruggiero, Michele. 1974. *Rivolta dei Contadini Piemontesi, 1796–1802*. Turin: Piemonte in bancarella.

Sarti, Raffaella, Anna Bellavitis, and Manuela Martini, eds. 2018. *What is work? Gender at the crossroads of home, family, and business from the early modern era to the present*. New York-Oxford: Berghahn.

Steinberg, Ronen. 2019. *The afterlives of the Terror. Facing the legacies of mass violence in Postrevolutionary France*. Ithaca: Cornell University Press.

Talamo, Giuseppe. 2000. Società segrete e gruppi politici liberali e democratici sino al 1848. In *Storia di Torino VI*, ed. Umberto Levra, 461–491. Turin: Einaudi.

Toffanin, Tania. 2016. *Fabbriche Invisibili. Storie di donne, lavoranti a domicilio*. Verona: Ombre corte.

Tolaini, Roberto. 1997a. Istituzioni, mercato, fiducia. Le misure della seta nell'Ottocento. *Quaderni storici* 96 (3): 769–794.

Tolaini, Roberto. 1997b. *Filande, mercato e innovazioni nell'industria serica italiana. Gli Scoti di Pescia (1750–1860)*. Florence: Olschki.

Tolaini, Roberto. 2023. Qualità e differenziazione: per una fenomenologia delle misure della seta (XVII-XIX secoli). *RiSES—Ricerche di storia economica e sociale* 9 (1–2): 123–153.

Toninelli, Pier Angelo. 2006. *Storia d'impresa*. Bologna: Il Mulino.

Trinchero, Cristina. 2009. Napoleone al Moncenisio: l'avvio di grandi opere in Val di Susa tra Sette e Ottocento. In *Pietra tempo parola. Sistemi di difesa nella Valle di Susa*, ed. Isabella Maria Zoppi, 39–43. Turin: Omega.

Tuninetti, Giuseppe, and Pietro Stella. 2000. I cattolici. In *Storia di Torino VI*, ed. Umberto Levra, 799–838. Turin: Einaudi.

Vaccarino, Giorgio. 1953. *I giacobini "anarchici" e l'idea dell'unità italiana*. Turin: Einaudi.

Vaccarino, Giorgio. 1965. *L'Inchiesta del 1799 sui Giacobini in Piemonte*. Naples: Edizioni Scientifiche Italiane.

Vaccarino, Giorgio. 1989. *I giacobini piemontesi 1794–1814*. Rome: Ministero per i beni culturali e ambientali.

Vaccarino, Giorgio. 1990. Annessionisti e autonomisti piemontesi sotto il Direttorio e il Consolato (1796–1802). In *Ville de Turin, 1798–1814, II*, ed. Giuseppe Bracco, 9–31. Turin: Archivio Storico della Città di Torino.

Woolf, Stuart. 1986. *The poor in Western Europe in the eighteenth and nineteenth centuries*. London: Methuen.

Woolf, Stuart. 2002. Napoléon et l'Italie. In *Napoléon et l'Europe. Colloque de la Roche-sur-Yon*, ed. Martin Jean-Clément, 115–124. Rennes: Presses Universitaires de Rennes.

Zaghi, Carlo. 1986. *L'Italia di Napoleone dalla Cisalpina al Regno. Storia d'Italia 18/1*. Turin: UTET.

Zaninelli, Sergio, ed. 1988. *Storia dell'industria lombarda*. Milan: Polifilo.

Zucca Micheletto, Beatrice. 2012. La migration comme processus: dynamiques patrimoniales et parcours d'installation des immigrés dans l'Italie moderne (Turin au XVIIIe siècle). *Annales de démographie historique* 124 (2): 43–64.

Zucca Micheletto, Beatrice. 2014. Only unpaid labour force? Women's and girls' work and property in family business in early modern Italy. *The History of the Family* 19 (3): 323–340.

CHAPTER 10

Epilogue: The Crystallization of the Glass Beads Paradox

1 Leaving Montreuil-sur-Mer

At the beginning of this book, the Montreuil-sur-Mer episode in *Les Misérables* offers a clear yet paradoxical image of how technology, labor, and society intersect at a moment of emerging innovation. In Hugo's narrative, a simple technical gesture transforms an entire community, as the industrial outcome of human ingenuity appears to align with social renewal: work expands, poverty recedes, and moral order emerges newly constituted. Yet within this same scene, Hugo intertwines the rise of manufacturing with the tragic fate of a woman—Fantine—who, in her desperate search for work, finds employment in a glass-bead workshop, only to be brutally dismissed once her secret is exposed: she has a daughter, Cosette, born outside marriage. She then descends into a spiral of misery, exploitation, and stigma that ultimately ends in death. In her, progress born of innovation encounters its own shadow: Fantine's downfall suggests that when innovation becomes detached from the society that sustains it and is treated as an autonomous driver of change, even productive success begins to falter. The town, once flourishing through technical refinement, falls back into the misery from which it had emerged, revealing the limits of a material progress that remains material—unable to evolve into institutional, social, and moral advancement. The fate of Montreuil-sur-Mer mirrors Fantine's own—rising and falling in tragic symmetry.

M. Grassi, *The Silk Industry in Early Modern Piedmont*, Labour in History and Society,
https://doi.org/10.1007/978-3-032-15353-1_10

Writing with the moral clarity of his century, Hugo seems to warn that wherever the economy of technology prospers while the economy of humanity withers, the promise of modernity begins to fracture. His vision suggests that innovation is never neutral: its effectiveness rests on the social and institutional fabric that gives it form and meaning. It is not merely a question of ingenuity or technique, but a fragile balance between matter and morality, between progress and justice, between labor and dignity. The vitality of technological change, he suggests, ultimately rests on the harmony between material practice and social order.

A similar dynamic, as traced in these pages, shaped the history of silk production in Piedmont during the early modern period. It reveals how technical excellence could be achieved and sustained through the combined efforts of society—from above and below—and how, at the same time, that very excellence could undermine the prosperity it had helped create, exposing the structural fragilities of a flourishing economy. By adopting a close-up perspective—through the lens of workshops, biographies, and domestic economies—it becomes possible to grasp the full scope of this process and to illuminate the history of industrial progress through a microhistorical lens on everyday practice. In this sense, the rapid development of the Piedmontese silk sector, which made the *organzino alla piemontese* an international standard of quality, must be understood as an ongoing process of small adjustments, serial refinements, and the transmission of skills across both formal and informal settings. What emerges, then, is not so much a rupture or a revolution as a process of continuity—one defined by an inner capacity for reform, yet always open to external currents. As this book has demonstrated, the Piedmontese silk industry prospered not through technological innovation alone, but through the interaction of regulatory institutions, market actors, and artisanal labor. The state's legal architecture transformed local knowledge into economic stability, while the resilience of workers—particularly women drawn from rural labor—anchored innovation in lived experience. Yet the same mechanisms that produced excellence—standardization, precision, discipline—gradually constrained adaptability, exposing the paradox of success without renewal. In this way, the Piedmontese case illuminates the historical dynamics of innovation as a social, not merely technical, achievement.

As argued in the introduction, what took shape was an innovation ecosystem in which actors, activities, and norms evolved together. To look at Piedmont from within and from without, from above and below, from near and afar, is to see innovation as a system of interdependence—a structure in which technique and materiality, labor and society, law and authority hold one another in balance. Within this structure, machines and know-how function as the keystone of the system, ensuring the stability of an arch composed of interwoven forces: economic, legal, and cultural components that define the society into which innovation was grafted. Technical progress—seen in the hydraulic spinning mill or the *alla piemontese* reeling method—grew out of knowledge condensed over generations: transfers of skill sustained by migrant labor and by collective experimentation. Yet, as the case of the Lombe brothers and the Bengal reeling facilities *alla piemontese* reveal, such technologies often turned into displacements of machinery, materials, and human craft. Yet abroad, such transfers frequently failed to find an innovation ecosystem ready to receive them—and without that context, even the most refined technology could not take root. In essence, every form of innovation requires not only skilled hands but a form of know-how shaped through embodied expertise: an intimate familiarity with the rules, rhythms, and habits of a productive community that adapts its pre-existing knowledge to new technical frameworks.

Identify machinery as a keystone means recognizing that it provides the stability on which further developments depend—allowing the structure to rise higher, with new walls and vaults built upon it. In much the same way, technology actively participates in shaping what follows its own introduction: the reconfiguration of professional, commercial, and cultural dynamics, and even of the urban fabric itself, within the society that receives it. The most visible expression of this process was the growing institutional attention to the productive sector—manifested in the creation of laws, administrative and judicial bodies, and systems of control governing both professional practice and product quality. These measures, however enlightened, risk remaining abstract formulas unless they find anchorage in the basic unit of the productive chain: labor itself—the concrete work of human hands. The strength of the Piedmontese reformist system, at least in its initial phase, lay precisely in shaping standardizing legislation around artisanal practice—an activity grounded in individual and largely informal knowledge of the trade, inseparable from lived experience. In doing so, it made embodied expertise a fundamental component of the capital that defined the sector. From this interplay of regulation and skill emerged a period of stability in Piedmont's silk sector—one that fostered a system grounded in a culture of craftsmanship, understood both as a professional ethic and as a productive policy.

At this institutional turning point, the state asserted itself as the principal architect of economic transformation, using policy as a means to consolidate its authority and to direct the development of Piedmont's silk economy. The case shows that the effectiveness of innovation depended on institutional coherence as much as on technical refinement. Savoy's mercantilism, reinterpreted in light of French experience, did not merely promote trade: it sought to organize its very foundations—to define its rules and structures, regulate the time of production, and expand its foreign trade. What emerged was a mercantilist partnership in which the state and the merchant class acted as allies in building an economy that translated trust—long embedded in commercial practice—into a recognized and regulated principle of prosperity. From the founding of the *Consolato di Commercio* to the reform season under Victor Amadeus II, through the Manifesto of April 8, 1724, and the stabilization of the guilds' role, legislation worked to turn innovation into a standard, the workshop into a system, and the artisan into a worker—an effort to make the quality of Piedmontese production reproducible within the state's borders and, in turn, to strengthen its position in international markets. These dynamics encouraged the emergence of a new kind of trader—one able to refine his expertise and direct his investments with increasing precision. This entrepreneurial figure gradually assumed control over the production process as a whole, integrating technical expertise with the organization of labor and the demands of the market. By overseeing the entire process—from the reeling phase to the sale of the finished fabric—these entrepreneurs gave form to a genuinely industrial mindset, grounded in the pursuit of quality.

However, this turn toward entrepreneurship can only be understood in relation to the society that made it possible and sustained it: a dense web of household relations, community ties and labor practices that translated both technical innovation and mercantile regulation into everyday practice. The silk industry was not only an economic engine but a social laboratory, where the stratification of labor and the differentiation of roles reshaped the connections between individual lives, the institutional structures, and the spaces in which production took place. Actors involved in the various phases of production, confronted with the consequences of innovation, experienced significant economic shifts and a reorganization of hierarchies and dependencies. State regulation, while safeguarding product quality and labor discipline, also reinforced a rigid social structure grounded in control and the supervision of the workforce. Furthermore, within this context, gender and class dynamics assumed a decisive role. The strong presence of women in the reeling facilities—generally confined to low-paid, repetitive tasks within rigid gendered divisions of labor—revealed the less visible side of the industry's prosperity: an economy that drew its strength from the flexibility of its labor force while reproducing structural hierarchies among merchants, masters, and wage earners. Institutions rendered this order both operative and visible: apprenticeship regulations and guild statutes codified dependence, defining access to work and the boundaries of professional recognition, while charitable manufactories such as the Albergo di Virtù organized and disciplined labor—including that of the poor and minors—and the royal manufactories regulated production, standardized quality, and concentrated control, binding inclusion to subordination. In this context, figures such as Anna Maria Pajsio—one of the few women to attain the status of master weaver and to facilitate the informal transmission of skills that enabled her niece Rosa Orsola's guild admission—embody the contradictions of the Piedmontese silk industry, where women's skill and recognition were grounded in dependence and exclusion. Ultimately, the political and economic crises of 1789–1792 laid bare the instability of this system, revealing the limits of women's fragile advancement. In this sense, the reorganization of the silk sector acted as a social and institutional device, turning Piedmont into a laboratory where the logic of industrialization took shape.

Significantly, in an economy undergoing rapid transformation, the pursuit of perfection through standardization proved to be a trap: what had once secured Piedmont's primacy in silk eventually made it less adaptable to change. European taste, shaped by Lyonnais fashion, began to favor lightness and novelty over durability and regularity of texture. At the same time, cotton gradually eroded the markets for silk and fostered a broader culture of consumption. The very innovations from which Piedmont had long benefited, such as the hydraulic spinning mill and the *alla piemontese* reeling method, began—though not without difficulty—to spread beyond the borders of the state, reaching as far as Sweden and Portugal. Their technical excellence thus became, albeit slowly and with some difficulty, replicable elsewhere, gradually draining away the competitive advantage that had sustained its reputation for decades. To these external pressures were added internal fragilities: the silk industry remained deeply dependent on environmental and agricultural conditions. A poor harvest or a silkworm disease was enough to compromise entire seasons of cocoon production, significantly affecting the whole sector. So it was during the crisis of 1787 when adverse climate patterns and collapsing production triggered mass unemployment, affecting tens of thousands of workers. Faced with this emergency, the state responded by shifting from economic instruments to mechanisms of social containment—measures aimed at mitigating misery without addressing its structural causes.

Amid these tensions, the political upheavals that marked the final years of the eighteenth century sealed the last act of Piedmont's silk supremacy. The Napoleonic annexation turned the region into a productive and peripheral outpost of France, compelled to supply semi-finished silk to the looms of Lyon. The guild structures were dismantled, the institutions that had once guaranteed the system's cohesion dissolved, and the Restoration of 1814—though it sought to revive the ancien régime—failed to mend an economic fabric already torn apart, giving way to a new social divide increasingly defined by the owner–worker relationship. The world had changed: new markets, new fibers, and new actors were redefining Europe's industrial geography—particularly in Italy, with Lombardy now emerging as the leading center of the silk industry.

2 The Crystallization of the Glass Beads Paradox

At its height, as in its decline, the Piedmontese experience reveals that innovation is not a fixed condition but a dynamic process shaped by the constant negotiation between perfection and adaptation, between refinement and renewal, between the weight of tradition and the impulse to change. Its trajectory reveals how technical ingenuity and social discipline evolved together in shaping the industrial order of early modern Europe. In this perspective, the history of Piedmont's silk industry demonstrates that no achievement is ever final: technical mastery endures only when it remains attuned to the human dimension of labor.

The Piedmontese experience thus embodies, in historical form, the same dynamic that Hugo captured in fiction: the moment when innovation, once a source of vitality, becomes the mechanism of its own exhaustion. The enduring quest for the stabilization of product quality—born of technical ambition and unfolding in economic and social consequences—emerges as the counterpoint to the very ecosystem of innovation that once sustained progress. In this tension lies the glass beads paradox: once institutionalized, the aspiration to maintain perfected standards risks crystallizing and can preserve the warmth that gave it life only by renewing itself. When renewal fails, observation turns inward, dialogue with the outside world weakens, creativity fades, and the system that once ensured prosperity loses its flexibility and capacity to adapt. In both cases—the historical Piedmont and the Montreuil-sur-Mer transfigured by Hugo's imagination—the promise of innovation yields to its own paradox: once technique no longer serves the social bonds that gave it meaning, progress begins to erode. In its pursuit of perfection, both moral and mechanical, the factory mistakes obedience for virtue and discipline for skill. Its strength ebbs away: the machinery keeps moving, yet the life that sustained it has disappeared. Madeleine—the industrial persona assumed by Valjean, the entrepreneur of Montreuil-sur-Mer—discovers Fantine's expulsion too late. His gesture of aid, the adoption of her daughter Cosette, arises from personal conscience rather than systemic awareness and cannot reverse the town's industrial decline. Cosette's social ascent marks a widening distance from the world that made it possible. Between her and the world from which Valjean once drew the wealth that secured her dowry—and which has long since fallen silent—only ruins remain: the sound of the glass beads no longer echoes through Montreuil-sur-Mer, and Fantine's voice has long faded away. In this silence, the passage from the moral economy of the ancien régime to the impersonal logic of capitalism emerges as a form of continuity. Hugo intuits this very continuity in Valjean's final gesture, where moral redemption and material progress collapse into the same silence—the silence of a pen that no longer writes. As he begins to write his final letter, seeking to justify the origin of Cosette's dowry, his words return to the very act of invention that had once transformed Montreuil-sur-Mer—the technical gesture that gave birth to its prosperity. Breaking down in tears, he recognizes that recording the innovation which once made the city flourish is futile. It belongs to a world that no longer exists. In the stillness of his unfinished letter, the gesture of invention finds its mirror: the same motion that once gave form to life now traces its crystallization.

> Cosette, I give you my blessing. I am going to explain. Your husband was quite right to make me realize that I ought to stay away, although he is a little mistaken in what he believed, but he was right. He is a good man. Always love him dearly after I am dead. Monsieur Pontmercy, always love my darling child. Cosette, someone will find this note, this is what I want to

tell you, you will see from the figures, if I have the strength to remember them, listen carefully, that money is rightfully yours. To explain everything: white jet comes from Norway, black jet comes from England, black glass jewellery comes from Germany. Jet is lighter, more precious, more costly. We can make imitation jet in France as in Germany. What is needed is a little anvil two inches square, and a spirit lamp to soften the wax. The wax used to be made with resin and lampblack, and cost four francs a pound. I thought of making it with shellac and turpentine. It cost no more than thirty sous, and is much better. Earrings are made out of violet glass glued with this wax to a little black iron mounting. The glass must be violet for iron-mounted jewellery, and black for gold-mounted jewellery. Spain buys a great deal of it. It is the country of jet...

Here he broke off, the pen fell from his fingers, he was overcome by one of those desperate sobs that at times welled up from the depths of his being; the poor man held his head in both hands, and pondered. (Hugo 2016, 1280)[1]

Bibliography

Hugo, Victor. 1862. *Les Misérables,* v. 10.2. Paris: Pagnerre
Hugo, Victor. 2016. *Les Misérables.* Translated by C. Donougher. London: Penguin

[1] "Cosette, je te bénis. Je vais t'expliquer. Ton mari a eu raison de me faire comprendre que je devais m'en aller; cependant il y a un peu d'erreur dans ce qu'il a cru, mais il a eu raison. Il est excellent. Aime-le toujours bien quand je serai mort. Monsieur Pontmercy, aimez toujours mon enfant bien-aimé. Cosette, on trouvera ce papier-ci, voici ce que je veux te dire, tu vas voir les chiffres, si j'ai la force de me les rappeler, écoute bien, cet argent est bien à toi. Voici toute la chose: Le jais blanc vient de Norvège, le jais noir vient d'Angleterre, la verroterie noire vient d'Allemagne. Le jais est plus léger, plus précieux, plus cher. On peut faire en France des imitations comme en Allemagne. Il faut une petite enclume de deux pouces carrés et une lampe à esprit de vin pour amollir la cire. La cire autrefois se faisait avec de la résine et du noir de fumée et coûtait quatre francs la livre. J'ai imaginé de la faire avec de la gomme laque et de la térébenthine. Elle ne coûte plus que trente sous, et elle est bien meilleure. Les boucles se font avec un verre violet qu'on colle au moyen de cette cire sur une petite monture en fer noir. Le verre doit être violet pour les bijoux de fer et noir pour les bijoux d'or. L'Espagne en achète beaucoup. C'est le pays du jais... ». Ici il s'interrompit, la plume tomba de ses doigts, il lui vint un de ces sanglots désespérés qui montaient par moments des profondeurs de son être, le pauvre homme prit sa tête dans ses deux mains, et songea" (Hugo 1862, 242–244).

Index[1]

[1] Note: Page numbers followed by 'n' refer to notes.

M. Grassi, *The Silk Industry in Early Modern Piedmont*, Labour in History and Society,
https://doi.org/10.1007/978-3-032-15353-1

M

N

O

P

Q

Kolibri 360 GmbH
Ferdinand-Jühlke-Straße 7
99095 Erfurt, Deutschland
produktsicherheit@kolibri360.de